THE FIGHTS ON THE LITTLE HORN

THE FIGHTS ON
THE LITTLE HORN

Unveiling the Mysteries
of Custer's Last Stand

GORDON CLINTON HARPER

with assistance from
Gordon Richard & Monte Akers

CASEMATE
Philadelphia & Oxford

First published in the United States of America and Great Britain in 2014 by
CASEMATE PUBLISHERS
1950 Lawrence Road, Havertown, PA 19083, USA
and
The Old Music Hall, 106–108 Cowley Road, Oxford OX4 1JE, UK

© Gordon Clinton Harper 2014
Reprinted in paperback 2017

Paperback edition: ISBN 978-1-61200-563-8
Digital edition: ISBN 978-1-61200-215-6

Cataloging-in-publication data is available from the Library of Congress and
the British Library.

Printed and bound in the United States of America

For a complete list of Casemate titles, please contact:

CASEMATE PUBLISHERS (US)
Telephone (610) 853-9131
Fax (610) 853-9146
Email: casemate@casematepublishers.com
www.casematepublishers.com

CASEMATE PUBLISHERS (UK)
Telephone (01865) 241249
Email: casemate-uk@casematepublishers.co.uk
www.casematepublishers.co.uk

Front cover: Sitting Bull by D. F. Barry, 1885 (licensed under the Creative Commons
Attribution-Share Alike 4.0 International license); and Brevet Major General George
Armstrong Custer in field uniform (Public Domain).

Back cover: scene of General Custer's last stand, *c.* 1877 (U.S. National Archives and Records
Administration, Public Domain)

CONTENTS

FOREWORD

Tori Harper

I loved the author of this book, Gordon Clinton Harper; but then he was my dad, a sometime guitarist, song lyricist, minor league baseball player, cowboy and soldier, who also spent over two-thirds of his life seeking out every last piece of information he could find about the battle on June 25, 1876, commonly known as Custer's Last Stand or the Battle of the Little Big Horn. He was also a private investigator, a designer of bank security systems and the head of corporate security and security training, which may account for his determination to dig deep, investigate thoroughly, and make certain his information was correct.

As readers will see, my dad preferred to call it the Fights on the Little Horn because that was the original name of the river where the great Indian village was sited on that fateful day, and because there were essentially two different battles—the Reno/Benteen fight and the Custer fight. Because Lieutenant Colonel George Armstrong Custer and all his immediate command were killed in the latter, and there was no white man left to tell the world exactly what happened, that has become the most famous, and the most mysterious, aspect of the fights. Many people have spent years since trying to piece together what might have happened, but Gordon Harper had advantages others did not have.

First, he spent the summer of 1960 living near the battlefield and rode around it many times with Northern Cheyennes as his guides. Second, he gained the confidence of some Mnicoujou Lakota. In both cases the Native Americans gave him insights into their oral histories of the battle. The Cheyennes even gave him a name in their language, "Nanotameocz," meaning "Wind-Walker" because they observed that the wind blew in his face whichever direction he took.

As he said of that summer, "I left with a greater understanding of events and possibilities, and an indefinable feeling of both fulfillment and emptiness." He also left with an intense desire to find out from primary sources the truth about the Little Horn fights as far as that was possible, and therein lay his other advantage—he was a relentless, objective researcher willing to deal only in facts.

He said that his focus was to answer all of the outstanding questions about the two fights, without being judgmental, and based almost exclusively on primary resources. While he recognized the value of many secondary sources, he believed that others were based on insubstantial foundations and legends that could not be traced back to reliable origins. To that end he tracked down even the most remote of published articles and letters connected to the fights. His goal was to present the reader with all diverse and contradictory evidence so that each one could make up his own mind. "I never debate theories," he said, "as everyone is entitled to his or her own."

It may be said that this book constitutes his own particular theory, because it comprises what he gleaned from all of the primary material that he compiled and that he believed constituted reliable, even when contradictory, sources. However, his additional goal was to strip the story of two battles down to the bare, reliable facts. He believed that too much of the legend of the battle was just that—secondary interpretation founded on other secondary interpretation that had grown into common acceptance that would not withstand close scrutiny. He wanted to consult, and then make available to all readers and scholars, those primary materials, annotated with his commentary, that are the foundation for what really happened, as witnessed by those who were present, in order to allow everyone to formulate their own conclusions. Accordingly, he amassed nearly 2,000 pages of reports, letters, interviews, memoirs, testimony, and other documents—not every possible or potential primary source that is known to exist—but all those he considered significant and worthy of consideration—and intended to publish them along with this manuscript.

Needless to say, a publication of that size is not reasonable for publication as a printed book in today's publishing industry, but modern technology has nevertheless made those sources available, in electronic book form. Readers desiring only to read and possess my father's conclusions and analyses of the fights on the Little Horn are holding that volume. Those readers, students and scholars who desire to obtain the appendices as well may obtain them in an electronic book format from the publisher of this book, Casemate. Included with those appendices is my father's bibliography for this book, which is nearly 30,000 words in length.

My father despised footnotes and endnotes, and he included in his original manuscript a rather lengthy explanation of why, as well as what he intended for his book. In his opinion, footnotes interrupted rather than embellished the narrative. The reader was given a choice of pausing and consulting each note, which distracted from the account, or ignoring it, which made it useless. As he said, "I have found, and still find, these types of notes terribly intrusive and disruptive while reading, and of little help in establishing the quality of the author's research." Because Gordie's intent was to include all of the primary sources upon which his narrative was based as appendices to his manuscript, he inserted occasional parenthetical references to particular appendices when he believed it would assist the reader, saying "[i]n most instances, the entire, or excerpted, source material is reproduced in the Appendices so that you can study it at your leisure and determine for yourself what a particular source had to say about something—other than what I selected for use in the text." Because those appendices cannot be included at the back of the printed version of this book, they have been replaced with endnotes in lieu of his parenthetical references (some include references to corresponding ebook appendices). Dad would not have been pleased, but I'm betting he will forgive us.

My dad also devoted a great deal of his time to discussing aspects of the fights on website forums dedicated to the Little Bighorn, and while I know very little about either George Armstrong Custer or the famous battle in which he met his death, I do know that many Custer scholars who debated on those forums held my father in high esteem. The posts there contain numerous comments such as "Well said Gordie" or "Gordie—good points," even when the writer did not agree with him. That was the measure of the man, the greatest man I have ever known, my dad, a proud, stubborn man who loved with all of his heart and wasn't afraid to tell people that they were wrong.

My father died quietly in his sleep on May 17, 2009, without having finished his book or getting it published. I knew how much the book meant to him so I was determined to get it published as a fitting memorial to him and to all those years he spent patiently researching and putting all the information into writing. With the help of two good friends, Gordon Richard and Monte Akers, I have achieved that ambition.

Unfortunately, or perhaps fortunately, Dad saved until the very end the drafting of what many will consider the most important portion of the book—his presentation of the Custer fight and what happened that no soldier or white man lived to describe. He had sketched it out and had shared its substance with a few other Little Bighorn enthusiasts, however, and Gordon Richard was as devoted to the subject as my father. Accordingly, with his assistance, the "missing chapter" was completed and is contained herein as chapter 9.

What you have in your hands, then, is what Gordon Harper believed that the available, reliable primary sources reveal as what really happened; unadorned with speculation and theories from other experts, but filtered through the mind and knowledge of a man who literally devoted half a century to studying what occurred on one particular day in history. It is presented in two sections—nine chapters of chronological narrative and eight chapters of analysis, each of the latter being devoted to a topic of particular interest or controversy. It is a labor of love—my father's for the story of the fights on the Little Horn, and mine for him. I am honored to share both with the world.

PROLOGUE

*" . . . you will proceed up the Rosebud in pursuit of the Indians
whose trail was discovered by Major Reno a few days since."*
—FROM THE LETTER OF INSTRUCTIONS FROM BRIG. GEN.
A.H. TERRY TO LT. COL. G.A. CUSTER, JUNE 22, 1876

What led General Terry to send Custer "in pursuit of the Indians" on June 22, 1876?

The origins go back to one economic disaster after another, starting in 1869. On September 24 of that year came Black Friday, the collapse of gold premiums. Then on October 8–9, 1871, Chicago suffered its great fire, causing property loss to the value of nearly $200 million, made worse by other destructive fires in Michigan and Wisconsin. Closely following came the equine influenza epidemic of 1872, which affected every aspect of transport, and the Coinage Act of 1873, which depressed silver prices. Only one more such event was needed to create a depression. That came in September 1873, when Jay Cooke & Company, a major force in U.S. banking circles, lost its creditworthiness over its inability to sell several million dollars' worth of Northern Pacific Railway bonds, and the firm declared itself bankrupt.

The Grant administration was in dire financial straits but was heartened when the U.S. Cavalry expedition of July and August 1874—led, ironically, by Custer—announced the discovery of mineral wealth, particularly gold, in the Black Hills of Dakota. There was only one snag, but a big one—the Black Hills belonged to the Lakota Sioux.

Nevertheless, gold seekers began to flood into this sacred Sioux land, and by late 1875 Grant and his cohorts were looking for a way to obtain the legally required three-fourths majority of the Sioux Nation to sign over the Black Hills. The solution they came up with was to force the free-roaming bands to go to reservations, where they could be more easily pressured into agreeing to the sale of their land. This plan was put into operation in December, when the Indian agents were directed to advise the free-roamers to give themselves up at their agencies by January 31, 1876. The wintry conditions would have made it impossible for most of the scattered bands to reach the agencies in time, and as the ultimatum also breached the obligations of the Sioux Treaty of 1868, it was largely ignored.

This gave the government spurious justification to turn matters over to the War Department. Originally a winter campaign was planned, but because of bad winter weather only Col. J.J. Reynolds, with Gen. George Crook as an observer, took the field. This was significant because on March 17 part of his force botched an attack on the village of the Northern Cheyenne, Old Bear, who happened to be on his way in to his agency! This communicated to the Indians that the white men were determined to end their way of life, thus leading to the coming together of various roaming bands for self-protection and a huge gathering of them at the Little Horn, although the annual sun dance ceremony was also a factor.

By mid-May 1876, the army had started out once more against the so-called "hostiles." Brig. General Alfred Terry commanded the Dakota Column out of Fort Abraham Lincoln, Dakota Territory, Colonel John Gibbon led the Montana Column out of Fort Ellis, Montana Territory, and General George Crook led the Wyoming Column out of Fort Fetterman, Wyoming Territory. There followed a month of fruitless searching for the elusive Indian bands until on June 19, when Major Marcus Reno returned from a scouting expedition with the news that he had discovered a relatively fresh Indian trail leading southwest up the Rosebud valley. On June 22, therefore, following a conference with his officers the previous day, Terry handed Custer his letter of instructions, and the lieutenant colonel led his 7th Cavalry up the Rosebud to follow the trail found by Reno.

Follow it he did, for two and a half days, until on the evening of June 24, his Crow scouts discovered that it led into the Little Horn valley. However, they were unsure whether the quarry had gone downstream or upstream after moving through the Rosebud/Little Horn divide. Being advised that the

Crows knew of a promontory called the Crow's Nest from which they could spy on the enemy without being seen the next morning, Custer sent the scouts off, then moved his command into the divide from where he could react quickly to the intelligence the Crows would provide him the next day. At 7:30 a.m. on June 25, Custer learned that the great village had moved downstream and, having gone to view the position himself, he decided he would keep his command hidden that day and attack at dawn on June 26.

That plan was abandoned when it was believed his force had been seen by the Indians, and with the likelihood that the village would flee and scatter once warned, Custer made ready to move against the enemy at once. According to Lieutenant George Wallace's official itinerary and every other credible witness on the subject, it was exactly noon when Custer led his regiment across the divide between Davis and Ash Creeks and began the descent into the valley of Ash Creek. About seven minutes—and slightly less than half a mile—later, Custer halted the command and drew off to the side of the trail with his adjutant, Lieutenant Cooke. The two men engaged in conversation for a few minutes, with Cooke making notations in a small notebook that he carried with him. These notations were evidently the record of the battalion assignments that Custer then proceeded to make.

At about 12:12 p.m., Custer motioned for Captain Benteen, whose company was leading the main column, to join him. Adjutant Cooke met Benteen as he came up and delivered verbal orders to him. Benteen, with companies D, H and K, then moved off on a left oblique, while Major Reno, with companies A, G and M, together with Custer with companies C, E, F, I and L, moved to the left and right banks of the Middle Fork of Ash Creek respectively.

The die was cast.

CHAPTER 1

THE APPROACH TO THE LITTLE HORN: BENTEEN'S MARCH

"Half a league, half a league, half a league onward"
—ALFRED, LORD TENNYSON

CUSTER'S ORDERS TO BENTEEN

Battalion assignments having been made just past the divide, Custer and Reno moved down Ash Creek while Benteen bore off to the left, following his verbal orders. Although it has become fashionable in some circles to theorize that Benteen's task was to enter the Little Horn valley and to sweep north, there is no doubt as to what was intended, except perhaps in Benteen's own musings.

Later, at the Reno Court of Inquiry in 1879, Benteen would say: "My orders were to proceed out into a line of bluffs about 4 or 5 miles away, to pitch into anything I came across, and to send back word to General Custer at once if I came across anything." He stated that these orders were amplified by both the chief trumpeter and the sergeant-major of the regiment to require him to go on to the next line of bluffs and the next, and then "to go on to the valley—and if there was nothing in the valley, to go on to the next valley."

He testified that these orders constituted nothing more than:

> valley hunting ad infinitum . . . scarcely knew what I had to do . . . I
> was sent off to hunt up some Indians. . . . I could have gone on in as

5

straight a line as the country would admit, all the way to Fort Benton
... I might have gone on 20 miles in a straight line without finding
a valley ... those were exact orders. No interpretation at all ... I understood it as a rather senseless order. ... If I had gone on to the second valley, I would have been 25 miles away. I don't know where I
would have been.[1]

Benteen responded to questions about his returning to the main trail by
stating that "it was scarcely a compliance" with his orders, and "I must say I
did" consider it a violation of his instructions. The truth of the matter is considerably different.

When Custer launched his regiment against the village discovered by
his scouts at the Crow's nest, he had only an approximate fix on its location.
The scouts had located it around the mouth of Ash Creek, but there was the
distinct possibility that it or other villages lay upriver or downriver. Those
scouts included six Crow Indians and their interpreter Michel "Mitch" Boyer.
Boyer was born in 1839 of a French father and Lakota mother and lived with
the Crows. He had been mentored by Jim Bridger, and Boyer was considered
second only as a guide and scout to that famous mountain man. Mitch Boyer
and his Crows knew the area intimately, so from them and the surprisingly
good maps which he had, Custer also knew that there were several tributaries
flowing into Ash Creek from the west/southwest, i.e. from his left, and that
the Sioux used these smaller creeks for campsites, and their valleys as road-
ways to the Little Horn. His orders to Benteen were designed to ensure that
these smaller valleys and the larger valley of the Little Horn were seen in
order to determine whether, in fact, Indian camps were located there.

Although Custer had Varnum and some of the scouts going ahead over
much of this same ground, he obviously wanted a larger force in the vicinity,
in case it should be needed quickly. Whatever written notes or orders that existed were lost to posterity—unlike the famous later order from Custer to
Benteen—but sufficient witnesses to the verbal orders left a record, including
Benteen himself, that there is no need to guess what they indeed were.

Lieutenant Frank Gibson, Benteen's own lieutenant, wrote his wife on
July 4, 1876 that: "Benteen's battalion ... was sent to the left about five miles
to see if the Indians were trying to escape up the valley of the Little Big Horn,
after which we were to hurry and rejoin the command as quickly as possible
..."[2]

Edward Godfrey, who commanded K Company of Benteen's battalion, wrote in his 1892 *Century Magazine* article: "Benteen's battalion was ordered to the left and front, to a line of high bluffs about three or four miles distant. Benteen was ordered if he saw anything to send word to Custer, but to pitch into anything he came across; if when he arrived at the high bluffs he could not see any enemy, he should continue his march . . . until he could see the Little Big Horn valley . . . "[3] Godfrey told Walter Camp that "Cooke came up after passing the divide, and gave Benteen his orders to make scout to the left. . . . Reason for sending Benteen off to left was that Custer expected to find Indians scattered along the river, and did not know whether he would find them down stream or up stream from the point he would strike the river."[4]

Lieutenant Winfield Edgerly was second in command of D Company of Benteen's battalion. He also left a record. In a letter to his wife dated July 4, 1876, he wrote: "We were in Benteen's battalion, and our orders were to go over to the left and charge the Indians as soon as we saw them, and keep an officer with about six men in advance . . . to report anything they might see."[5] Edgerly was also interviewed by Walter Camp, and Camp's notes say that Edgerly told him: "Custer's idea was that they would scatter and run in all directions, hence he sent Benteen to southwest."

Benteen himself seemed to understand his orders quite clearly prior to his testimony quoted above. In a letter of July 2, 1876 to his wife, he wrote: "I was ordered with 3 Co.'s . . . to go to the left for the purpose of hunting for the valley of the river—Indian camp—or anything I could find." And on July 4, 1876, also to his wife: "I was ordered . . . to go over the immense hills to the left, in search of the valley, which was supposed to be very near by."[6]

In his official report dated July 4, 1876, Benteen had no difficulty in recounting his orders in detail:

> The directions I received from Lieutenant-Colonel Custer were, to move with my command to the left, to send well-mounted officers with about six men who would ride rapidly to a line of bluffs about five miles to our left and front, with instructions to report at once to me if anything of Indians could be seen from that point. I was to follow the movement of this detachment as rapidly as possible . . . the other instructions, which were, that if in my judgment there was nothing to be seen of Indians, Valleys &c, in the direction I was going, to return with the battalion to the trail the command was following.[7]

Benteen said much the same in an interview published in the *New York Herald* on August 8, 1876, and repeated the basic contents of his official report, with a few extra details, in both of the narratives he wrote in the 1890s. It is only in his Reno Inquiry testimony that he mischaracterized his instructions; but it is exactly that testimony which has colored most histories of the Little Horn ever since.

Benteen's battalion was to consist of three companies—Weir's D and Godfrey's K, in addition to his own H—and although many writers have tried to make something of significance out of Custer's choice of the delegated companies, including one writer who went to great lengths to show that Custer had divided up the combat-experienced companies among the various battalions, and others who have tried to show that Custer kept his favorite company commanders with himself, the more prosaic truth is that these three were simply half of the left-wing organization of the regiment. Benteen had, in fact, commanded this wing during the march from Fort Lincoln up until the evening of June 22 when Custer had temporarily abolished the wing organizations. All of the other battalion assignments were similarly constructed. Custer did, however, make a minor adjustment in that he switched companies A and K (the previous alignment had been ADH and GMK). He made the same minor adjustment in the battalions of the right wing, switching L and C (the original alignment had been CIB and EFL). His reasons for these changes are not readily apparent.

According to Benteen, the troops were in column dismounted when he received his orders. He had his three companies move out on their left oblique mission, sending his own first lieutenant, Frank Gibson, ahead with an escort of about eight men. The number is variously given as six or ten or a dozen, or just "some," but it makes sense that two sets of four would be selected for the duty. The time was approximately 12:15 p.m., and Benteen would not rejoin the main command for another four hours.

BENTEEN'S LEFT OBLIQUE AND RETURN TO ASH CREEK

Although his orders called for a rapid movement, Benteen moved along only at a fairly fast walk. To be sure, the nature of the terrain—though not nearly so forbidding as it has been made out to be—had an effect upon the pace. Not everyone, however, was slowed by the ground, for after the battalion had been marching for about fifteen minutes and had covered something less than a mile, Chief Trumpeter Henry Voss galloped up with additional instructions for Benteen.

After proffering the usual "with the compliments of General Custer," Voss instructed Benteen that should nothing be observed from the first ridge of hills about a quarter mile off, then Benteen should carry on to the next line of bluffs, the remainder of the orders remaining in effect. Voss then galloped away to rejoin the main command on Ash Creek. Custer, on the main trail, could see that this first divide did not appear to be promising in terms of viewing the Little Horn valley.

As Benteen started up again, Gibson crested the first ridgeline and saw that the small valley of the dry creek below was devoid of life. There is no record of how he did so, whether by signal or by courier, but Gibson did report that nothing of any consequence could be seen. Benteen's instruction to keep on going was relayed to Gibson, again by unknown means—although it may simply have been shouted, since Gibson was not that far in front of Benteen. Gibson and his party dropped down over the ridgeline, through the narrow bottom and up the other side.

As this was transpiring, Benteen was overtaken by another messenger from Custer, this time in the person of Regimental Sergeant Major William Sharrow. Sharrow brought Custer's compliments along with orders that if nothing could be seen from the second ridgeline, then Benteen was to keep on until he could see the valley of the Little Horn and whatever might be visible therein. The remainder of the orders as to rapidity, reporting and rejoining was repeated.[8]

It must be noted that nothing in Benteen's orders, notwithstanding his later statements to the contrary, told him to "pitch into anything he came across." This is evident for the following reasons: 1) his official report mentions nothing of the kind and he would not have omitted something so significant; 2) he was not provided with any medical services or supplies, not even an enlisted medical attendant; 3) Benteen would not have failed to capitalize on that failure, had it truly been an oversight or deliberate act on Custer's part. He did not however, mention it at any time, even when he was telling the Reno inquiry that he would have been beyond Custer's aid, had he in fact been forced to fight any major action.

The battalion kept on to the next ridgeline, with Gibson keeping to the high ground and Benteen staying on the lower ground as much as possible by edging to the right. The rate of travel was, on average, a fast walk, perhaps averaging as much as three and a half miles an hour. As Benteen topped the western ridge of the unnamed creek, the valley of which Gibson had crossed and examined some minutes earlier, he could see Gibson on a higher ridge ahead, signaling that there was nothing in the valley of the Little Horn.

Benteen would later say that he had never seen the valley, which was true since it was not viewable from the lower ridges at the nameless creek; but Gibson did see it, of that there can be no doubt. In a letter to Godfrey dated August 9, 1908, Gibson wrote:

> I can state definitely that I did find and see it . . . I crossed one insignificant stream running through a narrow valley, which I knew was not the Little Big Horn valley, so I kept on to the high divide on the other side of it, and from the top of it I could see plainly up the Little Big Horn Valley for a long distance, with the aid of the glasses; but in the direction of the village, I could not see far on account of a sharp turn in it . . . I saw not a living thing on it, and I hurried back and reported to Benteen, who then altered his course so as to pick up the main trail.

Some writers have speculated that Gibson was mistaken, and that he was referencing the south fork of Reno Creek, and it is true that in later years, Gibson himself thought he might have been in error; however, it is impossible to confuse the two valleys and it would not have required the use of glasses to see down the rather narrow valley (as compared with the Little Horn valley) of the south fork.

In addition, Gibson stated in a narrative written sometime after 1880 that: "After a fatiguing march over the hills, we reached a point from which the valley of the Little Big Horn could be seen for a distance of ten miles in a southerly direction, but on the North, towards the village, the view was obstructed by very broken country and high hills. We found no Indians and retraced our steps as rapidly as possible."[9]

Benteen, with his orderly and the Gibson party, descended back into the nameless creek bottom, and led his battalion along it to the valley of Ash Creek and the trail being followed by Custer and the remainder of the regiment. He did so in compliance with his original orders, not in disobedience of them; but he did not increase his rate of march to rejoin the command, nor did he dispatch a courier to Custer with the important intelligence he had gathered—this was a direct contravention of his orders, one which he consistently tried to hide or gloss over.

The squadron walked down the little creek bottom until it came out into the valley of Ash Creek at almost exactly 2:00 p.m. The pack train was in sight coming down the trail, about a half-mile away, according to every witness on the topic, and Benteen hurried onto the trail so as to put some space between the train and himself. It would not have looked good on the record should he have allowed the train to beat him down the trail. At this point in time, the Custer/Reno commands were only about three miles ahead of Benteen, and had passed the mouth of the little creek just twenty-five to thirty minutes before. Benteen had been off on his scout for slightly more than an hour and a half, and had covered almost exactly six miles. The time and distance involved in this scout has been the subject of some little controversy and speculation in the intervening years—mainly because of Benteen's obfuscating testimony at the Reno court of inquiry. The contemporary record however, is quite clear, and the sighting of the pack train, which is mentioned by virtually every witness, establishes the truth beyond any doubt.

Gibson, to his wife July 4, 1876: ". . . sent to the left about five miles . . ." Edgerly, in the *Leavenworth Times* August 18, 1881: ". . . and about five or six miles from the starting point we came upon Reno's trail." Benteen, in the *New York Herald* August 8, 1876: "The whole time occupied in this march was about an hour and a half . . ." Edgerly, in Walter Camp's notes, no date: ". . . having gone 5 or 6 miles from where the regiment divided . . ." Benteen, from his official report: "I had then gone about fully ten miles . . ." Edgerly, to his wife, July 4, 1876: "After we went about two or three miles, we found it impracticable to keep to the left, and came down into the valley.

During the march on the left oblique, several members of Benteen's battalion, including both Godfrey and Benteen, heard gunshots, and caught glimpses of Custer's command moving down the trail. Godfrey wrote in his 1892 narrative: "During this march to the left we could see occasionally the battalion under Custer, distinguished by the troop mounted on gray horses, marching at a rapid gait. Two or three times we heard loud cheering and also some few shots, but the occasion of these demonstrations is not known."

Benteen, in his second narrative, recalled: "The last glimpse we had gotten of General Custer's column was the sight of the gray-horse troop at a gallop. Well one couldn't tell much about the simple fact of seeing that much at an increased pace, as, owing to the roughness of the country, the troop might have lost distance, and had only increased the pace to recover its distance."[10]

STOPS FOR WATER AND THE FIRST COURIER FROM CUSTER
Neither the gunshots nor the "demonstrations" caused Benteen to increase his pace; nor did the sight of the gray horse troop "at a gallop," nor his original orders to rejoin the command quickly spur him on—but the sight of the pack train made him move more quickly into the trail and trot down it, the obvious purpose being to distance himself from the train and to keep from dragging up the rear.

This worked to his advantage, for another half-mile down the trail, Benteen came upon a morass "at which a stream of running water had its source," according to Godfrey, 1892. Godfrey's description has served to mislead researchers as to the location of this morass, for it was not so much a watering hole or a source for a stream as it was a section of Ash Creek which had some water in it—much of the creek was dry.

Benteen halted his battalion and allowed the men to water their horses. The horses, said Benteen in his report, "had been without water since about 8 p.m. of the day before." He also reported that this watering of the animals did not take more than fifteen minutes. In his Reno court testimony, Edgerly thought it more like eight to ten minutes. Godfrey, however, told the inquiry that the watering took between twenty and thirty minutes. Since the companies could not all water at the same time, Godfrey's estimate is likely much closer to the actual interval.

In his statements to Walter Camp, Godfrey was much more voluble about the stop at the morass. The halt there took so long, he said, that:

> Some of his [Benteen's] officers began to get uneasy, especially as they were hearing firing. Capt. Weir, especially, became impatient and wanted to go on. One officer inquired of another: "I wonder what the old man [Benteen] is keeping us here so long for?" . . . finally this uneasy feeling among the subordinate officers became known to Benteen, in some manner, and Weir said they "ought to be over there" [where the fighting was going on], and being at the head of the column, started out with his co.

In his 1892 narrative, Godfrey did not go into so much detail, but wrote:

"While watering, we heard some firing in advance, and Weir became a little impatient at the delay of watering and started off with his troop, taking the advance, whereas his place in column was second."

No other witness to the stop at the morass associated it with hearing gunfire in advance, although none of them were asked specifically about it; but at least one other person did associate gunfire with a stop for watering. In a letter to C.T. Brady dated September 21, 1904, William E. Morris, a private of M Company, wrote:

> Benteen, arriving about an hour later, came up as slow as though he were going to a funeral. By this statement I do not desire to reflect in any way upon him; he was simply in no hurry; and Muller [Jan Moller, of H troop], who occupied an adjoining cot to mine in the hospital at Fort Abraham Lincoln, told me that they walked all the way, and that they heard the heavy firing while they were watering their horses.[11]

It would have been impossible to have heard any heavy firing from the morass, as there was no fighting going on at that time, even if there had not been almost seven miles distance and sound-blocking hills between the morass and the site of Reno's fight in the bottom. Godfrey, as a matter of fact, was a bit hard of hearing, and probably couldn't have heard firing at that distance anyway. The only possible conclusion, other than discrediting both Godfrey and Moller, is that Benteen stopped another time to water the horses, but closer to the Little Horn. This is exactly what did happen.

Captain Weir grew impatient at the morass, not because of any gunfire, but simply because of the delay. Ten minutes would not have upset him, but almost half an hour did. That is why he pulled his company out in front without observing the military niceties, as Godfrey later emphasized. Benteen, no doubt upset at Weir's attitude, put the battalion in motion and overtook him—but he did not put Weir back in his proper place in the order of march, as will become evident. Benteen continued to set the pace, and the pace was still a walk.

It was at this juncture, approximately 2:30 p.m., that Boston Custer passed the Benteen column on his way from the pack train to join his brothers up ahead. Edgerly said in his 1894 monograph that "the General's youngest brother rode by on his pony. He had been back with the pack train, and was now hurrying up to join the General's immediate command. He gave me a cheery salutation as he passed. " The evidence clearly shows that Boston, who had gone back to the train to get a fresher horse, did join his brothers and died with them on Custer's Field. He obviously came back before Benteen reached the main trail.

The sight of Benteen's column no doubt led Boston Custer to feel that the main command was not far ahead, and that it would be safe to go ahead alone to try to find his brothers. Until Benteen swung into the trail from his scout, the trail ahead of the train had been empty, since the Custer/Reno commands had traveled at a much faster rate than the packs. Boston was neither the most robust nor adventurous of men. He would never have left the security of either the packs or Benteen's squadron had there been heavy gunfire audible ahead.

Benteen's command pulled out of the morass just as the first of the pack mules arrived and plunged into the mucky water, "in spite of the efforts of the packers to prevent them, for they had not had water since the previous evening," wrote Godfrey in 1892. Leaving the mules in his wake Benteen marched down the trail slightly more than three miles until he reached the old camp location commonly known as the Lone Tipi site. In fact, there were two tipis, one of which had been left standing, and which contained the body of a warrior slain in the fight against Crook the previous week; and one which had been knocked down or partially wrecked, probably as a sign of mourning.

Some historians believe that this site was abandoned quickly as the Custer/Reno command approached and that it was a rearguard of forty to fifty warriors from this fleeing village that was seen by Fred Gerard. This was simply not the case. For one, it would have to have been a fair-sized camp—about twenty-five lodges—to afford a rearguard of forty or fifty men, and hence would have been plainly visible from the Crow's Nest. For another, there are witnesses to the fact that the site was not occupied by a camp that morning. Wooden Leg, a Cheyenne, said that he thought that "the Sioux were left in burial tepees . . . when we left there . . . early the next morning after the Rosebud battle." This would mean that the camp was moved on June 18.

Obviously, another group might have occupied the same ground, despite it being contrary to Indian custom to camp on ground occupied by the dead, but Charles Varnum would later write in his unfinished memoirs, in reference to what he saw from the Crow's Nest: "I could see on a branch between me and the river one tepee standing and one partly wrecked. They proved to be full of dead bodies from the fight of Genl. Crook." And later: "I could see down the valley of a stream flowing into the Little Big Horn, two tepees, one partly wrecked or fallen over." Varnum also mentioned this sighting in a letter to Walter Camp dated April 14, 1909: "Another led down to the Little Big Horn. On this were the two lodges you know of . . . "

The march to the Lone Tipi site, which was located near the forks of Ash Creek and its major southern tributary, took a little over forty-five minutes. The time was about 3:15 p.m. Benteen rode around the standing lodge, which had been fired by troopers from the Custer/Reno command and was still smoldering, and looked into it. It is clear from his two narratives that he stopped and dismounted to do so. It is also clear that he halted his command in this vicinity to water the horses again. It could be that some had not been watered at the previous stop; that he was giving the men a chance to fill their canteens; or that he was simply following the custom of either halting or dismounting and walking the horses for five minutes every hour; but there is no doubt that this second watering did occur, and that it was here, not at the morass, that firing was heard up ahead.

Patrick Corcoran, a private of K Company, told Walter Camp that he "saw Knipe ride up and speak to Benteen, when Benteen just got through watering horses." Dennis Lynch, a private of F who was with the pack train, told Camp: "When Benteen was watering horses, the pack train came up to him, and he saw Sergeant Knipe ride up and speak to Benteen."

B.F. Churchill, a civilian packer, also associated Knipe's arrival with the tipi. He testified at the Reno inquiry that he was at the head of the train, and that: "The first we heard of it [the fighting] was about two and a half miles from the Little Big Horn near a tepee. It [the news] was brought to us." His confrere, John Frett, confirmed Knipe's arrival as being near the tipi, and also associated it with watering. He testified at the Reno court: "We were at the watering place near the tepee, the last tepee that was there before we got to the battlefield, the one with the dead Indian in it, when a sergeant came from some company of the 7th Cavalry, I don't know what company, and said that we should hurry up, that General Custer was attacking the Indians."

But it was Sergeant Daniel Knipe himself who defined the situation beyond any doubt. In his 1903 account, he stated that when he first saw Benteen: "He and his men were watering their horses when first seen."[12] He later confirmed this in a letter of October 9, 1910, to Walter Camp: "In regards to the place that I met Benteen he had left the place where he was watering his horses. When I first saw him that was what he was doing, watering, and it was about one mile as you say from where I met McDougall."

The firing caused Weir to push out ahead with his company. This is borne out by the fact that Edgerly testified that he saw Knipe arrive and speak with Benteen. He would not have seen this had D Company not been in the advance. The pace was now a more rapid walk, and a mile brought the first news from up ahead in the person of Sergeant Daniel Knipe of Captain Tom Custer's C Company, as mentioned above. The time was approximately 3:35 p.m. and Benteen was now more than an hour behind Custer.

Sergeant Knipe had been sent back by Captain Custer for a twofold purpose, as revealed in the oral orders given him. Knipe told Walter Camp in June 1908 that his orders were to go to McDougall and tell him to hurry and bring the packs straight across country and that if any packs came loose to leave them unless they contained ammunition, "and if you see Benteen, tell him to come on quick—a big Indian camp."

Knipe followed back on Custer's trail. On his way he saw a band of Rees driving captured Sioux ponies along to the east, and as he topped the hills above the north fork of Ash Creek he saw Benteen watering his horses. He angled off to the right and "waved his hat and Benteen turned to right (north) and came over that way and Knipe turned to right and passed Benteen and told him that 'they want you up there as quick as you can get there—they have struck a big Indian camp'." Knipe also repeated his orders about hurrying up the packs.

Benteen's reaction was amazing and virtually unbelievable. By his own testimony at the Reno inquiry, "A mile or so from that tepee I met a sergeant coming back with instructions to the commanding officer of the pack train to 'hurry up the packs.' I told him the pack train, I thought, was about seven miles back, and he could take the order back as I had nothing to do with that, that Captain McDougall was in charge of the pack train and would attend to the order." He later repeated this under direct questioning by Reno's attorney: "He simply had verbal instructions to the commanding officer of the pack train and I did not consider that an order to me." Benteen did not mention, and was not asked about, the portion of the instructions which applied to him—and Knipe, who was no longer in the army, was not called as a witness. Benteen also hid the fact that he had actually left the packs only slightly more than three miles behind him, and that that had been more than an hour before his meeting with Knipe. Knipe himself said that it was about a mile back to McDougall.

According to all witnesses, including the sergeant himself, Knipe then passed down the length of the Benteen battalion on his way back to the packs. Godfrey would write in 1892 that: "... as he passed the column he said to the men 'We've got 'em boys.'" Later, to Walter Camp, Godfrey was a little more expressive: "As he passed, someone asked him what was going on up ahead, and Knipe said: 'They are licking the stuffing out of them.'" Edgerly in his later narrative used Godfrey's exact 1892 wording, and may well have taken it from Godfrey's article. There is no doubt at all about two things: Knipe did ride back to the pack train and he did say something that indicated that there was action going on ahead.

None of this had any effect on Benteen—not the firing heard in advance; not the impatience of Weir and other officers; not the orders to hurry up; not the remarks of Sergeant Knipe. He continued to march at a brisk walk, not changing the pace one whit. It was not until he had gone another mile that circumstances caused him to move more rapidly.

THE SECOND COURIER FROM CUSTER AND BENTEEN'S RESPONSE
At approximately 3:50 p.m., a second messenger from Armstrong Custer met Benteen. This was one of the orderly trumpeters, John Martin of Benteen's own H Company, and he was carrying a written order that could not be ignored. Martin had been sent back from near the head of the coulee east of Sharpshooter's Ridge, and his horse had been wounded on the trip. He met Benteen at the flat where the north fork enters Ash Creek and handed him one of the most famous orders in U.S. military history:

Benteen.
Come on. Big Village. Be quick.
Bring Packs.
W. W. Cooke
P.S. Bring Pac's.

Benteen testified, and always maintained, that Martin told him the Indians were "skedaddling, therefore there was less necessity for me going back for the packs." W.A. Graham, Benteen's champion, repeated this in his 1923 *Cavalry Journal* article, published the year after Martin's death. However, Walter Camp's notes of an interview with Martin on October 24, 1908 contain the following: "Martin says when he gave message to Benteen, Benteen asked: 'Where is General Custer?' Martin said: 'About 3 miles from here.' Benteen said: 'Is being attacked or not?' and Martin said: 'Yes is being attacked' and said no more. Martin is positive that he did not tell Benteen . . . that Indians were skiddaddling." What is absolutely certain is that Martin remained with Benteen's command, and did not go back to the packs.[13]

This note from Custer has been the subject of controversy ever since it saw the light of day. Historians have argued over what it meant; how Benteen could be quick and still bring the packs; where was he supposed to "Come on" to? Benteen himself supposedly asked, "How can I be of service to him if I have to await the packs?" or words to that effect. It has been postulated that Custer was referring to the ammunition packs and/or that he was more anxious to have the extra manpower than anything else. Some have guessed that Custer expected Benteen to join Reno in the valley, not come to him. In reality, in the actual circumstances as they existed and as Custer obviously saw them, there is nothing whatsoever mysterious or vague about this order. It is, in fact, explicit and peremptory. What is also absolutely certain is that Benteen did not obey any part of the order, except to "Come on."

Instead of responding immediately to the order, Benteen waited until Weir came up with his company and then halted D Company while he showed Weir the order. "I asked him no questions, nor did he volunteer any advice," said Benteen at the Reno court. This was the same Thomas Weir who was supposedly a close friend of Custer, who had twice pushed on ahead without orders or observing military courtesy and who would later do exactly the same thing. Then "when the command came up near enough to me, I ordered a trot," testified Benteen, indicating quite clearly that he did not even send Martin back to hurry up the rest of his own battalion, let alone the packs. Benteen's response to "Be quick" was to increase the pace from about four miles per hour to about six miles per hour. He did nothing to speed up the packs or to let McDougall and Mathey know that something big was happening ahead of them. His testified excuse for this was that "the Indians could not get to the pack train without coming by us," which was patently an absurd statement, especially as he also testified that the packs were seven miles behind him. The statement was not challenged, however.

As the battalion trotted down the trail toward the mouth of Ash Creek, with Benteen in the advance, they came to the spot where the trails divided,

Reno's continuing toward the Little Horn and Custer's diverging to the right to the higher ground. According to Benteen, he himself carried on to the ford. "There I saw an engagement going on and I supposed it was the whole regiment. There were twelve or thirteen men in skirmish line that appeared to have been beaten back," he testified. "The line was then parallel with the river and the Indians were charging and recharging through those men. I thought the whole command was thrashed, and that was not a good place to cross." How he equated "twelve or thirteen men" with the whole regiment was neither asked nor explained.

Had Benteen actually gone to the ford, as claimed, he could have seen nothing of the sort, for the valley proper was not visible from the ford, because of intervening timber. Nobody but Benteen puts him anywhere near the ford. Godfrey "does not think Benteen could have seen Reno's retreat until he (Benteen) got to the ridge," recorded Walter Camp in his interview notes. The matter is resolved by Benteen himself. In a letter of July 4, 1876 to his wife he wrote: "When getting on top of hill so that the village could be seen—I saw an immense number of Indians on the plain—mounted of course and charging down on some dismounted men of Reno's command; the balance of R's command were mounted, and flying for dear life to the bluffs on the same side of river that I was."[14]

What really happened, according to Frank Gibson, was that "When came to point where Custer's trail parted from Reno's Benteen said: 'Here we have the horns of a dilemma.' Gibson advised taking the right hand trail and says that Co. H, at least, took it. He does not remember Co. D taking the left, but sure that H took to right. Does not recall about Benteen personally taking to center between two trails."[15] According to Godfrey, Gibson remembered correctly:

> When they came to point where Custer's trail separated from that of Reno there was some discussion as to which one should be followed. The debate was settled by Weir starting off on the left-hand trail, following on after Reno, while the other two companies followed the right-hand trail. Benteen, with his orderly, took a mid-position between the two trails and went on ahead.[16]

Edgerly also recalled that his company—Weir's—"got down near river."[17] Here again Weir took the initiative. One can only wonder why Benteen did not ask Martin, who had just come from Custer, which trail to follow.[18]

Because Custer actually headed to the high ground some distance from the Reno ford area, there is little doubt but that one of the two trails was Reno's and the other had been made by Indians traveling to the valley. Reno's trail crossed Ash Creek before nearing the ford.

As the command approached the Little Horn, firing could be plainly heard in advance. Edgerly informed Walter Camp, "When got down near river saw horsemen scampering toward bluffs and thought must be Indians Reno was driving out of village."[19] Again, this viewing must have been from ground higher up than the ford. The advance was checked when three horsemen appeared on the higher ground to the right, and beckoned to the command to come over to them.[20] These proved to be three of the four Crows who had gone with Custer: Goes Ahead, White Man Runs Him and Hairy Moccasin. The other, Curley, had disappeared. Although most accounts (especially Edgerly and Godfrey) indicate that it was Half Yellow Face who beckoned to the command, this was impossible as Half Yellow Face was still in the valley, forted up with his friend White Swan, who had been wounded.

It was now approximately 4:10 p.m., and about a mile down the bluffs a growing group of men and animals could be seen. One of the Crows said or signed "soldiers," and Benteen led his battalion toward these men. William Morris wrote to C.T. Brady in 1904 that: "Benteen . . . came up as slow as though he were going to a funeral," and said that Jan Moller told him: "They walked all the way, and that they heard the heavy firing while they were watering their horses."[21] In fairness to Benteen, he did not walk, but trotted the mile or so to the soldiers, who turned out to be Major Reno and the remnant of his command, some of whom were still struggling up the steep bluffs. Reno had lost his hat and had a bandana tied around his head. As Benteen came near, Reno went out to meet him. John Martin recalled that Reno said: "For God's sake, Benteen, halt your command and wait until I can organize my men."[22] Some accounts include a more plaintive plea to "help me, I've lost half my men." Whatever Reno actually said, it was enough to stop Benteen from carrying out the part of his written orders he had been following. Even the "Come on" was now ignored. It was, according to Edward Godfrey's memorandum book and the elapsed time, about 4:20 p.m.

What then had happened to Custer and Reno since Benteen had parted from them? Let us rejoin them as they started their journey down into Ash Creek valley.

NOTES

1. Frederick W. Benteen: narratives and testimony before the Reno Court of Inquiry; [ebook] Appendix 3.4.
2. Francis M. Gibson: a letter to his wife, July 4, 1876; [ebook] Appendix 2.14.
3. Edward S. Godfrey: narratives of 1892 and 1908; [ebook] Appendix 3.37.
4. Walter Mason Camp (1867–1925) was a railroad expert, editor, author and historical researcher who is best remembered as the man who interviewed scores of white and Indian witnesses to the various Indian wars in the latter half of the 19th century. His interview notes relating to the Fights on the Little Horn have become primary sources for historians and researchers writing about those engagements. Camp used parentheses in his note, but any square brackets in Camp's notes are Gordon Harper's.
5. Winfield Scott Edgerly: a letter to his wife, July 4, 1876; [ebook] Appendix 2.10.
6. Frederick Benteen: a letter to his wife, written in dated installments, commencing July 2, 1876; [ebook] Appendix 2.2.
7. Captain Frederick W. Benteen: report of July 4, 1876; [ebook] Appendix 4.1.
8. Frederick W. Benteen: narratives and testimony before the Reno Court of Inquiry; Francis M. Gibson, his account, undated, from a manuscript in the collections of the North Dakota Historical Society; Edward S. Godfrey: narratives of 1892 and 1908, and his testimony before the Reno Court of Inquiry; [ebook] Appendices 3.4, 3.36, 3.37, 3.38, 3.39.
9. Francis M. Gibson: account, undated, from a manuscript in the collections of the North Dakota Historical Society; [ebook] Appendix 3.36.
10. Frederick William Benteen: narrative c. 1891; [ebook] Appendix 3.4.
11. William E. Morris: letter to C. T. Brady, September 21, 1904; [ebook] Appendix 3.80.
12. Daniel Knipe: account, 1903, from *Montana Historical Society Contributions* (Volume 4, 1903); [ebook] Appendix 3.64.
13. Orderly-trumpeter John Martin: stories from various sources, plus his testimony before the Reno Court of Inquiry; [ebook] Appendix 3.70.
14. Frederick W. Benteen: letter to his wife, July 4, 1876; [ebook] Appendix 2.1.
15. Francis M. Gibson: letter to his wife, July 4, 1876; and his account, undated, from a manuscript in the collections of the North Dakota Historical Society; Kenneth Hammer (ed.), *Custer in '76: Walter Camp's Notes on the Custer Fight* (Provo, Utah: Brigham Young University Press, 1976) p.175; Kenneth Hammer, *Men With Custer* (Hardin: Custer Battlefield Historical & Museum Association, 1885); [ebook] Appendices 2.14, 3.36.
16. Edward S. Godfrey: narratives of 1892 and 1908; his testimony before the Reno Court of Inquiry, 1879; and excerpts from his field diary, June 1876; [ebook] Appendices 3.37, 3.38, 3.39.
17. Winfield S. Edgerly: account, given at Fort Yates, Dakota Territory, July 30, 1881, as published in the *Leavenworth Weekly Times*, August 18, 1881; his later narrative, date unknown but definitely after 1909; Edward S. Godfrey: narratives of 1892 and 1908; [ebook] Appendices 3.19, 3.20, 3.37.

18. Francis M. Gibson: account, undated, from a manuscript in the collections of the North Dakota Historical Society; [ebook] Appendix 3.36.

19. Frederick W. Benteen: narratives and his testimony before the Reno Court of Inquiry; Winfield S. Edgerly: account, given at Fort Yates, Dakota Territory, July 30, 1881, as published in the *Leavenworth Weekly Times*, August 18, 1881; Edgerly: later narrative, date unknown but definitely after 1909; Edgerly: later narrative, date unknown but definitely after 1909; Edward S. Godfrey: narratives of 1892 and 1908; Godfrey: testimony before the Reno Court of Inquiry, 1879; Godfrey: excerpts from his field diary, June 1876; [ebook] Appendices 3.4, 3.19, 3.20, 3.37, 3.38, 3.39.

20. Frederick W. Benteen: narratives and testimony before the Reno Court of Inquiry; Winfield S. Edgerly: account, given at Fort Yates, Dakota Territory, July 30, 1881, as published in the *Leavenworth Weekly Times*, August 18, 1881; Edgerly: later narrative, date unknown but definitely after 1909; Edgerly: account, undated, from a manuscript in the collections of the North Dakota Historical Society; [ebook] Appendices 3.4, 3.19, 3.20, 3.37.

21. William E. Morris: excerpts from his accounts from correspondence and as published in an unidentified newspaper, in the period 1894–1923; [ebook] Appendix 3.80.

22. Orderly-trumpeter John Martin: stories from various sources, plus his testimony before the Reno Court of Inquiry; [ebook] Appendix 3.70.

CHAPTER 2

THE APPROACH TO THE LITTLE
HORN: RENO'S AND CUSTER'S MARCH

*"The tactics of cavalry are not capable of being reduced to rule . . .
with the cavalry commander everything depends upon his coup
d'oueil . . . "*—CAPTAIN LEWIS EDWARD NOLAN,
Cavalry—Its History and Tactics

ACROSS THE DIVIDE—TO ASH CREEK

Lieutenant George Wallace, the acting topographical/engineering officer, noted in his official itinerary that the regiment crossed the divide between Davis and Ash Creeks at exactly 12:00 noon. No one has ever been able to show any convincing evidence to the contrary, and this noted time dovetails with the only other precise times noted by Wallace that day.[1] There is some doubt as to whether the time kept by Wallace was the local time, the "sun time," or St. Paul time. Rather than try to reconcile the various time estimates given by other participants, Wallace's time notations will be used as a basis for elapsed time, distance and speed calculations, where such are made.

Approximately seven minutes after crossing the divide and having his first good look at the panorama spread before him, Armstrong Custer halted the command and drew off to the side of the trail with his adjutant, First Lieutenant William Winer Cooke. Although the jottings which Cooke made in his notebook did not survive the campaign, it is evident from what transpired that Custer divided the regiment into four battalions, each formed of half of the left or right wing organizations of the regiment. These battalions were the same as had marched from Fort Lincoln, except that in the right wing, companies C and L were switched, and in the left wing, companies A and K were similarly swapped. What Custer's reasoning was for these minor changes will never be known. It might have been a question of manpower or of personalities. As it transpired, each of the "new" battalions had two captains, although this may have been coincidental.

The battalion assignments have already been detailed, except for Captain McDougall's B Company which, reportedly on account of having been the last to report compliance with standing orders, had been assigned rearguard duty protecting the pack train. Lieutenant Winfield Edgerly noted in a letter to his wife July 4, 1876 that: "Gen'l Custer, reassigned the companies into battalions, giving three companies each to Reno, Benteen, Keogh and Yates. We were in Benteen's battalion, and our orders were to go over to the left."[2] That Yates had three companies is confirmed from the fact that the gray horse troop, E Company, was part of his command and was continually noted as being in the center of Custer's column. It would not have been there had it been a part of a two-company squadron.

Although some historians have tried to make it appear that Armstrong Custer kept his favorite company commanders and assigned the others away from himself, the assignments were actually made in strict accordance with military requirements as to seniority, and precisely the same way that they had been previously—the only exceptions being that Reno and Benteen commanded battalions instead of wings as they had done on the march from Fort Lincoln, and the reconfiguration of the battalions as noted above. It should be noted that Custer had abolished the wing organization at an officers' meeting on June 22. Here it stayed abolished, with the battalions going to the senior commanders.

As Benteen passed by Major Reno on his way to the left, Reno asked him where he was going, and Benteen replied jokingly that he was going to scout the hills and drive everything before him. Reno testifying at his inquiry said:

> Colonel Cooke came to me and said, "The General directs you to take specific command of Companies M, A, and G." I turned and said to him, "Is that all?" He said, "Yes" ... Previous to that, Captain Benteen had started to the left up the hill. I had no instructions in

reference to him, and I asked him where he was going and what he was going to do. I don't recall his reply exactly, but it was to the effect that he was to drive everything before him on the hill . . .[3]

TO THE LONE TIPI

Reno drew his three companies to the left of the trail, while Custer maintained position on the right. Custer started his column forward at a brisk walk, with the companies sometimes breaking into a bit of a trot as the ground afforded, and as required to maintain the formation. As Lieutenant Charles Varnum would later testify: "General Custer generally rode a very fast-walking horse that made nearly the whole column trot to keep up with him."[4] Reno started his column into motion a few seconds later, keeping to the left so as to keep the dust down as much as possible. He gradually fell slightly behind Custer, as the ground over which he marched was somewhat rougher than that taken by Custer. The pace was deliberate, but not slow. "I . . . moved with my column to the second ridge, and between myself and the column commanded by General Custer was a small ravine which developed further down into a tributary of the . . . River," recalled Reno. This, of course, was the source of, and grew into, Ash Creek. "I moved my column nearly parallel to General Custer for some time."[5]

Custer had sent his scouts ahead of both the main body of troops and Benteen's battalion over to the left. Lieutenant Varnum was on the left with most of the Rees, while Lieutenant Luther Hare, who had been seconded to Varnum the previous night, was on the right with Mitch Boyer, the Crows, and a handful of Rees. The Rees were not overly familiar with this country and were used mostly as couriers back to Custer. Far from a headlong, mad dash to come to grips with the hostiles, Custer was making a very professional and even somewhat cautious advance toward an enemy whose location he had not yet firmly fixed. Whether by design or not, he was husbanding his horses for the fight or pursuit which was soon and inevitably to come.

Instead of being an attack, as has been suggested over the years, this movement was on the order of a reconnaissance-in-force, or, probably more accurately, a movement-to-contact, much like what would nowadays be called a "search and destroy" mission.

Varnum wrote in his unfinished memoir: "Lieut. Hare reported to me the night before for duty and I sent him to the right front and I took the left front of the advance. From every hill where I could see the valley I saw Indians mounted . . . I reported my observations several times."[6] Hare, on the right flank and front, no doubt did likewise, although he never was asked, nor did he ever write, so far as is known, about his scouting mission. Trumpeter John Martin told W.A. Graham: "All the time as we rode, scouts were riding in and out, and the General would listen to them and sometimes gallop away a short distance to look around. Sometimes Reno's column was several hundred yards away and sometimes it was close to us, and then the General motioned with his hat and they crossed over to where we were."[7]

Lieutenant Wallace testified:

> After Captain Benteen started to the left, General Custer and Major Reno moved down this little stream, one on the right and the other on the left bank. They were moving from 100 to 300 yards apart owing to the nature of the ground. After going ten or twelve miles, Major Reno was called across to the same side of the stream on which General Custer was moving. The two battalions then moved along parallel to each other for some distance further . . . I remember looking at my watch when General Custer brought Major Reno's battalion on the same side of the little stream with him. As we crossed that little stream, I took out my watch and looked at it, and it was then two o'clock.[8]

This crossing was made very near the confluence of the main and south forks of Ash Creek. Major Reno would later testify: "The crossing was a little difficult, so that when I got on that side the battalion was somewhat scattered, and I was about opposite the rear of the column commanded by General Custer. I received an order from Lieutenant Cooke to move my command to the front."[9] The confluence of the creek branches was the only spot nearby where a crossing could have been effected without more difficulty than Reno mentioned, and the location is confirmed by artifact evidence in the form of an army horseshoe of the proper pattern found on the Reno side some years later.

Wallace's estimate of the distance covered was reasonably good, at least as compared with mileage estimates given by others for various marches or intervals, which may have been one of the reasons he was selected to be the topographical officer and itinerary keeper on the march. It was just under eight miles from the divide when Reno crossed over and just before the Lone Tipi site was reached. The march had consumed one hour forty-eight minutes; about three miles behind, Benteen was coming out into the valley of Ash Creek from his scouting mission, just ahead of the pack train. The regiment was at this time fairly well closed-up and the several units were well within co-operating distance of each other.

AT THE LONE TIPI AND BEYOND

The site of the Lone Tipi was west of some white bluffs on the right side of Ash Creek, and Reno's crossing place.[10] This misnamed site actually contained one standing lodge and one that had been mostly knocked down. The standing lodge contained the body of a Sans Arc warrior, a brother of Turning Bear, who had been mortally wounded in the Crook fight on the Rosebud a week earlier.[11]

The abandoned village site became the focal point for a more rapid advance. The majority of Varnum's Rees had already drifted over toward the command, and most were already at the Lone Tipi site. Hare came down from the right flank with Herendeen, Boyer and the Crows. Reno had moved his battalion to the front, as ordered, and found: "When I got up there, there was a turmoil among the Indians that were with us as scouts. They were stripping themselves and preparing for a fight. I afterwards understood that they would not go forward, and General Custer had ordered them to give up their guns and horses."[12]

Although some writers have attributed this reluctance on the part of the scouts to advance as a frightened response to the dead warrior lodge, or to the first concrete sign of the nearness of the hostiles, it was in reality a simple misunderstanding. When Custer ordered the Ree scouts to move ahead, some mistake in translation led them to think that they were to go ahead while the troops remained behind. This, of course, made it seem to the Rees as if they were to be put on some sort of sacrificial mission, and what their nominal leader, Bobtailed-Bull said, was that they would not go ahead unless the soldiers did as well. When Custer ordered them stripped of their guns and horses, and told them to stand aside while the soldiers went ahead, the misunderstanding became apparent and was cleared up.[13]

The Rees led out, with Reno and his battalion immediately behind on the left, and Custer's column to the right and with its leading elements just behind the head of Reno's command. The entire force was on the right bank of Ash Creek. As the troops passed the single still-standing lodge, some of them, most witnesses agree, set it afire.

Fred Gerard, who had ridden a little further to the right and up a higher knoll, called out to Custer that he could see the hostiles up ahead. Although what he said has been misrepresented over the years, his testimony at the Reno inquiry is very clear as to what he saw and what he said. Gerard testified: "A few minutes before Major Reno received his orders, I rode up a little knoll . . . and from this knoll I could see the town, the Indian tepees and ponies. I turned my horse sideways and took off my hat and waved it and then I hallooed to General Custer, 'Here are your Indians, running like devils!'"[14]

Gerard placed this occurrence at the abandoned village site. He was very specific as to where he was:

It was very close to the lodge where the dead Indians were . . . To the right it was a broken country. It was a small hill 20 or 25 feet higher than where the lodge was standing, and a short distance from it. There was where I first saw the Indians to know they were Indians. In the morning I had seen them from the mountain top where Lieutenant Varnum was. That is, I saw a large black mass moving, which I supposed to be Indians and ponies.

When asked where the Indians were that he saw from the little hill, he replied, "They were down in the bottom of the Little Big Horn River. I should say over three miles from where we were, and I judged them to be on the left bank of the river."

His observation that the Indians were "running like devils" was not accurate, although it must have appeared so to him. As he testified, what he saw included the ponies, or at least some of them, as well as lodges, and since everything was moving, it is obvious that this was a camp moving toward the gathering farther down the river. It is obvious from other evidence that ponies were also being driven in to the camp circles so that the warriors could be mounted. To Gerard, and to every other observer, the driving in of the ponies indicated that the Indians were preparing to flee, because that is what everyone was predisposed to think, and to fear—not that the Indians would stand and fight, but that they would scatter to the four winds.

There has been speculation that Gerard was referencing a body of warriors on the east side of the Little Horn, and this speculation grew to include a fleeing village, with these warriors as a rearguard, and further that the village had recently been where the lone tipi still stood. There is no basis whatsoever for this speculation, as witnessed by Gerard's testimony. There had been no village on that site for several days. None had been seen from the Crow's Nest—just a single standing lodge and one broken down. The idea that Boyer and the Crows had been watching this village all morning is a mistaken reading of the account by White Man Runs Him that mentions that they had been watching "the village" through field glasses from the high white bluffs. It would hardly have been necessary to watch through glasses any camp at the Lone Tipi site. The Crows and Boyer were, in fact, looking at the northern camps across the Little Horn, which would have been perfectly visible, though not in detail, from those bluffs, utilizing glasses.

Gerard's shouted observation spurred Custer into immediate action. He and other officers, according to Gerard, rode up onto the hill from which Gerard had just come down. He was not sure whether Reno was among them, but said: "My impression is he was close there."

THE ATTACK ORDER TO RENO

The two commands were still in motion, and when Custer had seen whatever he saw from the vantage point of the hill, he issued an order to Major Reno. This order was transmitted to Reno very near the flat where Ash Creek and its main northern arm meet. The exact wording of the order, how it was delivered, and what it meant, are still in dispute. The importance of the order cannot be overstated, for it was this order which launched Reno into his fight in the valley, and the interpretation of which is the basis for the defense of his subsequent actions.

Five persons survived the fights and testified to having heard this order delivered. Two were officers of the regiment—Major Reno and Lieutenant Wallace; two were civilians—Interpreter Fred Gerard and Scout George Herendeen; one was an enlisted man—Sergeant, then Private, Edward Davern, who was Reno's orderly on June 25, 1876.

Wallace's testimony was rather sketchy and self-contradictory, leaving the impression that he might have been testifying from later knowledge:

> We passed a tepee which had some dead bodies in, and soon after passing that, the adjutant came to Major Reno and said that the Indians were about two miles and a half ahead, and Major Reno was ordered forward as fast as he could go, and to charge them and the

others would support him. . . . I think it was promulgated through Major Reno's adjutant [Hodgson] I don't know that. I think so.

The order was about this, "The Indians are about two miles and a half ahead, on the jump, follow them as fast as you can, and charge them wherever you find them, and we will support you." I think those were the words. The term "we" I am not positive of.

Lieutenant Cooke, the adjutant of the regiment, came from General Custer to Major Reno and said to him, "The Indians are about two miles and a half ahead. They are on the jump. Go forward as fast as you think proper, and charge them wherever you find them, and he will support you." My mind is not exactly clear. I know he was to be supported.[15]

Wallace could not be sure whether the order came direct from Cooke to Reno, or came to Reno through Lieutenant Hodgson, his adjutant, and he was not consistent as to the gait Reno was to use, whether "as fast as you can," or perhaps "as fast as you think proper." He also forgot to say that the Indians were "on the jump" in his first version and was not certain as to who would do the supporting—"we" or "he." He summed up his testimony quite nicely, however, when he got in the last "I know he was to be supported"; and it may well be that that was his sole purpose. Lieutenant Varnum, however, recalled in his unfinished memoirs that Wallace was actually with Custer, not Reno, when Reno launched his pursuit.

Wallace's testimony dovetailed nicely with Reno's. Reno said: "I moved forward in accordance with the order received from Lieutenant Cooke to the head of the column. Soon after that, Lieutenant Cooke came to me and said, 'General Custer directs you to take as rapid a gait as you think prudent, and charge the village afterwards, and you will be supported by the whole outfit.'" Reno repeated this order exactly under cross-examination, adding, "I think those were the exact words." For more than a hundred years, writers have accepted, and used, the Reno version as historical fact, which is passing strange since he was the "defendant" at the inquiry.

The testimony of the non-officers is not quite so cut and dried. What George Herendeen had to say was very brief, but he was certain that the order came directly from Custer to Reno. "I heard General Custer tell Major Reno to lead out and he would be with him. Those were about the words I understood him to use. That is all I heard."

Fred Gerard was a bit more detailed in his description, while still indicating that Custer gave Reno the orders directly:

> The General hallooed over to Major Reno and beckoned to him with his finger, and the Major rode over, and he told Major Reno, "You will take your battalion and try and overtake and bring them to battle and I will support you." And as the Major was going off, he said, "And take the scouts along with you." He gave him orders to take the scouts along, and that is how I heard it. . . . The order I heard was direct from General Custer to Major Reno. I do not pretend to say Lieutenant Cooke did not communicate the order first.

Orderly Edward Davern had an entirely different version of the order and stated that he was right beside Reno when it was given:

> I heard Adjutant Cooke give him an order. The order was, "Girard comes back and reports the Indian village three miles ahead and moving. The General directs you to take your three companies and drive everything before you." These I believe were the exact words . . . "Colonel Benteen will be on your left and will have the same instructions."

Davern repeated these words exactly when cross-examined by Reno's attorney.

It is, of course, impossible to easily reconcile these various accounts, but it is not necessary to reconcile them to understand what Major Reno did in the valley—it is only when examining the aftermath of the battle that knowing the actual order would prove invaluable. It is evident, however, that Custer gave Reno two separate and distinct orders. The first, given near the Lone Tipi, was to take his battalion into the lead. This may have been what Herendeen meant by his evidence. The second, transmitted near the flat, was the "pursue and attack" order. This order was given at approximately 2:15 p.m., according to Wallace's time estimate.

After receiving the order, Reno led his command, consisting of three combat companies, the Ree scouts under Varnum and Hare, several civilians and two surgeons, down Ash Creek at a quickened pace toward the Little Horn. Also accompanying him were two of the Crow scouts, Half Yellow Face and White Swan, who had misunderstood a direction to them and went with Reno instead of staying with Custer. Although it is common to see the number 112 given as the strength of Reno's battalion, he actually had more than 170 men with him on the way to the Little Horn. Not all of them, however, would cross into the valley bottom with him.

At about this same time, or possibly very shortly before, Mitch Boyer and the Crows, who had been on top of the chalk bluffs most of the morning, came down to the command. Whether Boyer reported through Hare or directly to Custer, there is no doubt that he reported that he had seen lodges stretching far to the north down the Little Horn.

Charles Varnum, who had gradually become aware that he was alone with only his orderly, out on the hills to the left of Ash Creek, had ridden back looking for his scouts and had just reported to Armstrong Custer when Reno was pulling out:

> Major Reno with three troops of the 7th Cavy., was passing in front at the trot. I reported to the General saying I guess he could see about all I could of the situation. "I don't know. What can you see?" said the General. "The whole valley in front is full of Indians," I replied, "& you can see them when you take that rise" (pointing to the right front).
>
> I asked where Reno was going & he [Custer] told me he was to attack. I asked if I was to go with him [Reno]. He said I might. Fred Gerard, the interpreter, shouted a lot of Indian language to the scouts & we started at the gallop. My classmate, Lt. Wallace, was riding with the General as topographical officer. I turned back & shouted to him, "Come on, Nick, don't stay back with the coffee coolers." Custer laughed & made a sign to Wallace who joined me.[16]

Varnum always remembered Custer's laughing reaction to the "coffee coolers" remark and put it down as a sign of Custer's special affection for him. The comment might have seemed impudent had it come from some other officer, he thought. He also thought it showed that Custer was far from depressed in spirit.

When Varnum, Hare, Gerard and the scouts started their gallop, they were about halfway down Reno's column, which was moving at a quick trot or hand gallop. According to Varnum, he reached the river just as the leading company of the squadron was climbing out on the other side. Back on the trail, Benteen was walking down the trail after watering his horses in the morass. Custer meanwhile had paused to water his in the north branch of Ash Creek. It was now 2:30 p.m., and though he did not know it, his next move would set him on a walk with destiny.

NOTES

1. First Lieutenant George D. Wallace: testimony before the Reno Court of Inquiry, 1879; his report and the question of rapid and excessive marches, worn-out horses and exhausted men; [ebook] Appendices 3.113, 4.14.
2. Winfield Scott Edgerly: a letter to his wife, July 4, 1876; [ebook] Appendix 2.10.
3. Major Marcus A. Reno testimony at Reno Court of Inquiry; [ebook] Appendix 3.96.
4. Charles A. Varnum: testimony before the Reno Court of Inquiry; [ebook] Appendix 3.111.
5. Major Marcus A. Reno testimony at Reno Court of Inquiry; [ebook] Appendix 3.96.
6. Charles A. Varnum: two narratives, date unknown; [ebook] Appendix 3.112.
7. Orderly-trumpeter John Martin: account as contained in *The Cavalry Journal* July 1923); [ebook] Appendix 3.69.
8. First Lieutenant George D. Wallace: testimony before the Reno Court of Inquiry, 1879; [ebook] Appendix 3.113.
9. Major Marcus A. Reno testimony at Reno Court of Inquiry; [ebook] Appendix 3.96.
10. Curley: narrative as told to Charles Francis Roe, 1881, from the *Army and Navy Journal* (March 25, 1882); Goes Ahead the Crow scout: narratives from *The Arikara Narrative* and as given to Walter Camp, August 5, 1909; Hairy Moccasin, Crow scout, His narratives from *The Tepee Book* 1916 and as related to Walter Camp, February 23, 1911; White Man Runs Him, Crow scout: narratives; Curley, Crow scout: several and varied narratives of 1876 et sub.; [ebook] Appendices 3.15, 3.16, 3.40, 3.44, 3.116.
11. Francis Johnson (Kennedy): account *c.* 1899; [ebook] Appendix 3.61.
12. Major Marcus A. Reno testimony at Reno Court of Inquiry; [ebook] Appendix 3.96.
13. Fred Gerard: testimony before the Reno Court of Inquiry, 1879; Charles A. Varnum: testimony before the Reno Court of Inquiry, 1879; First Lieutenant George D. Wallace: testimony before the Reno Court of Inquiry 1879; [ebook] Appendices 3.33, 3.111 3.113.
14. Fred Gerard: testimony before the Reno Court of Inquiry, 1879; [ebook] Appendices 3.33.
15. First Lieutenant George D. Wallace: testimony before the Reno Court of Inquiry, 1879; [ebook] Appendix 3.113.
16. Charles A. Varnum: undated statement found among the papers of Charles Francis Bates; [ebook] Appendix 3.110.

CHAPTER 3

THE APPROACH TO THE LITTLE HORN: CUSTER'S MARCH TO MEDICINE TAIL COULEE

". . . looking on the bluffs across the river to our right.
I saw the gray horse company of the regiment moving
down along the bluffs."—FIRST LIEUTENANT CHARLES
VARNUM AT THE RENO INQUIRY, 1879

THE SWERVE TO THE RIGHT AND THE FIRST COURIER

At 2:30 p.m., while Reno's command moved toward the Little Horn, Custer turned a little to his right and watered his horses in a small creek. Lieutenant Cooke and Captain Myles Keogh, who was in command of one of the two battalions with Custer, spurred ahead to see Reno across the river. Before they quite got to the river they were met by Fred Gerard, who was coming back with what he thought was some important information for Custer.

Gerard had ridden to the river with the scouts, and when he reached the eastern bank and had stopped to enter the water, one of the Crows called out to him that the hostiles were not running away, but were, to the contrary, coming forward to meet the troops. In his testimony and in 1909 interviews with Walter Camp, he described the sequence of events thusly:

The scouts were to my left, and called my attention to the fact that all the Indians were coming up the valley. I called Major Reno's attention to [this] . . . I halted there a little time. I thought it was of importance enough that General Custer should know it, and I rode back towards Custer's command. At this knoll I met Colonel Cooke and he asked me where I was going. I told him I had come back to report to him that the Indians were coming up the valley to meet us, and he says, "All right, I'll go back and report." And he wheeled around and went toward [General Custer's] command . . . This knoll was right on the edge of the river's bank.

And also:

I told him that Reno and his battalion had forded and that the Indians were coming up the valley to meet him, and I thought the General ought to know that the Indians were showing fight instead of running away. He said: "All right, Gerard, you go ahead, and I will go back and report." I turned and rode back toward the river, and before I reached it met a mounted soldier hurrying east.[1]

This soldier, Private Archibald McIlhargey, was a messenger from Reno to Custer, bearing the news that Reno had everything in front of him. Edward Davern remembered seeing McIlhargey: "I saw him recross the river coming back from Major Reno's command . . . he said he was going to see General Custer." Reno was more explicit: "First I sent a man who was known in army parlance as my striker, named McIlhargey, to General Custer with my compliments, and to say that the Indians were in front of me and in strong force."[2]

It is impossible to know exactly what Custer had in mind when he sent Reno ahead with his orders to bring the Indians to battle—whether he intended to support Reno from the rear and changed his mind when Cooke and McIlhargey independently brought their news; if he had intended all along to throw his own battalions in on the flank of what he thought was a fleeing enemy; to attack and capture the village from the rear, thus forcing the warriors into a desperate fight; or if his subsequent action was spurred by the reports he had received from Lieutenant Varnum and Mitch Boyer.

He had finished up the watering, which John Martin testified took only about ten minutes: "He sent his compliments to the commanders and directed them not to let the horses drink too much, that they had too much traveling to do that day," and started on after Reno; but he turned to the right almost immediately, and led his command up to the higher ground.[3] It is obvious, however, that he would not have taken his whole command with him if all he wanted to do was to view the valley himself.

It is popularly supposed that a further impetus for this move to the higher ground was the observation by Sergeant Daniel Knipe of C Company of a few dozen Indians up on those bluffs. Walter Camp mentions this in his interview notes, giving the number as sixty to seventy-five, but not as a direct quote from Knipe, and says that these Indians were "north of where Reno was corralled." They could not, therefore, have been seen from the lower ground. Knipe, in a letter dated July 20, 1908 to Camp, a month after the interviews, wrote: "Custer with his five companies followed Reno's trail on after him, some distance down Benteen's (Ash) Creek; seeing about fifty or a hundred Indians up on the bluff to the right of Little Big Horn, he turned square to the right."

This would tend to indicate that it was Custer, not Knipe, who saw the Indians, but Knipe did say in his 1924 narrative that he and Custer saw the Indians at about the same time and that when they reached the top of the rise the Indians had gone.[4] In his 1903 narrative Knipe states that it was Custer who saw the Indians.[5] Perhaps the most interesting aspect of this story is that not one single Indian source, and there are many, mentions any sizeable number of Sioux or Cheyenne on the east side of the river at this time, nor did the Crow scouts ever mention anything like this in any of their many and varied accounts. Plus Knipe, who went up on this higher ground near the head of the column, never said what happened to these "fifty or a hundred" hostiles, only that they "were gone"—and John Martin, one of Custer's orderly trumpeters, who was riding near Custer all the time, told Walter Camp that he never saw them.

There is an Indian source which claims that the Indians were aware of Custer's approach and had set up a decoy party for him—one of the classic "trap" scenarios employed by the warriors. Had this been the case, the warriors supposedly seen would have remained in sight so as to entice the troops into whatever ambuscade had been laid out for them.

Be that as it may, Custer did climb the hills and did proceed along the high ground, sending flankers off to his right to a broken line of ridges that might mask a hidden enemy. Although there is no definite way of knowing to which company these troopers belonged, it would be natural for them to have been detached from L Company, which was now on the right flank.

During the march down Ash Creek, Custer's five companies had been marched five abreast in column of twos, with—according to Knipe—C Company on the right. The order, then, from the creek toward the hills would have likely been L-I-E-F-C. After watering and starting along the long ridge that terminated in Sharpshooter's Ridge, the same formation was maintained, but the order now became the reverse of what it had previously been—from left to right C-F-E-I-L.

Custer may have asked Mitch Boyer if there was a way down the steep bluffs above the Little Horn and Boyer would have replied that there was a good ford a couple of miles downstream, one which was often used by the Crows or Sioux when moving horses or camps. Custer did not ask the Crow scouts directly.[6] The time was approximately 2:45 p.m. when Custer topped out on the high hills. Benteen had not yet cleared the Chalk Bluffs near the Lone Tipi site otherwise he might have spied the tail end of Custer's columns snaking over the crest.

Although there were no survivors of Custer's fight, there were more than seven survivors of his march along the bluffs. These were the two enlisted messengers sent back—Knipe and Martin; four Crow scouts—Curley, Goes Ahead, Hairy Moccasin and White Man Runs Him; one Ree, Black Fox, and at least two enlisted men whose horses gave out. All of them, except Black Fox and some of the stragglers, have left accounts of what they saw and remembered. It should be noted that a third alleged messenger, Private Theodore Goldin, also left many accounts and voluminous correspondence. His claims to have been a messenger from Custer to Reno cannot, however, withstand close scrutiny, and his accounts of Custer's march have therefore not been considered,[7] nor has the fantastic tale of Peter Thompson, although there are doubtless some seeds of truth in the latter.[8]

Daniel Knipe, in a letter of July 20, 1908 to Walter Camp, wrote: "and when the command got up to the bluff where the Indians were supposed to have been seen [another indication that Knipe himself did not see them], we could see across the valley, see Reno and his three companies, about thirty-five Indian scouts, going right up to the Indian camps. We could see the Indian camp plainly." In fact the camps were not visible to most of the troops. In his 1924 narrative, Knipe said that:

> ... when the men of those four [five] troops saw the Indian camp down in the valley, they began to holler and yell, and we galloped

along to [toward] the far end of the bluffs. . . . Just then the captain [Tom Custer] told me to go back and find McDougall and the pack train and deliver to them orders that had just been issued by General Custer. "Tell McDougall," he said, "to bring the pack train straight across to high ground—if packs get loose don't stop to fix them, cut them off. Come quick. Big Indian camp."[9]

Walter Camp's notes of his June 1908 interviews with Knipe indicate that the packs were not to be cut loose if they were ammunition boxes and quoted Knipe as saying that Captain Custer added: "And if you see Benteen, tell him to come on quick—a big Indian camp."[10] Knipe immediately wheeled his mount around and set off on his assignment, while Armstrong Custer led his command ahead along the bluffs. Included in this movement was Knipe's fellow C Company sergeant, August Finkle, whose horse was starting to labor. Had it not been for this, it would have been Finkle rather than Knipe who carried the message back for McDougall and Benteen.[11] Finkle went on, and died in Custer's fight.

It was about 3:05 p.m. when Knipe started back on the ride that would prove to be rather uneventful and which would take him about half an hour before he reached Benteen between the flat and the abandoned village location. In that half hour, much would happen on the bluffs.

In recent years it has become fashionable to question Knipe's accounts of his having been a messenger and to accuse him of manufacturing the story to cover an act of cowardice. Supposedly, he was intent on deserting, or staying out of the coming fight, and came up with the messenger tale when he ran into Benteen while heading for safety. There are so many things which militate against these charges that it would take a separate chapter to enumerate them. Let it simply be said that nobody at the time questioned his motive or bravery, he fought during the siege on the hilltop, his later life showed no indications of cowardice, and he would have had to rely on everyone in Custer's command being killed so that no questions would have been asked.

ALONG THE BLUFFS AND THE SECOND COURIER

It is, of course, important to determine, if possible, just what Custer saw of Reno's action and where and when he saw it, since these observations naturally affected Custer's own decisions and actions. Knipe's evidence that they saw Reno riding toward the village and Custer's immediate dispatch of the message to McDougall and Benteen show clearly that at that point in time Custer thought that Reno could handle things in the valley and that he would throw in the rest of the regiment at another point to support Reno's attack, to threaten or capture the village, the full extent of which was not visible from the first viewpoint, which was on a small hill just north of where Reno later entrenched.

It is probably at about this same time that a second messenger from Reno arrived with a report for Custer. Reno stated that shortly after dispatching McIlhargey: "I sent a second time a man named Mitchell, who was about me in the capacity of cook . . . That was some minutes after. " Mitchell was to report that the hostiles were not running away, but were coming up to meet the troops. Since he was found among the dead on Custer's Field, it is apparent that he did join Custer's command, as had McIlhargey before him, so presumably he delivered his message.

Trumpeter Martin, in his several accounts, said only that the command moved at a gallop with the gray horse company in the middle and that they did not stop until they had reached the vicinity of Weir peaks. He also stated that Custer never saw Reno in the valley.[12] This is at variance not only with Knipe's evidence, but also with that of the Crow scouts, as well as the logic of the situation.

Hairy Moccasin told Walter Camp on February 23, 1911 that "Custer's command, as well as Bouyer and the 4 Crows saw Reno's fight in the valley;" but he is not specific as to what exactly they saw. In light of what he said later in the same interview, it would seem that it was the initial stages of the fight.[13] In the narrative attributed to him appearing in *The Tepee Book*, June 1916, Hairy Moccasin said:

Mitch Boyer was ahead with the four scouts right behind. Custer was ahead of his command a short distance behind us. Custer yelled to us to stop, then told us to go on the high hill ahead (the high point just north of where Reno later entrenched). From here we could see the village and see Reno fighting. . . . Everything was a scramble with lots of Sioux. The battle was over in a few minutes. We thought they were all killed. We four scouts turned and charged north to where Custer was headed for. Three of us stopped to fire into the village . . . When we met Custer, he asked, "How is it?" I said, "Reno's men are fighting hard."

It is difficult to reconcile the "fighting hard" response to Custer's query with the "We thought they were all killed" observation a scant few minutes before. It is obvious, however, that they did not see Reno's retreat to the bluffs, because the sound of battle would have been moving right toward Custer, and the head of Reno's fleeing column would have even then been coming up to the top of the bluffs; plus the timing is impossible. What Hairy Moccasin was describing was probably Reno's fight on the skirmish line.

Goes Ahead was interviewed by Camp on August 5, 1909 but only mentioned seeing Reno's battle as they were going back along the bluff after leaving Custer. In *The Arikara Narrative*, Goes Ahead was much more expansive in his descriptions:

> As Custer swung off from the trail after Reno left him to cross the upper ford, there was an Arikara scout and four Crow scouts with him. Custer rode to the edge of the high bank and looked over to the place where Reno's men were, as though planning the next move. When they arrived at about the point where Lieutenant Hodgson's headstone was placed later, the three Crow scouts saw the soldiers dismounting in front of the Dakota camp and thought the enemy were "too many."[14]

In an undated interview with Camp, White Man Runs Him says that the Crows "Went with Custer all way to mouth [of] Dry Creek . . . Custer sat on bluff and saw all of Reno's valley fight."[15] This latter observation would appear to be patently absurd. Had Custer seen all of Reno's fight while on the bluff, he would simply have stayed there to consolidate the commands and to offer protection for Reno's retreat from the valley. He was obviously not anywhere to be seen on the bluff when the leading elements of Reno's command reached the top.

In his 1919 interview on the ground with General Hugh Scott, White Man Runs Him said that Mitch Boyer called to the scouts:

> "Let us go over to the ridge and look at the lodges." When we reached there we saw that the lodges were over in the valley quite a ways down the river, so we went on ahead, Custer following. . . . Custer moved slowly and took his time and stopped occasionally. He did not leave that place until Reno had started skirmishing. Reno was

fighting long before Custer moved . . . Custer believed that Reno's command was all killed because they were retreating into the bluff and the dust was flying.

But later in the same interview he said, "No. I saw him [Reno] fighting across the river, but didn't know he had retreated back to the bluffs," which directly contradicts his previous statement.[16] This was in answer to a specific question about seeing Reno retreat. Since the Crows retraced their steps along the bluffs before Reno had retreated there, it is clear that Custer could not have known of Reno's retreat.

In an account published in the same year by Colonel Tim McCoy, and which probably was based on the same interviews as was General Scott's—McCoy was with Scott—White Man Runs Him is much more consistent in his story and clarifies some of the information contained in the Scott interviews. He makes it clear that the "going slow" remark pertains to Custer's movement from the flat to the bluffs:

> . . . so we moved on ahead, Custer following. . . . Custer and his brother went to the right of us and halted on a small hill. His troops were moving forward below him. . . . Custer then proceeded on up the ridge and his men followed. They were moving rapidly, and the scouts were forced to gallop their ponies sometimes to keep up with them. At a certain point on the ridge, they turned to the right and rode down a coulee in a northerly direction. The scouts took up a position on the high bluffs where we could look down into the Sioux camp.

In this account, there is no mention of seeing Reno in the valley, either on the way down the bluffs or on the way back.

The other Crow scout, Curley, then the youngest at seventeen, has become undoubtedly the most controversial due to the many and very dramatic accounts he left or which have been attributed to him.[17] Although his more Hollywood-style tales are largely discredited, there is no doubt that he did accompany Custer's command down the bluffs to a point short of Medicine Tail Coulee, and his picture of that advance must be considered.

In his first account, given briefly at the steamer *Far West*, and in the first attributed story, published in the *Helena Herald*, July 15, 1876, Curley gave no details of the movement down the bluffs. Later Curley did, however, take Fred Miller, a clerk at Crow Agency, over the ground and said that: "he started toward the Custer men after General Custer had left the bluffs where he first looked at the Reno men going to the charge," indicating that Custer had seen at least Reno's advance down the valley.[18] This corroborates Knipe.

Curley was interviewed by Walter Camp on four separate occasions from 1908 to 1913. Although there are a number of glaring discrepancies in his accounts to Camp, he was very consistent as to the movement down the bluffs. In 1908, Camp recorded that Custer turned to the right about a mile and a quarter from the Little Horn and that:

Custer's route from this point was directly across the country, on the crest of a long ridge, running to the bluffs and coming out at a point about 500 feet north of the Reno corral. From here Custer passed along the crest of the bluffs for fully 3/4 mile, in full view of the river and of the valley over across it. Custer hurried his men, going at a gallop most of the time. Reno and his command were plainly seen by Custer's whole command while marching this ¾ mile . . . Custer's command passed into the valley of a tributary of Reno [Medicine Tail] Creek . . . and went down it, going in a direction directly north and coming out into the bed of Reno Creek about a mile from its mouth . . . From the moment Custer's command commenced to descend . . . it passed out of the view of Reno's battalion, but Bouyer and his four scouts kept to the left of Custer, on the crest of the high ridge and peaks and at all times could command a view of the river and the bottoms beyond. . . . When they [Curley and Boyer] got to the top of the first of these peaks, they looked across and observed that Reno's command was fighting. At the sight of this, Bouyer could hardly restrain himself and shouted and waved his hat. . . . Undoubtedly Bouyer is the man seen by some in Reno's command to wave his hat, for Custer never went to the peaks or high ridge.[19]

In 1910, Curley reiterated that:

Custer did not see Reno's fight. Mitch Bouyer and myself did. . . . Before [he] got to Crow Hill, Bouyer waved hat to Custer from here. Saw Reno fighting from Edgerly [Weir] peaks . . . saw retreat and

Bouyer then gave signal to Custer. Custer and Tom Custer returned signal by waving hats, and men cheered. Bouyer probably told Custer Reno had been defeated, for Bouyer did a whole lot of talking to Custer.

In 1913, Curley told Camp that he and Boyer joined Custer in Medicine Tail Coulee and that: "I had seen Reno defeated in the bottom and discussed it with Mitch. I saw Mitch say something to General Custer when we met him and presumed that he must have informed him about Reno's situation."

In 1932, a few days before his death, Curley was interviewed by Russell White Bear, a friend who had interpreted for him many times and who wanted to get the story straight. Curley told him:

We rode to the north fork of Reno [Ash] Creek and crossed it, going to the hill, turning westward on the ridge—we could see nothing of the valley where the village was located—Custer's troops were not hurrying—they rode at a walk—probably because they were going up a grade. When we reached the ridge the soldiers kept marching on the east side of Reno Hill and going down to the west side of the ridge—down a ravine, running northward. At this point Custer and two other soldiers besides Bouyer and I rode over to a high point that overlooks the Little Big Horn Valley to see what was going on— we could see the dust rising everywhere down the valley. Reno's men were riding toward the Indians—Custer nor any of us dismounted. Custer made a brief survey of the situation and turned and rode to his command. He did not ask Bouyer or me about the country—we rode following the creek as you know. . . . Custer, turning left, rode down Medicine Tail. After riding awhile, he halted the command.

The least florid of Curley's accounts was that given to General Hugh Scott in 1919. It has none of the theatrics of some of his other accounts, does not mention his going with Custer beyond Medicine Tail, but to the contrary indicates clearly that he left the bluffs at almost the same time as the other Crows. It may be that the presence of White Man Runs Him tempered the story—it is the only time Curley told his story with one of the other scouts present—in any event it is by far the most credible of the Curley accounts and it contains some internal verification.[20]

Curley basically told Scott that Custer moved down the ridge after reaching the high ground and:

> ... then turned to the right and followed a coulee down in a northerly direction. When Custer left, Mitch Boyer and we Scouts remained on the point [that Custer had just left]. When we looked down to the camp we noticed there were not many around and Mitch Boyer said he thought the Indians were out campaigning somewhere and suggested we hurry down and fight them [indicating that they had not yet seen any of Reno's fight]. There were 5 of us altogether. We went further north on the high bluffs and came near the Indian camp just below the bluffs. Each of us fired 2 or 3 shots at the camp. Custer had reached the river when we were at this point on the bluffs. . . . When Custer reached the river we turned . . . Mitch Boyer said he was going down to Custer and his men and for the rest of us to go back to the pack outfit. Being on the hill we could see Reno was retreating and was well to the foot of the hills. The Arapahoe [Arikara/Ree] scouts of Custer had some of the Sioux horses and brought them across the river just below the ridge on the east side. We also met two groups of soldiers on the ridge just north of where Reno made his stand [probably the stragglers from Custer's command]. . . . I left the others and traveled toward the mouth of Reno [Ash] Creek in a southwest direction. The others yelled to me and asked where I was going. I answered, "I am going down to see if I can reach the river and get some water."[21]

The final surviving witness, and the last of the known messengers from Custer, was orderly trumpeter John Martin, who left one lengthy account, as supposedly told to Colonel W.A. Graham, two interviews with Walter Camp, and his testimony at the Reno inquiry.[22]

From his vantage point on Sharpshooter's Ridge, Custer looked behind him for any sign of Benteen's command, which no doubt his brother Boston had informed him was fairly close behind and which Knipe had been instructed to hurry forward if encountered. He was rewarded by seeing two columns of dust rising above the Ash Creek valley, apparently close together and also apparently representing both Benteen and the pack train. He had no means of knowing which was which. This was doubtless the genesis of the message sent to Benteen via Trumpeter Martin.

In Graham's 1923 *Cavalry Journal* article, Martin says that after Reno departed to his attack:

> We went at a gallop, too. (Just stopped once to water the horses.).
> The General seemed to be in a big hurry. After we had gone about a
> mile or two we came to a big hill that overlooked the valley, and we
> rode around the base of it and halted. Then the General took me with
> him, and we rode to the top of the hill, where he could see the village
> . . . we couldn't see it all from there . . . but several hundred tepees
> were in plain sight . . . There were no bucks to be seen; all we could
> see was some squaws and children playing. . . . We did not see any-
> thing of Reno's column when we were up on the hill. . . . We rode on,
> pretty fast, until we came to a big ravine that led in the direction of
> the river, and the General pointed down there and then called me.
> This was about a mile down the river from where we went up on
> the hill [this would put "the hill" in the vicinity of the Reno defense
> position], and we had been going at a trot and gallop all the way . . .
>
> The General said to me, "Orderly, I want you to take a message
> to Colonel Benteen. Ride as fast as you can and tell him to hurry. Tell
> him it's a big village and I want him to be quick, and to bring the am-
> munition packs." He didn't stop at all when he was telling me this,
> and I just said, "Yes, sir," and checked my horse, when the Adjutant
> said, "Wait orderly, I'll give you a message," and he stopped and wrote
> it in a big hurry, in a little book, and then tore out the leaf and gave
> it to me. And then he told me, "Now, orderly, ride as fast as you can
> to Colonel Benteen. Take the same trail we came down. If you have
> time, and there is no danger, come back; but otherwise stay with your
> company."[23]

This account agrees entirely with Martin's testimony, which is perhaps
not so surprising, since Graham based almost all of his writings on the Reno
inquiry testimony. The only substantial difference is that Martin told the
court that Custer dictated the message to Cooke and that Cooke then gave
the paper to Martin with the same instructions noted above. This is a more
believable scenario, for Custer would not be likely to give a verbal order to an
orderly when his adjutant was right beside him. In his interviews with Camp,
Martin is again consistent with the exception of the viewing of the village:

"Then Custer halted the command on the high ridge about 10 minutes, and officers looked at village through glasses," and the message: "Cooke halted and wrote message to Benteen and gave to Martin and then Custer spoke to Martin and said: 'Trumpeter, go back on our trail and see if you can discover Benteen and give him this message. If you see no danger come back to us, but if you find Indians in your way stay with Benteen and return with him and when you get back to us report.'"

It is important to note that Martin was instructed to follow on the trail that the command had taken and that nothing was said about seeking Benteen in the hills on the opposite side of Ash Creek. This makes it clear that Custer expected Benteen to be on the trail. The admonition about returning with Benteen and reporting indicates that Custer wanted Benteen with him, not either in the valley with Reno or somewhere unspecified acting as a reserve—both of which eventualities have been put forward by some researchers.

From all of the evidence, it becomes evident that Custer first saw part of the village from a point just north of the later entrenchments on the hills and both the evidence and the timing indicate that he saw Reno advancing down the valley toward the village and the masking force of warriors. It is also obvious that he could not see the entire extent of the camps from this point, from the evidence and from the topography. His observations here caused him to send back Knipe to Benteen and the pack train at 3:05 p.m.

In less than ten minutes Custer had marched a mile farther to the Weir peaks area. From a vantage point here, most likely on Sharpshooter's Ridge,[24] he could, and from all evidence did, see dust and smoke rising from the valley and no doubt also heard the sounds of Reno's fight, which was still raging below and to his left. He could also see dust, people and horses moving to the north across the river and camps spread along the banks for miles to the north.

He did not go to the highest peak,[25] and could not have seen everything even if he had done so. The terrain forbade that. He may earlier have seen Reno on the skirmish line—he could not possibly have seen him on the line in the timber, because of the intervening trees—but there is absolutely no question but that Reno was still fighting. White Man Runs Him told General Scott: "Custer saw the camp from the highest point on the ridge to the right of the first entrenchment. He just saw Reno going down the valley but did not see him come back." The immense size of the village, only part of which was visible, caused Custer to send back Trumpeter Martin with the message to Benteen, but there was no desperation hinted at, merely the necessity for speed. Custer still believed that Reno would handle things in the bottoms. It was just past 3:15 p.m., and Custer could see that his quarry was to the north and apparently running.

DOWN AND INTO MEDICINE TAIL

The Custer command had skirted the Weir peaks area to the right and had just started to descend to Medicine Tail Coulee—named for a Crow Indian who later owned the land—which was the horse/lodge trail probably mentioned by Boyer to Custer and which led directly to a useful ford of the meandering Little Horn River. The command moved down a wide slope east of Sharpshooter's Ridge, still in formation, and came out into Medicine Tail on a flat about a mile and three quarters from the Little Horn. The last glimpse Martin had of them was when they were going down this slope: "The last I saw of the command they were going down into the ravine. The gray horse troop was in the center and they were galloping." Although most accounts state that Custer used Cedar Coulee as his route for this movement, Cedar Coulee (misnamed, as there were no cedars in it) did not lend itself to such a movement, especially at such a pace as described by Martin. It was and is, a relatively narrow, sharply defined ravine, clogged by juniper bushes. It is not the route a horseman would have chosen and definitely not if that man was in a hurry. Custer's command could not have negotiated this ravine at speed and would have found the going troublesome even in column of twos with the five companies following one after the other, at any pace.

Custer's march down to Medicine Tail encompassed approximately a half-mile and took less than five minutes. Upon reaching the floor of the coulee at the flat, Custer very briefly halted the command to allow the companies to close up, and reformed the battalions into two columns of fours, prior to a move to the higher ground to the north and east, from where he could gain a better view of matters as they stood and plan his next moves. One account states that this change to fours was effected before descending into Medicine Tail Coulee, while Custer was on Sharpshooter's Ridge.

He was satisfied that Reno was accomplishing his mission in the valley and that the camps were on the move north. Speed was of the essence and he could not wait for Benteen, who he believed would be along shortly. He moved the two battalions out of Medicine Tail to the higher ground north and east, with Yates on the left and Keogh on the right. The time was approximately 3:25 p.m., and Custer was eager to find a way to press home an attack on the village; but had his orders to the pack train commander via Sergeant Knipe been delivered and obeyed?

NOTES

1. Frederic F. Gerard: testimony before the Reno Court of Inquiry, 1879; [ebook] Appendix 3.33.
2. Private Edward Davern of F Company, Reno's orderly: testimony at the Reno Court of Inquiry, 1876; Major Marcus A. Reno: testimony at Reno Court of Inquiry, 1876; [ebook] Appendices 3.17, 3.96.
3. Orderly-trumpeter John Martin: stories from various sources and testimony from the Reno Court of Inquiry, 1876; [ebook] Appendix 3.70.
4. Daniel A. Knipe: narrative from the *Greensboro Daily Record*, April 27, 1924; [ebook] Appendix 3.65.
5. Daniel A. Knipe: account, 1903, from the *Montana Historical Society Contributions*, Vol. 4, 1903; [ebook] Appendix 3.64.
6. Curley: narrative, 1881, as told to Charles Francis Roe, from *The Army and Navy Journal* (March 25, 1882); Curley, Crow scout: the several and varied narratives of 1876 et sub.; Goes Ahead, the Crow scout: narratives from *The Arikara Narrative* and as given to Walter M. Camp August 5, 1909; Hairy Moccasin, Crow scout: narratives from *The Tepee Book* 1916, and as related to Walter M. Camp February 23, 1911; Hairy Moccasin, Crow scout: interview by Walter M. Camp, July 17, 1910 at Crow Agency; White Man Runs Him, Crow scout: narratives; [ebook] Appendices 3.15, 3.16, 3.40, 3.44, 3.45, 3.116.
7. Theodore W. Goldin: article in the *Army Magazine* and a letter to Frederick Benteen; Theodore W. Goldin: his stories as reflected in his correspondence from 1904 to 1934; [ebook] Appendices 3.41, 3.42.
8. Peter Thompson, *Thompson's Narrative of the Little Bighorn Campaign 1876* (Glendale, Calif.: The Arthur H. Clark Co. 1974).
9. Daniel A. Knipe: narrative from the *Greensboro Daily Record*, April 27, 1924; [ebook] Appendix 3.65.
10. Daniel A. Knipe: account, 1903, from the *Montana Historical Society Contributions* (Vol. 4, 1903); [ebook] Appendix 3.64.
11. Daniel A. Knipe: narrative from the *Greensboro Daily Record*, 27 April 1924; [ebook] Appendix 3.65.
12. Orderly trumpeter John Martin: his stories from various sources, plus his testimony before the Reno Court of Inquiry; [ebook] Appendix 3.70.
13. Hairy Moccasin, Crow scout, his narratives from *The Tepee Book*, 1916, and as related to Walter M. Camp February 23, 1911; [ebook] Appendix 3.44.
14. The Arikara Scouts with Custer on the Little Horn Campaign: accounts from *The*

Arikara Narrative; Little Sioux, Arikara scout: narratives from *The Arikara Narrative* and from a Walter Camp interview *c.* 1912; [ebook] Appendices 3.1, 3.67.

15. White Man Runs Him, Crow scout: narratives; [ebook] *Appendix 3.116.*

16. Ibid.

17. Curley, Crow scout: the several and varied narratives of 1876 et sub.; [ebook] Appendix 3.16.

18. Ibid.

19. Ibid.

20. Ibid.

21. Ibid.

22. Orderly trumpeter John Martin: stories from various sources, plus his testimony before the Reno Court of Inquiry; [ebook] Appendix 3.70.

23. Orderly trumpeter John Martin: account as contained in the *Cavalry Journal*, July 1923; [ebook] Appendix 3.69.

24. White Man Runs Him, Crow scout: narratives; [ebook] Appendix 3.116.

25. Curley, Crow scout: the several and varied narratives of 1876 et sub.; [ebook] Appendix 3.16.

CHAPTER 4

THE APPROACH TO THE LITTLE HORN: THE PACK TRAIN AND MESSENGERS

*"Tell McDougall to bring the pack train straight across
to high ground—if packs get loose don't stop to fix them,
cut them off. Come quick. Big Indian camp."*
—Captain Thomas W. Custer to
Sergeant Daniel Knipe, June 25, 1876

ACROSS THE DIVIDE AND DOWN ASH CREEK

When the 7th Cavalry crossed the divide between Davis and Ash Creeks at noon on June 25, 1876, the Indian scouts fanned out ahead with the eleven combat companies marching behind. To the rear of the eleven companies came the pack train—followed by the rear-guard, B Company under the command of Captain Thomas M. McDougall. Lieutenant Edward Mathey had charge of the pack train itself, and he was experienced in this type of duty, having had charge of the supply train at the Washita years before. McDougall provided the guard because he had been last to report his company ready in compliance with standing orders earlier in the morning. According to John Bailey, saddler private in B Company: "on June 25, McDougall was to have the advance, but he was asleep when Custer had officers' call, and Custer, hearing of this, told him he would have to take the rear guard that day . . . says some of the Company wept when they heard this."[1] Although it is often overlooked or given short shrift in histories of the campaign, this "fifth battalion" was a strong and important component of the advancing regiment.[2]

When Custer made the battalion assignments on the western slopes of the divide and sent Benteen off on his scout to the left, he instructed Mathey and McDougall to close up the train and to give the combat squadrons a head start before proceeding on the trail—Custer obviously had no worries about the train taking care of itself if it came to a fight. Captain McDougall testified: "We started about twenty minutes after the command left."

Prior to that, according to Lieutenant Mathey's testimony:

During that long halt I went to sleep. Somebody woke me up and said officers' call had sounded and I went to see what were the orders. The officers were coming away. General Custer had given them their orders, I supposed, and I had no further orders to ask, and I went back to the pack train. Everything got ready to move and I followed the command. After we had gone I suppose two miles, Captain Benteen turned to the left with his column. . . . That morning Lieutenant Cooke came back and brought me an order to keep the mules off the trail, they made so much dust. I sent a man to see about doing it, and while he was gone was when Lieutenant Cooke came and asked me if I had received the order. I said, "yes" and I was about doing it. When the man came back from giving the order, I asked Lieutenant Cooke how that was. He said that was better, they were not kicking up so much dust. That was the last order I ever got from that source.

Mathey continued:

We followed the main trail. Captain McDougall was urging me to get the packs along as fast as possible. I did so, but we had to repack a great deal. When a mule became unpacked, I would leave two men to pack him and go ahead with the main train, and leave them to bring up that mule. We pushed along with a good deal of trouble, as our command had not had too much to do with that [packs] before.[3]

In fact, the train had been nothing but trouble from the outset and had probably been a consideration in Custer's having followed the Indian trail up

Davis Creek. Mathey told Walter Camp on October 19, 1910 that Custer had asked him the previous evening to report which company's packs were giving the most trouble. Mathey said that he remarked that he did not like to make comparisons, seeing that all were doing the best they could, but if required to do so he would have to name the packs of Companies G and H. McIntosh took the criticism good-naturedly, but it made Benteen angry.

THE MORASS

The march continued down the main trail. McDougall followed the pack mules with his company, Mathey leading the train. Mathey testified: "After I had gone, I suppose a little over an hour, and I had a horse that was very warm, and I changed him for another one, and went to the head of the train to see how it was getting along. In a short time, I came to where a mule had been in the morass. Something was said about the mule being there. . . . The packs were very much scattered from the front to the rear of it."

Since the location of the morass is crucially important to the timing of the movements of the train and Benteen's battalion, it is necessary to note what various persons had to say on that point. One person who should know is Mathey, and his testimony is that: "It was four or five miles, I think," referring to the distance from Benteen's swing to the left, which ties in rather nicely with the timing of his switching of his horse for a fresh one. Captain Mc-Dougall could not remember the time or distance from the division of the regiment, but was able to say: "I only remember that from this morass to Major Reno's position, I think it was about 8 miles," which agrees with Mathey's location exactly.[4] The fact that it is measured from a different direction endorses the placement.

When Benteen came into the valley of Ash Creek and saw the pack train a half-mile up that valley, the train had traveled between three and a half and four miles and had done so at a marching rate of just under three miles per hour. Since the train had started some twenty minutes after the rest of the troops, that gives an extremely accurate fix on the timing of both Benteen's march and that of the train. It was almost exactly 2:00 p.m. when Benteen saw the pack train—a march of an hour and a half for the train, crossing the divide at 12:30 p.m.

The pack train's march to the morass had been rather uneventful, except for the apparently frequent slippage or "unpacking" of some of the loads. McDougall covered it just as succinctly as had Mathey:

We started about twenty minutes after the command left. Lieutenant Mathey in advance with the pack mules made the trail, and we followed in the rear. Whose trail he followed, I don't know, whether an Indian trail or that of General Custer. We proceeded along the trail till we came to a kind of nearby watering place, where I found 5 or 6 mules mired. I dismounted my company to assist the packers and we got them out in about twenty minutes. We adjusted the packs and started on. About four miles from there, we came to an Indian tepee.

Mathey said that he thought there were "three or four" mules stuck in the mud at the morass, that there was no delay to the train—"It seemed to move right along"—and that "After passing the morass, I judge about three miles, we came to a tepee. Someone said something about a dead Indian inside of it, but I did not look inside."

ORDERS FOR THE PACK TRAIN

Two citizen packers, John Frett and B.F. Churchill, testified before the Reno court. Neither had much of interest to say about the march down Ash Creek, except that the mules were never driven at more than a walk until the train reached the Lone Tipi site. It is here that the only real controversy regarding the train arises—and that is the question of whether or not Sergeant Daniel Knipe delivered the verbal orders to the train that he carried from Custer. It becomes necessary to retrace Knipe's steps to determine the truth of the matter.

Knipe started back from Custer at approximately 3:05 p.m. and reached Benteen with his message at about 3:35 p.m. after a ride of half an hour. When Knipe first saw Benteen's command, they were watering their horses near the Lone Tipi site, and he met Benteen about a mile nearer the Little Horn, between the tipi and the flat. Benteen told Knipe that he had nothing to do with the pack train and to take the order back to Captain McDougall "about seven miles back." He repeated the statement about sending Knipe back later in his testimony.

In his 1924 narrative, Knipe gets the positioning reversed, but is definite on the subject of delivering the order:

Reaching the pack train, I gave Captain McDougall the orders sent him, and went on toward Captain Benteen as I had been told to take them to him also. McDougall [read: Benteen] and his outfit rode on to the top of the hill and reinforced Major Reno as he retired from the bottom of the bluffs. . . . As I went back after Captain Benteen [McDougall] I saw some Indians running along. I thought they were hostile Indians and got ready to give them a few rounds before they got me, but they were scouts.[5]

In his letter to Walter Camp dated October 9, 1910, Knipe is even more emphatic, indicating where he met McDougall: "In regards to the place that I met Benteen . . . it was about one mile as you say from where I met McDougall. I was not in sight of McDougall when I met Benteen." Camp also noted from his interviews with Knipe that "Knipe rode back at head of pack train . . . " Since Knipe met Benteen about a mile west of the Lone Tipi site, he therefore met the train near that site.

Several members of the pack train also recalled Knipe, or at least a sergeant from one of the companies, arriving with news of the fight, just at about the Lone Tipi. All this is of importance only because both Mathey and McDougall denied under oath receiving any order through Knipe or, for that matter, anyone else.

Mathey testified before McDougall did, and was specifically asked by the Recorder:

Recorder: Who did you see near the tepee and what orders, if any, were received?

Mathey: After passing the tepee probably two or three miles, I don't remember the distance, I saw somebody coming back. One, I remember, was a half-breed, and I asked him if General Custer was whipping them, and he said there were too many for him . . .

Recorder: Did you receive orders from General Custer or Major Reno or Captain Benteen on that march?

Mathey: No, sir, only such as I received from Captain McDougall.

Recorder: Did any sergeant report to you with orders?

Mathey: No, sir.[6]

McDougall however, contradicted Mathey:

Recorder: Did you receive any orders during that march from the

place where you received General Custer's orders till you reached
Major Reno's command on the hill?

McDougall: No, sir, the only thing was Lieutenant Mathey said the
engagement was going on.

Recorder: You received no notification to hurry up the pack train?

McDougall: No, sir, I think Lieutenant Mathey got that order. He told
me about it, and I told him to hurry up, I was very anxious about
it.[7]

Walter Camp in his interviews with them never asked either Mathey or
McDougall about the order brought by Knipe. It is evident however, that
Knipe did take the order back to the packs and it would seem that he would
naturally give it to Mathey, since Mathey was at the head of the train and
McDougall at the rear. Knipe however, always said that he gave the order to
McDougall and went so far as to tell Walter Camp: ". . . met head end of pack
train about at lone tepee. Packs strung out about a mile and met McDougall
about ½ mile east of lone tepee." Why Mathey and McDougall would deny
receiving this order is a question that has no logical answer—no odium ever
really attached itself to the actions of either of them during their approach
to the Little Horn—but it is hardly likely that it was simply forgotten. That
McDougall remembers Mathey telling him about receiving the message is
puzzling, since Knipe says he gave it to McDougall.

Some critics make much of these disavowals and attempt to show that
the packs were not brought "straight across country" and nor were any packs
reported having been cut loose. In fact when Knipe arrived at the pack train,
at approximately 3:45 p.m., the mules were strung out for almost a mile and
the topography at the abandoned village location did not lend itself to a quick
right oblique. The northern side of the valley is hemmed in here by some
high bluffs known to the Crows as the "White Rocks," and it would have been
impossible to have simply made a sharp right turn.

Whether by design or by chance Mathey and McDougall waited until the
train was well clear of the bluffs and then prepared to move onto the higher
ground. This may have been in response to Custer's order sent via Knipe—
maybe they disremembered receiving it—or it may have been a military reaction to the scene unfolding before them. In any event, they did what had
to be done.

In the meantime, while Knipe was delivering his message, or not, and while the train was moving down the trail, Trumpeter Martin was completing his ride to Benteen with the famous "Be Quick" message. His ride back had also been mostly uneventful, although his stories tend to be somewhat confusing. Walter Camp noted from his 1908 interview that before Martin got back to the high point from which he said Custer had seen the village, and which he said the whole command had traversed, he heard heavy firing off to his right. Given his position, this can only have referred to the fight in the valley, since Custer's command was now directly behind him. He also told Camp that he saw hordes of Indians charging toward the ford at Medicine Tail and saw Custer "retreating up the open country in the direction of the battlefield." This is not only physically impossible, but is contradicted by all credible evidence, so either Martin was misquoted or else Camp had projected his own opinions onto Martin. Camp noted that Martin did not tell of this at the Reno inquiry because he was not asked, but in reality he was asked.

The Recorder asked Martin: "Tell what you saw going back." Here was the opportunity to tell what he saw and Martin replied: "After I started from General Custer to go back, I traveled 5 or 600 yards, perhaps ¾ of a mile. I got on the same high ridge where General Custer saw the village the first time. On going back over that ridge I looked down into the bottom, and I saw Major Reno's battalion was engaged. I paid no further attention to it but went forward on my business." No Indians charging toward the ford, no Custer command retreating up the country—what he saw was Reno "engaged" in the bottom and he paid no further attention to it, implying that there was nothing noteworthy, other than Reno was "engaged" and not retreating.

Later in his testimony, Martin amplified this observation by direct responses to questions from Major Reno's counsel:

Question: Where did you see Major Reno fighting?
Martin: I was up on the ridge and he was in the bottom.
Question: Where was that point from which you first saw Major Reno fighting? Was it further up the stream than where he made the stand, or at the same place?
Martin: About at the same place.
Question: Was his line deployed in skirmish form?
Martin: Yes, sir.[8]

That exchange should certainly settle exactly what Martin saw of Reno, and as to what he saw of Custer, there is this earlier question and reply: "Did you see General Custer after leaving him in sight of the Indian village?" Martin: "No, sir."

Lending credence to Martin's testimony is the fact that he met not only at least one lagging trooper whom he recognized as belonging to C Company but claimed to have encountered Boston Custer who had left the pack train some time before and was hurrying along to join his brothers. Boston had passed Benteen's battalion at the morass some seven and a half miles back and about an hour and twenty minutes before. Since Boston was able to join his brother's command and died not far from his two brothers near the Last Stand Hill, it is perfectly clear that Custer was not under attack at this time, about 3:25 p.m. There is considerable doubt that Martin actually did meet Boston since he did not mention this until his 1908 interview with Walter Camp. Some even doubt that he mentioned it then because he had testified that Custer was with "his brothers" on the high hill, but Camp's note of the matter is quite positive that Martin "says he met Boston Custer," so the mystery remains.

Martin backtracked along Custer's trail until he saw Benteen down in the valley of Ash Creek and rode down to him with Custer's message. He was moving at a "jogtrot"—slightly faster than a standard trot—and had covered the almost four miles to Benteen in just over half an hour. Martin's horse suffered a flesh wound somewhere along the way, probably from an almost-spent bullet, although Martin did not notice it until it was pointed out to him by Benteen. There now arises another conundrum in connection with the pack train.

In Graham's 1923 article, he reports Martin as saying:

He [Benteen] didn't give me any order to Captain McDougall, who was in command of the rear guard, or to Lieutenant Mathey, who had the packs. I told them so at Chicago in 1879, when they had the court of inquiry, but I didn't speak English so good then, and they misunderstood me and made the report of my testimony show that I took an order to Captain McDougall. But this is a mistake. . . . The pack-train was not very far behind then. It was in sight, maybe a mile away.[9]

How Martin's 1879 testimony could be misconstrued is truly mystifying—he did not respond confusedly to some vague question that could itself be misunderstood—since he responded to a lengthy set of simple questions, thusly:

> Recorder: What did you do?
>
> Martin: I delivered my dispatch. . . . Then Captain Benteen took the dispatch, read it, and put it in his pocket, and gave me an order to take to Captain McDougall to bring up the pack train and keep it well up.
>
> Recorder: You say Captain Benteen gave you an order to go to Captain McDougall?
>
> Martin: Yes, sir.
>
> Recorder: Did you start right off?
>
> Martin: Yes, sir.
>
> Recorder: How far did you go to find Captain McDougall?
>
> Martin: About 150 yards.
>
> Recorder: Captain McDougall was himself in front of his troops?
>
> Martin: Yes, sir.
>
> Recorder: How were the packs?
>
> Martin: They were pretty well together.
>
> Recorder: What did you say to Captain McDougall?
>
> Martin: I said Captain Benteen sent his compliments, and wanted him to hurry up the packs, and not get too far behind, and to keep them well closed up.
>
> Recorder: Then what did you do?
>
> Martin: I went back to my company and took my position on the left of it.
>
> Recorder: Did Captain McDougall close up the packs then?
>
> Martin: Yes, sir.[10]

Reno's counsel, Lyman Gilbert, cross-examined Martin at some length about time intervals and distances, but posed only one question as to the McDougall message: "Then you were sent back to Captain McDougall?" and Martin replied: "Yes, sir." The totality of Martin's testimony would seem to be determinative on the question, and certainly cannot be characterized in the way Graham's article did. The flies in the ointment are the disclaimers by Mathey and McDougall as to receiving any orders, although they were not asked specifically about Martin, only about "a sergeant." And even Benteen threw in a gratuitous denial, perhaps to take the heat off himself when the Recorder asked him about the gait he took after receiving Martin's dispatch:

> Recorder: After you received the order at the hands of Trumpeter Martin, was the gait of the command increased, and if not, why not?
>
> Benteen: I don't think the gait was increased, as we were going as fast as we could without going at a gallop; but I gave the command "trot." I don't think it increased the gait at all. Martin has testified that I sent him back to the pack train. I did no such thing. If he went back to the pack train, he went there of his own accord.
>
> Recorder: May you not at that time have said something about the packs?
>
> Benteen: I did not ask him about the packs or send him to them.
>
> Recorder: May you not have said something in his hearing by which he may have been honestly mistaken in the matter?
>
> Benteen: I think not.[11]

It is hard to see how Martin could have been so mistaken about the basics—one can always make mistakes in the details, such as the distance—of having gone back to McDougall. He had nothing to gain by making up such a story and nothing to lose by saying nothing of the matter. The only witnesses with any conceivable agenda were the officers who made the denials and especially Benteen, who would not want it known that the packs were fairly close behind him. It is difficult however, to see how Martin could have made a return trip to McDougall, even if only ten or fifteen minutes, in time to have accompanied Benteen up to the bluffs. It may be that Martin's testimony related to the advance to Weir Point later on and that he mistook the context of the questions.

The questions must remain unresolved: Did Knipe give his message to Mathey? To McDougall? To either? And did Martin take an order from Benteen to McDougall? Did it make any difference either way?

THE PACK TRAIN TO THE HILL

In any event, the train was now clear of the encroaching bluffs and from his vantage point at the head of the column, Lieutenant Mathey became aware of a fight up ahead, in the person of a half-breed who said there were too many Indians for General Custer. "I saw a great deal of smoke," testified Mathey, "When I first knew they were fighting, I stopped the head of the pack train, and sent word to Captain McDougall that they had been fighting, and I would wait for him to bring up the rear. When it came up, we went ahead." The halt to close up the packs was "Probably 10 or 15 minutes. It was not long," said Mathey.

McDougall thought it was his idea to stop: "From that point (the Lone Tipi vicinity) I saw in the distance a very large smoke, and I told Lieutenant Mathey to halt for a few minutes till we could close up the entire train and prepare for action, which we did. About a mile from that point, Lieutenant Mathey sent word to me that the fight was going on. I told him to hurry up with the mules as fast as possible."

The smoke seen was from the fires started by the hostiles to try to drive out the dozen or more troopers still in the timber in the bottom where Reno's fight had taken place. McDougall continued his testimony:

I went on about 2 miles (cutting across the high ground) and saw some black objects on the hill in a mass, and I thought they were Indians. I told my company we would have to charge that party and get to the command. We drew our pistols. I put one platoon in front of the pack train and one in the rear, and charged to where those persons were. I found out then that it was Major Reno and his command. I should state that about a quarter of an hour before reaching them, I heard firing to my right, and as soon as I arrived, I reported to Major Reno that I had brought up the pack train alright, without losing any of the animals, and that I heard firing to my right.

McDougall later in his testimony said that the "black objects" were about two miles away when he first saw them.

Starting from the place where the regrouping halt was made, the train then cut up to the higher ground and Mathey also saw smoke and men on the hill. He thought they were "probably two or three miles" from the halt. Shortly after reaching the high ground, Mathey saw Lieutenant Luther Hare coming toward him at a gallop. Hare was acting as Reno's adjutant and was on a special mission. "After we started," testified Mathey, "I saw Lieutenant Hare, who said he wanted the ammunition. I detached two mules from the train and ordered them to go with Lieutenant Hare." This represented the reserve ammunition of one company. Each mule carried "two boxes, each with a thousand rounds in each box," stated Mathey.

According to Lieutenant Hare's own testimony, he had ridden "about a mile and a half" before he met the train and delivered orders to "hurry up as soon as possible, and cut out the ammunition as soon as possible, and send it ahead." He continued: "I came back ahead of the pack train," and estimated that his return trip of three miles took "probably 20 minutes," indicating that he went at a full gallop the whole way. He did not see the ammunition packs come up, he said: "I got back before any of the packs came up."[12]

Since Hare stated that he had been given the order for the packs "as soon as we were joined by Captain Benteen's column," and since he found them about a mile and a half away after riding ten minutes, this would give approximate arrival times of 5:00 p.m. for the two ammunition mules sent on ahead and 5:20 p.m. for the head of the rest of the train. These times would have to be adjusted for any interval between the arrival of Benteen and Reno's issuing of the order to Hare. There is no doubt that there was such an interval and the actual times can be more accurately given as 5:15 p.m. and 5:35 p.m. This timing, taken from the Reno position viewpoint, is perfectly consistent with a timing taken from the Lone Tipi area and based solely on the pack train's speed of advance, i.e. four to five miles at a walk, with some allowance for moving uphill for part of the journey and for a slightly increased speed after Hare's arrival.

It can readily be seen that Mathey and McDougall, whether or not they truly received any messages through Knipe or Martin, did exactly what was indicated and necessary in the circumstances, but what had brought Reno with the remnants of his command to the hill on which now reposed virtually seven of the twelve companies that had marched from the divide?

NOTES

1. Bruce R Liddic and Paul Harbaugh (eds.), *Camp On Custer: Transcribing the Custer Myth* (Spokane: The Arthur Clark Co., 1995).

2. Harvey A. Fox and John A. Bailey: interview with Walter Camp, undated; [ebook] Appendix 3.25.

3. Captain E. G. Mathey: testimony at the Reno Court of Inquiry, 1879; [ebook] Appendix 3.71.

4. Captain Thomas M. McDougall: testimony at the Reno Court of Inquiry, 1879; [ebook] Appendix 3.75.

5. Daniel A. Knipe: narrative from the *Greensboro Daily Record*, April 27, 1924; [ebook] Appendix 3.65

6. Captain E. G. Mathey: testimony at the Reno Court of Inquiry, 1879; [ebook] Appendix 3.71.
7. Captain Thomas M. McDougall: testimony at the Reno Court of Inquiry, 1879; [ebook] Appendix 3.75.
8. Orderly trumpeter John Martin: his stories from various sources, plus his testimony before the Reno Court of Inquiry; [ebook] Appendix 3.70.
9. Orderly trumpeter John Martin: account as contained in *The Cavalry Journal* (July 1923); [ebook] Appendix 3.69.
10. Orderly trumpeter John Martin: his stories from various sources, plus his testimony before the Reno Court of Inquiry; [ebook] Appendix 3.70.
11. Frederick William Benteen: narratives and his testimony at the Reno Court of Inquiry, 1876; [ebook] Appendix 3.4.
12. Luther Rector Hare: testimony at the Reno Court of Inquiry, 1876; [ebook] Appendix 3.49.

CHAPTER 5

THE OPENING SHOTS: RENO'S FIGHT IN THE VALLEY

"The brigade will advance: Walk March, Trot."
—MAJOR GENERAL THE EARL OF CARDIGAN'S
INITIAL ORDERS TO THE BRIGADE OF LIGHT
CAVALRY AT BALACLAVA

OVER THE RIVER, THROUGH THE WOODS AND DOWN THE VALLEY

Major Marcus Reno, operating under orders to pursue and bring the hostiles to battle, reached a ford of the Little Horn River, very near where Ash Creek emptied into it, at 2:30 p.m. He was riding at the head of most of his command of three companies of cavalry and assorted scouts, at a fairly brisk trot or hand gallop, as the ground permitted.

The two Crow scouts who had accompanied Reno's command by mistake had already crossed over the Little Horn by the time Reno arrived, as had a few of the Arikaras. These latter had been spurred on by Custer's minor outburst at the Lone Tipi and were after Sioux horses as previously instructed. There were just as many stragglers.

Reno's orderly, Private Edward Davern, testified that he "stopped a short distance before I got to the river to fix my curb strap, as my horse was becoming unmanageable." Lieutenant DeRudio told Walter Camp in 1910 that he had stopped somewhere after passing the Lone Tipi to fill his canteen and had not caught up with the command until it reached the river. George Herendeen was quoted in the *New York Herald* on August 8, 1876 as saying: "My horse fell, and for a few moments I was delayed, but I caught up with Reno at the ford."

One of the most interesting of the stragglers was the Arikara scout Soldier, not in and of himself, but for his observations of other stragglers. In *The Arikara Narrative*, and in a 1912 interview with Walter Camp, Soldier said: "There were other stragglers between me and Custer. The ones nearest to me were White Eagle and Bull [Bellow]. Stabbed [Stab] was behind, came up behind me and explained that he had been out with a message to soldiers over to east [Benteen]."[1] Soldier would meet other stragglers later on.

Regimental Adjutant Cooke and battalion commander Captain Miles Keogh had ridden with Reno's command almost as far as the river. "We are all going with the advance, and Miles Keogh is coming too," Cooke laughingly remarked to Reno, although Keogh probably turned back before Cooke did.[2] Private James Wilber of M Company recalled that Cooke was right at the riverbank: "We were galloping fast," Wilber told Camp, "and just as we got to the river, Cooke called out, "'For God's sake, men, don't run those horses like that; you will need them in a few minutes.'" Wilber remarked that he did not see Keogh at the river.

The trail followed by the troops crossed back over to the left side of Ash Creek as it neared the Little Horn. Lieutenant George Wallace, speaking of Cooke and Keogh, testified: "They were with us when we started from General Custer, and were with us when we crossed back to the left of the little stream which runs into the Little Big Horn. I thought at the time that they went into the fight with us. When they turned back, I don't know."[3]

Approximately twenty yards from the river, there was a little knoll, or hill, which caused a fork in the trail. Most of the command went around to the left of this knoll, while a few, including Reno, took the right branch of the fork.[4] Private Thomas O'Neill of G Company described a very interesting scene at this piece of ground to Walter Camp, remembering that: "some of the Rees were sitting (on it), holding a council and discussing the numbers of the Sioux. One of these was picking up handfuls of grass and dropping it, and pointing to the Sioux, who could be seen down and across the river, indicating that the Sioux were as thick as the grass." O'Neill went down to the river to the left of the knoll, through a dry ravine, indicating that the majority of the command did not ford at the actual mouth of Ash Creek.

Fred Gerard, the interpreter for the Arikara scouts, was hailed by some of them, who signaled to him that the Sioux were not running, as had been thought, but were coming up the bottom lands on the west side of the Little Horn to meet the troops. Gerard, who was very near to Reno, passed this information to the Major. "The scouts were to my left, and called my attention to the fact that all the Indians were coming up the valley. I called Major Reno's attention to the fact that the Indians were all coming up the valley," Gerard recalled in his inquiry testimony. He repeated this statement in both *The Arikara Narrative* and in a 1909 letter to Walter Camp. Reno, for his part, denied that the incident ever occurred, testified that he would not have allowed Gerard to speak to him and would have believed nothing he said anyway.

Major Reno's testimony on the point is very illuminating of the man and of the relative positions of Gerard and himself, as the following excerpts will attest:

Q. State whether at the crossing "A" you received any communication through a man [named] Girard?

A. Never. He had no right to make any communication to me, officially I mean.

Q. You say you received no communication from Girard down at that crossing; that you would not permit him to communicate with you. Was he not there in the capacity of interpreter?

A. From the manner in which you ask the question, it would seem to indicate that he came to me in an official capacity which I would not recognize. Of course, if he had any information to convey to me, I should have listened to him; but I would not have believed it.

Q. How else could he communicate with you under such circumstances? He could not communicate with you socially?

A. We were not in the fight, and I would not let General Custer send an order to me through such a channel.

Q. Any information that Girard may have had about the Indians, or what some scout may have told him, would you have considered it improper for him to report to you?

A. As I say, I should have listened to it, and as I say again, I should not have believed it.[5]

Gerard however, was not the only person to warn Reno that the Indians were not running away. George Herendeen wrote to the *New York Herald* in January 1878 that: "As we were crossing I heard the Crow scouts call out to one another, 'The Sioux are coming up to meet us,' and understanding the language, I called to Reno, 'The Sioux are coming.'"[6]

That Gerard was close to Reno at the river is confirmed by Lieutenant Charles DeRudio. He testified: "I remember that Major Reno was the first man to go into the river. My horse was stubborn and would not go into the river, only on the jump, and when he jumped into the river, he splashed water on Major Reno." But he expanded on his description of this scene in a 1910 interview with Walter Camp: "Here he found Reno and Gerard sitting on horses in the river, Reno drinking from a bottle of whisky. DeRudio was the first man to ford the river, and as his horse surged ahead he splashed water on Reno," who said: "What are you trying to do? Drown me before I am killed?"[7]

Fred Gerard thought that the Indians' change in posture, from one of running from the troops—which was the "predictable" behavior—to one of confrontation, was important enough to be reported to Custer, and so he took it upon himself to take the information back. Gerard testified:

> I halted there a little time. I thought it was of importance enough that General Custer should know it, and I rode back towards Custer's command. At this knoll, I met Colonel Cooke, and he asked me where I was going. I told him I had come back to report to him that the Indians were coming up the valley to meet us, and he says: "All right, I'll go back and report." And he wheeled around and went . . .

Gerard also stated that he met Cooke about seventy-five yards from the ford. He also recalled this incident in *The Arikara Narrative*, and in his correspondence with Walter Camp.[8]

While Gerard was going back with the information for Custer, Reno was taking his battalion across the river, through the timber and brush on the west side, and forming it up on the open prairie beyond. The crossing was totally unopposed and was accomplished with a minimum of fuss and bother, although many of the troops stopped to water their horses and/or to replenish their canteens.

Major Reno's official report of July 5, 1876 states that he "crossed immediately and halted about ten minutes or less to gather the battalion, sending word to Custer that I had everything in front of me and that they were strong."

His testimony at his court of inquiry provides no clue as to how long it took to cross over, but is simply: "I crossed the creek, and then formed my battalion with two companies in line and one in reserve. I had been a good deal in the Indian country, and I was convinced that the Indians were there in overwhelming numbers."[9] Other witnesses were more expansive on the crossing and watering. Sergeant Ferdinand Culbertson of A Company testified: "There was a short delay of about 5 to 8 minutes in closing up the column."

Lieutenant DeRudio told Walter Camp that: "At ford A Reno's battalion watered horses and when men got clear of timber formed the companies and went forward. . . . Does not think the delay here was long," although he testified: "There was no delay that I remember." Lieutenant Luther Hare, on duty with the scouts, supposedly told Walter Camp in 1910 that: "At the ford, the scouts watered, and pulled out just as Reno and his battalion came up. Reno stopped here and took plenty of time to water. Was here 10 or 15 mins." says Hare. "Hare says it is not true that Reno did not give his men time to water." Hare's earlier testimony on the point was consistent: "There was a halt at the head of the column, and some of the men were watering their horses when I passed them. I was delayed some time and did not pass them till I reached the ford. When I reached there, some of the men were watering, and some had halted."

Doctor Porter also stopped at the ford: "Some of the horses were watered at the stream. I watered my horse there," he testified. He also stated that there was no formal halt to water, that it was done "passing through" and that it took "five to ten minutes" to re-form on the other side. Lieutenant Varnum testified: "I don't know about any delay. The water was quite deep there, and the river was probably 25 or 30 feet wide, and in a column of troops getting across, there is necessarily some delay. They can't keep closed up in the water. How much stoppage, I can't say." Varnum did not see anybody stopping to water their horses but he also stated that only one company had crossed before he himself did. Lieutenant Wallace testified that he stopped to replenish his own canteen and could do so because there was an unavoidable delay in crossing: "I knew there would be a halt to close up, and I took advantage of it to fill my canteen."

The Arikara and Crow scouts were not the only men in the command to see indications of Indians down the bottom. Varnum had seen many during his scouting earlier that day and wrote in his first narrative that after coming out into the bottom and riding on ahead of the troops: "The valley was full of Indians riding madly in every direction." Sergeant Culbertson testified that he didn't see any Indians, but did see a lot of dust. Private Davern testified that he did see Indians, although not many:

> Q. What were the Indians doing after you crossed the river and the command was moving down the bottom?
>
> A. I first saw a few Indians away down the bottom. They appeared to be riding around in circles.
>
> Q. About how many do you think you saw there at that time?
>
> A. I cannot say; there may have been 20 or 30 or 40.
>
> Q. Where were you when you saw those few Indians?
>
> A. I saw those before I got to the ford.
>
> Q. How far from the ford were you when you saw them?
>
> A. But a short distance.[10]

Luther Hare testified: "I crossed the stream and rode out to the edge of the timber. I could see some Indians driving in some ponies downstream and to my left."

Fred Gerard testified: "I will have to go back to where we crossed the ford first. When we came to this ford and turned the knoll, I had a full view down the valley, and I could see Indians coming up. The bottom seemed to be just alive with Indians. As to the number, there seemed to be at least fifteen hundred coming up."

Gerard also noted that a very heavy trail led off to the right from the knoll—a lodge pole trail:

> Q. Now, go back from there to the time that you saw Lieutenant Cooke near the knoll that you have spoken of, and describe the trail or trails that you saw there, if any, or about that place.
>
> A. The trail before we turned around this knoll, going to the left of the ford, there was another trail going to the right, quite a large one.
>
> Q. What did it appear to be?
>
> A. A lodge trail.
>
> Q. Are you familiar with Indian trails?
>
> A. Yes, sir.
>
> Q. State what opportunities you have had of judging about those matters.
>
> A. I have been a resident in Indian country for thirty-one years, and I

think I ought to know an Indian trail when I see it.

Q. Then you know that was a large Indian trail?

A. Yes, sir—a lodge trail.

Q. State whether or not that was the trail that Major Reno's command took, that lodge trail you speak of, leading to the right.

A. No, sir. We took the left hand trail coming around the knoll.

Q. Which was the larger of the two trails?

A. I think the right hand trail. That is an impression, simply. I could not say now; it is so long ago.[11]

The belt of timber on the west side of the river was quite wide—DeRudio told Camp that "timber on west side was 200 yards wide." Tom O'Neill of G Company recalled: "On other side of river, there were timber and fallen logs, and took some time to get through." John Ryan, first sergeant of M Company, remembered that "there was a very strong current, and there was quicksand about three feet deep" at the ford.[12] Young Hawk, one of the Arikara scouts, said that he and a few companions crossed at the mouth of a dry coulee, and picked their way through a prairie dog village.[13] All things considered, it is clear that the crossing and re-forming, while done militarily and with little or no disruption, took more than a few minutes.

When Fred Gerard returned from his short ride back on the trail and his conversation with Lieutenant Cooke, he found one of the Indian scouts, whom he had told to wait, waiting for him at the ford.[14] "I turned and rode back toward the river, and before I reached it met a mounted soldier hurrying east . . ." he told Walter Camp in 1909, although in his testimony he stated otherwise:

Q. Now state whether in returning to Major Reno's command, you met anyone going back toward General Custer's column.

A. No, sir. I have no recollection of meeting anyone.

Q. State whether your route was such as to enable you to see anyone going back, communicating between the two commands.

A. I don't think anyone could have been by me without my seeing him.

This soldier hurrying east, whom Gerard saw or perhaps didn't, had been sent by Major Reno, as evidenced by his testimony: "I sent back word twice. First I sent a man who was known in army parlance as my striker, named

McIlhargey, to General Custer with my compliments, and to say that the Indians were in front of me and in strong force."

Archibald McIlhargey was a private of I Company and had earlier been detailed as Major Reno's striker. It is known that he was with Reno's command and since he was found dead on Custer's battlefield, it seems obvious that he had indeed been sent back by Reno, and it can be reasonably inferred that he delivered Reno's message, probably to Adjutant Cooke. He most likely overtook Cooke before the adjutant had rejoined Custer's column. McIlhargey was also seen by Private Davern.

It is also obvious that Reno sent McIlhargey back after seeing the hostiles down the valley, and that he waited a few minutes for a response from Custer, who he likely thought was following him, before moving on down, for Reno's testimony on the point continues:

> Receiving no instructions in response to that, I sent a second time, a man named Mitchell, who was about me in the capacity of cook. They were the nearest men I could get hold of quick. That was some minutes after, and I was convinced that my opinions were correct. I still heard nothing to guide my movements, and I went on down the valley to carry out my orders.

Private John Mitchell, also on detached duty from I Company, was also found dead on Custer's battlefield.

Gerard made his way across the Little Horn accompanied by the scout; the two men picked their way through the brush and timber on the west side, coming out onto the plain to see that Reno had already started down toward the hostiles:

> Q. How far from "A" (the ford) toward "C" (the point of timber where the skirmish line was drawn up) were the troops at the time you came back to the ford?
> A. I judge they were four or five hundred yards, possibly a quarter of a mile, from "A."
> Q. How long had you been gone from "A"?
> A. They were crossing when I left. I rode about 75 yards back, and stopped a few seconds or possibly a minute, and rode back. By the time I got back, they were probably 500 yards away.

Gerard may have been correct about the distance he rode back before he encountered Cooke, but he cannot be correct both as to the time that elapsed before he got out into the prairie on the west side of the Little Horn and the distance Reno had advanced. All of the many happenings at the ford and just beyond it—the crossing of the troops; the stopping of many to water their horses and fill canteens; the disorganization caused by the men picking their various ways through the brush and fallen timber on the west side; Reno's sending two messengers and waiting for replies; the reorganization of the companies on the open prairie—took time; and while it may not have been an inordinate delay under the circumstances, it certainly consumed more than three or four minutes. The best estimate is that it took about fifteen to twenty minutes.

There seems to be a small question as to exactly what happened after the companies cleared the timber on the west side of the Little Horn. According to Captain Myles Moylan, who commanded A Company:

> A slight pause was made there to allow the companies to close up after crossing the stream. When all were closed up, they moved forward again at a trot, the head of the column moving at a very fast trot, so that the two rear companies were galloping. They moved probably a third of a mile, when the companies were formed in line, before the crossing was made on a little high ground on that side of the river.[15]

Every other witness on the subject, and there are many, states that the companies were formed in line when they came out of the timber and advanced in that manner. Lieutenant DeRudio, to Walter Camp: "The column then left-fronted into line with A Company on right, G in center and M on left. The Indian scouts were ahead and to left going down valley," and in his testimony: "As soon as we cleared the woods on the other side of the river, Major Reno called the battalion into line-of-battle. As soon as the line was formed, Major Reno moved them at a gallop." Private William Morris of M Company remembered: "As soon as we forded, Reno gave the command, 'Left into line, gallop—forward, guide center' and away we went—faster than I had ever ridden before." Corporal Stanislas Roy of A Company told Camp: "After passing ford, we formed in line." Major Reno, Private John Sivertsen of M Company, George Herendeen, Lieutenant Wallace and First Sergeant John Ryan all said the same thing.

Reno began his advance at approximately 2:50 p.m., with two companies, A and M, in line abreast, holding G Company in reserve on the second line. As the battalion started to move down the valley, Varnum and Hare took the Indian scouts ahead and on the left of the soldiers. Varnum wrote in his second unpublished narrative: "... came out into the open valley ahead & covered the advance with my scouts, Lts. Wallace & Hare, Charlie Reynolds, Herendine, Boyer & Fred Gerard & Bloody Knife, with myself, leading but spread out across the front," and in his testimony noted that: "We started out 50 to 75 yards ahead of the command. The bottom opened out wider as we went down the stream."

The advance started at a trot, and a gallop was ordered shortly afterwards. First Sergeant Ryan recalled in the *Hardin Tribune,* June 22, 1923, that: "We started down on a trot and then on a slow gallop." George Herendeen wrote in 1878 to the *New York Herald* that: " ... the line kept moving, first at a trot, then at a gallop." In his testimony however, he characterized the gait as a "slow lope." Lieutenant Wallace also testified that the gait was first a trot and then a gallop. Major Reno was the only witness to characterize this movement as a "charge," doing so both in his original report and in his testimony, although when pressed to describe the actual gait when the reserve company was brought into line, stated that it was "then a gallop," indicating that it had not been until then. Reno obviously was careful to call it a charge so that he could be seen to have been in compliance with his orders to "pursue and charge"; but witnesses called upon to answer whether "charge" had been ordered verbally or by trumpet had to answer in the negative.[16]

All witnesses indicate that shortly after starting, the third company, G, was brought up on the left of the line, extending it further to the left, toward the foothills on the west. The impetus for this move by Reno was twofold. First, the bottom widened out very considerably as the troops advanced from the ford, and second, an immense and forbidding dust cloud ahead indicated that the enemy was present in strength and not running. M Company was on the right and A Company in the center, but although some witnesses indicate that M was on the left, those observations pertain to a later time on the skirmish line, as will be seen.

As the line advanced, several of the troopers noticed a column of troops on the bluffs across the river. Private Daniel Newell rather melodramatically recalled in the *Sunshine Magazine* that:

As we galloped down that bottom and into that nest of Sioux, I remember seeing Custer's command on the bluffs on the opposite side
of the river, marching along to the north, possibly a mile or so from
the point where we had left them. Captain Varnum said later that he
also saw them, and that they were moving at a trot. I didn't pay much
attention at the time. I had something else on my mind.[17]

Newell may have been remembering Varnum's sighting rather than one
of his own. Corporal Roy told Walter Camp that "while forming, I heard some
of the men say 'There goes Custer.' He could be seen over on hills to our right
and across river," indicating that he had not seen them himself.

Private Tom O'Neill told Camp: "When about half way down to where
skirmish line was formed, he saw Custer and his whole command on the
bluffs across the river, over to the east, at a point which he would think was
about where Reno afterward fortified, or perhaps a little south of this. Custer's
command were then going at a trot." Private Henry Petring of G Company
told Camp: "While in the bottom, going toward the skirmish line, I saw Custer
over across the river, on the bluffs, waving his hat. Some of the men said:
'There goes Custer. He is up to something, for he is waving his hat.'"

Since Varnum stated that he saw the troops, or at least E Company, as he
was coming into the skirmish line area, and the other statements, except perhaps for O'Neill's, either confirm this timing or do nothing to discredit it, it
is evident that Reno's advance of more or less two and a half miles took about
fifteen minutes, which would agree with the gaits already mentioned. It is
also very likely that elements of Custer's command were actually seen twice
in this time frame—once when Custer himself first approached the edge of
the bluffs and again when the column was moving down along the high
ground, back from the edge of the bluffs.

Reno led the advance toward the village, riding some forty yards ahead
of the line of troops, accompanied by his adjutant, Lieutenant Benny Hodgson. There was very little initial opposition to the advance of the troops by
the Sioux and Cheyennes, the reason being that the Indians had been taken
by surprise by the appearance and rapid movements of the soldiers.

The preponderance of the evidence of the Sioux and Cheyennes who
spoke to the matter indicated that the surprise was complete, and that the appearance of the troops sent the camps into panic and confusion. Although
the troops had been seen much earlier in the day by three parties of Indians,

one of these groups was returning to their agency, one other trailed along behind the soldiers and only the third went to alert the camp. The news that the troops were coming arrived just as Reno appeared in the bottom.

The Hunkpapa Iron Hawk told Eli S. Ricker in 1907 that two young men were going back on the Indian trail toward the east looking for ponies and they discovered the troops coming. One of these boys, whose name was Deeds, was killed. The other returned to camp and gave the alarm, and the camp was thrown into the utmost confusion.[18] This same informant gave John G. Neidhardt an expanded version of this story in 1931:

> A boy was out with the party that went hunting, and when they were coming back they stopped at Spring Creek. After they got there, his horse played out, and he was riding double with someone. Then when he returned, his father told him and another boy to go and get his horse; and this was the last of the boy. . . . The morning of the fight I was eating, and I heard someone say "Chargers are coming." When I heard this I jumped up and rushed out to get my horse. I roped one, and just then the horses stampeded. They all got away from me. As they got away from me, an older brother of mine headed them off. I got on my horse with a rope around his nose, and just then Reno was charging. Everyone left their children, and they all tried to catch their horses, which were stampeding. The children came out of the creek where they were swimming I fled with the horses among the Minneconjous—that is, I tried to get them out of the danger zone. I headed them off, and brought them back.

This same information was given to John P. Everitt by One Bull, a Hunkpapa, and published in *The Sunshine Magazine* in September 1930. One Bull identifies the boy who was killed as Deeds. One Bull said that:

> On the day of the fight, [he] was in his lodge when he saw a man named Fat Bear come running into camp, shouting that soldiers were across the river and had just killed a boy named Deeds who was out picketing his horse. One Bull came out of his tepee and saw troops charging down on the camp on the same side of the river. He went to the lodge of Sitting Bull, and said he was going out to fight. Sitting Bull said, "Go ahead. They have already fired."

Although the details are not always the same, the common thread in the stories of the Indians is that Reno's appearance was a surprise and a shock, and it doesn't matter what the tribal affiliation is, the general tenor of the statements hardly varies. Some remember that there had been a dance the previous evening and that almost everyone slept late on June 25. Some remember that many of the women were off digging wild turnips; that some hunters had gone north down the river after antelope; that many people, including a lot of children, were swimming in the Little Horn. Some remember that they were taking horses out to graze, or were looking after their ponies. Principal witnesses, aside from those previously quoted, include Mnicoujous: Standing Bear and White Bull; Hunkpapa: Mrs. Spotted Horn Bull; Oglalas: American Horse, He Dog, Black Elk, Thomas Disputed, Eagle Bear, Eagle Elk, Lone Bear, Red Feather and Respects Nothing; Cheyennes: Weasel Bear, White Bull, Tall Bull and Wooden Leg.[19] Although the testimony of the troops also differs in the particulars and especially as to the number of hostile Indians actually seen, most witnesses recall that there was an immense amount of dust obscuring the village, that there was very little gunfire and that no hostiles were very close to the command.

Sergeant Culbertson testified:

We moved down the valley, and after going about half way (toward the village) there were Indians coming in on our left and front. Most of them would circle off to our left. There were a few shots fired, some of which struck in front of A Company.

Q. How far was that from where the line halted?
A. About half a mile.
Q. Was that regular fire or a few scattered shots?
A. Scattering.
Q. In moving down, were you opposed at any time in front by Indians meeting you?
A. They were circling in our front. They were 5 or 600 yards in our front just before we halted.
Q. Could you tell about how many Indians you saw up to the time the command halted?
A. There were then, in our front, 200 to 250 riding back and forth, and some crossed over to the bluff on our left.

Q. How far were the hostile Indians from the command when they halted, and what were they doing?

A. They were firing on us as we were about 500 yards from them.[20]

Lieutenant DeRudio's testimony was that: "When we had got near to the woods on the right hand side of the line, I heard some bullets whistling but not the noise of the explosions. In front of us there was an immense, dense dust, and we could see the shadows of some Indians in that dust," although he told the *New York Herald* that the dust was so thick that nothing could be distinguished in it. Even the Indians he testified he could see through the dust were not doing anything to threaten the command:

Q. What were those Indians that you saw in the dust doing? Advancing toward Major Reno or running?

A. They were running around, making a dust.

Q. Were they advancing toward him at the time he halted?

A. No. They seemed to be standing, waiting for the command to come up.

Q. How far was that from the line?

A. 5 or 600 yards.[21]

According to First Sergeant Ryan, "Before we arrived at the timber, there was one shot fired away ahead of us."[22] Captain Moylan saw, as he testified, "an immense cloud of dust . . . down the valley, and a little opening in it occasionally where we could see figures moving through it." Lieutenant Wallace also saw "a big dust, but as we moved on, the dust cleared away and the Indians were seen coming back." Up until then, he testified, "The Indians . . . were apparently running from us." Wallace also thought that: "It was a good mile and three-quarters before the first shot was fired, and two miles to the timber where he dismounted. The ground over which he [Reno] passed was level, and there were no obstacles in the way till the Indians came there."

Major Reno however, saw things very differently. In his official report of July 5, 1876, he wrote:

I deployed and with the Ree scouts on my left charged down the valley driving the Indians with great ease for about 2½ miles. I however soon saw that I was being drawn into some trap as they would certainly fight harder and especially as we were nearing their village, which was still standing, besides I could not see Custer or any other support and at the same time the very earth seemed to grow Indians and they were running toward me in swarms and from all directions. . . . I saw I must defend myself and give up the attack mounted.

In his testimony at his court of inquiry, Reno drew an even more dramatic picture:

> I could see a disposition on the part of the Indians to lead us on, and that opinion was also confirmed when a little afterwards, on advancing a little further, I could see the Indians coming out from a ravine, where they evidently had hidden themselves. I think [this] ravine, as I saw it, was eight or nine hundred yards in front of me, and on what we called the foot hills on the left bank of the river, there were straggling parties of Indians making around to my rear. I said to myself at once that I could not successfully make an offensive charge. Their numbers had thrown me on the defensive.

This "ravine" was actually a semi-dry creek bed and was, as Reno stated, some eight hundred yards in front of him, and was, in fact a former channel of the Little Horn. There were not hundreds of Indians either hidden in the creek bed or boiling out of it, as the Indian evidence amply illustrates. They were coming from the camps beyond the bend in the river, which Reno could not see. It was Reno who commanded, however, and it was his perceptions that mattered most. He saw the ominous cloud of dust, which was caused both by the Indians driving in their ponies and by their riding back and forth to create a very typical diversion, the equivalent of a smokescreen. He thought he saw hordes of Indians waiting to lure him into a deadly trap; and one thing he was certain of—he obviously kept looking backward—there was no close support coming from behind him, as he said he had been led to expect. He therefore threw up his hand, ordered the line to halt, to dismount and prepare to fight on foot. While some participants credit this halt with saving the command, it was, in fact, Reno's first error of commission and the first intimation that he had perhaps been put in a position and circumstance for which he was not very well suited.

That there was no compelling reason for Reno to stop when he did is

amply shown by the Indian evidence and is confirmed by incidents that occurred coincidently. Private Roman Rutten had trouble controlling his horse
during the advance down the valley and had been forced to ride wide circles
around the troops to maintain contact. He told Walter Camp: ". . . when got
down near the skirmish line, the horse lunged ahead of the command, and
took him considerably nearer the Indians. He therefore circled him around
to the right, came back through the timber and joined command. Rutten was
not wounded in this movement, but was wounded in the shoulder on the hill
the next day." Private William Morris later wrote:

> John R. Meyer's [Meier, private of M] horse carried him down the
> valley, through the Indians, some of whom chased him two or three
> miles over the hills and back to the ford. He escaped with a gun-shot
> wound in the neck. Rutten's horse also ran away; but he succeeded
> in making a circle before reaching the Indians, and received only a
> gun-shot wound in the shoulder.[23]

Two other troopers could not control their high-spirited mounts, which
carried them straight ahead and into the fearsome dust cloud. Like Rutten
and Meier, they were privates of M Company and both of them—George
Smith and James Turley—were supposedly "never seen again." Private William Slaper told Earl Brininstool in 1920 that: "several [horses] became unmanageable and started straight for the open, among the Indians, carrying
their helpless riders with them. One of the boys, a young fellow named Smith,
of Boston, we never saw again, either dead or alive . . ." and First Sergeant
Ryan later reported: "Private James Turley of my troop when we arrived at
the timber and had orders to halt, could not control his horse which carried
him towards the Indian camp. That was the last I saw of him. He was a very
nice young man. " In fact both Smith and Turley were able to survive their
wild rides, only to be killed later.[24]

In addition to these four troopers who did not stop and were not killed,
there were a few other soldiers out in advance of the skirmish line. Reno's
own orderly, Private Davern, had gone ahead to join Lieutenant Hare:

Q. What were you doing at the time?
A. I got permission from Major Reno to go with Lieutenant Hare, and
went in advance of the line, about 200 yards.

Q. What did you do?

A. I moved on down the bottom about 200 yards ahead of the skirmish line to get a shot at some Indians about 200 yards to our left . . .

Q. You saw Indians 2 or 300 yards to the left of the line?

A. Yes, sir.

Q. Were those the nearest Indians you saw?

A. Yes, sir.

Q. Were they firing at you?

A. No, sir.

Q. Were the Indians firing at anybody about that time?

A. I heard no bullets at that time.

Lieutenant Varnum recalled in his testimony that he looked back and saw that the troops had halted: "I noticed all of a sudden that they [the Indians] stopped and turned backward, and I turned my head around and glanced back to see the cause, and I noticed a battalion deploying from column into line, and I supposed at the time that they supposed they were going to halt, and turned back on us at that time." He therefore rode back to rejoin his company:

I was not present and didn't hear any of the orders, and don't know what orders were given. When the line halted, I rode with Lieutenant Hare in toward the line, and the Indian scouts, as they generally fight in the Indian fashion, were gone, I don't know where, and my old company that I belonged to was in the line, Captain Moylan's company, and I went back and reported to him, and told him I should stop with his company during the fight . . . I think they were just coming from their horses at the time I rode up. . . . I saw, about the time Major Reno's command dismounted in the bottom, just as I joined it from the left and front, looking on the bluffs across the river to our right, I saw the Gray Horse Company of the regiment moving down along those bluffs. As I know now the Gray Horse Company was with his command, I know it was General Custer's column.

I just looked up and saw it. We had plenty to do there, and did not look any more. It was back from the actual edge of the bluffs. The head and the rear of the column were both behind the edge of the bluffs in a sort of hollow, and I just happened to catch sight of about the whole of the Gray Horse Company. . . . They were probably three-fourths of a mile from where we were. General Custer generally rode a very fast-walking horse that made nearly the whole column trot to keep up with him, and that is my impression of the gait they were moving at.

Varnum also contributed an interesting bit of evidence when he stated: "When his command was deployed from column-of-fours into line, the body of the Indians seemed to turn back toward us. When we started on again, they went on again. They kept a certain distance from us all the time, and when we finally halted and dismounted, they turned back again," indicating quite clearly that not only was Reno's command not threatened before it was halted, but that the hostiles did not actually turn back upon the troops until after the halt was made.

There has been some little confusion as to the relative positions of the three companies on the skirmish line when it was formed vis-à-vis their positions during the advance down the valley. It is clear that the positions from right to left during the advance were M-A-G, and on the skirmish line were G-A-M.[25] The confusion arose from the convoluted reasoning some historians used to reconcile these differences, when in fact the reconciliation is both straightforward and logical. All witnesses speak of a halt and a deployment, some without going into any detail as to exactly what they meant by "deployment," obviously assuming, and rightly so, that military men knew what was meant. Varnum's simple observation that "I think they were just coming from their horses" when he rode up, is a key piece of evidence that seems to have slipped into the cracks.

When the advance was halted near the point of timber, the line no longer existed as a line. The troops rode into the edge of the timber and dismounted. A detachment of M Company under the command of First Sergeant Ryan entered the woods to ensure that it was clear of any enemy prior to the horses being taken in.[26] First Sergeant Ryan was also very specific:

When we got to the timber we rode down an embankment and dismounted. This was where the channel of the river changed and was probably several feet lower than the level of the prairie. We dismounted in haste, number four of each set of four holding the horses. We came up onto higher ground forming a skirmish line from the timber towards the bluffs on the other side of the valley and facing downstream in the direction of the Indian camp ... some of the men laid down while others knelt down. At this particular place there was a prairie dog town and we used the mounds for temporary breastworks.[27]

Here is confirmation that M was on the right and the first company to reach the woods. Being the first to dismount and leave their horses, M troopers became the first to deploy out onto the bottom as skirmishers and the other companies followed in turn, A being next followed lastly by G. As the troopers came onto the skirmish line, it was simply extended out to the left, with M being followed over by A then A by G. Since Reno considered the left to be the weakest defense area and it was the only place he could readily be flanked by the warriors, it is logical to assume, and very correct military thinking, that the troops would be moved immediately toward the left as they came out on the line, not leapfrog each other from right to left.

Major Reno himself noted in his official report: " . . . taking possession of a point of woods, and which furnished (near its edges) a shelter for the horses, dismounted and fought on foot," and also testified: "I dismounted by telling the company officers. Lieutenant Hodgson gave the order to G Company, and I gave it to Companies M and A. I gave the order to dismount and prepare to fight on foot, and their horses would be sheltered in this point of timber." Reno could not have given the latter orders in this fashion had the command been driving forward at a gallop, especially since he was forty or so yards in advance of the line when it was moving.

Lieutenant DeRudio thought the deployment was made "very nicely. It surprised me much as there was a lot of recruits among them, and many of the horses were green. The battalion deployed, the right of the line at right angle with the woods." Captain Moylan wrote Fred Calhoun on July 6, 1876: "This was done very properly by the men, our line formed, and a very heavy fight commenced." Some witnesses, notably Reno, Wallace, Culbertson and Moylan, made a point of emphasizing the number of recruits or new men in the companies. In fact the majority of the newer enlistments had been detached at the Powder River supply depot, and there were very few with the battalion in the valley—only three green 1876 recruits in the three companies.[28]

Whether or not the deployment onto the skirmish line was made "very nicely" or "very properly," it was made without incident and very safely, for the hostile warriors had not yet opened any significant fire upon the troops. The troopers apparently kept reasonably standard intervals of five yards, although Sergeant Culbertson didn't think so. "The intervals were not kept up well. I judge we were deployed about 200 or 250 yards, perhaps more," he testified. Other estimates put the length of the skirmish line at, or above, four hundred yards and there is little doubt that this was the case. There were over a hundred men on the line, including several of the Indian scouts who had not gone off after enemy ponies.[29] Although it is popularly supposed and frequently written, that the scouts ran at the first sight of the Sioux—Reno testified to exactly that—many of them fought in the valley, either on the line or in the woods, or across the Little Horn below the bluffs.[30] When the line stretched out onto the bottom prairie, it formed an angle with the river, so that the left was farther from the village than was the right, which was resting on or very near the point of timber. The left of the line was advanced so that the angle was more of a right angle and during this movement the entire line advanced some seventy-five to one hundred yards, according to most witnesses,[31] and came to a halt about a half-mile from the tipis in the valley, although the right of the line was much closer to the Hunkpapa camps which were in a bend of the river just beyond the timber where the horses were located. As the troopers assumed their prone or kneeling firing positions on the line and settled in to fire on the apparently approaching warriors, it was approximately 3:15 p.m.

THE FIGHT ON THE SKIRMISH LINES—IN THE VALLEY AND IN THE WOODS

The disposition of the troops had taken place with absolutely no hindrance from the warriors of the camps. The surprise approach of the soldiers, the warriors' need to get their horses to hand, the prime directive of seeing their families on the way to safety, and, strangely enough, time taken to don best clothing, charms, paint and fetishes, all meant that no harm had been done to the troops prior to the formation of the skirmish line or immediately thereafter. Of course, no harm had been done to the hostile Indians either.

The skirmish line stayed on the plain only a very short time, mostly estimated by witnesses to have been ten to fifteen minutes. Sergeant Culbertson's description was that they "remained on the skirmish line, firing. Some of the men were firing very fast. We were on the skirmish line about 35 minutes." Culbertson was the only witness to give such an estimate of the time. Lieutenant DeRudio testified: "Q. How long did the skirmish line stay there before it came in? A. 10 or 12 minutes," and Private William Morris wrote: "Our line, deployed as skirmishers, had been fighting perhaps 15 minutes."

Charlie Varnum agreed with the lower estimate: "Q. Major Reno deployed his skirmish line, and they remained 10 or 15 minutes in position? A. Yes, sir," while Private Tom O'Neill told Walter Camp: "The skirmish line could not have stood to exceed 20 minutes," and Private Edward Pigford told Camp: "The skirmish line was no sooner formed than it broke up." Major Reno stated that the line was out on the plain for at least twenty minutes, for he had been there with it for that long: "We had been out there about 15 or 20 minutes, under a pretty hot fire." George Herendeen disagreed: "After skirmishing for a few minutes, Reno fell back to his horses in the timber," and Fred Gerard wrote to Walter Camp: "Charlie Reynolds and I . . . went out and took station just in rear of the skirmish line, where it rested on the timber, to watch the firing, which lasted about five minutes . . . ."[32]

There is positively no question that the skirmish line did not stay out on the grassy bottom for very long, for the majority of the Sioux and Cheyenne warriors who left accounts of the fighting in the valley do not mention this skirmish line at all, let alone as being of much importance or involving any hard fighting.

Of the Cheyennes, Soldier Wolf told George Bird Grinnell in 1898 that: "The people from the lower circles rushed toward the sounds of gunfire. The troops retreated and the Indians rushed in among them," clearly indicating that there was only one event of any consequence. Two Moon said in 1911: "The soldiers had come to the edge of the Sioux camp, got off their horses and gone into the brush and timber." Tall Bull told Grinnell, also in 1898, that: "The people from lower down heard the shooting and rushed up to confront the troops, who retreated into the timber when pressed." Tall Bull says: "They did not stop there, but ran right through it and out on the other side."

The Cheyennes may have come late to the fray, since their camp circle was a few miles down the river, but the Sioux gave similar descriptions, differing only in that the troops were driven into the timber. Gall was quoted in 1886: "The women and children caught the horses for the bucks to mount them; the bucks mounted and charged back Reno and checked him, and drove him into the timber." Iron Hawk told John Neidhardt in 1931: "I had only a bow and arrows. I got dressed for war as quickly as I could; but it took me a long time to put an eagle feather on my head! I painted my face a dark red. About the time I got through dressing for the war, the Reno troop was through fighting, so I did not get to fight any . . ." Turtle Rib told Camp: "The fighting against Reno did not last long. He could not say how many minutes, but only a few," and Flying By told him that: "Battle with Reno lasted only short time, and my horse shot. Soldiers went through timber and retreated to river." White Bull was interviewed by Walter S. Campbell in 1932 and stated: "Immediately after, the soldiers dismounted and formed a line in the open facing the north. White Bull saw them set up a flag [guidon]. White Bull yelled aloud, 'Whoever is a brave man will go get that flag.' But everybody was busy. Nobody volunteered, and before he himself could do anything the soldiers moved the flag, falling back into the timber along the river."

The action on the skirmish line was not only short-lived and insignificant, but was fought at long range and resulted in only one trooper being killed and one wounded. There were several non-combatant woman and children killed or wounded in the village, especially among the Hunkpapas, not purposely, but simply because the troops were firing at long range in the general direction of the village and at whatever warriors they could see through the dust. Several of the participants have left narratives.

Private Daniel Newell said:

> There we got down to real fighting. It was no trouble to find something to shoot at. They were soon on three sides of us, and fast getting on the fourth. We didn't fight there long until we got orders to fall back to the timber, nearer the river on our right. We went like a bunch of sheep. On the way, I came to a buffalo wallow, and I said to myself, "Here is a good breastworks." I dropped into it and fired five shots at the Indians with my carbine. Then I looked around, and could not see a blessed man, so I moved on for the timber.

William Morris remembered it pretty much the same and added an interesting observation:

> Ninety percent of the command went into the fight in shirts, gray or blue, their coats being on their saddles. Some of the officers or non-commissioned officers who wore coats threw them off, as the marks of rank singled them out to the Indians as chiefs. There weren't many

questions asked after the battle about where the coats of those above a private went to; but I guess everyone understands. While in this position, the man next on my right, Sergeant O'Hara, was killed [O'Hara was, according to other accounts, only wounded]. The smoke obscured the line, but bullets were taking effect all along it. We were perfectly cool, determined, and doing good execution, and expected to hear Custer attack. We had been fighting lying down about fifteen minutes, when one of our men came from the timber and reported that they were killing our horses in the rear. Reno then made his only error; he gave the command, "Retreat to your horses, men!" French immediately corrected the mistake with the command, "Steady, men—fall back slowly; face the enemy, and continue your fire."

As will be seen, Reno was not on the line when it fell back to the timber and did not give the order.

Private O'Neill however, saw it differently. He told Walter Camp that: ". . . on the skirmish line, there was no very hard fighting, and thinks that but few effective shots could have been fired. The men were in good spirits, talking and laughing, and not apprehensive of being defeated—and the Sioux toward the village were riding around, kicking up a big dust, but keeping pretty well out of range."

Most participants gave the skirmish line action very short shrift in their later recollections, although the casualties were mentioned by a great many of them. "One man was wounded on the skirmish line that I saw," testified Sergeant Culbertson. Lieutenant DeRudio told Walter Camp: "Says fight on skirmish line did not last over 10 minutes if it did that long. Does not remember sending from skirmish line for ammunition. On skirmish line he found Sergeant White wounded and took his gun and fired two shots at Indians over on hills to west . . ."

Private Edward Pigford was also interviewed by Camp: "Says Sgt. O'Hara was hit on the skirmish line and not killed. When Pigford left the skirmish line, O'Hara called to Pigford: 'For God's sake, don't leave me.' He personally fired only 4 or 5 shots. Says O'Hara was [then] killed about 40 or 50 yard from timber." Private Roman Rutten to Camp: "Says Sergt. O'Hara was first man killed, and he fell on skirmish line." Private James Wilber told Camp: "Sergeant O'Hara was killed near the tepees, and was first man killed in battle," but Private Frank Sniffin told him that: "Sgt. O'Hara was killed on our line in the bottom. He was dead, or supposed to be, when we left the firing line."

Whether O'Hara was killed, or only wounded and left on the line, he was remembered in more detail by First Sergeant John Ryan: "This was where the first man was killed, Sergt. Miles F. O'Hara of my troop M. He was a corporal going out on the expedition and was promoted to a sergeant a few days before his death to replace Sergt. John Dolan, who was discharged. . . . Sergeant O'Hara was considered a very fine soldier. "

Despite the few casualties and the lack of pressure from the Sioux and Cheyennes, the skirmish line rapidly withdrew into the belt of timber on its right. Major Reno and some of his officers, notably Wallace and Moylan, advanced two reasons for this movement—the Indians were passing around his left in great numbers, so as to completely surround the skirmish line on the plain, and the Indians were filtering into the timber, endangering the horses and hence the safety of the entire command. Wallace testified: "The Indians, instead of pressing our front, passed around to our left and opened a flank fire," and also: "After being in line some time, it was reported that the Indians were coming on the opposite side of the creek and trying to get our horses. Company G was then taken off the line and taken into the timber." Wallace described the actions of the warriors thusly: "They were fighting in regular Indian style, riding up and down, some few on foot and some few on the hills to the left, passing around and coming in our rear, filling the whole space in our rear, a mile or two, with scattered Indians riding about. Not a solid mass, but riding around, yelling and hooting, and those within range were shooting."

While it was true that warriors had circled around on the hills to the west in an attempt to flank and surround the troops' skirmish line, Captain French—who seems to have kept his wits about him—had refaced the line slightly and then more pronouncedly, so that part of his company was also facing west and then almost at a forty-five degree angle to the main line. This kept the warriors from rolling up the line.

In fact, neither proffered reason was true. Major Reno also stated that he went into the timber in order to lead a charge against the nearest part of the village. This too was a fabrication repeated by some of the officers. Reno's going into the woods was mere happenstance and the withdrawal of the skirmish line was not necessary at that time, nor controlled very well, or indeed even ordered by Reno. The relevant portions of Reno's testimony are: "Q. In making your estimate, did you have as one of the ingredients the fact that the Indians were circling to your rear, instead of remaining in your front? A. Yes, sir. I knew they were going there in small parties, at the same time there were many in front," and also:

> We had been out there about 15 or 20 minutes, under a pretty hot fire. I was on the line near Captain Moylan, when word came to me from out of the timber that the Indians were turning our right. I left Lieutenant Hodgson, my adjutant, to bring me word what went on there, and I went with Company G to the banks of the river. I suppose there were 40 men in it. When I got there, I had a good view of the tepees, and I could see many scattering tepees (some of the Hunk-papa camp). It was plain to me the Indians were using the woods as much as I was myself, in sheltering themselves and creeping up on me. I then rode out on the plain. There was firing there that I could hear, but not see. Lieutenant Hodgson came to me and said the Indians were passing to our left and rear, and I told him to bring the skirmishers in round the horses. After going down to the river there, and seeing the facilities they had, I knew I could not stay there unless I stayed forever.[33]

Lieutenant Wallace also remembered the Sioux and Cheyennes circling to the rear: "When we went on the skirmish line, I for the first time saw the village, and the Indians were thick in front, and were passing our left and rear." Private Davern, however, did not think that there were all that many warriors doing the circling: "Q. What were the Indians doing? A. Still circling around, and getting thicker in front. Q. Were any of them moving to the left? A. Yes, sir, Q. How many? A. I could not say. They were moving to the left all the time. Q. In squads or together? A. Mostly singly."

While some of the troopers and the officers seemed to know why the line was withdrawn, although not always agreeing as to the apparent reason, others had no idea of what was going on or why. Sergeant Culbertson, who on the whole tended to be a pro-Reno witness, had to admit that he was mystified:

> We remained there some time, when I heard the command given, I don't know by whom, to move by the right flank—every man moving

off toward the timber. I stopped on arriving at the timber with 3 other men, at the edge of the timber on the brow of the hill. The balance of the command went into the woods—I do not know for what purpose. I did not hear the command.

The real reason for the withdrawal had nothing to do with encircling Indians, casualties or military tactics. The movement was the result of a combination of errors that were themselves caused by erroneous reports by Lieutenant Wallace and Captain Moylan, and these, in hindsight to be sure, appear to have been nervous reactions to events that might have been possible, but which were not real.

Wallace, in his testimony, skirts the issue: "What disposition was made in there, I only know from hearsay. I remained on the picket line until the ammunition was getting exhausted, and the Indians were coming in our rear and on our left and in front, and the skirmish line had to fall back into the timber." Lieutenant DeRudio however, says it was Wallace who started things: "Pretty soon Lieutenant Wallace, as we were sitting together, called my attention to the Indians coming in on the other side of the woods. I started right down a little path with 5 or 6 men on the right of the line, to go and see." DeRudio continued:

Q. How did you come to leave that company and go into the woods?

A. I did not leave the company. The company was at the right of the line, right at the timber.

Q. You went into the timber?

A. Some of my men went into the timber, and I went with them.

Q. By whose orders did you go into the timber?

A. No one's. Lieutenant Wallace said some Indians were coming there, and I went in.

Q. You separated yourself from your command?

A. No, sir. The command came into the woods with me. Some of the men were in there when I went in.

Q. Did you follow them, or lead them in?

A. I followed them.

Q. By whose order did the men start to go into the woods?

A. I don't know of any order.

Q. Did Major Reno give an order to leave the line and go into the woods?

A. I don't know of any order.

Captain Moylan put the onus on Reno for the withdrawal:

Major Reno at that time was in the bottom superintending the movements of G Company that he had taken down there. Fearing that these Indians were turning the left of his line, and would close in from the left so as to necessarily cause a change of front on a portion of the front of the line [French had already moved part of his company—see above], at least, I went to the edge of the hill and called to him to come up there and look at the situation of affairs himself, so that he might see how the thing was going. He came in there, and soon took in the situation, and ordered the line to be withdrawn.

Moylan was telling an absolute lie and he knew it. Reno had never returned from his foray into the woods. Lieutenant Varnum makes this patently clear in his own testimony:

When I had been on the line ten or fifteen minutes, I heard somebody say that G Company was going to charge a portion of the village down through the woods, or something to that effect. I heard some of the men calling out: "G Company is going to charge!" I was on my horse, and I rode down into the timber to go with the company that was going to charge the village . . . I heard no orders. It was just a rumor that I followed, and I saw Colonel Reno there. He was right with G Company, evidently deploying it to go through the woods. The company was on the downstream side of the opening, and I said [to myself]: "I am going to charge!" or something like that, and I rode up to where the Colonel [Reno] was, and the Colonel asked me if I had just come from the line in front, and I told him I had a few moments ago . . . and he said: "I wish you would go back there and see how things are going on, and come back and report to me." I turned back on my horse and was riding across the opening when I met Lieutenant Hodgson . . . and told him that Major Reno wanted to know what was going on on the line, and if he would report to him, I would ride up and come down again . . . Then I went up to the line. . . . The line at that time appeared to have fallen back to the edge of the timber, that is, it was lying on the edge of the timber instead of being perpendicular to it.

This indicates quite clearly that the line was withdrawn while Reno was still in the timber, probably as battalion adjutant Hodgson was on his way to seek out Reno, and it is also obvious that Moylan must have precipitated the movement, since he is the one who went out of his way to lie about what happened—and as Private William Morris is quoted above, the withdrawal was so hasty that Captain French "immediately corrected the mistake with the command, 'Steady, men—fall back slowly; face the enemy, and continue your fire.'"[34] Why Moylan was never brought up short in his lie remains a mystery. It is sufficient at this point to understand that it was not a deliberate action by Reno, but a combination of circumstances that led to the change in front. The question must stand however, as to what exactly Reno was doing in the timber when he should have been controlling the skirmish line.

Across the Little Horn, Armstrong Custer had taken his command across Medicine Tail Coulee, unaware that Reno's line had withdrawn from the prairie; orderly trumpeter John Martin was on his ride to deliver a famous order to Captain Benteen; and Sergeant Daniel Knipe was speaking with that very same Benteen—telling him that he was wanted up ahead and being directed by Benteen to the pack train, which was still straggling back up Ash Creek.

It was approximately 3:35 p.m. as Reno's troopers reached the edge of the belt of timber, and dropped behind the shelter afforded by the bank which had been cut by a previous flow of the Little Horn and which delineated the proximate bottom land there. Now Reno's nervousness, echoed by Wallace and Moylan, was to escalate, causing him to make a desperate decision.

NOTES

1. Soldier, Arikara scout: from *The Arikara Narrative* and from an interview with William Mason Camp *c.* July 1912; [ebook] Appendix 3.101.
2. Reno: statement to the *New York Herald*, August 8, 1876; [ebook] Appendix 3.95.
3. First Lieutenant George D. Wallace: testimony at the Reno Court of Inquiry, 1876; [ebook] Appendix 3.113.
4. Frederic F. Gerard: testimony before the Reno Court of Inquiry, 1879; [ebook] Appendix 3.33.

5. Major Marcus A. Reno: testimony before the Reno Court of Inquiry, 1879; [ebook] Appendix 3.96.
6. George Herendeen: letter to the *New York Herald*, January 4, 1878; [ebook] Appendix 3.53.
7. Lieutenant Charles C. DeRudio: testimony at Reno Court of Inquiry, 1879; [ebook] Appendix 3.18.
8. Frederic F. Gerard: testimony at the Reno Court of Inquiry, 1879, and narrative of 1909; [ebook] Appendices 3.30, 3.33.
9. Marcus A. Reno: report of July 5, 1876; Major Marcus A. Reno: testimony at Reno Court of Inquiry, 1876; [ebook] Appendices 3.96, 4.9.
10. Private Edward Davern of F Company, Reno's orderly: testimony at the Reno Court of Inquiry, 1879; [ebook] Appendix 3.17.
11. Frederic F. Gerard: testimony at the Reno Court of Inquiry, 1879, and narrative of 1909; [ebook] Appendix 3.30.
12. John M. Ryan: narrative, published in the *Hardin Tribune*, June 22, 1923; [ebook] Appendix 3.99.
13. The Arikara scouts with Custer on the Little Horn Campaign: accounts from *The Arikara Narrative*; Young Hawk, Arikara scout: accounts from *The Arikara Narrative* and from interviews with Walter M. Camp *c.* 1912; [ebook] Appendices 3.1, 3.120, 3.121.
14. Frederic F. Gerard: testimony before the Reno Court of Inquiry, 1879; [ebook] Appendix 3.33.
15. Captain Myles Moylan: testimony at the Reno Court of Inquiry, 1879; [ebook] Appendix 3.81.
16. Lieutenant Charles C. DeRudio: stories from various sources, 1876 and subsequent testimony at the Reno Court of Inquiry, 1879; Captain Myles Moylan: testimony before the Reno Court of Inquiry, 1879; First Lieutenant George D. Wallace: testimony before the Reno Court of Inquiry, 1879; [ebook] Appendices 3.18, 3.81, 3.113.
17. Daniel Newell: account as given to John P. Everitt and published in *The Sunshine Magazine*, September 1930; [ebook] Appendix 3.82.
18. Hunkpapa and Brule participants: stories from the hostiles; [ebook] Appendix 3.58.
19. Cheyenne participants: stories from the hostiles; Hunkpapa and Brule participants: stories from the hostiles; Mnicoujou and Two Kettles: stories from the hostiles; Oglala: stories from the hostiles; [ebook] Appendices 3.9, 3.58, 3.78, 3.83.
20. Sergeant Ferdinand A. Culbertson: testimony at the Reno Court of Inquiry, 1879; [ebook] Appendix 3.14.
21. Lieutenant Charles C. DeRudio: stories from various sources, 1876 subsequent and testimony at the Reno Court of Inquiry 1879; [ebook] Appendix 3.18.
22. John M. Ryan: narrative published in the *Hardin Tribune*, June 22, 1923; [ebook] Appendix 3.99.
23. William E. Morris: excerpts from his accounts from correspondence and as published in an unidentified newspaper, in the period 1894–1923; [ebook] Appendix 3.80.
24. *See* [ebook] Appendix 5.17 for locations.
25. Charles A. Varnum: testimony before the Reno Court of Inquiry, 1879; First Lieutenant

George D. Wallace: testimony before the Reno Court of Inquiry, 1879; [ebook] Appendices 3.111, 3.113.

26. William E. Morris: excerpts from his accounts from correspondence and as published in an unidentified newspaper, in the period 1894–1923; John M. Ryan: narrative published in the *Hardin Tribune*, June 22, 1923; [ebook] *Appendices 3.80, 3.99.*

27. John M. Ryan: narrative published in the *Hardin Tribune*, June 22, 1923; [ebook] Appendix 3.99.

28. See Analysis 4.

29. The 7th Regiment of Cavalry, United States Army: Rosters pertaining to regimental assignments, strengths, casualties and battle statistics on the campaign which culminated in the series of actions known as the Battle of the Little Big Horn, June 25 and 26, 1876; [ebook] Appendix 5.17.

30. The 7th Regiment of Cavalry, United States Army: Rosters pertaining to regimental assignments, strengths, casualties and battle statistics on the campaign which culminated in the series of actions known as the Battle of the Little Big Horn, June 25 and 26, 1876; [ebook] Appendix 5.17.

31. Sergeant Ferdinand A. Culbertson: testimony at the Reno Court of Inquiry, 1879; Private Edward Davern of F Company, Reno's orderly: testimony at the Reno Court of Inquiry, 1879; Lieutenant Charles C. DeRudio: stories from various sources, 1876 and subsequent testimony at the Reno Court of Inquiry, 1879; First Lieutenant George D. Wallace: testimony before the Reno Court of Inquiry, 1879; [ebook] Appendices 3.14, 3.17, 3.18, & 3.113.

32. Frederic F. Gerard: narrative of 1909; [ebook] Appendix 3.30.

33. Major Marcus A. Reno: testimony at Reno Court of Inquiry, 1876; [ebook] Appendices 3.96.

34. William E. Morris: excerpts from his accounts from correspondence and as published in an unidentified newspaper, in the period 1894–1923;[ebook] Appendix 3.80.

CHAPTER **6**

ACROSS THE LITTLE HORN AND
UP A HILL: RENO'S RETREAT
FROM THE TIMBER

*"For God's sake, Sergeant, take your horse—we're going
to retreat."*—TRUMPETER DAVID MCVEIGH OF
A COMPANY TO SERGEANT WILLIAM HEYN,
WHILE IN THE TIMBER

Major Reno had started feeling anxious immediately after crossing the Little Horn at Ford A, when he understood that the Indians were coming out from the village to meet him and realized that Custer's immediate command was not following him across the river.

His nervous state was betrayed, as we have seen, when at the inquiry he testified, "I crossed the creek and then formed my battalion with two companies in line and one in reserve. I had been a good deal in the Indian country, and I was convinced that the Indians were there in overwhelming numbers," followed by his admission that he had sent two Privates, McIlhargey and Mitchell, to Custer in quick succession.[1] That nervousness had developed into alarm on the skirmish line when Lieutenant Wallace had called out that Indians were in the timber trying to get the command's horses. Instead of sending a subordinate, Reno left the skirmish line and took a number of G Company men into the timber to check out Wallace's claim.

Without their commanding officer in sight, some officers became worried to the extent that DeRudio quickly followed Reno into the timber with some A Company men, Lieutenant Varnum went into the timber to see what was happening there, Lieutenant Hodgson followed shortly after, and Captain Moylan, seeing the skirmish line numbers being depleted, with the Indians getting bolder, ordered the skirmish line back to the timber's edge.

Shortly thereafter the whole command was in the timber and Reno, who had remained in it, found himself under pressure to make a decision on what course of action to take. His state of mind can only be surmised from testimony given at the inquiry. Dr. Porter said, "I heard Major Reno say, 'We have got to get out of here, we have got to charge them' and I saw him getting out of the timber in the direction we came in." In response to the question "State your opinion, if you have any, in respect to the conduct of Major Reno at that timber, whether it was that of an officer manifesting courage, coolness and efficiency, such as would tend to inspire his men with confidence and fearlessness, or the reverse," he stated, "I saw nothing in his conduct particularly heroic or particularly the reverse. I think he was some little embarrassed and flurried. The bullets were coming in pretty fast and I think he did not know whether it was best to stay there or leave."[2]

So Reno was in a dilemma, with his scattered command waiting for orders and the Indians infiltrating, firing as targets presented themselves. George Herendeen's testimony describes what happened:

As I started to find the command they were standing still mounted in the park—what I could see of them . . .

Q. Did you see Major Reno there and, if so, what was he doing?

A. He was sitting on his horse in the park.

Q. Were you near him?

A. I rode to within about six feet of him on his right . . .

Q. Did you hear him give any orders or instructions at that time?

A. I heard him order the troops to dismount and there was a volley by the Indians, I judge the same Indians that came in and that I had been firing at. There was an Indian [Bloody Knife] standing on Major Reno's front, not more than eight or ten feet from him. As I rode in there and got straightened up and saw how everything lay, this volley was fired and this Indian and a soldier [were] hit. The soldier hallooed and Major Reno gave the order to dismount, and the soldiers had just struck the ground when he gave the order to mount and then everything left the timber on a run.

In later testimony Herendeen enlarged upon what happened to Reno after Bloody Knife was hit:

Q. State, if you know, what the effect of Bloody Knife being killed had on Major Reno?
A. All I know is what Major Reno told me.
Q. State what he told you.
A. I think it was on the 26th or the morning of the 27th when General Terry was advancing up. I was near Major Reno and knowing that Bloody Knife was killed near to where we were in the timber, I asked him if he remembered anything about that fact. I forget the exact words I used. He said, "Yes, his blood and brains spattered over me."[3]

Already highly agitated, it is understandable if Reno was further unnerved by that incident. Reno naturally, painted a different picture:

Q. How did you come to leave the timber, with what orders and in what manner?
A. I left the timber sending orders to Captain French by Lieutenant Hodgson, and giving the order in person to Captain Moylan and Lieutenant McIntosh to mount their men and bring them to the edge of the timber where they could be formed in column-of-fours. I had no other means of accomplishing that formation except through their action.

This scene of cool decision-taking does not gel with what Herendeen described, so the question is who was being truthful? Perhaps some earlier testimony from Reno throws some light: "The regiment had evidently got scattered or someone would have sent me an order or come to aid me. And in order to secure a union of the regiment, which I thought was absolutely necessary, I moved to the hill to get where I could be seen . . ." The salient point here is his comment "I moved to the hill" as if he already had a fixed target in mind, but from his position in the timber he could not see what became known as Reno Hill, so in his testimony he was obviously prepared to embroider the truth.

Moylan too described leaving the timber as a properly ordered, well-executed military maneuver:

The companies were mounted up and being unable to form in any order in the timber, I gave my men orders to mount up as rapidly as possibly individually and move up out of the timber in order that they might be formed out there. When about one half of my company was mounted up, I went out of the timber and formed the men in column-of-fours as they came up.[4]

It would indeed have been praiseworthy had it happened that way, yet the Lakota and Cheyenne accounts beg to differ. He Dog, Oglala, to Camp: ". . . Indians were getting ready for word to charge in a body on soldiers at timber. . . . Just as we charged, the soldiers left the timber in two bunches on their horses as fast as they could ride up the river."[5] Tall Bull, Cheyenne, to Grinnell, " The Indians . . . then charged down on the soldiers who retreated into the timber. They did not stop there, but ran right through it and out on the other side."[6] Wooden Leg, Cheyenne, to Thomas Marquis: "Our Indians crowded down toward the timber where were the soldiers. . . . Sioux were creeping forward to set fire to the timber. Suddenly the hidden soldiers came tearing out on horseback, from the woods."[7] These three accounts, and there are others in a similar vein, make no mention of troops taking the time to form up outside of the timber, just of soldiers suddenly appearing out of that timber and racing upriver to try to escape.

Even then Moylan's testimony could be credible if it were just Indian accounts that refuted it. Unfortunately, some other testimonies tend to agree with their opponents. Lieutenant Varnum for instance:

I heard from the woods cries of "Charge! Charge! We are going to charge!" There was quite a confusion, something about a charge down in the woods, and I jumped up and said, "What's that?" and started down into the woods and grabbed my horse . . . I didn't hear any orders . . . and I grabbed my horse and mounted him . . . I came out with the men. The head of the column was then about a couple of rods or something like that from the edge of the timber.[8]

F.F. Gerard testified: "Q. State the formation that you noticed of the troops in the timber after the skirmish line had swung around to the river as you have described. A. The troops I saw in the timber were in a great hurry to get off. There seemed to be no order at all. Every man was for himself."[9]

The reality then was that once all of his command had entered the timber, Reno had a stark choice, stay in the timber or move out, but moving out had its problems, namely, where could he move to? From his position in the woods he could not see across the river but he did know that by heading south he might be able to ford the river at some point. Whatever alternative he might have been entertaining evaporated when a volley from the Indians scattered the blood and brains of Bloody Knife all over him. Momentarily numbed, he called out "dismount" and then "mount" before spurring his horse to exit the timber. According to Private Roman Rutten of M Company in an interview with Camp, Reno cried out "Everybody follow me" as he rode past.[10]

Whatever hasty organization had taken place within the timber soon disintegrated as A Company dashed after Reno, followed by M Company, then a scattering of G Company. Evidence from every unbiased white source describes the desperate race of the soldiers as they tried to escape to safety. Varnum to Camp: " . . . left the timber late and before reached river overtook head of column, which was being led by Reno and Moylan, whom he did not at first notice, but upon making some remark about ought not to be retreating so disorderly, Reno made some reply to the effect that he was in command."[11] Hare to Camp: "In timber he did not hear any order to retreat. Clear brought his horse and said the command was leaving. When he started, A and M had gone quite some time and G had left just ahead of him, but he caught up to M. Co. M had taken off to right . . ."[12] Sergeant Roy of A Company to Camp: "Met Wallace mounted and leading G Troop out. . . . Wallace said 'Grab any horse you can get and get out of here.'"[13] Private Rutten of M Company to Camp: "When I reached the river, the water ahead of me was full of horses and men struggling to get across. . . . The opposite bank was high and steep, and men were riding both upstream and downstream trying to find some place to get up."[14] F. F. Gerard to Camp:

> Reno, however, seeing no support from the rear, lost his head, if he had any, and suddenly decided to run the gauntlet of the Sioux. In less than five minutes after entering the timber the men began to bolt from it in disorder and spur their horses toward Ford A. Some left the timber from the south side and some up the bank at the west and then turned in the direction of the general retreat.[15]

These descriptions are complemented by what the Lakota and Cheyenne warriors saw. The Northern Cheyenne American Horse to George B. Grinnell:

> When the troops reached this timber, they stopped and went into it, and stopped [again]. The Indians were all around them. Then the Sioux and the Cheyennes charged and the troops ran for the river. The Indians rode right up to them knocked some off their horses as they were running, and some fell off in the river. It was like chasing buffalo—a grand chase.[16]

Soldier Wolf, Northern Cheyenne, to Grinnell: "The soldiers retreated to the timber and fought behind cover. If they had remained in the timber, the Indians could not have killed them. But all at once—perhaps they got frightened—they rushed out and started to cross the creek. Then it was that the Indians rushed among them."[17] Wooden Leg, Northern Cheyenne, to Thomas Marquis, after telling him that "the hidden soldiers came tearing out on horseback, from the woods" said:

> I was around on that side where they came out. I whirled my horse and lashed it into a dash to escape from them. All others of my companions did the same. But soon we discovered they were not following us. They were running away from us. They were going as fast as their tired horses could carry them across an open valley space and toward the river. . . . We gained rapidly on them . . . I saw a Sioux put an arrow into the back of a soldier's head. . . . Others fell dead either from arrows or from stabbings or jabbing or from blows by the stone war clubs of the Sioux.[18]

Both the white and Indian accounts describe a scene of utter chaos in the mad dash Reno made with his command in a frantic attempt to reach a safer haven than he believed was possible in the timber. During that shambolic retreat to a hill that happened to be near the first fording place they came to, thirty-seven of Reno's men were killed, roughly one-third of his command. It was close to 4:00 p.m. as the survivors struggled to reach the comparative safety of the hilltop, but support was close to hand in the shape of Benteen's command.

NOTES

1. Major Marcus A. Reno testimony at Reno Court of Inquiry; [ebook] Appendix 3.96.
2. Doctor H. R. Porter: testimony at the Reno Court of Inquiry, 1879; [ebook] Appendix 3.88.
3. George Herendeen: testimony at the Reno Court of Inquiry, 1879; [ebook] Appendix 3.55.
4. Captain Myles Moylan: testimony at the Reno Court of Inquiry, 1879; [ebook] Appendix 3.81.
5. Kenneth Hammer (ed.), *Custer in '76: Walter Camp's Notes on the Custer Fight* (Provo, Utah: Brigham Young University Press, 1976), p.206.
6. Richard G. Hardorff, *Cheyenne Memories of the Custer Fight* (Spokane, Washington: The Arthur H. Clark Company, 1995), p.46.
7. Thomas B. Marquis, *Wooden Leg: A Warrior who Fought Custer* (Lincoln and London: University of Nebraska Press, 1971), p.220.
8. Charles A. Varnum: testimony before the Reno Court of Inquiry; [ebook] Appendix 3.111.
9. Fred Gerard: testimony before the Reno Court of Inquiry, 1879; [ebook] Appendix 3.33.
10. Hammer, *Custer in '76*, p.118.
11. Ibid., p.61.
12. Ibid., p.66.
13. Ibid., p.112.
14. Ibid., p.119.
15. Ibid., p.233.
16. Hardorff, *Cheyenne Memories*, p.28.
17. Ibid., p.42.
18. Marquis, *Wooden Leg*, pp. 220/221.

CHAPTER 7

STRANGE INTERLUDE: CHAOS ON RENO HILL AND THE WEIR ADVANCE

"If in doubt, always ride to the sound of the guns."
—A RULING PRINCIPLE OF CAVALRY TACTICS

REACHING THE TOP OF THE BLUFFS

It was just two or three minutes past 4:00 p.m. when the first of Reno's shattered command reached the relative safety of the top of the bluffs on the eastern bank of the Little Horn, and although it is widely believed that Reno was himself the first to climb the bluffs, there is no compelling evidence to support that belief. The thought probably originated in Lieutenant Frank Gibson's July 4, 1876 letter to his wife: "His three troops came riding back to us in disorder, and he at the head."

Whoever the first man or men to reach the top and to stop there, this act quite probably saved a great many of the following soldiers—simply from the fact of stopping and dismounting instead of blindly and madly riding on. Had what was left of the command not stopped, many of the Lakota and Cheyennes would undoubtedly have followed, and the slaughter would have continued until the fleeing troops ran into Benteen—had they, in fact, run in that direction. Had the flight continued in a straight line, the men would actually have been quartering away from assistance, and survival would have been very unlikely. Fortunately, circumstances dictated that that scenario never played out.

There are varying and conflicting accounts of what transpired when the bluff was topped. Most of the officers who had been in the valley with Reno painted a picture of military competence and more or less steadiness. Since they were in charge of and responsible for the situation, this is hardly surprising. Their reputations and careers were on the line, and their testimony and their reminiscences reflect this.

Reno himself testified: "After a glance about, I thought it as good a position as I could obtain with the time at my disposal. I immediately put the command in skirmish line dismounted, a movement that was accomplished through the company commanders."

Captain Myles Moylan paid more attention to the wounded, he said, but remembered that there was a skirmish line put out: "After we had gathered them [wounded men] together, we rode to the top of the hill and dismounted there and I turned my attention to getting my wounded men together and caring for them. . . . I got my wounded men together, five, and had Dr. Porter come there and attend to them and all that, and after doing this I heard voices saying there was a column of cavalry approaching." Moylan, who seemed to emphasize the care he gave to the wounded, went on to say:

> [The command] was not demoralized, neither was it very exultant. . . . Within a few moments after we got on the top of the hill, the command was in a tolerably good condition. A skirmish line had been thrown out. . . . I presume it was done by his [Reno's] orders. . . . I do not remember him giving any orders at all. . . . I was separated from the other portions of the command, and probably two-thirds of it had reached the top before I got there. . . . After [Benteen arrived things were regular as clockwork], it was not so regular before.[1]

"[As to the feelings of the command when it got to the top of the hill] I can't speak for anyone else. I can only speak for myself. I felt as though I had been pretty badly licked," testified Lieutenant Varnum, who didn't comment on any skirmish line. Lieutenant George Wallace didn't have a lot to say, but all of it was geared to showing a definite professional military reaction by the officers:

> The command was halted and preparations made to give them a standoff. It [the command] halted and dismounted and the first thing

done was to get the companies together, organize them, and then they had to count off again and dismount so as to make another stand. . . . They were first dismounted and deployed on the crest of the bluff and then mounted and moved back. . . . It must have been . . . Major Reno [who gave the orders].

Lieutenant Luther Hare testified that:

The command was necessarily scattered; but I don't think it was demoralized, from the very prompt way in which they rallied and formed. Before I got to the top of the hill, I heard Lieutenant Varnum calling to the men to halt, and when I got there Captain Moylan was forming his skirmish line. I didn't hear Major Reno say anything.[2]

In stark contrast to the battalion's officers, the enlisted soldiers from Reno's command and many of the officers of other units that arrived at the spot were not quite so complimentary in their reflections upon the scene.

Sergeant Ferdinand Culbertson testified: "The first officer I saw was Captain Moylan, and I heard him say he would not sell his horse for something. I don't know what." Edward Davern, Reno's orderly, recalled getting to the top of the bluff after having his horse stumble and being delayed in catching up an Indian pony: "Yes, sir. I saw Major Reno. I don't recollect exactly [what he said]. I think he asked me if I had any water. I said I had not, and he gave me some. I told Major Reno I had lost my carbine, and then he told me he had lost his carbine and pistol, both."

"Those that were alive were in pretty good order and well shaken up," testified Captain Benteen, "Men coming up on foot on a big bluff would be pretty well blown, and so would the horses. They were not in line of battle, but were scattered around at points, I suppose to the best advantage. They all thought there was a happier place than that, I guess."

Lieutenant W.S. Edgerly testified that:

One of the first officers I saw was Major Reno. He was on his horse, he had lost his hat and had a white handkerchief on his head. He was in an excited condition. As we came up he turned and discharged his pistol towards the Indians. . . . About a thousand yards [away] . . . I consider it done in a sort of defiance of the Indians. About the same time I saw Lieutenant Varnum. He had lost his hat and had a white handkerchief round his head. He was excited and crying and while telling us about what had occurred. He got mad and commenced swearing and called for a gun and commenced firing at the Indians. About that time Captain Moylan came up and said, "For God's sake give me some water!" He said he had 25 wounded men dying of thirst.

We very shortly formed a skirmish line after we got up.... There were a few Indians on points firing.... I was surprised after the ride they had they were so little excited. I remember one man who was perfectly cool. He came up the hill holding the scalp of an Indian in his hand which he had just taken. D Company [were deployed as skirmishers by order of] Captain Weir. Four or five (Indians were) at points at short range. We drove them away in a short time.[3]

Lieutenant Edward S. Godfrey had similar recollections about how the skirmish line was formed:

I was ordered by Captain Benteen to dismount my company and put it in skirmish line on the bluff toward the river. Lieutenant Hare, the second lieutenant of my company, but who had been detached to serve with the scouts, came up and said he was "damned glad to see me—that they had had a big fight in the bottom and got whipped like hell." He [Reno] gave me no instructions. Captain Benteen gave me all my orders at that time. He seemed to be giving the commands. Major Reno, if I recollect right, was making arrangements to go down after Lieutenant Hodgson's body or to get his effects.

Daniel Newell, a private of M Company, remembered:

As soon as we could, we crawled up on the hill, but there weren't many there. Captain Varnum was there, wearing his straw hat, and trying to rally enough men to go back for the wounded. The sergeant came up with ten men, and Burke [Edmund H.], blacksmith for K troop, said, "Where are all your men?" "Ten is all I can muster, Burke," he told us. They were all scattered around, and after a while we got together.

It is entirely possible that Charlie Varnum or Luther Hare, or both, were first to try to halt the flood of fleeing troopers. According to Private William Morris also of M Company:

> Capt. Moylan had started to continue on his own hook, with what was left of his men from the retreat ordered by Reno. Lieut. Hare, who had passed me on his fast horse across the stream, yelled out with a voice that could be heard all over the field: "If we've got to die, let's die here like men. I'm a fighting ----- from Texas." Then turning to Moylan, he called out: "Don't run off like a pack of whipped curs."

Doctor Porter recalled in his testimony that: "I saw first Lieutenant Varnum. He had his hat off, and he said, 'For God's sake men, don't run. There are a good many officers and men killed and wounded, and we have got to go back and get them.'" Porter also said that: "I went up to the Major and said, 'Major, the men were pretty well demoralized, weren't they?' and he replied, 'No, that was a charge, sir.' They were demoralized. They seemed to think they had been whipped."[4]

Morris said that Reno was spurred by Hare's stinging remark. "That gave Reno the cue, and recovering himself, he said, 'Captain Moylan, dismount those men.' Moylan didn't obey at once, and Reno repeated the order."

A halt was made. The officers and men rallied about the location, although not in any real semblance of military order; and a mere handful of the Indians followed, or were already across the river, keeping, for the most part, a wary, if not necessarily respectful, distance.

The majority of the Reno battalion survivors, except for those left behind in the timber, had reached the top of the bluffs by 4:10 p.m. To be sure, there were still a couple of wounded and dismounted men struggling up the hills and ravines, but by and large the battalion was up by the time Benteen came along ten minutes later.

BENTEEN'S BATTALION ARRIVES

According to Trumpeter Martin: "As we approached them, Colonel Reno came out to meet us. He was dismounted, his hat was gone, and he had a handkerchief around his forehead. He was out of breath and excited, and raised his hand and called to Colonel Benteen. We all heard him. He said, 'For God's sake, Benteen, halt your command and help me. I've lost half my men.'"[5]

Major Reno testified otherwise, however: "In a short time I rode out to see him [Benteen], he was not far off. I told him what I had done and I was glad to see him. He then moved his battalion up to where my battalion was. I rode up with him myself." Lieutenant Godfrey told the Reno Inquiry: "I saw him [Reno] soon after I got there, coming up to Captain Benteen or perhaps they were talking together. He had a handkerchief tied round his head and seemed somewhat excited," but didn't say whether or not Reno rode out to meet them.

Fred Benteen was the most voluble of the inquiry witnesses concerning his arrival at the Reno position, yet still managed to say very little, contenting himself with repetitions of virtually everything he did say. In his two later narratives and in his personal correspondence, Benteen always bragged that he arrived just in the nick of time to save Reno's command. He did not hint at any such extravagant claim at the inquiry, or in his other public utterances.

"On reaching the bluff," Captain Benteen told the *New York Herald* in August 1876, "I reported to Colonel Reno, and first learned that the command had been separated, and that Custer was not in that part of the field, and no one of Reno's command was able to inform me of the whereabouts of General Custer." He testified that: "I think the Indians saw me about the time I saw them, and that checked their pursuit. They came around, probably 4 or 5 or more, to the highest point of land there. Maybe they had been there all the time, I don't know about that. I would say they were nearly a mile away."

Benteen continued:

I showed him [Reno] the order . . . I asked him if he knew where General Custer was. He said he did not, that he had been sent in to charge those Indians on the plain, and that General Custer's instructions to him, through Adjutant Cooke, were that he would support him with the whole outfit, and that was the last he had seen or heard of him, and did not know where he was. I supposed he [Custer] was down the river. I don't remember having stated to him [Reno] anything about it. He should have known more about General Custer than I could. . . . I supposed General Custer was able to take care of himself. He [Reno] was about as cool as he is now. He had lost his hat in the run down below.

"I inquired where Custer was," repeated Benteen, in his later narrative:

... showing him the order I had gotten. Reno read the order, replying that, about an hour ago, Custer had sent him across the river with orders to charge a body of Indians in the valley, promising that he would support Reno with the whole outfit; that since that time, he had seen nothing of Custer, and knew nothing of his whereabouts, but had heard some firing down the river, and supposed he was in that direction.[6]

It is most interesting to note the repetition of the "will be supported by the whole outfit" characterization of the order to Reno from Custer, since that is exactly the phraseology used by Reno and echoed by Lieutenant Wallace.

The arrival of the Benteen battalion and the throwing out of the skirmish lines and driving off of the few Indians in the nearer vicinity should have allowed things to settle down and present an opportunity for Reno to catch his breath and to take stock of the situation. After all, Benteen had just showed him the "Be quick. Big Village. Bring Packs." message from Custer. There were, and are still, very real questions as to whether Benteen was militarily correct in disregarding the orders embodied in that message by stopping to assist Reno, and whether Reno had any authority over him while that order remained unfulfilled. The message itself indicated the need for speed—even Reno was impressed by the fact that it had been written in a hurry, for he testified that Cooke had been in such a rush that he did not have time to affix his official designation of "Adjutant."

RENO'S SEARCH FOR BENNY HODGSON

It has been popularly supposed that Reno lost his head, if he did, when brain tissue was splattered in his face prior to the run from the timber in the bottom. It is obvious however, from an examination of all of the evidence and especially of Reno's actions, that he only ceased to function as an effective commander when he reached the top of the bluffs. The reasons should not be at all mystifying.

First, his experiences in the valley were enough to shake any man, and indeed had shaken up the vast majority of the men and even such a seasoned veteran as Captain Moylan. Second, Reno had seen little service and no action on the plains. When he looked back from the crest of the bluffs, he saw more than what was left of his shattered command struggling up the hills—and much more than the Indians looting and mutilating the dead. What he saw was the probable end of his military career. He had been ordered to charge the enemy and had failed, albeit for possibly explainable reasons, to press home his attack—worse still he had been driven from the field of battle, but worst of all he had lost over thirty men killed, had abandoned others in the timber, and there was absolutely no question but that some wounded men had been left to the mercies of the hostiles. So far as Reno knew, he had lost three officers—McIntosh, DeRudio, and Hodgson—down there. It had been a disaster for the command and for Marcus Reno personally, so it is little wonder that his thinking was not entirely clear.

So, instead of sitting down with Benteen and other officers to go over the situation and to plan on their next moves, Reno got some men together and went down the hill to find Benny Hodgson's body. Before doing so, however, he did have the presence of mind to send Luther Hare after the pack train to hurry them up and to get some ammunition ahead as fast as possible—at least the timing of events leads to that conclusion. Had Reno sent Hare after returning from Hodgson's body, then the packs could not have come up when they did, and Hare could not have seen Weir's movement while he was returning from the packs.

Reno told the inquiry court:

> In crossing the ford, Lieutenant Hodgson, who was my adjutant and a great favorite and friend of mine, I was told had been shot. With the hopes that it might be only a wound, or that I might be able to do something for him, I went to the river, after Captain Benteen's arrival, with some men I called together, but whose names I can't remember. Sergeant Culbertson, I remember, was one I had to go, and went to the ford. I suppose I was gone a half an hour. Captain Benteen was the senior officer in command when I went down, and he was a man in whom I had the greatest confidence.

Sergeant Culbertson testified:

> I was called by Captain Moylan, and asked what men were wounded, and how many were missing. I told him, and then Lieutenant Varnum asked me if I had any water. While speaking to him and giving him a drink of water, he asked me if I had seen anything of Lieutenant Hodgson. I said I had, and gave him a description of where

I had seen him last. He either called Major Reno, or he came up about that time, and I told him I had seen Lieutenant Hodgson in the river. Major Reno asked me if I thought I could find him. I said I thought I could. He said he was going to find some water, and I should go along with him. . . . 10 or 12 men and myself went with Major Reno to the river. We went down to the river and I found the body of a man lying at the edge of the river . . . I at first thought it was Lieutenant Hodgson, and called Major Reno's attention to it; but it proved to be a man of my own company. We filled our canteens above where the man was lying in the river, and came up to a little bench again advancing up the hill, and a man of my company came across the body of Lieutenant Hodgson, and called Major Reno's attention to it, and he came up to the body. We found that his watch and chain had been taken off, except the little gold bar inside of his vest, and a plain gold ring. Major Reno took that off, and said it was his class ring. We went on up the hill, and found a man of G Company in the brush and took him out. He had lost his horse, and had hid in there until he got an opportunity to get out. We then went on to the top of the hill. I judge it took us half an hour to go and come back.

Some of those who tend to believe part of Theodore Goldin's accounts of being a messenger from Custer to Reno, have speculated that this G Company man might have been Goldin, who rather than attempt to deliver the message had stopped on the hillside when he saw the exodus from the valley beginning.

Both Reno and Culbertson give the same half-hour estimate of the time spent on this trip to the river. Both indicated that there was some scattered firing and the possibility that they might have been in danger, although there were no Indians visible to them and none of the party was actually hit. Since Reno had previously had time to give an order to Hare and to deny permission to Captain Weir to march down the bluffs, it seems safe to say that he started this Hodgson search after 4:30 p.m. and it was after 5:00 p.m. when he returned.

FIRING DOWN THE RIVER AND WEIR'S RESPONSE

In the meantime, things on the hill had started to deteriorate, despite Reno having left Benteen, "a man in whom I had the greatest confidence," in command during his absence. The details will be explored in some detail here, since many subsequent actions, subsequent recriminations and subsequent obfuscations have their genesis in this time period.

When the men of Benteen's battalion arrived at Reno's position, many of them, including most officers, heard firing from down the river—heavy firing, which could only denote an engagement of some kind, and which obviously meant that Custer was in a fight. In his testimony, Reno denied hearing any such firing or having been told of any:

> I don't remember such a report [of hearing firing, from McDougall] being made to me. If I had heard the firing, as they represent the firing, volley firing, I should have known he was engaged while I was on the hill, but I heard no such firing. [When I was down at the river, I was] possibly not [in a better position to have heard any firing] although I was nearer to what is termed the battlefield than the command.

However, in his report of July 5, 1876, Reno stated: "We had heard firing in that direction and knew it could only be Custer," indicating quite positively that either he had heard the firing himself or that it had been reported to him.[7]

Lieutenant Edgerly of D Company heard it and was very consistent in his descriptions. He told Walter Camp: "Heavy firing was heard in the direction of Custer, and clouds of dust were seen over in the village, and Indians riding back and forth . . . said that after Benteen met Reno on the bluff they could hear firing in the direction of Custer very plainly, and Weir said: 'Edgerly, will you go down with the troop if I will?' Edgerly said yes, and Weir said: 'Well, I will go and get permission'."

In his personal narrative written some fifteen years after the fights, Edgerly stated: "At this time we heard firing from Custer's direction, and Capt. Weir asked me if I would be willing to go to Custer if the rest of the command did not." His 1879 testimony on the point was:

> Shortly after I got on the hill, almost immediately, I heard firing and remarked it, heavy firing by volleys down the creek. Captain Weir came to me and said General Custer was engaged and we ought to

go down. I said I thought so, too. He went away, walking up and down rather anxiously. I heard the fire plainly. The first sergeant came up then and I saw a large cloud of dust and thought there must be a charge, and said, "There must be General Custer. I guess he is getting away with them." He said, "Yes, sir, and I think we ought to go there." I did not answer him.

In 1881 at Fort Yates, Edgerly said:

Then I heard heavy firing over in the direction in which we after-wards found the remains of Custer's portion of the command, and could see clouds of dust, and horsemen rushing back and forth on the opposite side of the river and about four miles away. While this firing was going on, Colonel Weir, my captain, came to me and asked me what I thought we ought to do. I told him I thought we ought by all means to go down to Custer's assistance. He thought so too, and I heard the first sergeant express himself to that effect. He then asked me if I would be willing to go down with only D troop, if he could get permission to go. I told him I would.[8]

Lieutenant Godfrey wrote in his 1892 narrative:

During a long time after the junction of Reno and Benteen we heard firing from down the river in the direction of Custer's command. We were satisfied that Custer was fighting the Indians somewhere, and the conviction was expressed that "our command ought to be doing something or Custer would be after Reno with a sharp stick." We heard two distinct volleys which elicited some surprise, and, if I mis-take not, brought out the remark from someone that "Custer was giving it to them for all he was worth." I have but little doubt now that these volleys were fired by Custer's orders as signals of distress and to indicate where he was.[9]

Captain Moylan of Reno's own battalion wrote on July 6, 1876 to Fred Calhoun—who was Jim Calhoun's brother, Moylan's brother-in-law, and a lieutenant of the 14th Infantry, stationed at Camp Robinson: "The Indians did [not] continue the fight with us after we crossed the river, but turned their attention to Custer's command. We could hear the fighting with Custer several miles away."

Doctor Porter also testified that he heard firing, but he wasn't so sure what it signified:

We hadn't been up there very long before I heard firing down the stream and a little to the left. I heard pretty sharp firing down there for a few minutes, and then scattering shots. I supposed it was Indians firing because they had driven us off the bottom. I had been in several Indian fights before that. I had heard some firing but not much. It sounded like heavy, sharp firing, and then there were scattering shots, and then it got less and less.

Lieutenant Varnum wrote his parents on July 4, 1876: "Indians did not press us very hard, and we knew from the fearful firing at the other end of the village that someone was getting it hot and heavy up there." In his testimony, he stated that:

About the time, or probably a few minutes after Captain Benteen came up, I heard firing from away down the stream and spoke of it to Lieutenant Wallace. I don't recollect except that one time. I had borrowed a rifle of Lieutenant Wallace, and had fired a couple of shots at long range, and as I handed the rifle back to him, I heard the firing and said, "Jesus Christ, Wallace, hear that! And that!" Those were my words. [It was] very soon after [Benteen arrived]. It was not like volley firing, but a heavy fire, a sort of crash, crash. I heard it only for a few minutes. It must have pertained to General Custer's command at the other end of the Indian village. It was from that end of the village where General Custer's body was afterwards found. . . . I thought he was having a warm time down there, a very hot fire evidently.[10]

Benteen did his best to back up Reno in his own testimony:

That was the firing I tried to describe I heard after my arrival there— 15 or 20 shots that seemed to have come from about the ford "B," about the central part of the village. The village ran in two divisions, and at the ford "B" was about the place where I heard the shots, and all I heard that were not in sight were from that direction. I have heard, as a matter of course, officers disputing amongst themselves about hearing volleys. I heard no volleys.

Frank Gibson, Benteen's lieutenant, did. He wrote his wife on July 4, 1876: "We heard Custer's command fighting about five miles off in our front." Sergeant Culbertson did not say so directly, but left no room for doubt that Reno must have heard the firing:

It was when Lieutenant Varnum called me to ask me for some water. He was sitting at the edge of a bank. While sitting there talking to Lieutenant Edgerly, we could hear the firing. At first it was a couple of volleys, very heavy, afterwards it was lighter, and appeared to be more distant. Lieutenant Varnum made the remark that General Custer was hotly engaged or was giving it to the Indians hot, or words to that effect, and in a few minutes after, Major Reno came up, and we went to the river, and I did not hear it anymore. If there had been any firing after that, the hills would have broke the sound.

Q. Was Major Reno on the hill at the time you heard the firing?
A. Yes, sir.
Q. Was he near you at the time?
A. He came up while the firing was going on.
Q. What did he do?
A. He came up and commenced to talk with Lieutenant Varnum, and I stepped back as soon as he came up.
Q. Was he looking down the river?
A. He was.
Q. By himself?
A. No, sir. Lieutenant Varnum was sitting there at the time, facing rather down the river.
Q. Could you hear the firing at that time?
A. Yes, sir.
Q. What position did Major Reno occupy with reference to the firing, as compared with your position?
A. He was a little in front and to my right.

Q. How long did you continue to hear that firing?

A. Only a few minutes.

Private Davern, Reno's orderly, not only heard the firing, but pointed it out to Captain Weir, possibly initiating Weir's going to Reno. Here are the questions and answers from his testimony:

Q. Did you hear any firing from any other direction? From downstream? Anywhere?

A. Shortly after I got on the hill I did.

Q. Describe that firing.

A. It was in volleys.

Q. Where did it seem to come from?

A. From downstream.

Q. How did you happen to hear it? Did you go out to any point, or were you there with the others?

A. On the hill, where the others were.

Q. Was the balance of the command there?

A. Yes, sir.

Q. Was the firing plain, or faint?

A. It was not very distinct, but a person could distinguish it was firing.

Q. You could tell it was volleys?

A. Yes, sir.

Q. Did you hear any firing between the volleys?

A. No, sir.

Q. What did you see in the direction from which the fire was coming at the time?

A. I saw what I supposed to be Indians, circling around in the bottom on the opposite side of the creek from where we had our fight, away down in the bottom.

Q. Could you tell, from where you were, on which side of the creek they were?

A. I might be deceived, because there were so many bends in the creek.

Q. About how many Indians did you see?

A. There were a good many there.

Q. Were they raising much dust?

A. Yes, sir. I called the attention of Captain Weir to it at the time.

Q. What did you say to him, and what did he say to you?

A. I said to Captain Weir, "That must be General Custer fighting down in the bottom." He asked me where, and I showed him. He said, "Yes, I believe it is."

Q. What did he do then?

A. Not anything.

Q. Where was Major Reno at that time?

A. I don't know. He was somewhere on the hill.

Q. About how long was that after you got on the hill?

A. Maybe half an hour after.

Q. Refresh your memory about what was done by any part of the command right away after that firing was heard.

A. Nothing was done . . .

A. . . . I remarked to Captain Weir that General Custer must be fighting the Indians—they were circling around in the bottom. He said, "Why do you think so?" I said, "I hear the firing and see the dust, and see the Indians have all left us."

Private Theodore Goldin, whose writings must be taken with more than a few grains of salt, wrote C.T. Brady in 1904: "As we were standing on the bluffs looking down into the valley, I heard some loud talk near me, and turning in that direction, I heard Capt. Weir say: 'Well, by God, if you won't go, I will, and if we ever live to get out of here, someone will suffer for this.'" To Fred Dustin in 1932, he softened this:

I do believe I did state in the article that there was some sort of an altercation between Weir and Reno, relative to a forward movement to locate and aid Custer. I did not hear it, as it was just about over when I climbed the hill. I heard some loud talking as I approached the place where the officers were gathered to report my escape, but what it was I cannot say. All I know is just as I came up, Weir separated himself from the group, evidently laboring under considerable excitement.[11]

Private John Fox of Weir's D Company told Walter Camp that he witnessed a similar scene:

. . . says he heard a conversation between Weir and Reno, before D

Company went out. He says Weir remarked: "Custer must be around here somewhere, and we ought to go to him." Reno said: "We are surrounded by Indians, and we ought to remain here." Weir said: "Well, if no one else goes to Custer, I will go." Reno replied: "No. You cannot go—for if you try to do it, you will get killed, and your company with you." Fox says Reno appeared to be intoxicated, or partially so. He says that Moylan and Benteen stood by and heard what Weir said, and they did not seem to approve of Weir going, and talked as though to discourage him. Finally, Weir said that he was going anyhow, and Reno did not object.

Trumpeter Martin heard both the firing and the exchange between Weir and Reno, according to W.A. Graham:

We heard a lot of firing down the river; it kept up for a half hour or maybe more. It sounded like a big fight was going on, and the men thought it was General Custer, and that he was whipping the Indians, and we all wanted to hurry on and join him, but they wouldn't let us go. Captain Weir had some words with Colonel Reno, and I could tell by the way he was acting that he was excited and angry. He waved his arms and gestured and pointed down the river. Then we heard some volleys, and Captain Weir jumped on his horse and started down the river all alone.[12]

Weir had previously asked Edgerly if he would go down with only their own troop, if nobody else would go and had said he would seek permission from Reno or Benteen. After having been denied permission from Reno, Weir paced up and down for a few minutes and then, not asking any permission from Benteen, he mounted up and started down the bluffs with only his orderly for company. His second lieutenant, Edgerly, thinking that permission had been granted, mounted D Troop and followed along behind, all of them advancing at a cautious walk toward the high ground in the direction of the firing they had heard.[13] This was the start of what has become known as the Weir Advance or the Advance to Weir Peaks/Point.

D Company left the position while Hare was on his trip to the pack train, since he saw them out toward the peaks when he was making his return trip. Edgerly testified: "[It was] about 30 or 35 minutes after we arrived that we went out," making the start time about 4:50 p.m., definitely while Reno was on his expedition to Hodgson's body. It is distinctly possible that Weir purposely waited until Reno was down the hill before setting out, so that Reno could not stop or recall him, and it is very interesting that Weir's commander, Captain Benteen, whom Reno had left in charge, did not either. In fact, Benteen seems to have not only lost control of his subordinate, but to have mislaid him, as will become evident later.

A LULL IN THE PROCEEDINGS

Of course, other things were going on simultaneously with Reno's side trip, Hare's journey to the packs and Weir's unauthorized ride along the bluffs. There were wounded to be attended to, companies to be re-organized and the gap left in the perimeter defenses by Weir to be filled in. Happily for all concerned, the main body of the Indians in the bottoms had disappeared downstream in the direction of their camps, so that the activities on the hilltop and on the hillside were unmolested, except for the occasional long-range sniping by a few hostiles concealed somewhere on distant higher ground. As Lieutenant Godfrey testified:

> There was some firing [by the Indians]. I could not see many Indians. They were in the ravines. The most I saw were in the bottom. I judge there were probably not less than six or seven hundred Indians in that bottom that I saw there. A great many starting up on our left, that is, going back up the Little Big Horn above us. They soon came back and went down the river till finally the bottom was nearly cleared and I saw none at all. [They went] down the river. Not more than ten minutes [after my arrival].

Every other witness, then or since, on the subject agrees with Edward Godfrey's observation, with the notable exception of Captain Benteen, who testified that: "The Indians were there some little time after we were together on the hill. I can't tell. Perhaps half an hour or an hour. I don't think they all left at any time."

Godfrey also testified that there was no fighting going on: "When my company was first put out, it was pretty heavy firing, on the part of the command, principally; but the Indians that could be seen were so far away that it seemed like a waste of ammunition, and I ordered the troops to stop firing."

The wounded were the principal responsibility of Doctor Porter, the only remaining medical officer. Said Porter: "After Colonel Benteen's command had joined Major Reno they went further back up the river and there was a little hollow where we had a hospital, and I remained there. . . . I am pretty sure Captain Weir left before the pack train came up. I wouldn't swear to it, but I am pretty positive of it."

Captain French tried to rally the remnant of his M Company. According to Private William Morris:

Corporal Sniffen, of my troop, was the guidon bearer. The guidons of the other two troops had been thrown away in the retreat; but Sniffen had torn his from the staff and stuffed them in his shirt. First thing when Captain French saw him on the hill, he said, "Corporal, you damned fool, where are your colors?" Sniffen pulled them out, and French had them put on a carbine and stuck in the ground.[14]

During this lull in the fighting, the first of the men left behind in the timber managed to reach the top of the hill—Private John Sivertsen of M Company. He told Colonel Hall in 1916:

The first man I met on top of the bluffs was Captain French. He was very much astonished and pleased. They had had a roll call when they got on the bluff, and all who were not present were marked dead or missing. He shook my hand and said, "Fritz, I'm glad to see you. You are on the list of dead, and here you are back to life again. You're wet from fording the river. Go to the sergeant and get a blanket, and sit down by the camp fire." So I found my troop, got a blanket and some food, partly dried my clothes, and got straightened out a little. The men knew nothing about Custer, but they had heard heavy firing after reaching the bluffs.

Although Lieutenant Hare had been sent back to the pack train to hurry up some ammunition, the lack thereof was actually made good by Benteen's companies sharing their own extras with the troopers of Reno's battalion. "Benteen's battalion was ordered to divide its ammunition with Reno's men, who had apparently expended nearly all in their personal possession," wrote Godfrey in 1892, "It has often been a matter of doubt whether this was a fact, or the

effect of imagination. It seems most improbable, in view of their active movements and the short time the command was firing, that the 'most of the men'
should have expended one hundred and fifty rounds of ammunition per man."

Benteen's testimony on this subject was another plea of ignorance: "I don't
remember that he said anything about it [being out of ammunition]. I know
he sent Lieutenant Hare back to hurry it up. I have heard Lieutenant Hare
speak of it."

It was also during this time, wrote Godfrey in 1892, that:

> A number of officers collected on the edge of the bluff overlooking
> the valley and were discussing the situation; among our number was
> Captain Moylan, a veteran soldier, and a good one too, watching in-
> tently the scene below. Moylan remarked, quite emphatically: "Gen-
> tlemen, in my opinion General Custer has made the biggest mistake
> of his life, by not taking the whole regiment in at the first attack."

In his 1908 revision however, Godfrey omitted this scene. Most observers
since have felt that this omission indicated a shift in Godfrey's thinking to a
more pro-Custer position, but it may well be that it reflected Godfrey's growing knowledge of the truth of what had transpired in the valley and that he
simply felt that his earlier comments about Moylan no longer applied. There
is however, little question but that such a scene took place.

This lengthy period of relative inactivity on the hill has been, for the most
part, overlooked by chroniclers of the Custer battle. This is, perhaps, explained by the almost unanimous tendency of the participants, whether in-
tentional or not, to "telescope" the time frame, making it appear that several
separated incidents were occurring at the same time. It is only through a
lengthy examination of the evidence that the actual times can be derived.

While Weir was marching slowly down the bluffs and Reno was visiting
Benny Hodgson's body, Luther Hare returned from his twenty-minute ride
to the pack train. He did not, he testified, bring any of the ammunition-laden
mules with him, although every history since says that he did.

Reno had sent Hare back to the pack train at approximately 4:40 p.m.,
had started on his excursion to Hodgson's body a few minutes later and Weir
had sallied out at about 4:50 p.m. Hare returned from his gallop to the packs
and back at almost exactly 5:00 p.m., returned Godfrey's horse, which he had
borrowed for the ride, Reno came back from his side trip at about 5:10 p.m.,

and the first of the mules, two of them carrying ammunition boxes, arrived at about 5:15 p.m.

As to his trip, Reno testified: "I took a ring from his [Hodgson's] finger and from his pocket a bunch of keys. The body had been rifled of the watch. I came back on the hill, the Indians withdrew from my front and around me, except a scattering fire." The party had no tools with which to bury Hodgson's body, however, so it was left where they had found it.

The wait for the ammunition has long been advanced as a reason why the Reno and Benteen commands lingered on the hills instead of marching toward the sound of the gunfire as Weir did, it being stated that no advance could be made until the men of Reno's battalion had replenished their supply. As noted above, this replenishment was, said Godfrey, made by sharing the reserve supply carried by Benteen's troopers. Other witnesses disagree as to whether or not any of the ammunition was actually distributed from the boxes carried by the two mules hurried ahead by Mathey.

Benteen testified: "I think so [Reno replenished his ammunition]. I did not see it; but I heard he did. It was over an hour [before the ammo packs came up]. I saw them coming. I did not want any ammunition, and was not particularly interested in them." He wrote in his later narrative however: "In about an hour or less, the pack-train came up. Some carbine ammunition was then unpacked from it; and it was issued to some of Reno's men."

Private John McGuire of C Company answered Walter Camp's question on the subject. "Q. Did he see any ammunition boxes opened while waiting to start? A. No." Captain Moylan testified: "Soon after the pack train came up, the order was given for the men to be supplied with ammunition, those who needed it, and to prepare themselves at once to move forward." Note however, that he does not say that he saw anyone being supplied. Lieutenant Edward Mathey, who was in charge of the packs and who should have known, testified: "Q. Did you see that ammunition taken out of the boxes? A. Not that I remember. Q. After starting the ammunition pack mules with Lieutenant Hare, how long was it till you arrived with the pack train? A. Something less than a half hour, probably 20 minutes."[15]

NOTICING CAPTAIN WEIR'S ABSENCE
AND THE ARRIVAL OF THE PACKS

When Reno came back from the river, Hare reported to him that he had accomplished his task, and no doubt also mentioned that he had heard firing from down the river and had seen a company moving in that direction. Hare told Walter Camp that "just as he got back, he heard firing in the direction of Custer, and was told that previous firing down there was heard while he had been gone . . . he looked and saw Co. D advancing toward Custer. They were some distance out, but still in sight. Reno sent him to go to Weir and tell Weir to connect with Custer."

It was at about this same time that Captain Benteen, who had been in command during Reno's absence, noticed that one of his companies had disappeared. Wrote Benteen in his first narrative: "After a few words with Col. Reno, I inquired as to the whereabouts of 'D' Troop of my battn., and was informed that Capt. Weir had, without orders, gone down the river. This being the case, I sallied after Weir . . . " In his later narrative he says: "About this time, I saw one of the troops of my battalion proceeding to the front, mounted, without order from me. Upon this, I followed with the other two troops, Major Reno having his trumpeter sound the 'Halt' continuously and assiduously; but I had to get in sight then of what I had left my valley-hunting mission for." Benteen testified, however, that: "Captain Weir sallied out in a fit of bravado, I think, without orders. I did not see him when he left . . ." so there is hardly any question that he hadn't seen Weir leave. One is left to ponder just exactly what Benteen had been doing during the half hour Reno was away.

It is generally believed that Benteen immediately set out after Weir, but the timing of events clearly shows that he did not do so until after the pack train and escort had arrived at approximately 5:35 p.m.

Before the train arrived, however, Major Reno, who was apparently at least temporarily obsessed with Benny Hodgson's body, told Charley Varnum to go and bury it. Testified Varnum: "Colonel Reno told me to take a detachment and go down and bury Lieutenant Hodgson's body. There was nothing there to bury it with, and I told him I would have to wait until the packs came up."

When the packs did come up, Captain McDougall immediately sought out Major Reno:

> About a quarter of an hour before reaching there, I heard firing to my right, and as soon as I arrived I reported to Major Reno that I had brought up the pack train alright, without losing any of the animals, and that I heard firing on my right . . .

I was going toward the Little Big Horn and to my right would be north. I did not know at the time, but when I got to the command I knew it was downstream. It was just two volleys. I told Major Reno about it and he said, "Captain, I lost your lieutenant, he is lying down there." Then I left Major Reno and went to my company and threw out a skirmish line.[16]

This was undoubtedly to fill in the gap left by Weir's departure downstream, a gap apparently unnoticed by either Reno or Benteen.

Lieutenant Varnum had waited for the packs so that he could accomplish his mission in respect to Lieutenant Hodgson's body. "We remained there until the packs came up about three-quarters of an hour afterward. Then I got two spades from the packs and started with about six men to go down to the river and bury the bodies. About two-thirds of the way down, I saw a lot of men coming out of the woods and I stopped to see what was up."

Lieutenant Mathey had also come up with the packs. He saw Indians away off down the river. "Someone gave me a glass, and I saw off at a distance of 3 miles or more, and could see Indians circling around, but no soldiers. . . . [They were] Downstream, about where the village was. On the left bank." He also saw Reno:

Yes, sir [I saw Major Reno] soon after my arrival. He was standing there and giving some orders to Captain French about going to bury Lieutenant Hodgson and some men at the foot of the hill. I remember Captain French rather seemed to want more men to go with him, and Major Reno told him to go on, and he went on. Shortly after that, he gave an order for Captain French to come back.

It would appear that Mathey confused French with Varnum, although it is hard to see how he could have done so, or else Reno had gone completely overboard in regard to Hodgson's body.

McDougall told Walter Camp about the firing. "Right away he heard firing, and asked Godfrey if he heard it. Godfrey, who was deaf, said he believed he did. McDougall then said: 'I think we ought to be down there with him,' and went up to where Reno and Benteen stood talking, and expressed to them the same opinion. Reno did not appear to regard the seriousness of the situation." Here is another definite indication that Benteen had not left yet to follow up Weir's advance. McDougall also testified that Reno should have been able to hear the gunfire:

> He [Reno] was about four or four and a half miles from the firing, and I was about the same. The sound could resound through the hills. It was a dull sound, just two volleys. I thought it was some of the command. I thought it must be General Custer and the Indians. [I reported the firing to Major Reno] only once, as soon as I arrived with the pack train. I walked right up to him, close enough to report to him. He just said, 'Captain, you have lost your lieutenant, he is lying down there.' I then walked off and formed a skirmish line. [Reno did not order it] I did it as any officer would do.
>
> . . . All [the troops there] were quiet, the same as at a halt . . . I did not know anything was going on with the command till I had thrown out the skirmish line, and went back and heard the officers talking about it.

WEIR AND EDGERLY AT WEIR PEAKS

It has frequently been written that Weir returned with his D Company to the Reno position and that then the whole command marched down the bluffs to Weir Point. This did not happen and the confusion may have arisen from the fact that Lieutenant Hare did return from Weir's advanced position to Major Reno. He brought the information that Indians were in sight in great numbers in the distance, but that Weir's troops had not been discovered and were not being molested in any way. Lieutenant Gibson contributed to the latter-day confusion by writing his wife on July 4, 1876 that: "Reno ordered Weir to take his company and try to make connection with Custer, but he returned saying he could find no sign of Custer's command and that there were enough Indians there to eat up his company a hundred times over." Reno testified that he in fact did not issue orders to Weir, but did so to Hare:

> When Lieutenant Hare returned from the pack train, I told him to go to Captain Weir who, on his own hook, had moved out his company, and tell him to communicate with General Custer if he could and tell him where we were. I knew in what direction to send him because General Custer's trail had been found. It was back of the position I took when I went on the hill.

Winfield Edgerly told Walter Camp that: "After they got out ahead, Lieutenant Hare came out with instructions from Reno to open up communication with Custer if they could. Hare returned to Reno, and then M, K and H came out. He thought they must have followed within ½ an hour of the time D left, and that no more of the troops followed—or, if they did, they did not advance very far." Hare himself testified: "As soon as I got back from the pack train I went to Captain Weir, and when I came back, I met Major Reno going down."

That the downstream movement by the rest of the command did not start until after the packs arrived is borne out by Trumpeter Martin: "The rest of us stayed there until the packs all arrived. The ammunition mules came first, in about fifteen minutes; but it was more than an hour before the last pack-mule was up." Further evidence is the statement of Captain McDougall above, wherein he says that he didn't know anything was amiss until he heard the other officers talking about it. If the three companies—H, M and K—had already left, there would have been no "other officers" present to be talking about anything, only Moylan and Reno and Wallace. Benteen mentions very briefly in his testimony that he saw the packs coming but wasn't much interested in them.

In the meanwhile, of course, Weir and Edgerly had long since reached the high ground down the bluffs, at approximately 5:10 p.m. Only Lieutenants Edgerly and Godfrey have left anything approaching a complete account of this movement, although other survivors have painted smaller vignettes. Godfrey, of course, was not part of the initial advance. In his testimony, Edgerly stated:

> We went down about a mile and a half, he [Captain Weir] keeping up on the ridge and I going in a sort of valley. When we got up on the ridge we saw a good many Indians riding up and down and firing at objects on the ground. They saw us about the same time we saw them. I went down this valley, Captain Weir keeping up on the ridge. Pretty soon he saw Indians start for me, and he signaled me to swing to the right.

Walter Camp's notes indicate that Edgerly told him much the same, with some additional comments: "When Weir and Edgerly went out from Reno, they did not see Custer's trail, at least Edgerly did not recall seeing it anywhere. He did not think they could have relieved Custer in any way by going toward him after Benteen met Reno, but so far as they had any information at that time, there was no reason why they should not have tried it." Edgerly repeated this sentiment to W.A. Graham in a letter dated December 5, 1923.

Camp's notes on his interview with Edgerly state, "Edgerly soon turned to the right, into a little valley, which must have been the one followed by Custer and his men, or nearly parallel to it." This could not have been the one used by Custer, since Edgerly said that he never saw Custer's trail at any time. The notes continue: "Weir had gone to a higher point, and standing there signaled that Indians were coming, and Edgerly therefore turned back and circled over to the left . . . ahead to the high ground in front of Weir. He was on the second Reno [Weir] Peak [farthest north]." The discrepancy of "left" and "right" in the two versions is accounted for by Edgerly's having turned about by the right and then making a right turn, which brought him to the left of his original position.

In his 1881 statement, Edgerly was very clear on this point:

After going a few hundred yards I swung off to the right with the troop and went into a little valley which must have been the one fol-lowed by Custer and his men, or nearly parallel to it, and moved right towards the great body of Indians, whom we had already seen from the highest point. After we had gone a short distance down the valley, Col. Weir, who had remained to our left, on the bluff, saw a large number of Indians coming toward us, and motioned with his hand for me to swing around with the troop to where he was, which I did. When I got up on the bluff, I saw Col. Benteen, Captain French and Lieutenant Godfrey coming toward us with their troops.

Edgerly here has also been guilty of "telescoping" events, since there is no question but that Lieutenant Hare returned to Reno before the other troops started down the bluffs. Edgerly mentioned this in his later narrative:

In a short time Lt. Hare came to Weir with an order from Reno to open communication with Reno [Hare testified that the opening of communications was to be with Custer] if possible, and M and K troops were sent to our support. I saw no Indians on the bluff during our advance until near the lowest point, where we could see the bod-ies of Custer's men and horses with swarms of Indians.

Edgerly moved ahead along the ridge, dismounted his men and began to return the fire of the few Indians who had come up. He said that he went to a point, which was identified by Camp as one of the two Weir peaks farthest north. There was another peak, in the direction of the ford at the bottom of Medicine Tail Coulee and somewhat lower than the one Edgerly was on, that was occupied by some Indians who began firing. Edgerly told Camp that when he looked over toward Custer battlefield, he saw Indians shooting as though at objects on the ground and one part of the hill on Custer battlefield was black with Indians and squaws standing there. In his later, personal narrative, Edgerly says that they "could see the bodies of Custer's men and horses."

It has been conjectured over the years as to exactly what was seen by the men on the Weir Point hills and ridges when they looked toward what they later knew to be Custer's battlefield. Most historians are of the opinion that there was nothing really to be seen—that the Custer fight was over and that if anything remotely resembling the last stages of that fight had been visible, that fact could never have been successfully covered up for over a hundred years. This last observation seems to embody the absolute logic of the situation, but it is not necessary to assume that the Custer fight was totally ended when the troops arrived on Weir Point, because it would have been virtually impossible to see much of anything beyond Calhoun Ridge and Hill.

Although there would be a sprinkle of rain later in the evening, the forenoon and afternoon of Sunday, June 25, 1876, had been very warm and very dry, as indeed had been the previous several days. The local terrain was treeless, except along the banks of the river, and the hills east of the river were covered sparsely by sagebrush also fairly thickly by short-rooted buffalo grass. There was a coating of fine dust over all of this rolling and somewhat broken country, and horses tended to kick up a cloud of dust with every step, especially if moving at anything more than a walk. In addition to the dust, the air over the Custer battlefield would have been thick with powder smoke, for none of the firearms at the Little Horn fights utilized smokeless powder—even the metallic cartridges of the day used black powder—and there was no breeze to speak of to carry away the choking clouds of powder smoke and dust.

The only evidence that exists as to what could have been seen and what actually was seen is the testimony of those who were there and who later committed their observations to paper. Lieutenant Edgerly's comments have already appeared above, but there were others who had something to say. The first commentary is from men who were first on the points.

Corporal George Wylie, of Weir's D Troop, described the scene to Walter Camp in 1910:

> The troop marched out along bluff until came to a jumping-off place, from which could look down upon the hollow of Medicine Tail coulee. Men dismounted and put horses behind Edgerly peaks and behind hill to east, and men formed line over this hill, from east to west. Seeing many horsemen over on distant ridge, with guidons flying, Weir said: "That is Custer over there," and mounted up ready to go over, when Sergt. (James) Flanagan said: "Here, Captain, you had better take a look through the glasses; I think those are Indians." Weir did so, and changed his mind about leaving the place. Accordingly, the men were dismounted and the horses led behind the hill.

Lieutenant Luther Hare told Camp that: "While out on the advance with Co. D, the Indians were thick over on Custer ridge and were firing, and at that moment Hare thought Custer was fighting them." This observation was made during Hare's first trip to the Weir ridges. Whatever he saw and heard, and unfortunately there is nothing in Camp's notes more explanatory than the simple statement above, it was sufficient to convince him that the Custer fight was still going on.

FOLLOWING AFTER WEIR

After the pack train came up, three of the other companies—K, M and H—started down the bluffs toward Weir Point. The time was about 5:40 p.m. Captain Benteen always maintained in his writings that he initiated this movement, that he did it on his own authority and that Reno even had his trumpeter sound "Halt" and "Recall" in order to stop him. In his testimony he flatly stated that Reno did not order this movement, but Major Reno just as flatly contradicted him, saying: "I formed the column with three companies on the left, the pack train in the middle, two companies on the right, and started down the river." Neither one of them was telling anything resembling the truth. That Reno in fact ordered the follow-up to Weir's advance is indicated by two facts: firstly, that Captain French's M Company, which was part of Reno's designated command and not even nominally under instructions from Benteen, actually led the three-company march; secondly, that Benteen's own H Company brought up the rear. Had Benteen started on his own hook as he claimed, his company would have most likely been in the lead and French would have stayed put—especially considering the casualties his company had suffered in both men and horses. The advance as made bore no similarity however, to the rock-solid military formation given by Reno in his testimony.

Although this secondary movement has usually been characterized as a failed and rather thoroughly botched attempt to save Custer's command—and has for that reason been severely criticized—no-one has ever been able to firmly establish exactly what it was supposed to achieve, and at the time there was nothing to indicate that Custer was in trouble or needed saving. The firing heard down the river was evidence only of action there. Reno never said anything authoritative on the subject and neither did anyone else, with the exception of Captain Benteen, who testified that he: "went there to see for myself what was going on around the whole country that could be seen." In his second narrative, Benteen wrote, rather cryptically: "I had to get in sight then of what I had left my valley-hunting mission for." In plain truth, once Weir had taken the initiative and had marched toward the sound of the guns, Reno could do nothing else but follow in his tracks. Ordering Weir to return would not have looked very good on the record.

While the three companies moved down the bluffs, Reno was finishing up getting the wounded and perhaps the pack train in condition to follow along. Some of the wounded men could ride and were mounted if there were sufficient mounts for them, but the more serious of the casualties had to be carried in blankets by dismounted troopers, after having been made as comfortable as possible. This duty fell to Moylan's depleted A Company and probably to the remnant of G, although the task proved so onerous that McDougall eventually had to lend a platoon from B to help out. Reno also sent Lieutenant Varnum, with a small detachment, to bury Lieutenant Hodgson's body, perhaps after Captain French had refused to do the same duty.[17]

Lieutenant Varnum remembered at the Reno Inquiry that:

We remained there until the packs came up about three-quarters of an hour afterward. Then I got two spades from the packs and started with about six men to go down to the river and bury the bodies. About two-thirds of the way down, I saw a lot of men coming out of the woods and I stopped to see what was up.

... There was a citizen and quite a number of soldiers who came from the woods dismounted and were climbing the bluffs, coming up out of the bottom. There was timber immediately in the rear of where the fight had occurred down in the bottom. As I started with the men to bury the bodies, somebody, I think Lieutenant Wallace, called to me that they wanted me to come back, and I then started immediately up the hill. I got up the hill and it was very hard, slow work, it was badlands there, and when I got there, most of the command had started to move on down the stream along the bluffs, with the exception, I think, of Captain Moylan's company and possibly some of the others. He had most of the wounded. I think they were all of his company, and the men that he had left when he got out of the bottom were hardly sufficient to carry them. There were very few men there belonging to A Company after the fight and they moved very slowly. I stayed with him some time, and I think Captain McDougall's Company B sent a platoon to assist him in carrying the wounded.

... After the pack train joined the command, I took the spades and started down the hill and was gone possible 20 or 25 minutes, and when I got back the command was all moving except perhaps Captain Moylan's company, which I am not certain about, as he was encumbered with wounded. . . . I guess it was about an hour and a half [after we first got to the top] before the whole thing started.

French, Godfrey and Benteen reached the Weir Point area at about 6:00 p.m., after marching for twenty minutes. French brought his M Company up onto a ridge just behind Weir's D, while Godfrey took position on a spur just to the east of both of them. Benteen, who had supposedly been so anxious to see what could be seen, put his H Troop by file along the lower ridge closest to the river. In both his testimony and his later writings, Benteen claimed to have gone to the highest points and to have planted guidons and had his company front into line, so that any troops in the vicinity might see the position. There is a smattering of truth in these often-repeated extravagant claims, but the overall picture is totally false and misleading. He never did see that for which he had left his valley-hunting mission.

In his first narrative, Benteen wrote only that: "from the top of the highest point in vicinity, saw Weir's troop returning, hordes of Indians hurrying them somewhat." He expands on this point in his second narrative:

On reaching the highest bluff in the vicinity, I saw what I estimated to be about 900 Indians in the valley from which Reno had just been driven. The officer who had preceded me on his "own hook" with his troop had gone down a gorge with it. Indians were riding around the bluff on either side of this troop, signaling. I then formed a troop, dismounted, at right angles with the river, and one on the bluffs, parallel with the river, so that, if Custer's forces were near, our position would be defined.

It is in his Reno Inquiry testimony that Benteen told the story of planting the guidon:

I went down the same direction that Captain Weir had gone, to the highest point of land, and had the troops by file on the river bluffs, and a company across at right angles from that line, on another ridge, with the intention of showing to General Custer, if he were down the river, our exact location as near as possible.

. . . That was my first sight of the village, after I arrived at that high point. That was the only point from which it could be seen, and I saw, as I supposed, about 1,800 tepees. There was no sign of any troops, or of any fighting going on. Nothing of the kind could be seen. The troops were by file on a line of river bluffs, and, as I have stated, another company was formed at right angles on another ridge. I planted a guidon at the highest point that looked over that country. Some of the officers say that the battlefield was in sight; but I know positively that it was not, having gone over it two or three times since.

. . . [The purpose of the guidon was] to present an object to attract the attention of General Custer's command, if it was in sight. . . . It could not be seen as far as the horses [could be seen]. It might attract attention by its fluttering, or by the point of brass on the end, though the horses would be more noticeable objects than the guidon.

When asked directly if he thought Custer was still alive at that time, Benteen replied: "I thought so." Contrast this response with his gratuitous statement when questioned about the order received via Trumpeter Martin: "I received an order to 'Come on, be quick, big village, bring packs, bring packs.' He then had found [the village]. I wish to say before [I received] that order that I believe that General Custer and his whole command were dead."

Benteen's supposed display of the guidon and having collected the troops on the highest point of land have in recent years seriously colored published histories of the campaign, with many historians using these assumed incidents to attribute motives and actions to Custer, who, they say, may have seen the men and horses. In fact, only Benteen mentioned any of this, while the bulk of the evidence is that he was never on the highest ground with or without his company and that he in truth was not at the advanced position for very long at all. His own contradictory testimony is absolutely clear on this point and is corroborated by others. Benteen himself testified: "We had not been more than 2 or 3 minutes at that high point before the gorge was filled with Indians rushing towards us. Then we fell back to where we were corralled." Lieutenant Edgerly swore that: "After a little while Captain Benteen moved back with his company towards the corral," and Edward Godfrey told Walter Camp that: "Benteen did not remain there long, but went back and joined Reno."

While Benteen claimed to have been unable to see Custer's battlefield or any sign of troops or fighting, while in his advanced position, several others who were there have left accounts of what they did see. Private Edward Pigford, of French's M Company, told Walter Camp:

> Co. M . . . went all way to Edgerly peaks [Weir Point], from which could look down in direction of Custer Ridge. Says at first when looked over toward Custer ridge, the Indians were firing from a big circle; but it gradually closed, until they seemed to converge into a large black mass on the side hill toward the river and all along the ridge. He thinks what they saw was the last stages of the fight. His description of what took place at Edgerly Hills while Co. M was there seems reliable.

Pigford's is perhaps the most dramatic of the many observations left behind and it is so non-specific that it is hard to tell whether it refers to Custer Hill, which most likely would not have been visible because of the smoke and dust, or to Calhoun Ridge, which was more clearly visible. Most historians, however, have generally discounted Pigford's story, since to accept it would cast doubt upon the sworn statements of some officers who testified at the Reno Court of Inquiry and would mean that part of the regiment sat by and watched the end of Custer's battalions.

Lieutenant Charles Varnum wrote in his second narrative: "After helping with the wounded I joined Capt. Weir with the advance. We moved to a point that overlooked where Custer's fight took place, but it was covered with Indians riding in every direction. A considerable firing was heard but there was no body of troops in sight. I saw some white objects that I thought were rocks, but found afterwards they were naked bodies of men," thus refuting Benteen's sworn testimony.

In 1923, Sergeant John Ryan, also of French's M Troop, wrote:

We went in that direction for probably half a mile until we gained a high point and could overlook the Indian camp and the battlefield. We saw at a distance of from a mile and a half to two miles parties whom we supposed were Indians, riding back and forth, firing scattering shots. We thought that they were disposing of Custer's wounded men, and this afterward proved to be true.[18]

The distance mentioned is consistent with Calhoun Ridge. The classic description and the one most often quoted in histories of the campaign, comes from Edward Godfrey's 1892 narrative:

Looking toward Custer's field, on a hill two miles away we saw a large assemblage. At first our command did not appear to attract their attention, although there was some commotion observable among those nearest to our position. We heard occasional shots, most of which seemed to be a great distance off, beyond the large groups on the hill. While watching this group the conclusion was arrived at that Custer had been repulsed, and the firing was the parting shots of the rear-guard.

Again, this is clearly a description of Calhoun Ridge and Hill.

But one of the most interesting comments is found in Walter Camp's notes of an interview conducted with Corporal George Wylie of D Troop in October 1910. In almost an aside to the main interview, Camp writes: "Says no other troop got as far in the advance as D troop. Does not recall seeing Corpl. Foley ride down pursued by Indians, and never heard of it. This refers to what Flanagan told me." The name Flanagan refers to Sergeant James Flanagan, also of D Troop and a veteran of several years, who obviously had told Camp that he had seen the death by suicide of Corporal John Foley of C Company.[19] Camp's notes relative to his interview with Flanagan have never surfaced.

In the meanwhile, Reno was heading down the bluffs, followed by the pack train, McDougall's B Company, and the wounded being carried by Moylan's company; Charley Varnum had returned from his abortive trip down the hill and was hurrying to get to the advanced position on Weir Point; and George Herendeen and some dozen men were joining the command from the river bottom. Most of these men—who had been left in the timber by Reno's precipitous retreat from the bottom—were from G Company. As Godfrey wrote in 1892:

> It was about this time that thirteen men and a scout named Herendeen rejoined the command; they had been missing since Reno's flight from the bottom; several of them were wounded. These men had lost their horses in the stampede from the bottom and had remained in the timber; when leaving the timber to rejoin, they were fired upon by five Indians, but they drove them away and were not again molested.

This whole late movement by Reno seems to have been a rather catch-as-catch-can affair. Captain McDougall told Walter Camp:

> All 7 cos. went out, Moylan with Co. A being the last to start. Moylan had the wounded. On the advance, Benteen's men were by file along ridge parallel with river. The pack train merely got started before it was ordered to fall back. The rear then became the head of the column. Moylan was having difficulty getting along with the wounded, and just as they were ordered to fall back, McDougall had offered to let Moylan have one of his platoons to assist with the wounded.

Lieutenant Mathey testified that:

> We got no orders until the command started to move down the river, then the pack train followed. I observed the movements of the troops and followed them. I think about half an hour [after we arrived]. I don't know exactly [what they were waiting for]. I remember Captain

Moylan said it would be difficult to go along with his wounded men. We made the movement very slowly.

BACK TO POINT A

As this portion of the command slowly started along the bluffs, Fred Benteen had already left the forward position with his troop and was discussing with Major Reno the need for falling back to what he thought was the more defensible position they had previously held. Lieutenant Hare told Walter Camp:

> Benteen and Reno were discussing matters (They were standing about ½ mile in rear of Co. D), and Benteen suggested to Reno that they fall back, as they were in a poor place for defense. Benteen remarked that Indians could pass around them to the east and also by river flat at the west, and would soon be in their rear if did not fall back. This was probably why Reno decided to fall back.

Although he tried to make it appear in both his testimony and his later writings that he had left instructions for the three companies still on Weir Point, Captain Benteen had in fact left them without even notifying the officers that he was going. That there was only light fire being exchanged between the troops and the Indians was absolutely no excuse for such conduct, especially in view of Benteen's subsequent inquiry testimony that:

> I had left one company [French] on the ridge with instructions to send their horses back dismounted, and to hold that ridge at all hazards. Mind you, I was looking after things probably more than it was my business or duty to do. This company, when we got back to the place where we were corralled, had left that point, and were in the line, coming back as rapidly as were any of the others. I then sent Captain Godfrey's company back to another hill to check the Indians till we formed, and that he was all right, that he would be looked out for—and they got in all right.

Although there wasn't much in the way of fighting going on at Weir Point, the troops had been discovered and hordes of warriors were streaming toward the position. Private Pigford remembered that "the appearance of Indians coming from Custer Ridge towards Weir hills looked as thick as grasshoppers in a harvest field," and George Glease said: "When we tried to get to Custer, we looked down and saw the country thick with Indians." Lieutenant Edgerly testified: "At this point there were a few Indians who commenced firing at us from behind some rocks. I dismounted the troop, and also from behind rocks, we had an interesting duel, until Capt. French called up to me that Reno had sent orders for us to return to his position."

There is some confusion as to how, and by whom, the order to retire was actually given. Major Reno swore that: "Lieutenant Hare came back and said he had taken the responsibility of using my name, and ordered the return of the command on account of the number of Indians he saw." Walter Camp's notes of his interview with Lieutenant Hare, however, say: "Says he [Hare] did not order any Co. back on his own authority. Hare does not remember who gave the order to fall back." Since Hare was acting as Reno's adjutant, he was perfectly entitled to give orders in Reno's name and there was nothing intrinsically wrong with the orders to retire, although they did catch most of the other officers by surprise.

Lieutenant Edgerly expanded on his previously cited testimony:

In a short time Captain Weir moved back by himself towards where Major Reno had selected a position. The next thing was Captain French spoke to me and said the order had been given to move back. I said to him I thought not, that I heard of no such order. He waited some time, probably five minutes, and then said the order had been given to go back and he was going. He mounted his men and moved off at a gallop.

Walter Camp's notes indicate that Edgerly told him: "When they retreated from the advance, there were not many Indians in their front, but they became more numerous as the troops retreated. He said that he obeyed reluctantly because of the few Indians in his front."

Lieutenant Godfrey told Camp: "Here Godfrey's impression was that a stand would be made, putting the packs in the hollow behind the surrounding hills, to the west, north and east. He was soon surprised however, by Hare riding up and saying that the commanding officer had ordered that they fall back. Directly M Troop came galloping up and went past." Godfrey said much the same in his 1892 *Century* article:

The firing ceased, the groups dispersed, clouds of dust arose from all parts of the field, and the horsemen converged toward our position. The command was now dismounted to fight on foot. Weir's and French's troops were posted on the high bluffs and to the front of them; my own troop along the crest of the bluffs next to the river; the rest of the command moved to the rear, as I supposed to occupy other points in the vicinity, to make this our defensive position. Busying myself with posting my men, giving directions about the use of ammunition, etc., I was a little startled by the remark that the command was out of sight. At this time, Weir's and French's troops were being attacked. Orders were soon brought to me by Lieutenant Hare, Acting-Adjutant, to join the main command.

WINFIELD EDGERLY AND VINCENT CHARLEY

The withdrawal from the Weir Peaks area led to three of the most dramatic scenes of this phase of the engagement. These were the difficulty Lieutenant Edgerly had in mounting his rambunctious horse, the death of D Company Farrier Vincent Charley, and the covering of the withdrawal by Lieutenants Godfrey and Hare with Godfrey's K Troop.

Captain French had taken his company back at a gallop, so Edgerly mounted up D Company and prepared to follow. He himself however, had trouble getting into the saddle as his horse kept turning away from him. He described the scene to Walter Camp:

> Edgerly said that when he fell back he had trouble getting on his horse, and that there were Indians within 15 feet of him firing at him and his orderly. Edgerly's horse kept swinging away from him, and his orderly had to keep riding around to stop the horse. All this time, the Indians were firing at them, and the orderly, an old veteran, kept smiling. Finally Edgerly mounted and they got out of there in a hurry. Afterward Edgerly enquired of the orderly why he had smiled, or what he saw to laugh at, and the man replied that it was the bad marksmanship of the Indians so close to them.

Sergeant Thomas Harrison of D Company was a part of this scene and in 1911 told Walter Camp:

... the place where Edgerly had trouble mounting his horse was at the mouth, or northeast, end of the sugarloaf, east of the two peaks. Weir and D Company had stopped back at the south end of this sugarloaf, and Edgerly said he would go out to the end of the sugarloaf, to look down and see if he could see Custer while they were out there. D Company started back on the retreat. Charley was hit in this retreat, back near a ravine to left, perhaps a ¼ mile or less from the two peaks. As Edgerly and Harrison were coming off the sugarloaf, [their horses became unmanageable and] they had to throw their bridles over their heads and draw revolvers, and ride through the Indians.

Corporal George Wylie, also of D Company, recalled the scene for Walter Camp in 1910:

The Indians soon came up in great force, and the men were mounted up and started back along the ridge in column of twos on a walk. After going some distance, the Indians had arrived on Edgerly peaks, and opened up a hot fire. Corpl. Wylie had a ball shot through his canteen, the staff of the guidon he was carrying was shot off, the flag dropped, and Vincent Charley was shot and fell off his horse. Wylie got down to pick up the guidon. At the same time, Edgerly was stooping over Charley, and told him to lie quiet and he would return and rescue him.

Edgerly's own testimony was that:

I then gave the command to mount and moved off at a trot. As we got within 60 yards from that point I saw Company K with Captain Godfrey and Lieutenant Hare, their men dismounted and their horses being led back. They had seen us coming and Captain Godfrey had turned back and covered our retreat in the most brave and fearless manner. On going back I passed a man of D Company wounded. He looked at me and I told him to get into a hole and I would form a line, come back and save him. As soon as I got by K Company I met Captain Weir and told him about the wounded soldier and that I had promised to save him and asked him to throw out a skirmish line for that purpose. He said he was very sorry but the orders were to go back on the hill. I said that I had promised to save the man. He said he could not help it, the orders were positive to go back and we must go back.

The abandonment of Vincent Charley was, Edgerly later wrote, the hardest thing he ever had to do during his military career. There were very good reasons for Edgerly's feeling this way. Walter Camp's notes indicate that Edgerly told him: "Vincent Charley was hit in the hips, and when he fell, he struck his head, which began to bleed. Edgerly told him to get into the ravine out of danger for awhile. Charley was killed, and his body when afterward found had a stick rammed down the throat."

Comments from Sergeant Harrison's interviews with Camp also revealed another painful truth:

Vincent Charley was killed between the two Edgerly Peaks. I was orderly for Lieutenant Edgerly. The Indians had gotten around behind us when Edgerly had problems mounting his horse. We had to draw our revolvers and cut our way through on the retreat. "As they came along by Charley, he [Charley] cried out that he was wounded and needed assistance. Edgerly stopped, and told him to get into a ravine, and he would try to come back and save him as soon as they could get reinforcements. After going a piece, they looked back and saw the Indians finishing up Charley. At the moment they were talking with Charley, perhaps 200 Indians were in the immediate neighborhood, all advancing. When D Troop retreated, they failed to rescue Charley, and when Lieutenant Edgerly and I got away from the peak it was occupied by Indians, and it was then too late to help Charley, who was shot through the hips and making his way to the rear the best he could, half crawling on his feet and one hand." He says Weir was with the Company on the peaks and sugarloaf.

GODFREY COVERS THE RETREAT

Godfrey, who had been so surprised to see that the previously advancing elements of the command had now started to retrace their steps and who had received absolutely no communications in regard to anything, was even more startled when French's troops came tearing past him toward the rear, followed by D Company, who were moving at a more measured pace. The just-vacated ridges were almost immediately occupied by hundreds of warriors who commenced firing at the retreating troops and who gave every sign of pursuing.

According to Walter Camp's Godfrey notes:

> ... and next Co. D went past without Edgerly, who was having difficulty in mounting his horse. After those two troops had passed, Godfrey said to Hare: "Look here, Hell's to pay," for the Indians were coming in swarms along the ridge which the troops had just left. (There were no Indians in the coulee to the east, so Godfrey says. By this I mean the coulee down which Custer marched). Godfrey, after passing along the ridge some distance, dismounted his men, forming a skirmish line at right angles to the river and began to hold the Indians in check, at the same time sending the led horses back on the line of retreat. (This corroborates what others have said, namely that Godfrey's covering of retreat was near where stand was made).

In his 1892 article, Lieutenant Godfrey described the action thusly:

> I had gone some distance in the execution of this order when, looking back, I saw French's troop come tearing over the bluffs, and soon after Weir's troop following in hot haste. Edgerly was near the top of the bluff trying to mount his frantic horse, and it did seem that he would not succeed, but he vaulted into his saddle and then joined the troop. The Indians almost immediately followed to the top of the bluff, and commenced firing into the retreating troops, killing one man, wounding others and several horses. They then started down the hillside in pursuit. I at once made up my mind that such a retreat and close pursuit would throw the whole command into confusion, and, perhaps, prove disastrous. I dismounted my men to fight on foot, deploying as rapidly as possible without waiting for the formation laid down in tactics. Lieutenant Hare expressed his intention of staying with me, "Adjutant or no Adjutant." The led horses were sent to the main command. Our fire in a short time compelled the Indians to halt and take cover, but before this was accomplished, a second order came for me to fall back as quickly as possible to the main command. Having checked the pursuit we began our retreat, slowly at first, but kept up our firing. After proceeding some distance the men

began to group together, and to move a little faster and faster, and our fire slackened. This was pretty good evidence that they were getting demoralized. The Indians were being heavily reinforced, and began to come from their cover, but kept up a heavy fire. I halted the line, made the men take their intervals, and again drove the Indians to cover; then once more began the retreat. The firing of the Indians was very heavy; the bullets struck the ground all about us; but the "ping-ping" of the bullets overhead seemed to have a more terrifying influence than the "swish-thud" of the bullets that struck the ground immediately about us. When we got close to the ridge in front of Reno's position I observed some Indians making all haste to get possession of a hill to the right. I could now see the rest of the command, and I knew that that hill would command Reno's position. Supposing that my troop was to occupy the line we were then on, I ordered Hare to take ten men and hold the hill, but, just as he was moving off, an order came from Reno to get back as quickly as possible; so I recalled Hare and ordered the men to run to the lines. This movement was executed, strange to say, without a single casualty.

The total withdrawal from the advance to Weir Point was accomplished at almost exactly H1830. Vincent Charley had been the sole casualty during the past two and a half hours—but there would be many more to come. The fight on the hilltop was about to commence.

NOTES

1. Major Marcus A. Reno: testimony at the Reno Court of Inquiry, 1879; Captain Myles Moylan: testimony at the Reno Court of Inquiry, 1879; [ebook] Appendices 3.81, 3.96.

2. Charles A. Varnum: testimony at the Reno Court of Inquiry, 1879; First Lieutenant George D. Wallace: testimony at the Reno Court of Inquiry, 1876; Luther Hare: testimony at the Reno Court of Inquiry; [ebook] Appendices 3.49, 3.111, 3.113.

3. Sergeant Ferdinand A. Culbertson: testimony at the Reno Court of Inquiry, 1879; Private Edward Davern of F Company, Reno's orderly: testimony at the Reno Court of Inquiry, 1879; Benteen: testimony at the Reno Court of Inquiry; Winfield Edgerly: testimony at the Reno Court of Inquiry, 1879; [ebook] Appendices 3.4, 3.14, 3.17, 3.21.

4. E. S. Godfrey: testimony at the Reno Court of Inquiry, 1879; Daniel Newell: account as given to John P. Everitt and published in *The Sunshine Magazine*, September 1930; William E. Morris: excerpts from his accounts from correspondence and as published

in an unidentified newspaper, in the period 1894–1923; Doctor H. R. Porter: testimony at the Reno Court of Inquiry, 1879; [ebook] Appendices 3.38, 3.80, 3.82, 3.88.

5. Orderly trumpeter John Martin: account as contained in *The Cavalry Journal*, July 1923; [ebook] *Appendix 3.69*.

6. Captain F. W. Benteen: statement to *The New York Herald*, August 8, 1876; Frederick William Benteen: lengthier narratives and his testimony at the Reno Court of Inquiry; [ebook] *Appendices 3.3, 3.4*.

7. Major Marcus Reno: report on the Fights on the Little Horn, July 5, 1876; [ebook] Appendix 4.9.

8. Winfield S. Edgerly: account given at Fort Yates, Dakota, July 30, 1881, as published in the *Leavenworth Weekly Times*, August 18, 1888; [ebook] Appendix 3.19.

9. Edward S. Godfrey: narrative of 1892; [ebook] Appendix 3.37.

10. Charles A. Varnum: letter to his parents, from the *Lowell Weekly Journal*, August 1876; Charles A. Varnum: testimony at the Reno Court of Inquiry, 1879; [ebook] *Appendices 2.28, 3.111*.

11. Theodore W. Goldin: the *Army Magazine* article and a letter to Frederick Benteen; Theodore W. Goldin—his stories as reflected in his correspondence from 1904 to 1934; [ebook] *Appendices 3.41, 3.42*.

12. W. A Graham, *Cavalry Journal* (1923).

13. Winfield S. Edgerly: later narrative, date unknown but definitely after 1909; Edgerly: account, undated, from a manuscript in the collections of the North Dakota Historical Society; [ebook] Appendices 3.4, 3.19, 3.20, 3.36, 3.37, 3.70.

14. William E. Morris: excerpts from his accounts from correspondence and as published in an unidentified newspaper, in the period 1894–1923;[ebook] *Appendix 3.80*.

15. Captain E. G. Mathey: testimony at the Reno Court of Inquiry, 1879; [ebook] Appendix 3.71.

16. Captain Thomas McDougall: testimony at the Reno Court of Inquiry, 1879; [ebook] Appendix 3.75.

17. Captain E. G. Mathey: testimony at the Reno Court of Inquiry, 1879; Edward G. Mathey: interview with Walter Camp January 19, 1910; [ebook] Appendices 3.71, 3.72.

18. John M. Ryan: narrative published in *The Hardin Tribune*, June 22, 1923. [ebook] Appendix 3.99.

19. The 7th Regiment of Cavalry, United States Army: Rosters pertaining to regimental assignments, strengths, casualties and battle statistics on the campaign which culminated in the series of actions known as the Battle of the Little Big Horn, June 25 and 26, 1876; [ebook] Appendix 5.17.

Lt. Col. George Armstrong Custer in the last photo taken of him, April 1876. *Courtesy of the Little Bighorn Battlefield National Monument*

Elizabeth "Libbie" Bacon Custer, along with her husband and his brother Tom, in a photo taken at the end of the Civil War in spring 1865. *Courtesy of The Library of Congress*

Captain Frederick William Benteen, who commanded the lefthand battalion at the battle on June 25, 1876. *Courtesy of the Little Bighorn Battlefield National Monument*

Major Marcus Albert Reno commanded the center battalion of Companies A, G, and M, tasked with attacking the Indian village head-on while Benteen probed to the left and Custer circled to the right. *Courtesy of the Little Bighorn Battlefield National Monument*

Mitch Bouyer, son of a French-Canadian blacksmith and a Santee Sioux mother, and married to a woman from the Crow tribe, served as an interpreter and guide with the 7th Cavalry. Killed with Custer, it was not until 1985 that some bones found on the South Skirmish Line were positively identified as his. *Courtesy of the Little Bighorn Battlefield National Monument*

Brig. Gen. Alfred Howe Terry commanded the Dakota Column, which included the 7th Cavalry in the campaign, and was first to arrive on the field after the battle had ended. *Courtesy of The Library of Congress*

Brig. Gen. George R. Crook commanded the Wyoming Column during the three-pronged campaign, but turned back to wait for reinforcements after clashing with the hostiles at the Battle of the Rosebud. *Courtesy of the Little Bighorn Battlefield National Monument*

Col. John Gibbon, whose greatest fame had come at Gettysburg, where he held Cemetery Ridge against Pickett's Charge, commanded the Montana Column during the campaign that included the Battle of the Little Bighorn. *Courtesy of The Library of Congress*

Captain Thomas Ward Custer, George's younger brother. Winner of two Medals of Honor during the Civil War, his body could only be recognized after the Battle of the Little Bighorn through a tattoo. *Courtesy of the Little Bighorn Battlefield National Monument*

Second Lt. John Jordan Crittenden, son of a Civil War major general, was detailed to Company L, 7th Cavalry at the Little Bighorn. When his body was found it was seen that his prosthetic glass eye had been shattered by an arrow. *Courtesy of the Little Bighorn Battlefield National Monument*

Boston Custer, younger brother of George and Tom, was employed by the quartermaster as a citizen guide during the campaign, but joined his brothers' battalion and was killed with it. *Courtesy of the Little Bighorn Battlefield National Monument*

Second Lt. Benjamin Hubert Hodgson, B Company, who acted as adjutant for Reno's battalion, was killed during the valley fight. *Courtesy of the Little Bighorn Battlefield National Monument*

The body of First Sgt. James Butler of L Company was found near the river fairly close to Reno's position. Empty cartridge cases found around his body gave rise to speculation that he was either escaping or serving as a courier for Custer when he was killed. *Courtesy of the Little Bighorn Battlefield National Monument*

Captain Thomas Benton Weir, commander of D Company, tried to lead his men from Reno's hilltop position to aid Custer, but was turned back by Indians at the prominence that today bears his name. He died the following December after suffering from a severe case of depression. *Courtesy of the Little Bighorn Battlefield National Monument*

Second Lt. Charles Albert Varnum, of Company A, who commanded the army's Indian Scouts at the Little Horn. He survived and later fought in the Spanish-American War, retiring as a colonel. *Courtesy of the Little Bighorn Battlefield National Monument*

First Lt. James Ezekiel Porter, of I Company. He was one of three officers with Custer whose body was never identified; however, his buckskin jacket with a bloody bullet hole near the heart was found in the abandoned Indian village after the battle. *Courtesy of the Little Bighorn Battlefield National Monument*

Second Lt. James Garland Sturgis, who served with Company E of Custer's battalion during the battle. Like Porter, his remains were never identified, although bloody underclothing bearing his name was found in the abandoned Indian village. *Courtesy of the Little Bighorn Battlefield National Monument*

Trumpeter John Martin of H Company was assigned to serve as a courier for Custer during the battle, and carried Custer's last message, to Benteen. *Courtesy of the Little Bighorn Battlefield National Monument*

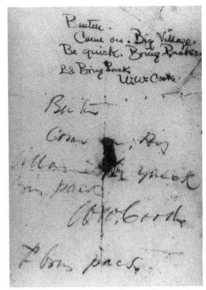

Custer's last written order, to Benteen, telling him "Come on. Big Village. Be Quick. Bring packs. PS Bring pacs." *Courtesy of the Little Bighorn Battlefield National Monument*

Captain Keogh's horse Comanche, the only living thing from Custer's command found on the battlefield. *Courtesy of the Little Bighorn Battlefield National Monument*

Irish-born Captain Myles Walter Keogh, commander of I Company. A professional warrior who had fought in Europe and in the Civil War, his body was found oddly unmutilated after the battle, as if he had earned unusual respect from his foes. *Courtesy of the Little Bighorn Battlefield National Monument*

Top left: Gall, Hunkpapa Lakota war chief, born in present-day South Dakota around 1840. *Courtesy of the Little Bighorn Battlefield National Monument*

Top right: Low Dog, Oglala Lakota minor chief. *Courtesy of the Little Bighorn Battlefield National Monument*

Left: Rain-in-the-Face, Hunkpapa Lakota war chief, born about 1835. Once arrested for murder by Tom Custer, he was said to have vowed to cut the officer's heart out. The state of Tom's body after the Battle of the Little Bighorn left it unclear whether the vow had been fulfilled. *Courtesy of the Little Bighorn Battlefield National Monument*

Right: Sitting Bull, Hunkpapa holy man and acknowledged spiritual leader of the Lakota Indians who gathered on the Little Horn in the summer of 1876. *Courtesy of the Little Bighorn Battlefield National Monument*

Bottom left: Crow King, Hunkpapa Lakota, who led approximately 80 warriors against Custer's troops on Calhoun Hill and Finley Ridge. *Courtesy of the Little Bighorn Battlefield National Monument*

Bottom right: Two Moon, minor Cheyenne chief, born about 1842. Said to be one of the models for the buffalo nickel, he traveled to Washington, DC several times, met with President Wilson in 1914, and attended Little Bighorn battle events. *Courtesy of the Little Bighorn Battlefield National Monument*

Left: Custer and three Arikara or "Ree" scouts in 1873. His favorite scout, Bloody Knife, who was killed during Reno's valley fight, is kneeling at left. *Courtesy of the Little Bighorn Battlefield National Monument*

Below: Officers of the Black Hills Expedition, 1874, many of whom were in the fights on the Little Horn. Custer is reclining in the center, with Bloody Knife standing behind him. *Courtesy of the Little Bighorn Battlefield National Monument*

First photograph of the battlefield, taken by John H. Fouch in early July 1877 shortly after the expedition to retrieve the bodies of the fallen officers. *Courtesy of Dr. James S. Brust*

Bones, principally horse ones, gathered from the battlefield in 1879 and piled on Last Stand Hill at or near the site where George Custer's body was found, prior to interment of the bones beneath the first monument constructed there. Photo by Stanley J. Morrow. *Courtesy of the Little Bighorn Battlefield National Monument*

False grave for Lt. James Sturgis. Although his body was not identified after the battle, a "grave" was constructed and marked with his name in 1879. *Courtesy of the Little Bighorn Battlefield National Monument*

The site where Captain Myles Keogh was found and originally buried, in a photo taken in 1879. *Courtesy of the Little Bighorn Battlefield National Monument*

Four of Custer's Crow Indian Scouts, photographed at his death site marker in 1908. From the left they are White Man Runs Him, Hairy Moccasin, Curley, and Goes Ahead. *Courtesy of the Little Bighorn Battlefield National Monument*

CHAPTER 8

UNDER SIEGE ON RENO HILL

"In fact the Indians were firing very rapidly at us and we just laid still and made no reply . . ."— 1ST LIEUTENANT CHARLES A. VARNUM—RENO COURT OF INQUIRY

The men on what would be known as Reno's Hill still had no idea what had happened to Custer and his immediate command, but their most pressing concern was the threatening horde of Indian warriors, many now armed with the Springfields and ammunition taken from the five companies with Custer as well as from those soldiers killed during Reno's retreat. The disciplined retreat of Godfrey's men had bought time for the rest of Reno's command to organize for the defense of the hill, and in his first narrative Captain Benteen told how Companies G and H formed a line on the right while the other companies formed a line on the left, forming an arc.[1]

Benteen described the scene thus: "The formation as described was dismounted, the horses of command being placed in a saucer depression of prairie. The lower rim of the saucer, instead of a rim was a gentle slope. The hospital was established at the upper rim, and was about as safe a place as there was around the vicinity, the blue canopy of heaven being the covering *[and]* the sage brushes *[and]* sand being the operating board; but the stout heart and nervy skill of Dr. Porter (the only surgeon of the three commands that hadn't been killed) was equal to the occasion."[2]

The soldiers came under heavy fire immediately and Lt. George Wallace testified how the warriors used the vantage points around Reno Hill to shoot at the soldiers:

Q. During this time what had been the conduct of the Indians?
A. They were surrounding us, and as we fell back to this position, they followed up the command, and occupied one or two high points, and then swung around and occupied every hill and point that would afford them a position to fire from.[3]

Commencing about H1830 the warriors kept up a more or less continuous firing until late in the evening, as Godfrey described, "The firing continued till nearly dark (between nine and ten o'clock), although after dusk but little attention was paid to the firing, as everybody moved about freely."[4] Dr. Porter, already busy with those wounded in the retreat from the timber, found himself busier still as the warriors' fire caused casualties among the soldiers in their unprotected positions. Without time to erect breastworks the soldiers were very exposed to Indian fire. Major Reno testified:

Q. What time were the troops put in position there on the hill, and what time did the firing commence?
A. The horses were put together hurriedly. We had hardly time to get in line dismounted, before they came at us in large numbers. The men threw themselves on the ground. They had no shelter. There was no protection except a growth, not exactly of sage brush, but it was what is called "grease wood"—forming no protection whatever.[5]

That lack of cover proved fatal to some soldiers and painful to others. Private Frank Braun of Company M was hit while in a stooped position, the bullet travelling up from his lower leg to lodge in the head of his thigh bone. He later died of his wounds.[6] Private William George of Company H was hit in the left side and also died later from the wound.[7] Private Henry C. Voight of Company M was killed by a bullet through the head as he tried to untangle badly frightened horses.[8] Private Julius Helmer and Sergeant DeWitt Winney, both of Company K, were killed almost simultaneously as evening drew on. Helmer was shot through the bowels and Winney received a fatal body wound.[9] Corporal George H. King of Company A received severe wounds to his left shoulder and died on July 2nd.[10] Edward Housen, a Private in Company D, was also killed. A Private in Company G, John McVay, was luckier, surviving a bad wound to his left hip. There were other, less serious wounds, as warrior bullets found targets among the hapless soldiers lying virtually in the open on Reno Hill. They would have found some relief at being taken to the hospital area which had been fortified to let Dr. Porter treat his charges in relative safety.

Captain E.G. Mathey testified:

Q. State where you went after you turned back with the pack train. What was done with it?

A. When we got on top of the hill it seemed to be a good position, and they halted as I was about to corral the mules and to tie them, when I received orders from Captain Benteen to put the men on the line, and I gave the order for the men to go on the line and let the mules go. I went out to see the line, and one man was wounded and brought back about to that place, and boxes were put around to afford protection, and after that the other wounded were brought to that place.

Q. What men were ordered to the line, the men of the different companies?

A. The men of the different companies. I heard Captain Benteen say, "Put all the men out on the line." The firing became heavy as soon as we halted.

Q. Go on and state anything about that matter that you recollect.

A. The firing kept on and we remained there. Sometime after dark Major Reno gave me an order to put boxes out to cover the front. There was quite a depression and the firing was heavy from that direction. With help, I put all the boxes in the place where I was directed. Captain Moylan's company was in that position.[11]

As darkness fell and the warriors' fire ceased, thoughts once more turned to the whereabouts of Custer and the companies with him. Lieutenant George Wallace testified:

Q. After Major Reno's command had taken its position on the hill, state whether there was any solicitude or uneasiness on the part of that command, or any portion of it, as to General Custer's column and, if so, state the nature of such solicitude or uneasiness.

A. There was no uneasiness whatever. I heard a great deal of swearing about General Custer running off and leaving us.[12]

Captain Edward S. Godfrey remembered things slightly differently:

Of course everybody was wondering about Custer, why he did not communicate by courier or signal. But the general opinion seemed to prevail that he had been defeated and driven down the river, where he would probably join General Terry, and with whom he would return to our relief. Quite frequently, too, the question, "What's the matter with Custer?" would evoke an impatient reply.[13]

Speculation was rife, but none of it extended as far as to consider the kind of tragedy that had actually befallen the Lt. Colonel and his immediate command.

Also under cover of darkness, the opportunity was taken to erect some fortifications for the men. Captain Miles Moylan testified:

During the night of the 25th, however, after the firing had ceased, by direction of Major Reno, the companies commenced to fortify themselves in this position. He gave orders that the dead animals, where they could be used, should be pulled out from among the herd, and put in position, and covered over with earth and so on, in order to establish the line. The most of that was done in front of my company, by my company. We took the dead animals and pulled them out and put them on the line and put packs on them and covered them over with earth as well as we could with the implements we had. We had only two or three spades in the command. With my company, we were occupied at night in throwing up these works so that during the 26th the casualties were very light.

Captain Benteen though, did not instruct his Company H to build any breastworks and in his testimony gave his reasons for omitting to do so:

Q. State whether or not you found it necessary to give orders or instructions, or suggestions, to more than your immediate company; and, if so, what were those instructions or suggestions? And what, in your judgment, was the necessity for so doing?

A. On the night of the 25th Major Reno was upon the hill where my company was stationed, after the firing ceased. It was about dark, and he instructed me to build breastworks. I was pretty tired, and did not think there was much necessity for building them, as I had an idea the Indians would leave us; but I sent for spades to carry out his instructions, but could get none. The next morning, the fire was very much heavier than it had been the day before and I had a great deal of trouble keeping my men on the line."

Benteen's decision not to let his men build cover for themselves would cost Company H dear on June 26th but the first casualty that morning was a Company B man, Private Richard B. Dorn. In his interview with Captain Thomas M. McDougall, Walter Camp's notes stated, "Dorn was killed while waking McDougall up."[14] With the warriors' fire increasing and the warriors themselves presenting very few targets it was not surprising that Reno's beleaguered command starting taking further casualties.

Another early casualty was Frank C. Mann, a civilian packer whose death was witnessed by Private William O. Taylor of Company A, "I know that during the forenoon of the 26th, I, with others, was ordered to take from our barricade anything we could carry up to the position held by H Troop. . . . Leaving our loads on the ground we returned at once to our barricade, where, a few moments later, F.C. Mann, a civilian packer, lying not over two feet from me was shot in the head and instantly killed."[15]

As the sun began to rise signaling another very hot day and without access to water, thirst was now becoming a worry. Three men, Private John Foley, together with Sergeants John Rafter and Louis Rott, all of Company K, agreed to dash for the river and fill some kettles with water, while Benteen organized some covering fire. The move was successful, but the water obtained only brought respite to a very few men.[16]

The firing from the warriors increased in intensity toward mid-morning as Captain McDougall stated in his testimony: "Then I went at nightfall and got some hardtack for my men, and a box of ammunition. The engagement began the next morning about half past two o'clock, being very heavy towards 10 o'clock."[17]

Almost certainly it was during that heavy bout of firing that Captain

Benteen's decision not to erect breastworks during the night brought calamity to Company H. Of the 39 men who had reached Reno Hill, 50% became casualties, being 17 wounded and 3 killed, as Indian bullets poured into the hapless soldiers. Of those wounded, nine were sufficiently serious for the men to be sent on the *Far West* to Fort Abraham Lincoln after the fighting was over. The three fatalities were Privates Julien J. Jones and Thomas E. Meador, plus Corporal George Lell. Jones and Meador were killed virtually at the same time according to Sergeant Charles Windolph. "On June 26, the Indians killed Jones on my right and Meador on my left."[18] Private Jacob Adams of Company H told how Meador initially received a bad wound to the right breast and how he, Adams, tried to carry the wounded man to safety, "when another bullet struck him in the head, ending his life instantly."[19] Adams also told how, after the head shot to Meador, "I dropped the body and hurried to shelter, and when I happened to look back I saw an Indian with a long stick adorned with feathers trying to reach Meador's form. I felt my whole nature revolt, and I assure you that Indian never attempted another such feat."[20] The Indian in question was the Sans Arc Lakota, Long Road, but whether or not Adams killed him is open to question, as in an interview with Walter Camp, Private Edward D. Pigford of Company M stated, ". . . the Indian killed near Co. H line was one who had charged up and stopped there. . . . Every little while this Indian would rise up and fire. Once when he rose up he exposed the upper half of his body, and [I] Pigford taking deliberate aim, killed him."[21] Oddly, Adams made no such claim in his Camp interview. Whatever the truth of that incident, Benteen's laxity had made his men pay a high price, yet ironically the Captain, who had been walking about totally exposed to the Indian fire, suffered only a superficial wound to his thumb and had a boot heel shot off.

While not at the same level as Company H, the other companies too had suffered casualties on June 26th. Company B had three wounded as had Company C. Company D had one, so too did Company E, while Company G had two. They also had their share of fatalities with Private James C. Bennett of Company C receiving a spinal wound from which he died on July 5th. Private Patrick M. Golden of Company D was killed just after the withdrawal of a move against encroaching warriors. Lieutenant Winfield S. Edgerly described what he witnessed: ". . . we were ordered to get into the pits again . . . saw Golden in the pit . . . Stivers and I got in. We hadn't been there a minute before a shot came throwing dirt all over us and striking Golden in the head. He never knew what hit him but died instantly."[22] Private Herod T. Liddiard of Company E was shot in the head as he was "taking aim at some Indians who Benteen was pointing out . . ."[23] Finally, Private Andrew J. Moore of Company G was ". . . shot through the kidneys just as we were getting up to charge out at the Indians."[24] Only one other Indian fatality occurred during this fighting, a Mnicoujou Lakota named Dog's Backbone as the Hunkpapa Lakota Old Bull recalled: "[A] fellow [named] Dog's Back was yelling, "Be careful—it is a long way from here but their bullets are coming fierce." As he finishes, [he] gets shot in [the] head and [was] killed. [This took place] in [the] middle [of the] day, day after Custer [was] killed . . ."[25]

The charge referred to in the previous paragraph was one of two aggressive moves made by the soldiers against encroaching warriors during the early afternoon. In his testimony, Captain Thomas M. McDougall described one of them:

A. Then I went at nightfall and got some hardtack for my men, and a box of ammunition. The engagement began the next morning about half past two o'clock, being very heavy towards 10 o'clock, when they made a general sally on us but we stood them off and drove them back. At about 2 o'clock Captain Benteen came down bareheaded to me and with his hat in his hand, said to me, "Captain, you will have to charge the Indians with your company, as they are firing into me pretty heavily, both with arrows and bullets, so get your men ready and start out," which I did, going about 60 yards, when the firing was so heavy on my right and rear that I had to retire to our original position.[26]

Lieutenant Charles A. Varnum's testimony echoed that of McDougall:

Q. Who led the charge? Who said it was a go?
A. Almost everybody. We were lying on the line, and he [Benteen] said that about this particular Indian on the point of this knoll, some such remark. I don't know that there was any special remark but it was "Is it a go?" or some such remark, and then everybody got up and it was a rush, it was not a charge. We ran to this point. We probably went up 15 to 20 yards and everybody scattered out of there. You could see the whole outfit skipping out to the hills beyond.[27]

The second of these forays was mentioned by Lieutenant Winfield S. Edgerly, both in his later narrative and in his testimony.

Narrative:
Benteen then charged with his troop, driving the Indians from his front. He then walked over to Reno's line, and saw a group of Indians to the north of Reno's position.

He told Reno of this, adding, "You ought to charge them," or words to that effect. Reno said, "If you can see them, give the command to charge." Benteen called out, "All ready now men, now's the time. Give them hell." Troops B, D, G and K charged and commenced firing, the Indians at the same time firing and running away. After we had advanced a short distance, Reno ordered us to get back in our pits.[28]

Testimony:
Q. At any time that morning did you observe anything about the fighting in the position Captain Benteen's company was in?
A. There was apparently a break in the company and I thought the men were rushing back to where I was. Pretty soon after that Captain Benteen came over and stood near where I was on a high point. The bullets were flying very fast there and I did not see why he was not riddled. He was perfectly calm, I remember there was a smile on his face. He said to Major Reno, "We have charged the Indians from our side and driven them out. They are coming to your left, and you ought to drive them out." Major Reno said, "Can you see the Indians from there?" He said "Yes." Major Reno said, "If you can see them, give the command to charge." Captain Benteen said, "All right, ready boys, now charge and give them hell!"[29]

Although the nearest warriors initially fell back before the advancing soldiers, as soon as they saw Reno's men withdraw they reoccupied their original positions, but earlier it was not the warriors causing the biggest problem for Reno. It was another blazing hot day, and without sufficient water thirst was continuing to be a major concern. In his narrative, Lieutenant Francis M. Gibson painted the picture:

The day was oppressively hot, and being cut off from water, our wounded suffered terrible from thirst. At last the demand for water became so frequent and so distressing that several nervy men volunteered to go for some, and taking their canteens with them, tried to steal down one of the deep and rugged ravines unobserved, but that unfortunately was not possible and two poor fellows lost their lives in this attempt to alleviate the sufferings of their comrades. Another sacrificed a leg in the same effort, but, at last, the water was obtained bringing fresh life to the wounded and temporary relief to the dying.[30]

In his *Century Magazine* article, Captain Edward S. Godfrey told a similar story:

Up to this time the command had been without water. The excitement and heat made our thirst almost maddening. The men were forbidden to use tobacco. They put pebbles in their mouths to excite the glands; some ate grass roots, but did not find relief; some tried to eat hard bread, but after chewing it awhile would blow it out of their mouths like so much flour. A few potatoes were given out and afforded some relief. About 11 a.m. the firing was slack, and parties of volunteers were formed to get water under the protection of Benteen's lines. The parties worked their way down the ravines to within a few yards of the river. The men would get ready, make a rush to the river, fill the camp-kettles, and return to fill the canteens. Some Indians stationed in a copse of woods, a short distance away, opened fire whenever a man exposed himself, which made this a particularly hazardous service. Several men were wounded, and the additional danger was then incurred of rescuing their wounded comrades. I think all these men were rewarded with medals of honor.[31]

After some discussion with the officers, twelve men volunteered to go for water. The water party set off about H1130 and Sergeant Stanislas Roy of Company A told Walter Camp how he and the eleven others, "In going down from the top of the bluff we had to run across an open space about 100 yards wide to get to head of ravine. From here to river we were concealed from Sioux. . . . Ravine 20 yds. from water. Madden was third man to rush for water and he was hit and leg broke, but he crawled back to cover unassisted."[32] According to Roy it took the water party about one and one half hours to finally get back to the Hill with the much needed water for the wounded. Apart from Saddler Michael P. Madden, who later had his leg amputated by Dr. Porter, Private Charles W. Campbell of Company G and Private James Wilber [a.k.a. James Wilber Darcy] of Company M, were also wounded.

When the warrior fire slackened toward mid-afternoon, other small parties went to the river for water. Altogether, some 34 men claimed to have gone for water and another four acted as sharpshooters for the later water carriers. Of these 38 men, 24 were awarded Medals of Honor, though the award should not be confused with the more modern Congressional Medal of Honor, as in 1876 it was the equivalent of today's Bronze Star. Nonetheless, the award recognized the gallantry of those who risked their lives that day so that water could be obtained for their comrades and the wounded in particular.

At about H1600 that afternoon most of the warriors had withdrawn, leaving only some sharpshooters to keep Reno's command pinned down. It was a prelude to the exodus of the whole village. Scouts had brought news to the Indians of the approach of the Montana Column, so with little hope of a speedy end to the siege of Reno Hill the chiefs decided to break the village up and disperse. A number of Indian accounts mention the circumstances. The Oglala Lakota He Dog said, "Did not have time to do Reno and Benteen up before Terry came."[33] Flying By, the Mnicoujou warrior, stated, "After Custer fight we went over the[n] fought soldiers with the pack mules until Indians reported other soldiers coming under officer called the Bear Coat [not so, as this refers to General Nelson A. Miles]."[34]

From the soldiers' point of view there was relief coupled with puzzlement. In his *Century Magazine* article, Captain Edward S. Godfrey reflects this dilemma: "Late in the afternoon we saw a few horsemen in the bottom apparently to observe us, and then fire was set to the grass in the valley. About 7 P.M. we saw emerge from behind this screen of smoke an immense moving mass crossing the plateau, going toward the Big Horn Mountains. A fervent "Thank God" that they had at last given up the contest was soon followed by grave doubts as to their motive for moving. Perhaps Custer had met Terry, and was coming to our relief. Perhaps they were short of ammunition, and were moving their village to a safe distance before making a final desperate effort to overwhelm us. Perhaps it was only a ruse to get us on the move, and then clean us out."[35]

At the Reno Court of Inquiry a number of officers were questioned about the Indian exodus.

Lieutenant George Wallace:
Q. At what time did the fire recommence in the morning?
A. Before it was clear daylight . . .
Q. How long was it continued?
A. It was continued heavily until after 10 o'clock. There was a good deal of firing from 10 to 12, but during the afternoon there was no continuous firing, but now and then. When we got the men at work, they would open fire on us again. Later there were just a few sharpshooters.
Q. At what time do you fix that?
A. It was after noon, about 4 o'clock.
Q. What followed then?
A. Well, later there was no firing at all and about sunset, or before sunset, I do not remember exactly when, my attention was called to the village. The Indians were moving on the opposite side of the stream, moving up this gentle slope which runs back to the Big Horn Mountains.[36]

Dr. Henry R. Porter:
Q. Did you see the Indian village move away on the 26th? Was your attention attracted to it, if so, by whom?
A. Ayes, sir. About 4 o'clock in the afternoon of the 26th, the firing ceased all together. Before that it had got less and less. A short time after it ceased, I could see the Indians moving away.
Q. Describe that movement, the length and width of the moving Indians, the length of time it was passing, and state, from any facts, your estimate of the number of Indians in the moving column.
A. There was a large body of Indians and ponies. It seemed to be a mile or two long. I judge there were two or three thousand, maybe four or five thousand Indians, men, women and children."[37]

Captain Miles Moylan:
Q. Did you see the village moving away?
A. Yes, sir.
Q. When was that?
A. About dusk of the 26th.

Q. What did its size appear to be, say in length and width, taking into consideration the time of your seeing it, and all the circumstances?

A. It was nearly dark at the time. The sun had gone down and it looked to me more like an immense buffalo herd than anything else. You could not distinguish mounted men from ponies. It was certainly two and a half or three miles long and it extended on the plain in front of our position across the river, covering nearly half of this plain, which was some six miles across. The moving village was probably several hundred yards wide. There was unquestionably a very large herd of ponies being driven. I think from one quarter to one half a mile would cover the width of the moving village.[38]

With darkness falling and uncertainty over the Indians' plans, Reno's command remained on the hill but shifted their positions to get away from the stink of dead animals, remaining apprehensive about further attacks by the warriors the next day. At around H0900 on June 27th a column of dust was seen and Indian scouts who had been sent out to check on it reported back that it was General Terry and the Montana Column approaching. Lieutenant Wallace testified:

Q. So you remained during that night?

A. Yes, sir.

Q. And how long the next morning?

A. The next morning we remained there until toward 9 o'clock. Then we saw a dust rising down the river, and by scouts being sent out, we found it was General Terry and then there wasn't much attention paid to this line.

Q. What communication, if any, did you have with General Terry and under whose orders?

A. When we found out who was coming, Major Reno directed me to go down to him and report to him who was up there, and show him how to get up, because the country was very rough.[39]

This was confirmed by 1st Lieutenant Edward Maguire, Terry's Engineering Officer in his testimony:

Q. Please state the condition of Major Reno's command at the time you reached them, whether exhausted or otherwise, and state any facts you may know in regard to the condition of his command, special or general, as they came under your observation.

A. The two officers I saw first were Lieutenants Wallace and Hare. They came riding rapidly towards us but did not appear to be very much excited. On going upon the hill General Terry and the rest of them rode up. There were shouts and there were enlisted men and also officers crying.[40]

When Reno's command had withdrawn from the Weir Point advance, the fate of Armstrong Custer and the five companies with him had been conjectured upon, but was then unknown. With the arrival of Terry and his force, the dreadful news was broken to them. Captain Godfrey described how he learned the news: "A white man, Harris, I think, soon came up with a note from General Terry, addressed to General Custer, dated June 26, stating that two of our Crow scouts had given information that our column had been whipped and nearly all had been killed; that he did not believe their story, but was coming with medical assistance. The scout said that he could not get to our lines the night before, as the Indians were on the alert. Very soon after this, Lieutenant Bradley, 7th Infantry, came into our lines, and asked where I was. Greeting most cordially my old friend, I immediately asked, "Where is Custer?" He replied, "I don't know, but I suppose he was killed, as we counted 197 dead bodies. I don't suppose any escaped." We were simply dumbfounded. This was the first intimation we had of his fate. It was hard to realize; it did seem impossible."[41]

Yet it was not impossible. Custer and the 209 men with him had all been killed. How it had happened would cause arguments for years to come, but on June 27th all that some of the officers could do was to visit Custer's Field and feel aghast at the sickening sight of so many bloated, often mutilated, corpses. Less than three days earlier those corpses had been five Companies of cavalrymen, making preparations in Medicine Tail Coulee to attack the Indian village, confident of a smashing victory. What had happened to change that into a disastrous defeat?

NOTES

1. See Appendix 3.4, p.7.
2. See Appendix 3.4, pp. 7 & 8
3. Ronald H. Nichols, *Reno Court of Inquiry Proceedings of a Court of Inquiry in the case of Major Marcus A. Reno* (Hardin, Montana: Custer Battlefield Historical & Museum Association, Inc., 1996) , p.62.
4. Captain E.S. Godfrey, 7th Cavalry, *Custer's Last Battle 1876* (Olympic Valley, California: Outbooks, 1976, reprinted from *The Century Magazine,* January 1892), p.24.
5. Nichols, *Reno Court of Inquiry,* p.568.
6. Richard G. Hardorff, *"The Custer Battle Casualties, II"* p.106.
7. Ibid p.108
8. Richard G. Hardorff , *"The Custer Battle Casualties"* p.166.
9. Ibid pp. 163 and 167
10. Hardorff, *Custer Battle Casualties II,* pp.110/111.
11. Nichols, *Reno Court of Inquiry,* p.516.
12. Ibid p.37.
13. Godfrey, *Custer's Last Battle 1876,* p.28.
14. Kenneth Hammer (ed.), *Custer in '76: Walter Camp's Notes on the Custer Fight* (Provo, Utah: Brigham Young University Press, 1976), p.71.
15. Richard G. Hardorff, *"On The Little Bighorn With Walter Camp"* p.98
16. Hammer, *Custer in '76,* p.147
17. Nichols, *Reno Court of Inquiry,* p.530
18. Hardorff, *Custer Battle Casualties II,* p.110.
19. Ibid p.113.
20. Ibid
21. Hammer, *Custer in'76,* p.144.
22. See Appendix 2.10
23. Hardorff, *Custer Battle Casualties"* p.165
24. Ibid
25. Richard G. Hardorff, *Indian Views of the Custer Fight,* p.122.
26. Nichols, *Reno Court of Inquiry,* p.530.
27. Ibid p.166
28. See Appendix 3.20, p.5.
29. Nichols, *Reno Court of Inquiry,* pp.449–450.
30. See Appendix 3.36, p.4.
31. Godfrey, *Custer's Last Battle 1876,* p.31.
32. Hammer, *Custer in'76,* p.114.
33. Hardorff, *Custer in '76,* p.208.
34. Ibid p.210
35. Godfrey, *Custer's Last Battle 1876,* pp.31–32
36. Nichols, *Reno Court of Inquiry,* p.63.
37. Ibid p.211

38. Ibid p.238.
39. Ibid p.64.
40. Ibid p.12.
41. Godfrey, *Custer's Last Battle 1876,* pp.35–36

CHAPTER 9

INTRODUCTION TO CUSTER'S FIGHT

"... it was a rout, a panic, till the last man was killed ... "
—Captain F.W. Benteen: testimony
at the Reno Court of Inquiry

G ordon "Gordie" Harper died in his sleep, in his study cum library, surrounded by all of the information he had accumulated on his life's passion, the Battle of the Little Big Horn, or as he preferred, the Battles of the Little Horn. He died before he had written in full the chapter covering his theory of what happened after Custer reached Medicine Tail Coulee. At first it was believed that it would not be possible for anyone else to know what information he would have used to develop his theory. Not only was it not contained in his manuscript, but it was based in part on sources that were private to him, probably obtained from Native Americans during the time that Gordie had lived near the battlefield, and which he said he had "agreed to hold close until such time as the true owners of the information decide that it can be brought out." In addition, Gordie had spent so much time at the battlefield, studying maps, measuring distances, reconstructing scenarios and comparing first-person accounts, that very few living persons were likely to be qualified to reconstruct his analysis.

Luckily, however, Gordie was an active contributor to a Little Big Horn message board as well as a regular correspondent with other Custer enthusiasts.

Based on explanations and answers to questions he posted to the message board and letters he wrote, plus the analysis of his close friend and fellow student of the battle, Gordon Richard, the "missing chapter" has been reconstructed. It may lack some shine and twists that only Gordie Harper could have provided, but it is presented here in what is believed to be a complete rendering of his description of that part of the Battles on the Little Horn.

These then, are Gordon Harper's thoughts on what he sometimes called "The Lop and Chop Scenario," or "Custer's Fight."

When assignments were made at 12:12 p.m., Custer assigned battalions to Captains Yates and Keogh. These consisted of companies C, E and F, and I and L respectively, and they operated later that afternoon as left and right wings. Initially, Custer, with those two battalions and Reno's battalion of companies A, G and M, marched down Ash Creek, initially on opposite sides, with Custer's five companies on the right side, abreast in column of twos, in the order of L-I-E-F-C from left to right, L being nearest the creek and C nearest the higher ground.

Reno crossed the creek to the same side as Custer at 2:00 p.m., very near the confluence of the main creek and its principal southern tributary (south fork). A few minutes later, Reno was ordered to take the lead with his battalion, and a few minutes after that Gerard spotted Indians across the Little Horn and Reno was ordered to pursue them and to bring them to battle.

After watering his horses for about ten minutes in the north fork of Ash Creek, Custer started after Reno, but almost immediately swung to the right and ascended onto the high ground. The five companies were still marching five abreast in column of twos, but the order had become reversed: C-F-E-I-L, from left to right.

The command proceeded in this formation until reaching Sharpshooter's Ridge, where Custer got his first look at the partial extent of the camps. After sending Sergeant Knipe back with a message to the pack train commander and for Benteen, if he was in sight, he continued north seeking a better vantage point. He halted his command near the top of a narrow ravine leading to Medicine Tail Coulee and sent Trumpeter Martin back with a message for Benteen. He then continued down into Medicine Tail. Either at this point, or down in the bottom of Medicine Tail Coulee, the columns of twos were transformed into columns of fours, with Yates' battalion on the left and Keogh's on the right. Yates, marching in order F, C to E and Keogh in I to L. The battalions were marched side by side down the east slope of Sharpshooter's Ridge to the flat in the bottom of Medicine Tail Coulee, or they assumed that formation upon reaching the bottom of the coulee. The time was now 3:25 p.m.

Custer led the command up onto the higher ridges to the east of Medicine Tail Coulee, reaching the Luce area at about 3:35 p.m., where he first viewed the true extent of the Indian camps. He perceived what he took to be a mass exodus of Indians to the north—clouds of dust, people on foot and on horseback, and concluded that a quick strike at the northern extremity of the camps would stop the exodus and bring the entire affair to a rapid end. There is evidence that he ran into a small party, or perhaps two parties, of hostiles, and brushed them aside without stopping or pausing. These warriors amounted to a mere handful—there were three or four toward the river and a couple or so to the east (compass directions are approximate). The Wolf Tooth party was just arriving in that area.

Custer hurried over Blummer–Nye/Cartwright Ridge toward what became Calhoun Hill, arriving there at about 3:45 p.m. and continuing on. He did not drop off Keogh's battalion at that point. Keogh, because of the terrain, was marching in the swale to the east of Battle Ridge, while Yates was moving along the top of the ridge. In the valley, Reno was just beginning to exit the timber, but masses of warriors were still engaged in that fight. Some warriors were coming up Medicine Tail Coulee and possibly Deep Coulee, but Custer did not consider them a threat to his consolidated command, with which he intended to get to the fleeing people to the north. The command passed Custer Hill at 3:53 p.m. and started downhill, toward the northern fords (usually called Ford D, although there was more than one usable ford in the area). They were basically still in the same formation, although it is likely that Keogh was slightly echeloned to the rear because he had farther to go around the hill, being on the outside of the arc.

At 4:00 p.m., while Reno was reaching his retreat hill, Custer was approaching the fords, when he discovered to his dismay that the fleeing Indians were not fleeing at all, but were racing down the valley to confront him. Many, perhaps a couple of hundred, were already across the river on his side, including eighty "suicide boys" led by Crazy Iron Horse (whose camp was almost directly across the river, being the northernmost of the camps, just beyond the Cheyennes') and Spotted Eagle, a horde of Cheyenne warriors who had not made it to the Reno fight, and the band of Cheyennes and Lakotas of which Wolf Tooth was a member (although not the leader), which had trailed after Custer from near Luce Ridge, and which were now above him at Custer Hill. All of these opened fire, not necessarily at the same time, but there was a sufficient volume of fire to cause Custer to rethink matters and consider a retreat.

By 4:00–4:15 p.m., Custer could see that hundreds of more warriors were coming rapidly down the valley, some even then crossing at Deep Ravine ford and—although he didn't know it—at Medicine Tail Coulee ford, and other fords. He could then see that he had no chance to force a crossing, and that he would be in dire trouble even if he could do so. Accordingly, he decided to get back to the high ground before being trapped between it and the river.

The battalions were ordered to fours right about and Smith's E Company was tasked with protecting the left flank and attempting to hold back the warriors coming across the river in that direction. The remaining companies were now in two columns going back up the slopes, with Keogh's battalion now in the order L–I and Yates' remaining two companies in the order C–F.

Smith's E Company moved across an intervening ridge and fired two massed volleys into the Cheyenne camps. E Company then turned its attention to the warriors crossing at Deep Ravine ford and attempting to come up Deep Ravine. These warriors were led initially by Waglula, the father of Crazy Horse, who had given his name to his son, but who was also still called Crazy Horse by some. Touch The Cloud was also among the leaders of these warriors, who numbered in the hundreds. Hump would later join in this general movement. Crazy Horse, the son, was coming with additional masses of warriors up Medicine Tail Coulee and across the ridges (after defeating Reno) toward Calhoun Hill, and so were others, getting between the troops and the camps, as well as Medicine Tail Coulee, so that Custer could no longer join up with Reno.

There was medium- to long-range firing between the troops and the Indians as the troops returned toward Custer Hill. There were probably a few troop casualties (bodies were found northwest of Custer Hill). The Wolf Tooth group had retreated before the troops, taking up positions behind the protection of the ridge east of Battle Ridge. There were warriors rushing up behind the Custer companies and warriors below Battle Ridge, having come up Deep Coulee and other routes.

Keogh's battalion was going back the way it came, along the swale, under fire from both sides and taking some casualties as it moved. Calhoun was in the lead. Custer was arriving at the Custer Hill area, with C Company leading, while E Company was trying to fight its way up the slope that terminates at Custer Hill, still trying to keep the Deep Ravine warriors at bay but with a notable lack of success. There were simply too many, and warriors had moved in behind E, firing both at them and at Custer's trailing company F. Custer formed a skirmish line near where the cemetery is now located and tried to hold the warriors at bay.

At 4:25–4:30 p.m., a massive charge from the north, led by the "suicide boys," and another from the south, crashed into Captain Tom Custer's C Company, smashing the troop into pieces and sending parts of it flying in disorder. Armstrong Custer was effectively lopped off from the balance of his command and was encircled with Yates and F Company on Custer Hill. C Company's men were either killed in place (about half of it), killed across Battle Ridge (another ten or so), or running toward Finley Ridge, where it was brought up short by warriors on Greasy Grass Hill and coming across from Medicine Tail Coulee. Algernon Smith's E Company was struggling mightily to move up the hill, but was under intense fire from Deep Ravine, and from the rear and flank. The men on Custer Hill were similarly engaged.

Meanwhile, at about 4:40–4:45 p.m., Calhoun and his L Company were blocked at Calhoun Hill by warriors coming across the eastern ridges and up Deep Coulee and Calhoun Coulee, following the troop trail and arriving at the same area as him at about the same time. He was subjected to a tremendous fire from three sides, and before he could think how to extricate his men, Lame White Man and Crazy Horse, the son, charged upon the remnants of his troops and lopped them off from the balance of Keogh's command. The remnants of L tried to get to Keogh, who with his I Company was now cut off from both directions and subjected to a crossfire from Battle Ridge and from the ridge to the east.

What was left of the Custer command was then in five distinct pieces— Custer at Custer Hill; Calhoun at Calhoun Hill, Battle Ridge and the Keogh Swale; Keogh in the middle of Keogh Swale and strung out back toward Custer Hill (where his dead became mingled with some of C Company); what was left of E Company trying to get up the hill and dying all along the way; and a handful of troopers on Finley Ridge. The warriors moved in to reduce pockets of resistance and finally rushed upon whoever was left alive, standing or otherwise.

By 5:00 p.m., both Keogh and Calhoun were finished and so probably was E Company. As each command was finished off, the warriors came into possession of more guns and ammunition to turn on those who remained.

By 5:30 p.m., the few remaining men at Finley were overrun and the few remaining men on Custer Hill were similarly dispatched. A very few E Company men had made it up the slope to Custer Hill. There may have been a few men who ran for their lives, or who may have been desperate messengers sent to Reno and Benteen for assistance, which accounts for the handful of bodies found toward the river or the "string" between the South Skirmish Line and Finley: Butler, Foley, Dose and the rest, although, as will be described in the next chapter, Foley and Dose probably died near the beginning of Custer's fight.

Hump, who had come from the Reno battlefield, was wounded and could not take part in the final rushes, but the senior Crazy Horse (Waglula), his son Crazy Horse, and Crazy Iron Horse were all there, and, obviously, many, many others, except that Crazy Horse the elder may have taken the wounded Hump down to the camps before the start of the final rushes.

Indian casualties were considerably higher than usually estimated—for example, it is believed that sixty-eight of the eighty suicide boys were killed.

Of course much was happening at the same time, and the timings are necessarily generalized, as is explained in greater detail following.

CHAPTER 10

DEATH OF THE VALIANT
BY GORDON RICHARD

"I guess we'll get through with them in one day."—LT. COL. GEORGE
ARMSTRONG CUSTER, ON THE MORNING OF JUNE 25, 1876

ANOTHER LOOK AT CUSTER'S FIGHT[1]

Very often, the focus of attention on what happened to the Custer battalions after they reached Medicine Tail Coulee means that the equally important question of their objective for being there in the first place is overlooked. Much criticism is leveled at Armstrong Custer for splitting his regiment in the face of the warrior numbers that were present, but I do not believe such criticism is justified.

The criticism would be justified in only two circumstances. First, if he had not expected the Indian village to flee and scatter, as Indians usually did when faced with a military force. The likelihood that the Indians would not stand and fight had been the major concern of the army command during the 1876 summer campaign. That the Indians had recently fought General George Crook's Wyoming Column to a standstill at the Battle of the Rosebud, causing Crook to retreat, was not known to Custer and would not be known to Terry until July. Custer therefore had no inkling that his opponents had an entirely different mindset than expected, and he could not have discovered it in any other way than by pitting his command against them. Criticism in this respect can only be made with the wisdom of hindsight.

Second, criticism would be acceptable if the deployments he made were haphazard and devoid of any known military strategy. If that had been the case, separating his command could only be seen as impulsive, because then he would have been reckless in exposing the separated elements to unnecessary risk. But on June 25, 1876 Custer had been a successful cavalry commander for over ten years, and did not abruptly forget what he had learned during that time. He once said, "It requires no extensive knowledge to inform me what is my duty to my country, my command. . . . First be sure you're right, then go ahead! I ask myself, 'Is it right?' Satisfied that it is so, I let nothing swerve me from my purpose."[2] It is unlikely then that Custer would have dispersed his forces other than with what he thought were sound military reasons at the time.

Yet at the Reno Court of Inquiry, both Major Reno and Captain Benteen denied that any strategy at all existed. Captain Benteen testified: a) "There was no plan at all" and b) "If there had been any plan of battle, enough of that plan would have been communicated to me so that I would have known what to do under certain circumstances. Not having done that I do not believe there was any plan."[3] Whilst Major Reno said: a) "There was no plan communicated to us if one existed. The subordinate commanders did not know of it" and b) "I might say there that I do not think there was any plan."[4] I believe Custer's subordinates were self-serving, as the suggested lack of a plan deflected attention away from their own shortcomings on June 25, 1876.

When Custer looked out for a second time from either the Crow's Nest or Varnum's Lookout that morning, those with him included Mitch Boyer and some Crow scouts, who were not only looking into a valley that was part of their homeland, but who had also camped in the area where the great Indian village was sited. Being made aware of that, Custer would not have spurned the chance to obtain all the information he could from them about the terrain from there to the Indian camps in preparation for his initial plan to approach the village at dawn the next morning. Returning to the command however, he was informed that Indians, rifling a lost hard-tack box, had seen the command. Believing that the village would scatter once warned, he decided on an immediate offensive. Lieutenant Godfrey confirms this, reporting Custer as saying, "At all events our presence has been discovered . . . that we would march at once to attack the village . . . "[5] Also, Lieutenant Edgerly recounted: " . . . as our presence had been discovered it would be necessary to attack at once."[6] George Herendeen recalled that Custer told him: " . . . besides they have discovered us. . . . The only thing to do is to push ahead and attack the camp as soon as possible."[7] And finally Reno said, " . . . .we could not surprise them and it was determined to move at once to the attack."[8]

Custer was therefore primed to move aggressively against the camps, and his subordinates were fully aware of that, so what tactics did he have in mind? The possibilities open to him would be dictated by what the Indians did. While they were expected to flee and scatter, their sheer numbers could well mean that much of the village would be intact when he reached it and the warriors would then be forced to put up some resistance to enable their families to escape. The comments of Crow scout Hairy Moccasin suggest that the latter scenario was the most likely. In a June 1916 interview he said:

> I was sent ahead [from the Crow's Nest]. Custer said, "You go and find that village." I went to a butte at the head of Reno Creek, from where I could see the village. I reported the camp to Custer. He asked if any were running about away from the camp. I said "No." We then came on down to the forks of Reno Creek. When we stopped there to divide up I could hear the Indians in camp shouting and whooping.[9]

The usual tactic against a standing village was envelopment, whereby a holding force would engage the enemy while other parts of the command swung to the left and/or right to hit him in the rear or on the flank. The late Jay Smith described such tactics in two articles he authored. In one, citing Von Clausewitz as his basis, he says, "Custer used an envelopment while employing the principles of offense, maneuver, and surprise,"[10] and in the other, "These were some of the best professional soldiers in the world. A few words or gestures were all that were needed to provide all the information required for a complete battle. Objectives and unit tactics were understood by all. Often a complete battle plan consisted only of stating which units would go where."[11] Viewed in this light, the deployment of the battalions commanded by Reno and Benteen can be seen to fit the requirements of an envelopment plan, which had of course, been used at the Washita and the Powder River fights, so it was widely known. There are corroborations that it was also to be used at the Little Big Horn from testimony and elsewhere.

At the inquiry, Sergeant Davern testified that Cooke said to Reno, "Girard comes back and reports the Indian village three miles ahead and moving. The General directs you to take your three companies and drive everything before you."[12] In answer to the question, "Was anything else said?" Davern replied, "Yes, sir; Colonel Benteen will be on your left and will have the same instructions."[13] Lieutenant Edgerly, in his papers, says, "Major Reno was ordered to 'march straight to the village, attack any Indians you may meet, and you will be supported.' Capt. Benteen was ordered to move to the left at an angle of about forty-five degrees from Reno's direction, attack any Indians he might meet, and he would be supported."[14] Plus we have Major Henry R. Lemly's assertion that Lieutenant Wallace told him that when Custer separated from Reno his plan was to march to the lower end of the village, crossing at one of the lower fords, and to make his attack there. His attack was to be the signal for Reno, just as soon as the latter saw or heard him, to press forward in the reasonable expectation that the combined pressure would stampede the Indians out of their villages.[15]

Perhaps the most significant evidence in terms of Benteen's intended role is Lieutenant Varnum's letter to his parents saying, "Just then Colonel Benteen and three companies came in from a trip they had endeavored to make to the rear of the village,"[16] which is endorsed by part of Captain Moylan's testimony where he is questioned regarding support for Reno:

Q. But at the time you were moving down this bottom and engaged in the timber and in going back to the top of the hill, was there any belief as to where the balance of the command was? What was your opinion?

A. My opinion was that it was on the rear of our trail and was coming to our assistance.

Q. And Captain Benteen's command?

A. That I do not know so much about. It passed away to the left and I thought might come in through the foothills.[17]

It is likely then that Benteen was meant to come to the village up the west bank of the river, possibly via the south fork of Reno Creek, as the entry to the Little Horn river valley course was almost certainly too far for Custer to have wanted him separated from the rest of the command.

Testimony which promotes the lack of an attack strategy is therefore false, contradicted by the weight of evidence demonstrating that Custer had planned the envelopment; but were the orders given by Custer to his senior subordinates as senseless as Benteen claimed? The only order Reno received was to attack the village and his command was supposed to be Custer's holding force, but it didn't hold for long. Benteen's column was ordered to the left to eventually find its way to the west of the river, probably via the south fork of Reno Creek, to block anyone from the camps fleeing that way and with the ultimate task of attacking the village from the south wherever he saw fit. By his own admission, Benteen disobeyed his orders by returning to the main trail instead of crossing one more hill into the valley of the south fork. Both officers therefore, had ample reason to avoid the truth at the court of inquiry, and we need to look at what Custer was trying to achieve with his immediate command in the light of what he expected his subordinates to be doing.

In his testimony at the court of inquiry Major Reno stated, "I moved forward in accordance with the orders received from Lieutenant Cooke to the head of the column. Soon after that Lieutenant Cooke came to me and said, 'General Custer directs you to take as rapid a gait as you think prudent, and charge the village afterwards, and you will be supported by the whole outfit.'" He also said, "From the manner I received the order I could not conceive of any other manner of being supported except from the rear"; yet in his Report of July 5, 1876, he wrote, "After traveling over his trail, it is evident to me that Custer intended to support me by moving further down the stream and attacking the village in the flank."[18] The latter comment was made, of course, in all rationality, without any idea that he would later have to justify his actions at a court of inquiry. The inference he made in his testimony was that Custer expected to follow him across the Little Horn but changed his mind and turned to the north. His report however, accurately describes Custer's adherence to the envelopment plan, a plan that would have been known to both Reno and Benteen.

Custer's turn to the north was therefore pre-determined by the tactics Reno describes in his report, and not for any other reason. Sergeant Knipe suggested that the move was because he saw some Indians on the bluffs, but Trumpeter Martin, who was also close to Custer, did not see them, so Knipe's tendency to embroider his own role appears to have come into play here. Some writers have suggested that Fred Gerard's news that the Indians were coming out to meet Reno prompted Custer to change his mind and move north instead of following Reno to attack the village. That theory is based on the idea that the warriors would stall the attack until their families had safely fled to the north and then flee themselves, the very scenario that was the biggest worry of all the military commanders. It was, in fact, their standard behavior in such circumstances, as Godfrey described:

If the advance to the attack be made in daylight it is next to impossible that a near approach can be made without discovery. In all our previous experiences, when the immediate presence of the troops was once known to them, the warriors swarmed to the attack, and resorted to all kinds of ruses to mislead the troops, to delay the advance toward their camp or village, while the squaws and children secured what personal effects they could, drove off the pony herd, and by flight put themselves beyond danger, and then scattering made successful pursuit next to impossible.[19]

Being aware of this meant that Custer was not only unsurprised by Gerard's news, but also delighted, because at that point the Indians were behaving as he expected them to. His turn to the north was therefore in response to what he had anticipated would happen, and he wanted to get to the northern end of the village to attack and crush the warriors between his battalions and those of Reno and Benteen. Initially of course, his movement was in the form of a reconnaissance-in-force, or, probably more accurately, a movement-to-contact—much like what would nowadays be called a "search and destroy" mission.

There is a great deal of argument about the route he took to get to Medicine Tail Coulee, but the details of that move are not so germane to the outcome of the battle, except for those interested in timings and where Custer was supposedly seen on the bluffs by some of Reno's men. For our purposes it suffices to say that after watering his horses for ten minutes in a small creek just off the north fork of Reno Creek, as testified to by Trumpeter Martini,[20] Custer took his five companies north along the bluffs that led past Reno Hill to Sharpshooter's Ridge, stopping on, or more likely near the latter feature, to view Reno's force in the valley. Having seen that the major had deployed a skirmish line, and being satisfied that his holding force was in place, Custer moved on, but not before sending Knipe off to the pack train and Benteen. It was about 3:00 p.m. and looking down into the valley, Custer could not only see Reno's skirmish line but also that that there were no Indians fleeing south, or coming up from the south behind the major. That told Custer that Benteen had not run into any Indians on his left oblique, and as he could see no sign of Benteen in the valley it also told him that the captain, against his orders, must have swung back to the main trail. In fact, Benteen was nearing the Lone Tipi at that time. As Knipe left on his mission, Custer headed for Medicine

Tail Coulee, entering it either by Cedar Coulee or by what came to be known as Godfrey's Gorge.[21]

One of the constant questions in this sequence of events is what happened to the Crow scouts and Boyer? Two of the Crows followed Reno into the valley by misunderstanding what Custer, via Boyer, asked them to do. The four others with Boyer then went to the ridges above the river whilst Custer took a different route to the bluffs and arrived there ahead of the scouts, as confirmed by Goes Ahead.[22] The scouts kept moving, however, passing Custer's command as he looked into the valley and at his behest they rode up Weir Point.[23] At that juncture Hairy Moccasin claimed that Curley was no longer with them.[24] From evidence supplied by Russell White Bear to Fred Dustin, it is likely that Curley had remained with Custer's men.[25] Whilst the Crows were on Weir Point the five companies, apparently without Curley, went with Custer west of Sharpshooter's Ridge and east of Weir Point, heading toward Medicine Tail Coulee via Godfrey's Gorge. This is where the Crow scouts and Boyer played a definite role in the events of that day. In 1909, Goes Ahead told Walter Camp that he and two fellow Crows did not see Custer "after he turned down the coulee to the right."[26] As they were on Weir Point, the Custer battalions would have been in clear sight if they had used Cedar Coulee, but as Boyer and the three Crows had passed Custer near Sharpshooter's Ridge, Boyer would have pointed out that Godfrey's Gorge was the easiest route into Medicine Tail Coulee, since it was not steep, narrow and shrub-lined like Cedar Coulee. Goes Ahead also told Camp:

> As to whether Curley left us and went back I decline to answer. I prefer that White Man [Runs Him] or Hairy Moccasin answer this question. . . . We saw Reno's battle and went back south along bluff and met Benteen's command. We three Crows did not see Custer after he turned down the coulee to right. Did not see Custer fight. Did not see beginning of it or any part of it. Do not know whether Custer went to river. We turned back too early to see where Custer went north of Dry Creek.[27]

This statement by Goes Ahead makes it clear that he, Hairy Moccasin and White Man Runs Him left Weir Point and moved a short distance north, where they fired on the Indian village before returning south, probably on the advice of Boyer. What they saw on the way is best summed up in the interview that White Man Runs Him had with General Scott at the mouth of Custer Creek or Medicine Tail Creek, 4 miles from Reno's entrenchement:

Q. How far down did Custer go?

A. Right down to the river.

Q. How far did they come?

A. They came down the ravine to the river here and started back.

Q. What did the scouts do then? Where was Mitch Boyer?

A. He was on that point there.

Q. Where was Curley?

A. He was back on the ridge.

Q. Where did you go then?

A. I went back.

Q. Why?

A. Mitch Boyer said, "You go back; I am going down to Custer."

Q. Did you see Reno go to the bluffs then?

A. No. I saw him fighting across the river but didn't know he had retreated back to the bluffs.

Q. When Custer came down here could he hear the shooting over there?

A. Didn't pay much attention; everybody around us was shooting and no one could tell the place where most of the firing was done.[28]

As Boyer was near them when they returned south, it makes it clear that he too could not have seen Reno's retreat, so Custer could not have learned of it from him. On their way south we know the three Crows met Benteen, as stated by Goes Ahead. They then spent some time on Reno Hill before making their way to safety during the evening of June 26, and a fortuitous meeting with Gibbon's column. Lieutenant Bradley described that meeting in his journal:

I took the trail of the four supposed Sioux in the hope of catching them in the Big Horn valley, toward which the trail led and where we thought they might have camped, as there was no convenient way of leaving the valley into which they had gone except that by which they had entered it. At the distance of less than two miles the trail struck the river, and we found that they had there crossed, leaving behind a horse and several articles of personal equipment, indicating

that they had fled in great haste. An examination of the articles disclosed to our great surprise that they belonged to some of the Crows
whom I had furnished to General Custer at the mouth of the Rosebud, which rendered it probable that the supposed Sioux were some
of our own scouts who had for some reason left Custer's command
and were returning to the Crow agency.[29]

What happened to Curley is not so clear because of the differing stories
he told during the years following the battle, but there are some acceptable
verifications, as Dr. Thomas B. Marquis shows in his 1934 booklet, *Curly, The
Crow* in which Marquis uses quotes by Thomas LeForge from *Memoirs of a
White Crow Indian*, another Marquis-backed work. In that book:

> LeForge tells of that interview wherein he interpreted while Lieu-
> tenant Bradley made notes of Curly's story. In the course of the nar-
> rative the young Crow repeatedly corrected an apparent impression
> that he had been in the fight. He declared clearly that he had not
> been in it. He was not present when the Custer engagement opened,
> but was on a hill in the background and saw its beginning. After a
> short time he went farther away, to another hill, and watched the
> struggle for awhile. He saw some loose horses running away over the
> hills, and he captured two of them. He started then to go entirely
> away from the scene. But the captive horses impeded his movements,
> so he let them loose and took himself on his own pony completely
> out of probabilities of any of the hostile Indians catching him.[30]

Marquis also quotes from *The Arikara Narrative*, in which:

> Red Star, an Arikara Indian who was one of the scouts under Var-
> num, says he saw Curly and Black Fox, an Arikara, with Custer at
> the time Custer looked from the bluffs bordering the east bank of
> the river just as the Reno men were going into their charge toward
> the Indian camps.[31] Goes Ahead, a Crow, also saw them. Curly and
> Black Fox remained together, or they got together soon afterward up
> the river, where Reno's soldiers had crossed for their first approach
> to the camps. Then Curly proposed that he would take Black Fox on
> the back trail of the soldiers to a place where he knew they had left

some hardtack. The two went toward the present Busby. Curly then said he was going to his home agency and he left the company of the Arikara. Darkness had come and the parting was 10 to 12 miles east of the battle scene.[32]

When Black Fox reached the mouth of the Rosebud he met the older scouts already there. They came out to meet him; he came on slowly. In answer to their queries he said he and Curley got together near Reno ford. Curley told Black Fox he would take him back to show him where the soldiers left some hard tack. So Curley took Black Fox to the flat below the hills overlooking the present town of Busby north side. Curley told Black Fox that for his part he was going home.[33]

That is as near as we can get to the truth about Curley's participation, for as a seventeen-year-old youth at the time of the battle, it would be surprising if he had not been affected by the amount of attention he received by newspapers wanting to hear his story. Loaded questions and distorted answers did not help his cause, but it is likely he began to believe his publicity and embellish it, rather than stick to the simple facts.

Mitch Boyer himself appears to have ridden north from Weir Point, caught up with Custer, and advised Curley to go home from there. He then found his way into Medicine Tail Coulee via a different route to join Custer. He met up with the command as they halted briefly in the coulee, a halt verified by Standing Bear.[34] Not having seen Reno's retreat he had nothing negative to report to Custer, which left the latter free to follow his original envelopment plan.

That he was expecting Benteen to join in the attack at the earliest opportunity is evidenced by the two messages he sent to the captain. Knipe, if indeed he was a messenger, carried the first and said in his 1903 interview, "Custer and his troops were within about one-half mile to the east side of the Indian camps when I received the following messages from Captain Thomas Custer, brother of the General: 'Go to Captain McDougall. Tell him to bring pack train straight across the country. If any packs come loose, cut them and come on quick—a big Indian camp.' 'If you see Captain Benteen, tell him to come quick—a big Indian camp.' "[35]

When he sent Trumpeter Martin to Benteen from the top of Medicine Tail Coulee, Armstrong Custer already knew from Boston Custer that the captain's command had not reached the west of the river, so the famous "Come on" message was surely exhorting Benteen to join in the action at the closest point possible. Custer believed Reno was still engaged as the holding force, and as Benteen was over an hour away, too long a time for Custer to wait around for him, Custer needed to find a point at which he could launch an attack at the north of the village while Reno and Benteen engaged warriors to the south.

At the core of most theories is a fascination with what, if anything, happened at Medicine Tail Ford, or "Ford B." The trouble is that a fascination can soon morph into an obsession, and so much attention has been focused on the "ifs," "buts" and "maybes" of Ford B that almost every piece of evidence about Custer being near the river has been taken as a reference to that ford. Unfortunately, the researcher Walter Camp reinforced that idea by his insistence that there had been action at that ford. He got that notion from the testimony of Lieutenant Maguire at the Reno Court of Inquiry, "The ground was all cut up by hoofs. My theory was that General Custer went to the ford and was met there and driven back and they separated into two bodies to concentrate on the hill at 'E' and I put those lines in as my idea of the route they took."[36] Both Maguire and Camp were wrong.

There is no concrete evidence to support any action at that ford, but the last person to see the command might have provided some helpful information. That was Trumpeter Martin, and although he told differing stories over the years, in his 1908 account to Camp he stated that on his way to deliver Custer's message to Benteen, when he got to the top of the ridge he saw "Indians charging like a swarm of bees towards the ford waving buffalo hides. At the same time he saw Custer retreating up the open country in the direction of the battlefield."[37] If true, by putting those two comments together we can surmise that the Indians in question were not armed with guns or there would have been no need for the buffalo hides to deter the soldiers, and that being the case, if Custer fell back it was not because he was driven away by a superior force. There is a simple explanation of his actions, and it has to do with what Custer could see, or rather what he could not see, as he paused in Medicine Tail Coulee. If he was looking to attack across Ford B he would have needed to be sure that it represented the northern extent of the village to ensure that he would not find warriors behind him if he did so. What could he see?

The camp across from that ford is generally assumed to be that of the

Cheyenne, but Wooden Leg describes their location on the day of the battle thus: "We were near the mouth of a small creek flowing from the southwestward into the river. Across the river east of us and a little upstream from us was a broad coulee, or little valley, having now the name Medicine Tail Coulee."[38] The small creek Wooden Leg mentions is probably Onion Creek, which does come in from the southwest to join the river, so the northern limit of the Cheyenne camp was about one mile downstream of Ford B, and it is possible that the entire Cheyenne camp was hidden from Custer by the timber along the river bank. To try and see more, Custer rode a short distance north to the height of Luce Ridge. The movement across Medicine Tail Coulee is described by some Indian accounts. The Oglala He Dog said, "Custer was coming from the north, across the dry creek,"[39] and ". . . saw other soldiers coming on the big hill right over east. They kept right on down the river and crossed Medicine Tail Coulee and onto a little rise."[40] Young Little Wolf, a Northern Cheyenne, stated that, "When Custer was first seen he was opposite Ford 'B' in Medicine Tail Coulee, traveling parallel with river, soldiers deployed and seemingly trying to circle the camp. After he passed Medicine Tail Coulee, Indians followed him."[41]

From Luce Ridge, Custer could see to the north a huge dust cloud and people running, which he deduced must be the non-combatants trying to escape. Still unable to see the full extent of the village, but alerted by Boyer to fords further north, Custer took the Left Wing—Companies E and F with his Headquarters Group—in that direction. The Right Wing—formed by Companies I and L, with C Company, and commanded by Captain Keogh—was deployed on Luce and possibly Butler Ridges menacing Ford B. It would have had been the prudent military option to agree that if anything went wrong, the best place for both wings to reunite would be on the high ground along what would come to be known as Battle Ridge, where their combined longer-range fire-power, used in a disciplined way, would keep the warriors at a distance and enable Custer to move south to organize a junction with Reno and Benteen.

It is my opinion that, at about 3:50 p.m. as he came down towards the river from Last Stand Hill, Custer's plan was to attack across the nearest available northern ford from which he could see the end of the village, then sweep south driving before him the little resistance he anticipated meeting, being joined by Keogh as Ford B was reached, with their combined forces subsequently routing an enemy caught between them and the Reno/Benteen commands. The idea that he would attack with only two companies and his Head-quarters Group has been decried by many as militarily rash in light of the Indian numbers, but what seems to get forgotten is that Custer believed that the main warrior force had gone to meet Reno, so he was not expecting much resistance. In the event, his part of the plan did not succeed, and there are various Indian accounts that perhaps explain why. It is necessary to understand that Indian accounts do not allow for the time lapse between one event and the next; however, by using a combination of them it proves beyond doubt that Custer went to the northern fords.

Wooden Leg saw that, "The soldiers had come along a high ridge about two miles east from the Cheyenne camp. They had gone on past us and then swerved off the high ridge to the lower ridge where most of them afterward were killed."[42] Two Moon said, "Custer marched up from behind the ridge on which his monument now stands, and deployed his soldiers along the entire line of the ridge. They rode over beyond where the monument stands down into the valley until we could not see them."[43]

The Cheyenne tribal historian John Stands In Timber relates that, knowing soldiers could be in the area, Wolf Tooth and Big Foot plus about fifty other young men had succeeded in slipping through the camp police and crossing the river under cover. They got together below Custer Creek north of the village and were about halfway up a wooded hill there when they heard someone shouting. "When they drew near, the rider began talking in Sioux. Big Foot could understand it. The soldiers had already ridden down toward the village. Then Wolf Tooth's party raced back up Custer Creek again to where they could follow one of the ridges to the top, and when they got there they saw the last few soldiers going down out of sight toward the river."[44] In view of Stand in Timber's statements that follow, I believe that this was Custer's five companies beginning their short journey down Medicine Tail Coulee:

> As the soldiers disappeared, Wolf Tooth's band split up. Some followed the soldiers, and the rest went on around a point to cut them off. They caught up there with some that were still going down, and came around them on both sides. The soldiers started shooting. It was the first skirmish of the battle, and it did not last very long. The Indians said they did not try to go in close. After some shooting both bunches of Indians retreated back to the hills, and the soldiers

crossed the south end of the ridge [where the monument now stands].[45]

The soldiers who crossed below the present monument site were, I believe, Custer's Left Wing on its way to the northern fords from Medicine Tail, but they were certainly not in that coulee since the monument is quite a bit north of that.

The soldiers followed the ridge down to the present cemetery site. Then this bunch of 40–50 Indians came out by the monument and started shooting down at them again. But they were moving on down toward the river, across from the Cheyenne camp. Some of the warriors there had come across, and they began firing at the soldiers from the brush in the river bottom. This made the soldiers turn north, but they went back in the direction they had come from, and stopped when they got to the cemetery site. And they waited there a long time—twenty minutes or more.[46]

Having moved north, the Left Wing was now across from the Cheyenne camp which, as Wooden Leg's account has shown, was not established opposite Ford B. Also, if they went back in the direction they had come from and stopped at the current cemetery site, again, they could not have been in Medicine Tail.

Is there any corroboration that some warriors shot at the soldiers from the river bottom? Stands In Timber says, "Hanging Wolf was one of the warriors who crossed the river and shot from the brush when Custer came to the bottom. He said they hit one horse down there, and it bucked off a soldier, but the rest took him along when they retreated north."[47] Also, parts of interviews with some Cheyennes in 1908 by George Bird Grinnell were summarized by Father P. J. Powell in *People of the Sacred Mountain* thus: "Bobtail Horse, Calf, Roan Bear, and two or three other men who had joined them pulled up close to the river. There, under cover of a low ridge, they opened fire on the advancing soldiers." In his interview, Brave Wolf also told Grinnell that he had first seen these soldiers riding down along the side of a little dry creek.[48] That description does not accord with Wooden Leg's view of Medicine Tail Coulee as a broad coulee, or little valley, so Brave Wolf is describing a different place, almost certainly the route that Wolf Tooth said the soldiers took down to the river. The "little dry creek," mentioned by Brave Wolf and others, could well be Cemetery Ravine.

Grinnell interviewed several Northern Cheyenne warriors between 1892 and 1925, and their accounts, which build on those of Wolf Tooth and Brave Wolf, appear in Richard Hardorff's book, *Cheyenne Memories*. American Horse said:

> . . . a man calling out that the troops were attacking the lower end of the village. Then they all rushed down below and saw Custer coming down the hill and almost at the river. I was one of the first to meet the troops and the Indians and the soldiers reached the flat about the same time. When Custer saw them coming he was down on the river bottom at the river's bank. The troops fought in line of battle, and they fought there for some little time. Then the troops gave way and were driven up the hill. The troops fought on horseback all the way up the hill.[49]

This narrative coincides with the Wolf Tooth description in three ways. First, Custer is going downhill and nearly at the river, second the troops are fighting, and thirdly the troops are then being driven up hill on horseback. Brave Wolf remembered:

> Then we heard the shooting below, and all rushed down the river. When I got to the Cheyenne camp, the fighting had been going on for some time. The soldiers were right down close to the stream, but none were on this side. Just as I got there, the soldiers began to retreat up the narrow gulch. . . . They still held their line of battle and kept fighting and falling from their horses . . . nearly up to where the monument now stands.[50]

Now we have four more points of coincidence with Wolf Tooth and three with American Horse. As with Wolf Tooth, the action is at the Cheyenne camp, then the troops are down close to the river, they then retreat and on horseback, agreeing with Wolf Tooth, who did not say they dismounted. Brave Wolf agrees with American Horse that the troops were right near the river, that they fought there and then retreated to the monument site on horseback. There is also one other very important piece of information, the comment that, "the soldiers began to retreat up the narrow gulch," because again, compared with Wooden Leg's description of Medicine Tail, it is plain that Brave Wolf is not talking about that place. White Bull (Ice) said, "Then word was brought that Custer was coming, and the Indians all began to go back to fight Custer. Custer rode down to the river bank and formed a line of battle and to charge. But he then stopped and fell back up the hill."[51] White Bull is basic, but his account agrees with the others. Soldier Wolf said:

> When these women were crossing the river and some were going to the hills, they discovered more troops coming. This was the Custer party . . . someone rode to where the men were fighting Reno and told them that more soldiers were coming below. Then all the men rushed down the creek again to where the women were. By this time, Custer had gotten down to the mouth of the dry creek and was on the level flat of the bottom. They began firing and for quite some time fought in the bottom, neither party giving back. There they killed quite a good many horses . . . and two soldiers were killed and left there. But soon the Indians overpowered the soldiers and they began to give way, retreating slowly, face to the front.[52]

As it is universally accepted that the women from the village had hidden themselves in Chasing—now known as Squaw—Creek, which is on the west side of the river opposite Cemetery Ridge and Custer Hill, this is further evidence that the actions described did not take place in or near Medicine Tail.

Soldier Wolf's account coincides on four points with previous accounts. He describes the "dry creek" that Bobtail Horse mentions; he speaks of the "level flat of the bottom" which agrees with American Horse; then there is the fact that the soldiers were firing as described by Wolf Tooth, American Horse, Brave Wolf and White Bull; plus the troops retreating, also recorded by the others. Tall Bull said:

> . . . news came to the Indians from down the creek that more soldiers were coming, and all turned back. All rushed back on the west side of the camp, down to a small dry run that comes in from the east, and there, down close to the river, were the soldiers. The Indians all crossed and they fought there. For quite a long time the troops stood their ground right there. Then they began to back off, fighting all the

time, for quite a distance, working up the hill, until they got pretty close to where the monument now is . . .[53]

Tall Bull's "small dry run that comes in from the east" coincides with the little dry creek mentioned by Bobtail Horse and Soldier Wolf. He also agrees that the soldiers were down close to the river, that there was a fight between Indians and soldiers, and then the soldiers retreated to near the monument. White Shield described how, "I looked back and saw soldiers in seven groups. One company could be seen a long way off, the horses were pretty white. . . . I went around and came in below, though the company was coming fast making for the Little Bighorn. Near me I could see only Roan Bear, Bobtail Horse and one other man."[54] Then, "When the Gray Horse Company got pretty close to the river, they dismounted, and all the soldiers back as far as I could see stopped and dismounted also. When the Gray Horse Company dismounted, the Indians began to fire at them, and the soldiers returned the fire."[55] Finally, "All the soldiers retreated back from the river, but the Gray Horse Company stood their ground."[56]

White Shield's account generally conforms to those cited previously. He confirms the presence of Roan Bear and Bobtail Horse near the action, also that E Company at least got close to the river, the exchange of fire between Indians and soldiers, and the soldiers retreating from the river.

In an interview in 1956 with Don Rickey, John Stands In Timber stated that Wolf Tooth had given him the following information:

> The Custer men tried to cross the river at a ford west of the present railroad tracks, on what is now the Willy Bends place. Cheyennes hidden in the brush on the south side of the ford drove the soldiers back and killed a couple of them in the brush by the river. Then the Custer men retreated to the flats below where the superintendent's house is now located. They waited there for about half an hour, whilst the Indians assembled in the vicinity and fired at the soldiers from the ridges north of the flats.[57]

The western ford mentioned is probably Ford D as originally shown on the 1877 map of Lieutenant W. Philo Clark. Wolf Tooth again refers to Indians, in this case Cheyennes, hidden in the brush by the river, but says that the brush was on the south side of the ford. The ford he mentions is likely the one used by Colonel Gibbon on June 29, 1876, which is north of Last Stand Hill and below the present National Cemetery. That makes the action described closer to Deep Ravine, but nowhere near as far south as Medicine Tail.

Of course, there may have been an added factor fueling the soldiers' retreat, a factor that could have been the pivotal moment in the battle. Recall that Hanging Wolf said ". . . they hit one horse down there, and it bucked off a soldier, but the rest took him along when they retreated north." The only soldiers important enough to be "taken along" in the midst of a gun battle were either Custer himself or his brother Tom, and if either one was not bucked off but hit and badly wounded, it might also account for the twenty-minute wait in the cemetery area whilst he was tended to by the doctor. There isn't, however, any firm evidence that this was the case.

There is one further piece of corroborating evidence. The body of newspaper correspondent Mark Kellogg, who was with the Headquarters Group, was discovered by Colonel John Gibbon as he crossed the river at the ford already mentioned on his way to Last Stand Hill. He wrote of his discovery:

> As we proceeded up the valley, now an open grassy slope, we suddenly came upon a body lying in the grass. It was lying on its back, and was in an advanced state of decomposition. It was not stripped, but had evidently been scalped and one ear cut off. The clothing was not that of a soldier, and, with the idea of identifying the remains, I caused one of the boots to be cut off and the stockings and drawers examined for a name, but none could be found. On looking at the boot, however, a curious construction was observed. The heel of the boot was reinforced by a piece of leather which in front terminated in two straps, one of which was furnished with a buckle, evidently for the purpose of tightening the boot. This led to the identification of the remains, for on being carried to camp the boot was recognized as one belonging to Mr. Kellogg . . ."[58]

Then there is the fascinating article by Bruce A. Trinque, "The Fight in Fishing Woman Ravine," which provided information from a Cheyenne family's oral history. It concerned the parents of Acker Standing Crane, his unnamed father, and his mother, Fishing Woman, who were involved in what happened as Custer's Left Wing approached the river near the Cheyenne camp.

Standing Crane's father told him that the soldiers were "riding down the trail . . . in little groups and had little flags. They were riding fast. They were headed for the creek."[59] When the Blackfoot woman he was helping to safety started screaming, he told her that "the soldiers were heading too far up river, that they were not headed for the women and children."[60] Soon after the woman started screaming again and he looked again. He says:

The soldiers had broken apart. Some were going on up the river. The rest had turned from the trail and were following a smaller trail toward where were the women. These soldiers were riding fast. They had two little flags in front of them. One had little white stars and a forked stem. In front of that little flag was another little flag. It had two tails and big white crossed knives . . . A little yellow bird sat on top of its pole.[61]

Once again we have soldiers riding down towards the river near the Cheyenne camp and we have confirmation of Soldier Wolf's account of rushing down the creek to where the women were. It is also clear that the Headquarters Group was leading the soldiers coming towards the women as the second flag mentioned is obviously Custer's personal flag. The trail referred to by Standing Crane's father was verified by two maps, one produced by Lieutenant William Philo Clark, the other by Captain R.E. Johnston on behalf of Chief Kill Eagle. These maps are reproduced in *Drawing Battle Lines*.[62] As Bruce Trinque says, on both maps the trail is shown leading from Custer Hill to the river and a ford some distance north of Deep Ravine, which is further corroboration that Medicine Tail was not the place where the Custer battalions fought near the river.

The soldiers observed by Standing Crane's father continuing northwards along the buffalo trail and rode horses which "were all pretty white."[63] Obviously that was E Company under Lieutenant A.E. Smith, and it is likely that they were heading for the far north ford to check the possibility of crossing there. The group heading for the place where the women were hiding would therefore have been the Headquarters Group and F Company commanded by Captain George Yates.

Standing Crane continues:

My father turned loose the Blackfeet woman and ran to where he thought the soldiers would strike the creek. It was just across the creek from where were the women. There were other Indians hurrying there. Some on horses, some on foot. There were not very many warriors. They ran to the edge of the creek and got behind a little rise. They started shooting at the soldiers. Five Indians, my father thought they were Cheyenne; they crossed the creek on horses. They charged the soldiers. The soldiers charged them back. The five Indians turned around. They rode for the creek. The Indians at the creek fired and killed some of the soldiers. Some of the soldiers stopped and got off their horses and the Indians and the soldiers shot back and forth across the river at each other. They did this for some time.[64]

This part of the account has the action taking place directly across the river from where the women were hiding, as described by Soldier Wolf. The five Cheyennes who attacked the soldiers compare very closely with those who were interviewed by Grinnell, and two of them were also named by White Shield. The warriors firing from a little rise at the edge of the river agrees with the information supplied by Wolf Tooth. The soldiers and the Indians firing at each other is in all accounts, and soldiers being killed appears in the Brave Wolf, Soldier Wolf and Wolf Tooth accounts. White Shield also talks of soldiers dismounting.

The few Indians who were fighting were then reinforced as others arrived, and Standing Crane's father's account continues: "Then an old man chief, he was Southern Cheyenne, came along. He saw that many Indians were coming up from the Skirt People and the Miniconjou camps. He called to his warriors to follow him. He rode across the creek. Not many Indians had their ponies. The ponies had not yet come into the camps."[65]

That Custer now found his Left Wing repulsed at the northern end of the camps was due to a combination of events that he could not have anticipated. The assumption had been that the majority of warriors would have swiftly moved to the south when Reno's force menaced that end of the village. What Custer did not realize was that at least two-thirds of the Indian fighting strength had been unable to find their horses in time to go and meet Reno. The vast herd seen from the Crow's Nest on the bench lands to the west of the camps was not, in fact, the only one. Wooden Leg told Marquis, "On the bench lands just east of us our horses found plenty of rich grass."[66] Later on he says, "The Cheyenne horses were put out to graze on the valley below our camp. Horses belonging to other tribes were placed at other feeding areas on the valley and on the bench hills just west of the combined Indian camps. The tribal herds were kept separate from each other."[67] There is also confirmation from Foolish Elk in his interview with Walter Camp: "The Indians were now getting their horses in from the hills and soon came up in large numbers. Some crossed the stream farther down and others crossed the ford and followed on after Custer in overwhelming numbers. They could not see how such a small force of soldiers had any chance to stand against them."[68]

The simplicity of what happened is clear from these Indian accounts, but the time frame is not, because when the Left Wing was baulked at the northern fords it set off a chain reaction that soon involved the Right Wing and took another hour and a half to unfold. As various actions were happening simultaneously, I have broken the time frame down into segments for the sake of convenience. Those segments are not however, meant to be other than approximate guidelines.

RIGHT WING, 3:45 P.M.

At about 3:45 p.m., acting on advice from Mitch Boyer, Custer had left for the northern fords, leaving the Right Wing in position on Luce and Butler Ridges overlooking Medicine Tail Coulee. It is likely that he told Keogh to allow about twenty minutes for the Left Wing to reach the northern ford crossing point, which was where, as already mentioned, they could reunite in case of trouble.

LEFT WING, 4:00–4:20 P.M.

At 4:00 p.m., as Custer with his Headquarters Group, accompanied by E and F Companies, descended from east of Last Stand Hill and down towards the northern fords, they were seen to divide into two parties. E Company on their gray horses turned further north, the rest moved down closer to the river in the direction of the noncombatants. Some five minutes later, as the Custer Group and F Company neared the river, the few Cheyenne warriors who had crossed the river to face the soldiers opened fire.

Whether or not any soldiers were hit is open to question, but nevertheless Custer ordered F Company to dismount and form a skirmish line to return fire. As the few warriors opposing them were hiding in the brush near the river, there were no easy targets for the soldiers to aim at; nevertheless the skirmish line fired a couple of volleys toward the source of the warrior fire.

By now, E Company had ridden fast from the far northern ford to the sound of firing and also dismounted into a skirmish line.

These events have already been described by American Horse and other Cheyennes in their interviews with Grinnell. They stated, "and there they fought for some little time," "The Indians all crossed and they fought there. For quite a long time the troops stood their ground right there," and "When the Gray Horse Company dismounted, the Indians began to fire at them, and the soldiers returned the fire." The reality of this episode was described by the Cheyenne minor chief Two Moon: "We hurriedly crossed the river, and some went up and some down, to get on each side of where the soldiers were intending to come. They came to the edge and stopped; then, almost in an instant the guns commenced to go, increasing to a roar-like thunder. Custer had started his last fight."[69]

The Indian accounts spell out quite clearly that the soldiers and warriors exchanged long-range, inconclusive gunfire for a period of time. This situation began to change as Custer saw, with some concern, warriors on foot and mounted racing through what he had believed was a deserted village; warriors he had expected to be engaging Reno's command at the southern end of the camps. Custer now accepted that he had to abort his original plan to get into the village at the northern fords. His force of fewer than one hundred men could not stand against the growing number of warriors he could see coming toward him. Indian accounts again confirm this. The Oglala Eagle Elk, " . . . noticed that the other Indians were charging from the south end. From that time, others were coming across the creek after the soldiers."[70] The Hunkpapa Iron Hawk said, " . . . the Indians crossed the river anywhere to confront Custer. The first Indians to reach Custer were about one hundred."[71] Hollow Horn Bear, a Brule, recalled, "They did not appear to want to cross the river after the warriors made their presence felt in such large numbers."[72]

It was now expedient for the Left Wing to go back the way it had come, reunite with Keogh's battalion, and buy time for Custer to plan again. Orders were therefore given for F Company to move back up toward the higher ground with the Headquarters Group, while E Company would act as rearguard to protect them. The ride down toward the river had been relatively easy. The return journey would be anything but. In temperatures of over 90 degrees, with horses already sweating, and dust-covered men perspiring heavily in their wool uniforms, that journey needed to be uphill. It was about 4:20 p.m. when the withdrawal began.

RIGHT WING, 4:00–4:20 P.M.

Captain Myles W. Keogh, commanding the Right Wing, was eager for the fighting to begin. For one reason or another he had missed the regiment's major engagements at the Washita in 1868 and during the Yellowstone Expedition in 1873. He had served with the Papal Guard and in the Union Army, so was no stranger to hot action, but had been pleasantly surprised when given command of a battalion at the Divide, as Custer had been cool toward him for some time after Keogh had struck up a close friendship with Libbie Custer. Now the Irishman relished taking his battalion across Ford B and smashing into the flank of any opposition Custer might have run into.

Keogh had deployed his three companies north of Medicine Tail Coulee, along Butler and Luce Ridges. From east to west the order was I–L–C. About 4:10 p.m., waiting to attack across Ford B, Keogh had cause for some unease. He could no longer hear the sound of Springfield carbine fire from Reno's command in the valley, only the spasmodic cracks of lighter weapons. But at around the same time he could hear gunshots to his north, including Springfield volley firing. Suddenly warriors started to cross Ford B and move up Medicine Tail Coulee, having, unknown to him, responded to the Left Wing's approach to the northern fords. Keogh quickly appreciated that the situation had changed. The planned joint attack was no longer possible, so in accordance with orders he began a move to the high ground to try to reunite with the Left Wing as he assumed they were faced with the same problem. Keogh began a disciplined withdrawal from his original position to the Nye/Cartwright Ridge area. I Company provided covering fire to deter the warriors moving up Medicine Tail. The quantity of cartridges that has been found along this line of retreat indicates that at least part of the Right Wing stayed on the ridges for a while. As C Company exited Butler's Ridge, Corporal John Foley became its first casualty, probably shot by some nimble warrior who had rapidly scaled the gently sloping ridge below the C Company position. The corporal would achieve far more recognition in death than he ever had in his rather undistinguished life.

Tall Bull was one of the warriors who mentioned this action: "Custer [Keogh] got onto flat near Ford B within easy gunshot of village, and Indians drove him back. By time I got there, had driven the soldiers to the first rise [where Foley lay], and they were going up the ridge to the right of Custer coulee and the Indians driving them. The men who had no horses to go to Reno first began the attack on Custer, and I did not see the first of it."[73]

That phrase in parentheses—"where Foley lay"—was inserted by Camp when he transcribed his July 22, 1910 interview with Tall Bull. The location of Foley's body had been quite accurately fixed by a number of the 7th Cavalry survivors when they had helped to bury the bodies of their dead comrades on June 28, 1876. In particular, Sergeant Stanislaus Roy of A Company, who in his interview with Camp said:

> We then formed skirmish line and buried the dead. On the way over we followed what we supposed was Custer's trail and at one point it led down pretty close to the river.
>
> The first dead body we came to was that of Corpl. John Foley. I heard several say: "There lies Foley of C Company." I saw him and recognized him easily, as he had [a] bald head and black hair. He was of middle age and I knew him well. Foley was at least three-fourths mile in advance of the first group of dead at C.
>
> The next body we came to was that of Sergt. Butler, and from him to first group of dead at C the distance was considerable. He lay probably one-half way from Foley to C. There was no dead horse near either Foley or Butler. I helped to bury the bodies on west slope of ridge, and we wound up with E Troop men over near the gully.
>
> ... When we went to bury the dead on June 28 we did not follow Dry Creek to the river but cut straight across to the battlefield, going over the little rise between the two coulees. The first body we saw was that of Corpl. Foley of Co. C on this rise, just over toward the coulee running up to the battlefield. Butler lay 200 or 300 yds. beyond and across the ravine."[74]

In his own records Camp noted, "Ford B is 800 feet from the top of the slope of the little hill on which Foley was found. The edge of the rise of ground on which Foley was found is 800 feet from the river, while Foley's body was found 300 feet farther, he lying about 1,100 feet from the river."[75]

The location of Foley's body is therefore not in dispute, but when he was killed most certainly is. A number of Camp's Indian accounts speak of a mounted man who escaped either from the final moments on Last Stand Hill or the destruction of C Company and fled south before shooting himself in the head. They include the Mnicoujou Turtle Rib, in the fighting near Battle Ridge, who " ... saw one soldier ride across a hollow and try to get away....

The soldier rode like the wind and appeared to be getting away from them, when he killed himself."[76] The Oglala He Dog said something similar but places the man's escape from Last Stand Hill. "Says location of Foley is right and he the one who shot himself . . . Foley rode out of fight from H [Last Stand Hill]."[77] The Oglala Red Feather, near Battle Ridge, stated, "One soldier on a sorrel horse tried to get round the Indians. . . . They saw some smoke and the report of a gun . . . (they concluded) he had shot himself.[78] Finally the Cheyenne Wooden Leg told Marquis:

> A Cheyenne told me that four soldiers from that part of the ridge [near Keogh's stand] had turned their horses and tried to escape. . . . Three of these men were killed quickly. The fourth one got across a gulch and over a ridge eastward before the pursuing group of Sioux got close to him. . . . Suddenly his right hand went up to his head. With his revolver he shot himself and fell dead from his horse.[79]

In yet another Camp interview, this time in 1920 with Colonel Herbert J. Slocum, who had joined the 7th Cavalry as a second lieutenant on July 28, 1876, Camp noted how Slocum told him that during the 1886 tenth anniversary trip to the battlefield, "Gall showed them where the lone soldier rode away . . . and finally shot himself. . . . It corroborates my information about Corpl. Foley, as told me by Turtle Rib. Gall told them that this soldier had chevrons on his sleeve."[80]

Two things become clear from these accounts. The first is that at some point in the fighting, either from near Battle Ridge or from Last Stand Hill, one soldier fled southeast on horseback and eventually shot himself in the head. The second is that in his eagerness to corroborate his own ideas, Camp, albeit unwittingly, either directly or via third parties, posed leading questions to the interviewees. There is no other explanation for He Dog apparently mentioning Foley by name, or for Gall stating that "this soldier had chevrons on his sleeve," as He Dog could not possibly have known Foley's name and Gall would not have had the word chevrons in his vocabulary. In both cases the Indian warriors were pointed to their answers by the questions they were asked.

Whilst that does not rule out the possibility that the escapee was Foley, one other thing does. Each of the five warrior accounts cited tells of the escapee shooting himself, and one specifically saying in the head. There are at least seven other accounts which state that the man shot himself in the head, and it takes little imagination to picture how disfigured his head would have looked after being hit at close range by a bullet from a Colt .45 Single-Action revolver. Add to that three days decomposing in blazing heat and the end result would not have been pretty. Yet Sergeant Roy, who was with the group that found Foley's body, said several of them immediately knew who the dead man was, and Roy "recognized him easily." It is highly unlikely therefore, that the escapee was Corporal Foley.

The unfortunate corporal's name has also become synonymous with what has become known as the Culbertson Guidon. According to Sergeant Ferdinand Culbertson of A Company, he was a member of the burial party which came across Foley's body, and in turning the corpse over discovered the bloodstained guidon of Foley's C Company under it. It is odd then, that neither this event nor the presence of Culbertson in the burial party was ever mentioned by Sergeant Roy in his various dealings with Walter Camp, who noted, regarding Culbertson, that he "found a bloodstained guidon torn from its staff beneath a soldier's body on Custer's battlefield says himself."[81] That Camp added "says himself" is a clear indication that he was skeptical. That Culbertson did not tell him the dead soldier was the clearly identifiable Foley when he later claimed that it was makes that later claim dubious.

As the Culbertson Guidon, with authenticating provenance, was auctioned in December 2010 for $2.2m, it has to be accepted that Culbertson did have a guidon of the period, possibly one he recovered at the battlefield. What is very much in dispute is that he found it on, or under, Foley's body. He may indeed, have found the G Company guidon which had been abandoned during the flight from the timber, when he went to look for Hodgson's body for Reno, but as A Company was deployed to look for bodies on Custer's Field, it is perhaps more likely that he did find the C Company guidon, but not on Foley. Sergeant Roy, in his letter of March 4, 1909 to Camp revealed, "It was not my troop that covered Foley and Butler,"[82] so it casts doubt on the likelihood of Culbertson having the opportunity of turning over Foley's corpse. The bodies of C Company men were scattered all over the battlefield, so it is much more of a probability that if Culbertson did recover their guidon, it was from one of these dead men. The provenance for the auction was apparently contained in letters from Roy to Sergeant Samuel Alcott, also of A Company, and from Alcott to Walter Camp, plus an unpublished memoir by Alcott. There is nothing in Camp's notes to suggest he took what Alcott had to say seriously, and Camp was like a dog with a bone when he believed in something. The reason for his lack of interest may well have been the fact that Alcott was shown as on detached service at the Powder River Depot, not at the Little Horn, so whatever the Sergeant was telling him was merely hearsay. Why Roy would confirm Culbertson's story is uncertain, except perhaps he did not witness the finding of the guidon, but simply believed what Culbertson told him.

The real impact of Culbertson's story has been to distort the history of the Fights. By placing the torn guidon with Foley, who was also erroneously believed by Camp to have been the escapee who had shot himself, it has been assumed that the corporal was the C Company guidon holder who, in a last desperate bid to escape, rather than let go of his flag, tore it from its staff and thrust it into his tunic before fleeing from the overrunning of his company. That would place him as an escapee late in the fighting rather than as a casualty in the early withdrawal from the ridges above Medicine Tail Coulee. Yet if, and there is a lot of doubt, Foley was the color bearer for his company, the guidon could just as easily have been torn from its staff by him in the sudden withdrawal from near Butler Ridge, as it is obvious that he could not ride up the ridges holding on to the staff with one hand whilst guiding his horse with the other. Because his body lay in a place relatively isolated from the main warrior surge after the retreating Right Wing, it is not surprising that it was left alone, other than with boys' arrows in it, easily recognizable to Roy and others, with the guidon, if ever with him, still on it. Whilst Foley's body was overlooked by the warriors when he became the first casualty of Keogh's command, the remainder of his company would not fare as well. They would become the catalyst for the collapse of the Right Wing.

RIGHT WING, 4:20–4:30 P.M.

At roughly the same time as the Left Wing began its withdrawal, Keogh's battalion had moved on to the Nye/Cartwright Ridge area. From there L Company began firing at warriors moving up to Luce Ridge from Medicine Tail Coulee, as Keogh's other two companies moved the mile to Battle Ridge, past Calhoun Hill via the ravine to the north of Nye/Cartwright and across the Deep Coulee flats. The Oglala Respects Nothing noticed this movement: "The soldiers came up to Calhoun Hill diagonally from the east [south] and the Indians came up diagonally from the river crossing to Calhoun Hill."[83] The Brule warrior Two Eagles told Walter Camp that, "There were a few [soldiers] went from 'E' [The Luce–Nye/Cartwright Ridge complex] to 'D' [Calhoun Hill]."[84] In one interview, the Mnicoujou White Bull related that he and other warriors rode up Medicine Tail Coulee and joined a "horde of others" in pursuit of L Company, which was bringing up the rear of the fleeing battalions, and "The Indians kept up a constant fire. Two soldiers fell from their horses. The other troopers opened such an intense fire from their saddles that the Indians were forced back."[85] The discovery of Springfield cartridge cases and Indian bullets in this area confirm the action at this location.[86]

Keogh's command was controlling the situation, but it was the calm before the storm. The warriors who had forced Crook to retreat at the Rosebud were fired up and ready to do the same to Keogh's force.

LEFT WING, 4:20 P.M.

To the north, with E Company acting as skirmishers for protection, the Headquarters Group and F Company started their ascent to a position where they could deploy a skirmish line to cover the withdrawal of E Company. They had not gone far when they suffered their first casualty. Mark Kellogg the newspaper correspondent was riding a mule and was about to discover why that species had a reputation for stubbornness. On that hot day his mount was thirsty, it could smell the river but its rider was moving him away from it. The beast stopped and refused to move, despite the urging of its rider. Then "The old man chief [Lame White Man] hit him on the head with his rifle as he rode by. Then the man on the mule fell off on to the ground. The Indians on foot got him."[87] A very few moments later the Headquarters Group sustained its second casualty: Corporal Henry C. Dose, a trumpeter, felled by an Indian bullet. His body was described by Lieutenant DeRudio as " . . . so much disfigured that I did not know who he was, only the marks on his pants showed me he was a trumpeter."[88]

The Cheyenne White Shield confirmed the E Company action: "All the soldiers retreated back from the river, but the Gray Horse Company stood their ground."[89] But whooping warriors, both mounted and on foot, were moving against them. Individuals were riding up closer to the troopers in acts of bravery. Yellow Nose told how "The soldiers soon changed from a stand to a retreat."[90] With bullets whistling past his head, the Cheyenne/Ute warrior circled in front of the soldiers and noticed a pretty flag being held on a long pole by one of the troopers. Yellow Nose decided he wanted that flag.

The warriors rode back and forth in front of E Company as the Headquarters Group and F Company retreated to the northeast. Unfortunately for them, a hunting party of about twenty Cheyenne was coming down from the northwest.[91] They stopped behind a small ridge north of Last Stand Hill and fired at the Custer group retreating in that direction. Archaeological evidence bears this out.[92]

LEFT WING, 4:30 P.M.

Having noted that the rest had retreated while E Company "stood their ground," White Shield observed how pressure grew on Smith's command: "After they had been shooting for some time, Contrary Big Belly made a charge down in front of the Gray Horse Company, and from where the Indians were, they saw that the horses of one other company began to get frightened and started to circle around the men who were holding them. When Contrary Big Belly got back, the companies began shooting fast."[93] White Cow Bull too saw the troops redeploy, "Now I saw the soldiers were split into two bands, most of them on foot and shooting as they fell back to higher ground, so we made no more mounted charges."[94]

As that pressure started to impact on the dismounted E Company skirmishers, their horse-holders were finding it harder and harder to keep control of the mounts in their charge. The Cheyenne Two Moon described what he saw at this point, "Those who were on the hill where the monument now stands, and where I am now standing, had gray horses and they were all in the open. The Sioux and Cheyenne came up the valley swarming like ants toward the bunch of gray horses where Long Hair stood."[95]

Prevented from going northeast by the Cheyenne hunters and being fired at by the Wolf Tooth group from the ridges to the north of Last Stand Hill, the sweat-drenched men of the Custer group had struggled to a wide, flat ridge sloping west from Last Stand Hill near the present visitor center, known now as Cemetery Ridge, and dismounted. Because they were receiving fire from the northeast, southeast, and some from the west, they formed circular skirmish lines with their nervous, excited horses in the center. White Cow Bull boastfully recounted his own exploits during this action: "I found cover and began shooting at the soldiers. I was a good shot and had one of the few repeating rifles carried by any of our warriors. It was up to me to use it the best way I could. I kept firing at the two bands of soldiers, first at one, then at the other. It was hard to see through the smoke and dust, but I saw five soldiers go down when I shot at them."[96]

With the Custer group on Cemetery Ridge and E Company skirmishers both firing as well, there was a cacophony of noise with gun smoke and dust filling the air to add to the confusion. Some of the Custer group soldiers were firing at the warriors who were menacing the stationary skirmishers of E Company. Looking down from his position overlooking Last Stand Hill, Wolf Tooth remarked on what was happening to E Company, "When the Gray Horse Company moved south they were confronted by a large number of Indians in and near the big Ravine."[97] The situation was becoming grim for the Left Wing, especially for E Company, and it was soon to get considerably worse.

RIGHT WING, 4:30–4:40 P.M.

Approximately a mile to the south, First Lieutenant James Calhoun had moved his L Company to the hill that would later bear his name, just south of C Company on Battle Ridge. The two soldier casualties mentioned by White Bull must have only been wounded as no bodies were found on Nye/Cartwright Ridge. The Right Wing deployment is noted by Standing Bear: "Custer [Keogh] came down the ridge across the creek—the second or rear ridge from the river. He made no known attempt to reach the river to cross. He went right up to Calhoun Hill and disposed his forces along the top of the ridge to Custer Hill."[98] Dismounting his company, Lieutenant Calhoun placed his horses in the small cleft slightly west of the hill, between it and Battle Ridge, and deployed his men as skirmishers in the form of a semi-circle around the military crest of the hill. Long-range firing kept the out-ranged warriors at a respectable distance, but individuals began to try to infiltrate closer to the soldier lines. Showers of arcing arrows began to cause problems to both men and horses. Said Wooden Leg:

> Most of the Indians were working around the ridge now occupied by the soldiers. We were lying down in gullies and behind sagebrush hillocks. The shooting at first was at a distance, but we kept creeping in closer all around the ridge. Bows and arrows were used much more than guns. From the hiding-places of the Indians, the arrows could be shot in a high and long curve, to fall upon the soldiers or their horses.[99]

Other warriors noted the long-distance stalemate and the first Indian attack. Runs the Enemy: "While Custer [Keogh] was all surrounded, there had been no firing from either side. The Sioux then made a charge from the rear side shooting into the men, and the shooting frightened the horses so that they rushed upon the ridge and many horses were shot. The return fire was so strong that the Sioux had to retreat back over the hill again."[100] With no clear targets to sight on, the L Company skirmishers caused very few warrior casualties, and could not stop the stealthy warriors beginning to surround them and the rest of Keogh's battalion. They were now taking gunfire from Greasy Grass Ridge to their west and upper Deep Coulee, now known as Henryville, to their east, as well as taking hits from the arrows falling from the sky. Facing one platoon to the east, Lieutenant Calhoun began to return the fire from Henryville and helped to repulse the first Indian charge described by Runs the Enemy.

Although many hundreds of warriors were already confronting Keogh's command, what the soldiers did not know was that following Reno's retreat, many more warriors were arriving from the south. Foremost among them and destined to have an important impact on events was the Oglala Lakota Crazy Horse. Revered by his people as remarkably brave and someone to follow in battle, Crazy Horse had already been effective in crushing Reno's command. Now he was racing down through the village to help protect the families from the menace of the five Custer companies.

LEFT WING, 4:40–4:50 P.M.

For a while the long-range firing from both E Company and the Yates group on Cemetery Ridge held the warriors back, but the soldiers were finding that there was a big difference between stationary targets on a practice range and the constantly moving warriors. Those on horseback weaved back and forth, and those on foot used every ridge and hollow to hide behind, making targets difficult to hit.

Mounted at the rear of his E Company, First Lieutenant Algernon "Fresh" Smith had organized his men into two lines to face the warriors coming at them from the direction of the river, "some kneeling and some standing" as seen by Two Moon.[101] However there was now a threat to his rear from the ravine to the east as warriors crept up behind its protective banks. The plight of E Company is recorded in Cheyenne oral history: "But by the time some of them (gray horses) did move toward the big ravine on the battlefield (E Company ravine), it was too late and the Indians were all around them in large numbers."[102]

A worried Smith knew it was time to withdraw and unite with the rest of the Left Wing Group on Cemetery Ridge. It was to prove an impossible task. Unable to control their wildly plunging animals, the E Company horse-holders could not get them to the troopers as Lieutenant Smith ordered his company to withdraw from their skirmish-line positions. The troopers found that the combined tasks of trying to climb the slope to their mounts and reloading their carbines in the midst of all the turmoil were beyond them. Eager to mount and ride to a safer position, the firing wavered. That was all the encouragement the warriors needed. The bolder spirits among them began to close on the soldiers of E Company.

The Cheyenne White Shield gave a vivid description of what he saw: "When the Gray Horse company dismounted, the Indians began to fire at them and the soldiers returned the fire. It was not long before the Indians began to gather in large numbers where I was. After they had been shooting for some time, Contrary Big Belly made a charge down in front of the Gray Horse Company . . ."[103] Another version of these events came from the Oglala White Cow Bull: "Another warrior named Yellow Nose, a Sapawicasa who had been captured as a boy by the Shahiyela and had grown up with them, was very brave that day. After we chased the soldiers back from the ford, he galloped out in front of us and got very close to them, then raced back to safety."[104] Yellow Nose was not, however, to be denied his flag, as White Cow Bull explained:

> I kept riding with the Shahiyelas still hoping that some of them might tell Meotzi later about my courage. We massed for another charge. The Shahiyela chief, Comes-in-Sight, and a warrior named Contrary Belly led us that time. The soldiers' horses were so frightened by all the noise we made that they began to bolt in all directions. The soldiers held their fire while they tried to catch their horses. Just then Yellow Nose rushed in again and grabbed a small flag from where the soldiers had stuck it in the ground. He carried it off and counted coup on a soldier with its sharp end. He was proving his courage more by counting that coup than if he had killed the soldier.[105]

The momentum was now with the warriors, and Lieutenant Colonel George Armstrong Custer was going to need every bit of his legendary "Custer's Luck" to extricate the Gray Horse Company from its predicament.

RIGHT WING, 4:40–4:50 P.M.

After reaching the Oglala camp in the village and checking that the families were safe, Crazy Horse, with a group of between fifty and one hundred warriors, moved from the west bank of the river via Deep Ravine ford and up the ravine. Surveying things from the top of Deep Ravine he quickly realized that he could not go straight across Battle Ridge from there or he would be an easy target for the soldiers on the crest of the ridge, Keogh's I Company. He therefore turned left, toward the basin area, then up, passing south around Last Stand Hill ridge, before moving into the ravine that now bears his name, north of Battle Ridge. Here he paused. The ravine led directly into the guns of the soldiers on the ridge. He needed a different route.

Unsurprisingly, every move of the great Oglala warrior was noted by his people. Flying By told how, "Crazy Horse and I left the crowd and rode down along the river. We came to a ravine; then we followed up the gulch to a place in the rear of the soldiers that were making the stand on the hill."[106] Pretty White Buffalo, the wife of Spotted Horn Bull, observed, "I saw Crazy Horse lead the Cheyennes into the water and up the ravine; Crow King and the Hunkpapa went after them;"[107] Wherever Crazy Horse went in this fight he would not go unnoticed.

Once Calhoun's L Company had taken its place south of C Company, Myles Keogh felt confident that his companies could hold their positions until the Yates group reunited with them. The range of the Springfield carbines was deterring the warriors from getting too close to his command, and the longer that lasted, the more time it gave Custer to join him. He knew that the Left Wing was also under attack, but believed they would be able to withdraw safely. Meantime, his battalion would give a good account of themselves.

For a while, after some volley firing from Calhoun's company had made the Indians more cautious, the only action was between his skirmishers and individual warriors trying to infiltrate closer to the soldier lines. Runs The Enemy has already described how the first Indian charge was repulsed, and the Lakota White Bull told his biographer how the warriors went on the offensive, but were beaten back by the soldiers' firepower. "The soldiers fired back from the saddle. Their fire was so effective that some of the Indians, including White Bull, fell back to the south."[108]

That situation prevailed only until more and more warriors arrived on the scene and began to look for ways to surround the Keogh positions. The Oglala Foolish Elk remembered:

The Indians were now getting their horses in from the hills and soon came up in large numbers. Some crossed the stream farther down and others crossed the ford and followed on after Custer [Keogh] in overwhelming numbers. They could not see how such a small force of soldiers had any chance to stand against them. The Indians were between Custer [Keogh] and the river and all the time coming up and getting around to the east of him passing around both his front and rear. Custer [Keogh] was following the ridges, and the Indians were keeping abreast of him in the hollows and ravines. Personally, he was with the Indians to the east, or on Custer's [Keogh's] right.[109]

For the next ten minutes or so the status quo seemed to prevail, but it was the warriors who were making the positive moves. Crazy Horse and his followers were moving along behind the eastern ridges, while others were in Deep Coulee and hiding in the upper part of the Coulee, now known as Henryville. The noose was tightening around the Keogh battalion. That was how Wooden Leg saw things:

The Indians all the time could see where were the soldiers, because the white men were mostly on a ridge and their horses with them. But the soldiers could not see our warriors, as they had left their ponies and were crawling in the gullies through the sagebrush. A warrior would jump up, shoot, jerk himself down quickly, and then crawl forward a little further. All around the soldier ridge our men were doing this. So not many of them got hit by the soldier bullets during this time of fighting.[110]

Captain Keogh watched the Indian movements carefully. He wanted to be sure that the warriors did not get too close to the horses in the gully behind Calhoun Hill or to the L Company skirmishers on their hill, as that would negate the superior range of the Springfield carbines. He sent a messenger to Harrington to be ready to move quickly with C Company if required.

LEFT WING, 4:50–5:00 P.M.
From his vantage point on Cemetery Ridge, Lt. Colonel Custer could see that E Company was in trouble. He could also see Indians moving up past Last Stand Hill and became concerned that a combination of these facts would

seriously compromise his anticipated reunion with Keogh's battalion. Swiftly Custer made up his mind and gave two orders to Captain Yates. The first was to send a squad of eight mounted F Company men to immediately aid Smith's beleaguered command, and the second was to mount up the rest of F Company and charge to drive off the warriors menacing Smith's men. At the same time, the Headquarters Group would move to the lower slope of the hill and Yates was to rejoin them there. Once there Custer believed that a strong defensive position could be established from which an effective field of fire would allow E Company to withdraw and reunite with the rest of the Left Wing.

The Yates group had barely left Cemetery Ridge when Sergeant Major William H. Sharrow was cut down by the firing from the northern ridge. The squad of eight F Company men led by 2nd Lt. William Reily mounted and galloped down to the E Company position as the Headquarters Group moved as planned. The bulk of F Company charged down the flats at the warriors threatening Smith and his men. The charge had its effect, as Wooden Leg described: "After a long time of slow fighting, about forty of the soldiers came galloping from the east part of the ridge down toward the river, toward where most of the Cheyennes and many Oglalas were hiding. The Indians ran back to a deep gulch."[111]

The arrival of the F Company squad was remarked on by Young Two Moon:

At the 4th charge on Yellow Nose's orders, all Indians mounted and Yellow Nose made a charge, and all Indians followed. They crowded the company furthest north and they started to run down the ridge. As they got down part way toward the Gray Horse Company, the latter began to fire and drove the Indians off, and the soldiers reached the Gray Horse Company. Some were killed, however, when they reached the Gray Horse Company. The latter shot at the Indians so fast that they drove the Indians back out of sight over the hill toward the agency.[112]

The bodies of F Company men Corporal John Briody and Private Timothy Donnelly, found in the Deep Ravine area, and perhaps Private William Brown, who was found in the village opposite Deep Ravine ford, testify to the observations of Young Two Moon.

Having successfully relieved Smith's command, Yates withdrew to reunite with Custer, who gave the order for F Company to form a skirmish line on lower Last Stand Hill. Custer himself, with Adjutant Cooke, Dr. Lord, Chief Trumpeter Voss and Sergeant John Vickory, his color bearer, set up a command post and hospital to the north of the skirmish line. His brother Tom and scout Mitch Boyer joined the skirmish line, relishing the action to come. Armstrong Custer was ready to cover the withdrawal of E Company.

RIGHT WING, 4:50–5:00 P.M.

On the crest of Battle Ridge, Myles Keogh had I Company containing the warriors to his east and southeast because they had no cover in that bare terrain. To the north, northwest and west though, the broken ground was ideal for infiltration. With the firing from Henryville obliging Lieutenant Calhoun to face part of his skirmish line in that direction under the command of Second Lieutenant J.J. Crittenden, the shooting at warriors near Greasy Grass Ridge was diminished. Some of the Indians took advantage of this and began to infiltrate from the northwest into Calhoun Coulee just below what became known as Finley Ridge. The Lakota White Bull described what he saw of this situation: "Some Indians went up draw to Custer [Keogh]. White Bull with them—a lot of them. When up in draw, Custer [Keogh] saw them and took shots at them, so they moved back south a ways. Custer [Keogh] was at a standstill, and get off horses to shoot, then got back on and made 4 companies, and one company was shooting at them in the draw."[113] Captain Moylan's testimony at the Reno Court of Inquiry confirms the White Bull view: "The evidences of fighting were a great many dead men lying about there. I saw Lieutenant Calhoun's company were killed in regular position of skirmishers. I counted twenty-eight cartridge shells around one man, and between the intervals there were shells scattered."[114]

Though L Company was being kept busy, up to now C Company had been relatively inactive, dismounted and deployed along the southern end of Battle Ridge between Keogh and Lieutenant Calhoun. In the absence of Captain Tom Custer, acting as an aide to his brother George, C Company was commanded by Second Lieutenant H.H. Harrington, who was a West Point graduate but possessing very little combat experience. Nevertheless, he had been alerted to be ready to move his company at a moment's notice. Keogh, acutely aware of the constantly increasing warrior numbers, and the threat they posed for his command and the horses being held in upper Calhoun Coulee, knew he could not afford to be passive. He ordered Harrington to mount his troopers and charge to drive the warriors out of Calhoun Coulee.

Harrington was then to hold the coulee to prevent further infiltration, so taking pressure off L Company.

The lieutenant got his company mounted and led them into a quarter-mile charge with revolvers blazing. The warriors in the coulee hastily retreated, seeking shelter behind Greasy Grass Ridge. The Oglala Eagle Elk remembered the event: "Just at this moment, we noticed that the other Indians were charging from the south end. From that time the others were coming across the creek after the soldiers. The soldiers were shooting a lot, so the Indians were thrown back."[115]

But what neither Harrington nor Keogh knew was that the ridge was hiding a great many more warriors than the ones chased from the coulee, as Pretty White Buffalo revealed:

> To get to the butte Long Hair [Harrington] must cross the ravine;
> but from where he was marching with his soldiers, he could not see
> into the ravine nor down to the banks of the river. . . . And I knew
> that the fighting men of the Sioux, many hundreds in number, were
> hidden in the ravine behind the hill upon which Long Hair was
> marching, and he would be attacked from both sides.[116]

Having cleared the coulee, Harrington halted his men just southwest of Finley Ridge and had them dismount. What the dismounted soldiers of C Company had now lost was mobility and a quarter of their firepower, as the number fours took the horses to the rear. These lost assets would prove to be critical, as would their empty revolvers, because even as the lieutenant followed the manual by dismounting his command in order to deploy as skirmishers with their carbines, the hidden warriors were primed to counterattack.

Taking some fire from Greasy Grass Ridge, the C Company troopers were just beginning to load their Springfields when a swarm of warriors erupted from behind that ridge. Screaming their war cries and with some firing arrows, the Indians closed rapidly on the startled soldiers. Some of Harrington's men got shots off, but that did not stop the warrior force, some of whom were more interested in capturing the company's horses. All the noise and dust had already frightened the cavalry mounts, and now warriors with flapping blankets added to their alarm. The bucking, frenzied animals became unmanageable and broke free from the number fours.

Said She Walks With Her Shawl, of the Hunkpapa, "We crossed the Greasy Grass below a beaver dam [where the water is not so deep] and came upon many horses. One soldier was holding the reins of eight or ten horses. An Indian waved his blanket and scared all the horses. They got away from the men [troopers]."[117] Though horses were always a great prize for the Indians, the majority of the warriors were hell-bent on attacking the soldiers, and swept up Calhoun Coulee into a hand-to-hand fight with the soldiers. At close-quarter combat the warriors held the advantage. Trained from a very young age in that style of fighting, they were in their element. Clubs and axes of stone, hatchets of metal, and vicious-looking knives began to crunch, cut and stab into the white men, who could only try to defend themselves with empty carbines and revolvers. With more raw recruits than any other company, Harrington's command yielded first to fear, then to panic. Those not already dead or badly wounded began to flee up the slope to seek the protection of L Company. Harrington and the three company sergeants, Bobo, Finkle and Finley, all still mounted, tried to rally their men in vain. Finley and Finkle fell yards apart on the ridge that bears Finley's name. Bobo whirled his horse around and rode furiously towards his battalion commander with I Company on Battle Ridge. An emotionally distraught Lieutenant Harrington rode straight at the mass of warriors clubbing at them with his empty revolver until he was engulfed by them and pulled from his mount. His body was never identified, but Reno claimed to have seen through field glasses "the Indians engaged in the war dance about three captives, who were tied to the stake, and my impression is that Harrington was among the unfortunates."[118]

The death knell of the Keogh battalion had begun to toll, for Crazy Horse, too, had not been passive. Moving east he had arrived behind a ridge that was sheltering a great many other warriors who had used Deep Coulee. The Mnicoujou White Bull met him there, "I rode around the ridge and dodged the bullets until I met a party of warriors with Crazy Horse. He was a chief of the Oglala and a brave fighter. He wore plain white buckskins and let his hair hang loose with no feathers in it. He had white spots painted here and there on his face for protection in battle, and it was said he was bulletproof."[119] Said Flying Hawk, "Crazy Horse and I left the crowd and rode down along the river. We came to a ravine; then we followed up the gulch to a place in the rear of the soldiers that were making the stand on the hill. Crazy Horse gave his horse to me to hold along with my horse. He crawled up the ravine to where he could see the soldiers."[120] Crazy Horse led them to the crest of the ridge. From there they could see that they were behind the soldiers on Battle Ridge. Crazy Horse would now show why he was held in such esteem.

LEFT WING, 5:00–5:10 P.M.

Even though the warriors had run to hide in Deep Ravine when F Company charged, E Company with the eight F reinforcements was still caught between Cemetery Ravine and Deep Ravine with the skirmishers facing both west toward the river and southeast toward Deep Ravine. It only needed a spark to ignite the powder keg that menaced them. That spark came in the form of the Southern Cheyenne chief, Lame White Man. After knocking Mark Kellogg from his mule, Lame White Man had watched the action for a while. Seeing the warriors flee from the soldiers' charge, he rode up and "called us to come back and fight. In a few minutes the warriors were all around these soldiers."[121] He then led the charge against Smith's command, calling out, "Come. We can kill them all."[122]

From behind their ridge, Wolf Tooth's band heard a Lakota crier calling out "to get ready and watch for the suicide boys. They said they were getting ready down below to charge."[123] This group of young men, who had made a pact to die rather than yield to the soldiers, were about to make a significant impact on the fighting. As Wolf Tooth watched, the boys galloped up to Cemetery Ridge, then turned and while "some stampeded the gray horses"[124] the rest "charged right in at the place where the soldiers were making their stand."[125] Already reeling from the charge led by Lame White Man, Lieutenant Smith's command now found itself in a deadly hand-to-hand fight with a vastly superior number of the enemy. Unable to use their carbines, once they had emptied their revolvers the soldiers used both weapons as clubs against the war clubs and hatchets of the warriors, in a reprise of C Company's demise. As wood, stone and metal crunched into the heads and bodies of the soldiers, desperation tuned to panic, and panic to thoughts of flight.

In the midst of this wild melee, Lame White Man was killed. Waterman, one of the five Arapahoes present, told Colonel Tim McCoy in 1920: "The soldiers were on the high ground and in one of the first charges we made a Cheyenne Chief named White Man Cripple was killed."[126] Yates' second-in-command, Second Lieutenant William Van Wyck Reily, fought his way a little further north but was then killed by Yellow Nose:

Custer [Reily] shouted loudly to his men and drew nearer to them when he found that they did [not] hear his voice. His appearance attracted the attention of Yellow Nose, who was armed with an old saber, having lost his gun. Custer's [Reily's] men had fallen beside him like grain before a sickle, and he stood alone when Yellow Nose drew his saber and tried to cut him down. The Indian's pony was wild, and when Custer [Reily] fired a pistol at close range the already wounded animal bolted and ran beyond him. Yellow Nose charged the second time, and again Custer [Reily] fired and the pony sprang to one side. Getting his pony firmly in hand for the onslaughts, Yellow Nose rode squarely down upon Custer [Reily], and without danger, as Custer [Reily] had fired his last shot. Custer [Reily] bent his knees as if to ward off the blow of the uplifted sword. He was struck on the back of his head and sank to the ground . . .[127]

Utterly routed, E Company was almost completely destroyed, but had taken most of the suicide boys with them. Wooden Leg named some of them: "Noisy Walking, Hump Nose, Whirlwind and Limber Bones."[128] Apart from Limber Bones all these young men were under twenty years old. Many warriors had also suffered a variety of wounds as they charged into the soldiers: "I saw one Sioux walking slowly toward the gulch, going away from where were the soldiers. . . . As he passed near to where I was I saw that his whole lower jaw was shot away. The sight of him made me sick. I had to vomit."[129] Amidst the heated cauldron of the close-quarter combat, it was almost inevitable that allies were mistaken for enemies. The Mnicoujou Standing Bear was involved in such an incident:

Burst Thunder . . . came up to us and told us to go down a little ways that there was a dead man here whom we should scalp (a Ree). So we went down and just as they scalped him there were two Cheyennes that came up to us. . . . One of the Cheyennes got off and turned the body over and found it was a Cheyenne that they had scalped. (This man was identified as Lame White Man.)[130]

Left Hand, one of the five Arapahoes present, made a similar mistake:

The soldiers were up on the ridge and the Indians were all around them. There was lots of shooting all around, and the Indians were all yelling. . . . I saw an Indian on foot, who was wounded in the leg, and, thinking he was one of the Crow or Arikara scouts with the soldiers, I rode at him, striking him with a long lance which I carried. The head of the lance was sharpened like an arrow. It struck him in the chest and went clear through him . . . Afterward I found out he was a Sioux . . .[131]

Many more warriors also died in the frantic fight for survival.

The survivors of E Company were few. Three, including "Fresh" Smith, did manage to escape to the relative safety of the F Company skirmish line on the lower slope of Last Stand Hill. Five others tried to escape to the east but were chased down and killed. Of the eight F Company men who had been sent to support E Company, three were found where the Deep Ravine fighting had taken place and the other five escaped with Smith to the north.

The seriousness of the situation was not lost on Armstrong Custer. He immediately sent Trumpeter Voss to Captain Yates with an order to shoot all the remaining horses for use as a defensive barricade. Some of the men wept as they shot the mounts that had been their faithful friends for so long, and the horses began to scream as they smelled the blood from those already killed. Higher up the slope, Lt. Colonel Custer still sat astride his ex-racehorse, the spirited gelding Vic, watching the warriors beginning to advance toward his remaining force. He could hear firing from the east which gave him one positive to pin some hopes on; there were no warriors attacking him from that direction, which he believed meant that Keogh's battalion was still holding its own and keeping warriors from coming up the eastern slopes. He could only hope now that Myles Keogh would find a way to unite with him.

RIGHT WING, 5:00–5:20 P.M.

Captain Keogh could only watch in dismay as C Company disintegrated under the warrior onslaught. Some survivors on foot were running towards L Company on Calhoun Hill whilst Sergeant Bobo was heading straight at Keogh's I Company position, closely followed by five other C Company men who had managed to mount their sorrel horses. Warrior fire killed Bobo's horse and he jumped from it as its lifeless body slid down from the crest of the ridge.[132]

Lieutenant Calhoun could see the panic-stricken men from C Company running to his position, though taking casualties all the time. Behind them came a mass of screaming warriors, some firing guns and arrows, some wielding their fearsome close-combat weapons, already dripping blood. To meet this imminent threat, Calhoun ordered Crittenden to switch the south-facing part of the skirmish line to face west. Waiting until the C Company men had cleared his line of fire, he ordered his skirmishers to open fire at the warriors. Many fell but the relentless swarm charged on.

The Oglala Red Hawk described the collapse of C Company and the charge against Calhoun's company:

> The officers tried their utmost to keep the soldiers together at this point, but the horses were unmanageable; they would rear up and fall backward with their riders; some would get away. The Indians forced the troopers back to where the first stand was made on Calhoun Hill and the ridge running from there to the river. At this place the soldiers stood in line and made a very good fight. The soldiers delivered volley after volley into the dense ranks of the Indians without any perceptible effect on account of their great numbers.[133]

Red Horse, a Mnicoujou, was equally graphic:

> One band of soldiers was right in rear of us; when they charged we fell back and stood for one moment facing each other. Then the Indians got courage and started for them in a solid body. We went but a little distance, when we spread out and encircled them. All the time I could see their officers riding in front, and hear them shouting to their men. It was in this charge that most of the Indians were killed. We lost 136 killed and 160 wounded. We finished up this party right there in the ravine.[134]

The heavy casualties did not deter the fired-up warriors, and as they got closer, some of the soldiers, already alarmed by seeing the frightened men of C Company running away, began to lose discipline. They began to edge closer to the men next to them instead of keeping their intervals. Their sweating hands fumbled the task of reloading their carbines, and the firing at the Indians became ragged. Even as the warrior horde crashed into them, some of Calhoun's men started fleeing towards Keogh's position on Battle Ridge. Calhoun and Crittenden tried desperately to rally their troopers but died in the attempt. Their bodies were found close together behind the line of their dead men. The fate of L Company was related by Red Hawk: "The Indians kept coming like an increasing flood which could not be checked. The soldiers were swept off their feet; they could not stay; the Indians were overwhelming. Here the troopers divided and retreated on each side of the ridge, falling back steadily to Custer Hill [Battle Ridge] where another stand was made."[135] Flying Hawk recounted: "When they found they were being killed so fast, the ones that were left broke and ran as fast as their horses could go to some other soldiers that were further along the ridge toward Custer."[136]

One soldier who did not take that course of action was the company's first sergeant, James Butler, a thirty-four-year-old veteran of known courage who raced to the south pursued by several warriors. His badly mutilated body, surrounded by a large number of cartridge shells, was found on the promontory that now bears his name, west of Luce Ridge. Dr. Charles Eastman, the Santee/white physician, was told about this by participants: "One company was chased along the ridge to the south, out of which a man got away. A mighty yell went up from the Indians as he cleared the attacking forces, as if they were glad that he succeeded. Away he went toward Reno's position."[137] Said Lieutenant Godfrey: "One of the first bodies I recognized . . . was that of Sergeant Butler. . . . The indications were that he sold his life dearly, for near and under him were found many empty cartridge-shells."[138] That is confirmed by the mutilations. The warriors did not want to face him again in the afterlife.

When Myles Keogh saw the huge numbers of warriors appear from behind Greasy Grass Ridge, almost immediately after Harrington's charge had chased away the infiltrators, he expected C Company to withdraw in orderly fashion after stopping the Indians with their firepower. What he saw instead was Harrington's command overrun and cut to pieces, with a few survivors running towards Calhoun, chased by scores of yelling warriors. He applauded silently when Lieutenant Calhoun swung Crittenden's squad to face the new threat. That confidence swiftly changed to alarm as the warriors kept on coming despite the withering fire from the L Company skirmish line. Now some of the warriors were firing at his own I Company exposed on the western military crest of Battle Ridge. He quickly ordered them to move over to the eastern military crest, even though they were exposed to some longer-distance firing from the Crazy Horse group behind the eastern ridge. It was there that Sergeant Bobo and the other five C Company men joined him.

Mounted on his horse Comanche, Keogh watched as L Company was in turn overwhelmed, and he prepared to organize his own company into the best defensive position he could. Before he could do that, events started to move rapidly out of his control. The survivors from his other two companies were running to their horses behind Calhoun Hill, but firing from Crazy Horse killed some of them and the horse-holders. As Flying Hawk recalled, "He shot them as fast as he could load his gun. They fell off their horses as fast as he could shoot. [Here the chief swayed rapidly back and forth to show how fast they fell.]"[139]

To assist the Calhoun Hill survivors to reach him safely, Keogh sent a squad from his company forward to fire at the chasing warriors. This distraction presented an opportunity for Crazy Horse to demonstrate just why he had such a highly respected reputation. Seeing the gap open up between the two sections of I Company, the Oglala war chief leaped on his pony and executed a bravery run through that gap. Several soldiers fired at him but none hit. Making a pirouette on his pony, Crazy Horse made a return run and again came through unscathed. His fellow tribesman Red Feather painted a picture of the incident. "While they were lying there, shooting at one another, Crazy Horse came up on horseback—with an eagle horn—and rode between the two parties. The soldiers all fired at once, but didn't hit him."[140] Other warriors, too, recalled this pivotal event. Another Oglala, He Dog stated, "Stretched along the ridge [on which the monument is now], there is a sort of gap in the ridge which Crazy Horse broke thru, cutting the line in two,"[141] and, "at Keogh is where Crazy Horse charged and broke through and split up soldiers in two bunches."[142]

Myles Keogh instantly recalled his forward squad, and the united I Company, with the remnants of the rest of the battalion, began to slowly move towards Last Stand Hill. But the bravery runs of Crazy Horse had fired up his followers even more, and he led them in a smashing charge against Keogh's back-pedaling force. This was immediately followed by an attack of the warriors coming from Calhoun Hill. Before he could rally his troops, Indian bullets shattered the left leg and knee of Myles Keogh and penetrated the right shoulder of Comanche. Squealing in pain the horse bucked wildly, throwing its rider as it galloped off toward the river. The gallant Irishman, crippled, unable to move but still clutching his revolver, died firing at the warriors who killed him. Two of his NCOs, Sergeant Bustard and First Sergeant Varden, tried to protect him but died in the attempt. Trumpeter John Patton fell dead across Keogh's body, while Private John Wild was also killed nearby. In fact nearly all of Keogh's I Company, only moments before a fighting force, now lay in heaps around their commander. Keogh's second in command, First Lieutenant James E. Porter, was not among them and his remains were never formally identified; but the finding of his bloodstained buckskin-coat lining with a bullet hole in the back left no doubt about his fate. Fate also caught up with Sergeant Bobo, who had escaped the annihilation of C Company, only to be killed with Keogh.[143] The five C Company men who had followed Bobo did not stop long once they saw the oncoming Indian threat. They spurred their horses toward Last Stand Hill.

Some warrior accounts tell of the last throes of Keogh's panic-stricken command. Having described how Crazy Horse had shot at the horse-holders behind Calhoun Hill, Flying Hawk went on: ". . . we rushed them on along the ridge to where Custer was. Then they made another stand (the third) and rallied a few minutes. They went on along the ridge and got with Custer's men. . . . Other Indians came to us after we got most of the men at ravine. We all kept after them until they got to where Custer was. There was only a few of them left then."[144]

The Mnicoujou warrior Hump observed, "The first charge the Indians made they never slacked up or stopped. They made a finish of it. The Indians and whites were so mixed up that you could hardly tell anything about it. The first dash the Indians made my horse was shot from under me and I was wounded—shot above the knee, and the ball came out at the hip . . . and I fell and lay right there."[145]

Having seen the Crazy Horse bravery runs, Red Feather said, "The Indians got the idea the soldiers' guns were empty and charged immediately on the soldiers. They charged right over the hill. Red Feather, yelling, shot into the soldiers who tried to get away. That made it easier for the Indians, who shot them from behind."[146] The effect of all this on the soldiers was noticed by Red Horse. "When we attacked the other party, we swarmed down on them and drove them in confusion. The soldiers became panic-stricken many of them throwing down their arms and throwing up their hands."[147]

Indian accounts also tell of how some survivors, both on foot and mounted, fled in the direction of Last Stand Hill. Foolish Elk said:

> It did not appear to him that a stand was made by Custer's men any-
> where except at the monument. He was in the gully and saw the sol-

diers killed on the side hill [Keogh] as they "marched" toward the high ground at end of ridge [monument]. They made no stand here, but all were going toward the high ground at end of ridge. . . . The men on horses did not stop to fight. . . . The men on foot, however, were shooting as they passed along.[148]

Turtle Rib, too, remarked: "When he got up with the soldiers, there was a running fight with some of the soldiers on foot. Those who kept their horses seemed to be stampeded. Some were going toward the monument, and some were trying to go back the way they came."[149]

However many may have tried to escape to join the Headquarters Group, some did not make it. Only about ten utterly traumatized soldiers reached the Left Wing's position on the hill. The escapees must have been overcome with relief at avoiding the fate of their comrades on Battle Ridge; they could not know that their reprieve was only temporary.

LEFT WING, 5:10–5:20 P.M.

Whatever hope Armstrong Custer entertained of being reunited with Keogh's battalion was even now being destroyed by Crazy Horse and a host of other warriors in the swale to the east of Battle Ridge. Of course he did not know that, but in any case he was faced with pressing problems of his own. Warriors were flooding through Deep Ravine and the coulees around his position, as well as using every piece of cover on the terrain leading up from the river.

Having overcome E Company, the warriors' blood was up and they were determined to come to grips with what remained of the Yates group. Following the destruction of the Right Wing, Crazy Horse and his victorious fighters now also swept towards Last Stand Hill from the east. The Hunkpapa Iron Hawk modestly described the impending storm: "Crazy Horse at one end, and Iron Hawk was on the side toward the ridge and between the ridge and the river in the attack on Custer. They surrounded Custer."[150]

Before this new throng of warriors reached him, Custer's hopes of a union with Keogh were totally shattered when the five C Company men galloped into view. They quickly confirmed that the Right Wing had been destroyed by warriors attacking from the eastern slopes of Battle Ridge, and Custer instantly knew that he would have to organize a defense against the inevitable attack from that direction. He ordered the C Company men to lead their horses to the crest of the hill where they were to shoot them for use as a protective barrier against firing from the east and southeast. As soon as that had been done, Custer deployed a small force to defend the position until Yates could redeploy F Company. Apart from himself there were his brothers Tom and Boston, his nephew Autie Reed, Adjutant Cooke, Mitch Boyer, Sergeant Robert Hughes, Sergeant John Vickory and Chief Trumpeter Henry Voss, plus the five C Company escapees. They waited for the onslaught as the pounding of Indian ponies' hooves could be heard coming closer.

Lower down the hill, Captain George Yates and his F Company lay behind the barriers of dead horses they had created earlier, already receiving bullets and arrows as the wily warriors used every scrap of cover to creep closer. Runs The Enemy, who had just come from fighting near Battle Ridge, told how:

> I left my men there and told them to hold that position and then I rushed around the hills and came up to the north end of the field near where the monument now stands. And I saw hundreds and hundreds of Indians in the coulees all around. The Indians dismounted and tied their horses in a bunch and got down into the coulees, shooting at the soldiers from all sides.[151]

Gall related what he saw of the F Company defense: "They were fighting good. The men were loading and firing, but they could not hit the warriors in the gully and in the ravine. The dust and smoke was as black evening."[152]

Just below the crest of the hill and behind the five dead horses, Armstrong Custer and his small group had now come under fire from the warriors coming from the Right Wing fight. Among them was Crazy Horse. Time was running out for the Boy General of the Civil War.

LEFT WING, 5:20–5:30 P.M.

Without horses there were no longer any cavalrymen on Last Stand Hill, and they were ill-prepared to fight an infantry action against a highly mobile foe. The Cheyenne woman Kate Big Head, or Antelope Woman, observed how the warriors were able to avoid being hit: "At that time there must have been hundreds of warriors for every white soldier left alive. The warriors around them were shifting from shelter to shelter, each of them trying to get close enough to strike a coup blow. . . . The remaining soldiers were keeping themselves behind their dead horses."[153] Individual warriors dared to dart forward and kill a soldier with a club or axe, but not all escaped unscathed. Kate Big Head saw "one Sioux boy killed by a soldier bullet,"[154] and Wooden Leg described how, "A Sioux wearing a warbonnet was lying down behind a clump of sagebrush on the hillside. . . . The Sioux was peeping up and firing a rifle from time to time. At one of these times a soldier bullet hit him exactly in the middle of the forehead."[155]

With little effective fire coming from the soldiers, it only needed a catalyst to spur the warriors into direct action. A lull in the firing was all the warriors needed. Believing most of the soldiers dead, they rushed forward, only to be met by the majority of F Company, very much alive. Hand-to-hand fighting followed, and what happened made a lasting impression on the warriors who were there. Said Turtle Rib, "No stand was made except at the end of the long ridge (where Custer fell), and here the bay and gray horses were all mixed together. There was a big dust, and the Indians were running all around the locality much excited and shooting into the soldiers."[156] Red Hawk stated, "Here the troopers divided and retreated on each side of the ridge, falling back steadily to Custer Hill where another stand was made. By this time the Indians were taking the guns and cartridges of the dead soldiers and putting these to use and were more active in the struggle. Here the soldiers made a desperate fight."[157]

Even as this desperate fighting was going on, the Custer group at the top of the hill was coming under increasing pressure. Subjected to rifle fire from the east, southeast, north and northwest, the ten men did not have enough firepower to hurt the warriors. Having watched the action for a while, Crazy Horse thought it was time he took a hand. He mounted his pony and led a charge over the dead horses atop Last Stand Hill. The result was devastating for the gallant little band of defenders. Brevet Major General George Armstrong Custer suffered a severe chest wound and Cooke, Vickory and Voss were left dead or dying, leaving only Tom Custer, brother Boston, Autie Reed, Mitch Boyer, Sergeant Hughes and perhaps some of the C Company men to fight on. The impact of Crazy Horse was recorded by the Arapahoe Waterman: "There was a great deal of noise and confusion. The air was heavy with powder smoke, and the Indians were all yelling. Crazy Horse, the Sioux Chief, was the bravest man I ever saw. He rode closest to the soldiers, yelling to his warriors. All the soldiers were shooting at him, but he was never hit."[158] It was nearing the end for the five companies that had ridden with Custer.

NO SURVIVORS, 5:30 P.M.

The tide of battle that had swept over the Keogh battalion now became a tsunami that destroyed what remained of the Left Wing, as the shrieking, whooping warriors swarmed over them. The frenzy of the fighting was graphically depicted by the Mnicoujou, Beard:

> Hundreds of other warriors joined us as we splashed across the ford near our camp and raced up the hills to charge into the thickest of the fighting. This new battle was a turmoil of dust and warriors and soldiers, with bullets whining and arrows hissing all around. Sometimes a bugle would sound and the shooting would get louder. Some of the soldiers were firing pistols at close range. Our knives and war clubs flashed in the sun. I could hear bullets whiz past my ears. But I kept going and shouting, "It's a good day to die!" so that everyone who heard would know I was not afraid of being killed in battle.[159]

The soldiers' revolvers were only effective for a very short time, for once emptied there was no time to reload. As clubs they were no match for the lethal close-combat weapons of the warriors. Once the high-pitched cracks of the six-shooters fell silent, the troopers received wicked blows to their heads, some from stone-headed clubs that caved their skulls in, splattering their brains and further unnerving their comrades. It was a charnel house of death from which no white man survived. Some did try to flee to safety and several warriors noticed them. Waterman remarked, "The soldiers were entirely surrounded and the whole country was alive with Indians. There were thousands of them. A few soldiers tried to get away and reach the river, but they were all killed."[160] Lone Bear responded to Camp, "Q: In the last stand at 'G' (Last Stand Hill), did the soldiers all fight to the last, or did some try to break away and escape? A: Soldiers were fighting hard at 'G.' There were a few who tried to get away."[161] And Respects Nothing told Eli Ricker:

> At any rate, he said that those were all killed at Custer Hill before those were down along the ravine. These latter, when the others were down, made a break through a narrow gap in the Indian line and ran toward the river trying to escape. They were on foot. The Indians followed them and killed them with war clubs of stone and wooden clubs, some of the latter having lance spears on them. In this pursuit

one Indian stumbled into a low place, among the soldiers, and was killed by them.[162]

The few at the top of the Hill fared no better. A badly wounded Armstrong Custer was spared the possibility of being captured alive when brother Tom shot him in the head with a small-caliber Colt carried by his elder brother.[163] Tom—twice a Medal of Honor winner in the Civil War and a fierce fighter—took some warriors with him as he died, and his body was therefore savagely dealt with later. The Ree interpreter Frederic F. Gerard told Walter Camp, "Tom Custer—they had smashed back of his head in with a stone or hammer and shot an arrow into top of his skull."[164] Adjutant Cooke's Dundreary whiskers were commented on by Wooden Leg: "Here is a new kind of scalp,"[165] as he skinned one side of Cooke's face. Others who had been in the hilltop group tried frantically to flee to what they saw as the safety of the timbered river area. They did not make it. Custer's brother Boston and their cousin Autie Reed were killed quite soon after they ran from the knoll. Near them fell Private Weston Harrington of L Company, then lower down, near Deep Ravine, the scout Mitch Boyer and Sergeant Robert H. Hughes of the Headquarters Group, both slain by the frenzied warriors. Private Timothy Donnelly of F Company also made it that far but no further. Red Hawk saw it all: "What was left of them retreated to (what he calls) the third stand. These were surrounded and the Indians rushed on the soldiers. Some of the soldiers broke through the Indians and ran for the ravine, but were all killed without getting into it."[166]

These final scenes were etched into the memory of Runs The Enemy:

The soldiers then gathered in a group, where the monument now stands—I visited the monument today and confirmed my memory of it—and then the soldiers and Indians were all mixed up. You could not tell one from the other. In this final charge I took part and when the last soldier was killed the smoke rolled up like a mountain above our heads, and the soldiers were piled one on top of another, dead, and here and there an Indian among the soldiers. I saw one that had been hit across the head with a war axe, and others had been hit with arrows. After we were done, we went back to the camp.[167]

It would be a camp where many Cheyenne and Lakota lodges would be in mourning. Their dead warriors would be sent to the afterworld with all their lives' honors intoned over their bodies. Many of the corpses of the white soldiers were so badly mutilated that their initial shallow gravesites would be marked with just one word—"Unknown."

NOTES

1. Naturally, the conclusions drawn in this chapter are Gordon Richard's, but they are drawn from mostly primary sources to which, in some cases, has been added reasonable possibility. Like all theories about what happened to Armstrong Custer and the five companies of his regiment after they reached Medicine Tail Coulee, these will be hotly debated, and no doubt hotly disputed by some. That is to be expected, because the fate of Custer and his 209 men will ever remain a mystery.

2. Marguerite Merington, *The Custer Story: The Life and Intimate Letters of General George A. Custer and His Wife Elizabeth* (Lincoln & London: University of Nebraska Press, 1987), p.65.

3. Ronald H. Nichols, *Reno Court of Inquiry Proceedings of a Court of Inquiry in the case of Major Marcus A. Reno* (Hardin, Montana: Custer Battlefield Historical & Museum Association, Inc., 1996), pp.421, 427.

4. Ibid, pp.563, 580.

5. W. A. Graham, *The Custer Myth: A Source Book of Custeriana* (Harrisburg, Pennsylvania: The Stackpole Company, 1953), p.138.

6. George M. Clark, *Scalp Dance: The Edgerly Papers on the Battle of the Little Big Horn* (Oswego, New York: Heritage Press, 1985), p.16.

7. Barry C. Johnson, *George Herendeen: The Life of a Montana Scout in "More Sidelights of the Sioux Wars"* (London: Westerners Publications Limited, 2004), p.18.

8. J. M. Carroll, *General Custer and the Battle of the Little Big Horn: The Federal View* (New Brunswick, New Jersey: The Garry Owen Press, 1976), p.102.

9. Herbert A. Coffeen, *The Tepee Book* (Volume II, No.VI, June 1916, Sheridan, Wyoming: Coffeen).

10. Jay Smith, "What Did Not Happen at The Battle of the Little Big Horn," *Research Review: The Journal of the Little Big Horn Associates* (Vol. 6, No.2, Saline, June 1992, MI: McNaughton & Gunn, Inc.), p.10.

11. Jay Smith, "The Indian Fighting Army," *Research Review: The Journal of the Little Big Horn Associates* (Vol. 3, No.1, June 1989, Dexter, MI: Thomson-Shore, Inc.), p.8.

12. Nichols, *Reno Court of Inquiry*, p.332.

13. Ibid.

14. Clark, *Scalp Dance*, pp.16–17.

15. John D. Mackintosh, *Custer's Southern Officer: Captain George D. Wallace 7th U.S. Cavalry* (Lexington, South Carolina: Cloud Creek Press, 2002), pp.110–111 and endnote.

16. Charles Varnum, "A Letter of July 4 1876, to his Parents," printed in the Lowell Weekly Journal (August 1876).

17. Nichols, Reno Court of Inquiry, p.235.
18. Carroll, *General Custer and the Battle of the Little Big Horn: The Federal View*, p.105.
19. Captain E. S. Godfrey, 7th Cavalry, *Custer's Last Battle 1876* (Olympic Valley, California: Outbooks, 1976, reprinted from *The Century Magazine*, January 1892), p.19.
20. Nichols, *Reno Court of Inquiry*, p.388.
21. Edward Settle Godfrey, *The Field Diary* (Portland, Oregon: The Champoeg Press, 1957), p.20.
22. O. G. Libby, *The Arikara Narrative of the Campaign Against the Hostile Dakotas June, 1876* (New York: Sol Lewis, 1973), p.159.
23. Herbert A. Coffeen, *The Custer Battle Book* (New York: Carlton Press, 1964), pp.48–49.
24. Ibid, p.49.
25. Fred Dustin, *The Custer Tragedy* (El Segundo, California: Upton & Sons Publishers, 1987), xiv.
26. Kenneth Hammer (ed.), *Custer in '76: Walter Camp's Notes on the Custer Fight* (Provo, Utah: Brigham Young University Press, 1976), p.175.
27. Ibid, pp.174, 175.
28. Graham, *The Custer Myth*, pp. 17, 18.
29. James H. Bradley, *The March of the Montana Column* (Norman: University of Oklahoma Press, 1961), pp.152, 153.
30. Thomas B. Marquis, *Rain-in-the-Face/Curly, The Crow* (Scottsdale, Arizona: Cactus Pony, 1934), p.6.
31. Ibid, p.7.
32. Ibid.
33. Libby, *The Arikara Narrative*, pp.119–120.
34. Hammer, *Custer in '76*, p.214.
35. Daniel Knipe: account from *Montana Historical Society Contributions* (Volume 4, 1903, Helena, Montana: Rocky Mountain Publishing Company) [ebook] Appendix, 3.64.
36. Nichols, *Reno Court of Inquiry*, p.16.
37. Hammer, *Custer in '76*, p.101.
38. Thomas B. Marquis, *Wooden Leg: A Warrior who Fought Custer* (Lincoln and London: University of Nebraska Press, 1971), p.206.
39. Richard G. Hardorff, *Lakota Recollections of the Custer Fight* (Spokane, Washington: The Arthur H. Clark Company, 1991), p.75.
40. Hammer, *Custer in '76*, p.206.
41. Richard G. Hardorff, *Cheyenne Memories of the Custer Fight* (Spokane, Washington: The Arthur H. Clark Company, 1995), p.90.
42. Marquis, *Wooden Leg*, p.229.
43. Joseph K. Dixon, *The Vanishing Race: The Last Great Indian Council* (Amsterdam, The Netherlands: Fredonia Books, 2004), p.181.
44. John Stands In Timber & Margot Liberty, *Cheyenne Memories* (Lincoln & London: University of Nebraska Press, 1972), p.198.
45. Ibid.
46. Ibid, p.199.

47. Ibid

48. George Bird Grinnell, *The Fighting Cheyennes* (Norman: University of Oklahoma Press, 1983), p.350.

49. Hardorff, *Cheyenne Memories*, p.29.

50. Ibid, pp.35, 36.

51. Ibid, pp.39, 40.

52. Ibid, p.43.

53. Ibid, p.47.

54. Ibid, p.51.

55. Ibid, p.52.

56. Ibid, p.53.

57. Ibid, p.169.

58. John Gibbon, *Gibbon on the Sioux Campaign of 1876: Hunting Sitting Bull* (Bellevue, Nebraska: The Old Army Press, 1970, Reprinted from The American Catholic Quarterly Review, October 1877), p.39.

59. Bruce A. Trinque, "The Fight in Fishing Woman Ravine" in John P. Hart, *Custer and His Times Book Four* (Dexter, Michigan: Thomson-Shore, Inc., Little Big Horn Associates, Inc., 2002), p.214.

60. Ibid.

61. Ibid.

62. Michael N. Donahue, *Drawing Battle Lines: The Map Testimony of Custer's Last Fight* (El Segundo, California: Upton and Sons, Publishers, 2008), pp.97, 139.

63. Trinque, "The Fight in Fishing Woman Ravine," p.216.

64. Ibid, p.217.

65. Ibid.

66. Marquis, *Wooden Leg*, p.204.

67. Ibid, p.214.

68. Hammer, *Custer in '76*, p.198.

69. Hardorff, *Lakota Recollections*, p.137.

70. Ibid, p.104.

71. Ibid, p.68.

72. Ibid, p.181.

73. Hammer, *Custer in '76*, pp.212, 213.

74. Ibid, p.116.

75. Richard G. Hardorff, *The Custer Battle Casualties: Burials, Exhumations and Reinterments* (El Segundo, California: Upton and Sons, Publishers, 1990), p.114.

76. Hammer, *Custer in '76*, p.202.

77. Ibid, p.207.

78. Hardorff, *Lakota Recollections*, p.86.

79. Marquis, *Wooden Leg*, p.232.

80. Hammer, *Custer in '76*, p.254.

81. Richard G. Hardorff, *Walter M. Camp's Little Bighorn Rosters* (Spokane, Washington, The Arthur H. Clark Company, 2002), p.61.

82. Richard G. Hardorff, *On the Little Bighorn with Walter Camp: A Collection of W. M.*

Camp's Letters, Notes and Opinions on Custer's Last Fight (El Segundo, California, Upton & Sons, Publishers, 2002), p.41.

83. Hardorff, *Lakota Recollections*, p.31.

84. Ibid, p.143.

85. David Humphreys Miller, *Custer's Fall: The Indian Side of the Story* (Lincoln & London: University of Nebraska Press, 1985), p.139.

86. Richard Allan Fox, Jr., *Archaeology, History, and Custer's Last Battle* (Norman & London: University of Oklahoma Press, 1993), p.245.

87. Trinque, "The Fight in Fishing Woman Ravine," p.219.

88. Nichols, *Reno Court of Inquiry*, p.322.

89. Hardorff, *Cheyenne Memories*, p.53.

90. Yellow Nose, "Yellow Nose Tells of Custer's Last Stand," *Bighorn Yellowstone Journal* (Howell: Powder River Press, Vol.1. No.3, Summer 1992; taken from the *Indian School Journal*, November 1908), p.16.

91. Unpublished Mnicoujou oral history in the collection of Gordon Harper.

92. Douglas D. Scott, Richard A. Fox, Jr., Melissa A. Connor and Dick Harmon, *Archaeological Perspectives on the Battle of the Little Bighorn* (Norman and London: University of Oklahoma Press, 1989), p.121.

93. Hardorff, *Cheyenne Memories*, pp.52, 53.

94. D. H. Miller, "Echoes of the Little Bighorn" (*American Heritage* 22 (4), 28–39, 1971), p.34.

95. Dixon, *The Vanishing Race*, p.181.

96. Miller, "Echoes of the Little Bighorn", p.34.

97. Hardorff, *Cheyenne Memories*, p.170.

98. Hardorff, *Lakota Recollections*, p.59.

99. Marquis, *Wooden Leg*, p.230.

100. Dixon, *The Vanishing Race*, p.175.

101. Graham, *The Custer Myth*, p.103.

102. Hardorff, *Cheyenne Memories*, p.170.

103. Ibid, p.52.

104. Miller, "Echoes of the Little Bighorn", p.34.

105. Ibid.

106. M. I. McCreight, *Firewater and Forked Tongues: A Sioux Chief Interprets U.S. History* (Pasadena, California: Trails End Publishing, 1947), pp.112–113.

107. James McLaughlin, *My Friend The Indian* (Boston & New York: Houghton Mifflin Company, 1910), p.174.

108. Stanley Vestal, *Warpath: The True Story of the Fighting Sioux: Told in a Biography of Chief White Bull* (Lincoln & London: University of Nebraska Press, 1984), p.195.

109. Hammer, *Custer in '76*, pp.198, 199.

110. Marquis, *Wooden Leg*, pp.230, 231.

111. Ibid, p.231.

112. Hardorff, *Cheyenne Memories*, pp.66, 67.

113. Stanley Vestal, *Interview with White Bull (Mnicoujou) in 1932* (in the personal papers of Walter Stanley Campbell at The University of Oklahoma Libraries).

114. Nichols, *Reno Court of Inquiry*, p.236.

115. Hardorff, *Lakota Recollections*, p.104.

116. McLaughlin, *My Friend The Indian*, p.173.

117. Hardorff, *Lakota Recollections*, p.95.

118. Carroll, John M. (ed.), *A Seventh Cavalry Scrapbook #11* (Bryan, Tx), pp.9–10; Reno, Major Marcus A., Interview in Philadelphia Press reported in the *Army & Navy Journal* (November 26, 1887).

119. Miller, "Echoes of the Little Bighorn," p.35.

120. McCreight, *Firewater*, p.113.

121. Marquis, *Wooden Leg*, p.231.

122. Ibid.

123. John Stands In Timber, *Cheyenne Memories*, pp.200, 201.

124. Ibid.

125. Ibid.

126. Graham, *The Custer Myth*, p.110.

127. Yellow Nose, *Yellow Nose Tells of Custer's Last Stand*. Yellow Nose misidentifies Reily as Custer, but only officer fitting Yellow Nose's description is Reily.

128. Marquis, *Wooden Leg*, p.268.

129. Ibid, 234.

130. Raymond J. DeMallie, *The Sixth Grandfather: Black Elk's Teachings Given to John G. Neihardt* (Lincoln & London: University of Nebraska Press, 1984), p.186.

131. Graham, *The Custer Myth*, p.111.

132. Hardorff, *The Custer Battle Casualties: Burials*, p.108.

133. Hardorff, *Lakota Recollections*, p.43.

134. Graham, *The Custer Myth*, p.60.

135. Hardorff, *Lakota Recollections*, p.44.

136. McCreight, *Firewater*, p.113.

137 Dr. Charles Eastman, "The Story of the Little Big Horn," *Chautauquan Magazine* (Volume XXXI, No.4, 1900).

138. Godfrey, *Custer's Last Battle*, p.35.

139. McCreight, *Firewater*, p.113.

140. Hardorff, *Lakota Recollections*, pp.87, 88.

141. Ibid, p.75.

142. Hammer, *Custer in '76*, p.207.

143. Hammer, *Custer in '76*, p.95.

144. McCreight, *Firewater*, p.113.

145. Graham, *The Custer Myth*, p.78.

146. Hardorff, *Lakota Recollections*, p.88.

147. Graham, *The Custer Myth*, p.60.

148. Hammer, *Custer in '76*, p.199.

149. Ibid, p.201.

150. Hardorff, *Lakota Recollections*, p.66.

151. Dixon, *The Vanishing Race*, p.175.

152. Usher L. Burdick, *David F. Barry's Indian Notes on "The Custer Battle"* (Baltimore:

Wirth Brothers, 1949), p.27.

153. Thomas B. Marquis, *Custer On The Little Bighorn: She Watched Custer's Last Battle* (Lodi, California: End-Kian Publishing Company, 1967), p.39.

154. Leslie Tillett, *Wind On The Buffalo Grass: The Indians' Own Account of the Battle at the Little Big Horn River, & the Death of their life on the Plains* (New York: Thomas Y. Crowell Company, 1976), p.54.

155. Marquis, *Wooden Leg*, p.236.

156. Hammer, *Custer in '76*, pp.201, 202.

157. Hardorff, *Lakota Recollections*, p.44.

158. Graham, *The Custer Myth*, p.110.

159. Miller, "Echoes of the Little Bighorn", p.38.

160. Graham, *The Custer Myth*, p.110.

161. Hardorff, *Lakota Recollections*, p.157.

162. Ibid, p.32.

163. Ralph Heinz, "Bigelow Neal and Dr. Porter" in John B. Hart, *Custer and His Times: Book Four* (Dexter, Michigan: Thomson-Shore, Inc., Little Big Horn Associates, Inc., 2002), p.228. Porter thought that Armstrong Custer shot himself. As the wound was in his left temple and he was right-handed, I believe otherwise.

164. Hammer, *Custer in '76*, p.237.

165. Marquis, *Wooden Leg*, p.240.

166. Hardorff, *Lakota Recollections*, p.44.

167. Tillett, *Wind On The Buffalo Grass*, pp.81, 82.

ANALYSES

THE QUESTION OF
DISOBEDIENCE

*"I do not tell you this to cast any reflection upon Custer...
but I feel that our plan must have been successful had it
been carried out ..."*—BRIGADIER GENERAL A.H.
TERRY: CONFIDENTIAL REPORT OF JULY 2, 1876

No narrative of the Little Horn campaign would be complete without a
close look at one of the most controversial and lingering questions:
did George Armstrong Custer disobey his orders? If he did so, did he
do it deliberately and "with malice aforethought"? That is, had he planned
to do so all along, and was he just waiting for the right opportunity?

Despite the stated opinions of some other writers, the controversy had
its roots in actions taken immediately after the battle. That is not difficult to
understand. Imagine yourself as one of the major players; suppose you were
Reno or Benteen or Terry or Gibbon, or even Sheridan, Sherman or Grant.
How would you have felt when the initial shock of learning of the Custer disaster abated? Do you think you might have been a bit apprehensive of the
public's reaction and your superiors' easily anticipated search for scapegoats?
Is it surprising to learn that the defensive works started going up right away?
I think not.

It is all these defensive mechanisms that have raised the question at all.
It should have been a fairly simple exercise to determine whether Custer

violated the letter or spirit of his orders and it should be just as simple today. Actually, it is: it is only the attempts to obfuscate the truth over the years that make it at all difficult. To see the truth one must first clear away the fog and the obfuscations that have been heaped upon one another.

Simple logic says that either Custer received orders or he did not; that he either obeyed them or he did not; that whatever he did, he did deliberately or he did not. There are not a great many permutations and combinations involved here. The problems arise only because one must deal with all of the obfuscating analyses that have been introduced into the process, and the historian has to present the divergent views and the reasons for them, in order for the simple truth to emerge.

Let us examine the first variable. Either Custer received orders or he did not—very straightforward, right? Wrong! Certainly Custer received instructions, but were they positive orders in the military sense? Some say yes and some say no. The actual document reads as follows:

>   Headquarters Department of Dakota (In the Field)
>   Camp at Mouth of Rosebud River
>   Montana, June 22, 1876
>
> Lieut. Col. G.A. Custer, 7th Cavalry
> Colonel:
> The Brigadier-General commanding directs that as soon as your regiment can be made ready for the march, you will proceed up the Rosebud in pursuit of the Indians whose trail was discovered by Major Reno a few days since. It is, of course, impossible to give you any definite instructions in regard to this movement, and were it not impossible to do so, the Department Commander places too much confidence in your zeal, energy, and ability to wish to impose upon you precise orders which might hamper your action when nearly in contact with the enemy. He will, however, indicate to you his own views of what your action should be, and he desires that you should conform to them unless you shall see sufficient reason for departing from them. He thinks that you should proceed up the Rosebud until you ascertain definitely the direction in which the trail above spoken of leads. Should it be found (as it appears almost certain that it will be found) to turn towards the Little Horn, he thinks that you should still proceed southward, perhaps as far as the headwaters of the

Tongue, and then turn towards the Little Horn, feeling constantly, however, to your left, so as to preclude the possibility of the escape of the Indians to the south or southeast by passing around your left flank. The column of Colonel Gibbon is now in motion for the mouth of the Big Horn. As soon as it reaches that point it will cross the Yellowstone and move up at least as far as the forks of the Big and Little Horns. Of course its future movements must be controlled by circumstances as they arise, but it is hoped that the Indians, if upon the Little Horn, may be so nearly enclosed by the two columns that their escape will be impossible.

The Department Commander desires that on your way up the Rosebud you should thoroughly examine the upper part of Tullock's Creek, and that you should endeavor to send a scout through to Colonel Gibbon's column, with information of the result of your examination. The lower part of the creek will be examined by a detachment from Colonel Gibbon's command. The supply steamer will be pushed up the Big Horn as far as the forks if the river is found to be navigable for that distance, and the Department Commander, who will accompany the column of Colonel Gibbon, desires you to report to him there not later than the expiration of the time for which your troops are rationed, unless in the meantime you receive further orders.

Very respectfully,

Your obedient servant,

E.W. Smith, Captain, 18th Infantry,

Acting Assistant Adjutant-General.[1]

These are the only written instructions that Custer received in regard to his movement up the Rosebud. They seem rather explicit and remarkably straightforward. But before we consider them, we have to deal with one of those obfuscating analyses mentioned earlier.

In 1892, Edward S. Godfrey, commander of K Company at the Little Horn, published a lengthy article in *The Century Magazine* on the battle. In it, he reproduced the written instructions under which Custer operated. One result of the article was a letter to Godfrey from James Brisbin, who was Gibbon's cavalry commander. In his diatribe to Godfrey, Brisbin condemns Custer as a madman and says, among other things:

I read the order you print as being the one given to Custer by Terry for his march. If that is the order Custer got, it is not the one copied in Terry's books at Department Headquarters. You will remember that after Custer fell, Terry appointed me his chief of cavalry. I looked over all the papers affecting the march and battle of Little Big Horn and took a copy of the order sending you up the Rosebud. That order now lies before me, and it says: "It is desired that you conform as nearly as possible to these instructions, and that you do not depart from them unless you see absolute necessity for doing so."[2]

Brisbin however, was in error. The written instructions were exactly as Godfrey had stated in his article and exactly as reproduced *in toto* above. Brisbin was a bitter and jealous man when he wrote to Godfrey. He had his own axe to grind, but it would be charitable to take the view that his memory simply played tricks on him. His letter contains a great many other inaccuracies and unfortunately was used by several writers to buttress their own recriminations against Custer.

So the one document remains. The initial question is: "Are these orders?" The answer is: "No, they are not!" It is a letter of instructions, which is something quite different. This is evident from the fact that the document is not identified by Terry as an order, as it is not numbered as such (and is the only instruction associated with an independent movement during the Indian Campaign of 1876 that is not so identified and so numbered); and from the actual wording of the document, which contains only one order: ". . . directs that, as soon as your regiment can be made ready for the march, you will proceed . . ." That is the typical wording of an order, the commander "directs" or else he "orders." He does not "suggest" or "desire" and he does not use the word "should" as in "you should." He says: "you will."

Several writers who should have known better have claimed that the "suggests" and the "desires" and the "shoulds" have all the import and force of the more formal words, but that is untrue. It is also unnecessary.

Within the body of the instructions there are many indications that Terry did not and could not have considered the instructions to be either orders or, what is more important, binding upon Custer in any real sense of the word. How can one know this? He says so!

After giving Custer a direct order in the first sentence of the letter, Terry says: "It is, of course, impossible to give you any definite instructions in regard to this movement . . . " Does any person possessed of reasonable intelligence believe that he would then go on to do what he has just said it was impossible to do? The Custer detractors believe that—or would have everyone believe that. Then Terry says that even if it were not impossible he "places too much confidence in your . . . ability to wish to impose upon you precise orders."

Of Gibbon's column Terry says ". . . its future movements must be controlled by circumstances as they arise . . . " and of the Indians he states that ". . . it is hoped that the Indians, if upon the Little Horn, may be nearly enclosed . . . that their escape will be impossible." Of the supposed rendezvous with Gibbon's column on the Little Horn, he says nothing and gives no date or timetable other than " . . . report to him there not later than the expiration of the time for which your troops are rationed . . . " Hardly the background for orders, but precisely the wording one would expect in a letter of instructions.

So here is Terry saying, in effect, that he is ordering Custer "in pursuit" of the Indians who may be on the Little Horn, that he can't give Custer precise orders—and wouldn't do so even if he could—that Gibbon's column is moving " . . . at least as far as the forks of the Big and Little Horns . . . " in a movement which " . . . must be controlled by circumstances . . . " and that he desires that Custer report to him there "no later than the expiration of the time for which you troops are rationed . . . " How anyone can construe this document as conveying anything other than the one specific order is simply beyond understanding, and it is perfectly obvious that Terry, who was nobody's fool, never intended them to be other than what they are.

It becomes obvious then that Custer could not disobey his orders, since he did not receive any—except the pursuit order, which he certainly obeyed.

Custer's apologists have argued that even if these were orders, he was given wide latitude in digressing from them, especially "when nearly in contact with the enemy," and they go on to show what circumstances arose and why Custer did what he did. All of which may be true, but none of which is necessary. And the Custer "antis" go to great lengths to refute all of the "pros'" efforts, again something which is not necessary. They especially argue that Custer would never have come "nearly in contact" had he not disobeyed his instructions.

The phrase "when nearly in contact with the enemy" appears in the second sentence of the letter, and is followed immediately by the "he will, however, indicate" portion. It is obvious that the "when nearly in contact" phrase refers to the date and place of the issuance of the instructions, not to some distant time and place. Even if it did not—even if all of the logic applied so far has failed to establish the sole truth—there is one tiny word that almost every writer/historian/critic has overlooked—although John Gray and Larry Frost noticed it—it is the word "you." As in " . . . unless you should see sufficient reason for departing from them . . . " Thus it is Custer, not Terry, nor anyone else, who had the final say in what he did and more importantly, why he did it. That one little word simply means that Custer could not disobey his orders, even if it is conceded that they were orders.

One other person who noticed the little word was Jacob Greene, who had been Custer's adjutant during the Civil War. In Cyrus Brady's book *Indian Fights and Fighters*, there is a very interesting and comprehensive discussion of whether or not Custer disobeyed his orders—Brady thinks he did—and Greene was asked by Libbie Custer to reply to Brady on her behalf. Greene's letter, dated September 1, 1904, is a masterpiece of logic and simplicity, as demonstrated in the following excerpt:

> In other words, the charge of disobedience can never be proved. The proof does not exist. The evidence in the case forever lacks the principal witness whose one and only definite order was to take his regiment and go "in pursuit of the Indians whose trail was discovered by Major Reno a few days since." They were the objective; they were to be located and their escape prevented. That was Custer's task. All the details were left, and necessarily left, to his discretion. All else in the order of June 22nd conveys merely the views of the commander to be followed "unless you should see sufficient reasons for departing from them." The argument that Custer disobeyed this order seems to resolve itself into two main forms. One is trying to read into the order a precision and a peremptory character which are not there and which no ingenuity can put there, and to empty it of a discretion which is there and is absolute; the other is in assuming or asserting that Custer departed from General Terry's views without "sufficient reasons." And this line of argument rests in part upon the imputation to Custer of a motive and intent which was evil throughout, and in part upon what his critic, in the light of later knowledge and the vain regrets of hindsight, thinks he ought to have done, and all in utter ignorance of Custer's own views of the conditions in which, when he met them, he was to find his own reasons for whatever he did or did

not do. Under that order, it was Custer's views of the conditions when they confronted him that were to govern his actions, whether they contravened General Terry's views or not. If in the presence of the actual conditions, in the light of his great experience and knowledge in handling Indians, he deemed it wise to follow the trail, knowing it would reach them, and deeming that so to locate them would be the best way to prevent their escape, then he obeyed that order just as exactly as if, thinking otherwise, he had gone scouting southward where they were not, and neither Terry nor he expected them to be.

To charge disobedience is to say that he willfully and with a wrong motive and intent did that which his own military judgment forbade; for it was his own military judgment, right or wrong, that was to govern his own actions under the terms of that order. The quality of his judgment does not touch the question of disobedience. If he disobeyed that order, it was by going contrary to his own judgment. That was the only way he could disobey it. If men differ as to whether he did that, they will differ.

Respectfully yours,

Jacob L. Greene.[3]

Greene's letter is probably the most cogent analysis of the question of disobedience and for any thinking person, must put the question to rest once and for all. But as he says: "If men differ . . . they will differ." One of the other important items brought out in the Brady discussion was the existence of an affidavit that purported to absolve Custer by giving him complete freedom of action, which he already had anyway. Although the question of disobedience should already be resolved, an examination of this affidavit follows, since to ignore it would be to ignore another controversy.

The affidavit was first mentioned by Nelson Miles in his memoirs *Personal Recollections of General Nelson A. Miles*, and since Miles retired as Commanding General of the Army, the affidavit and Miles' views carried a great deal of weight. Miles says in his book:

But we have positive evidence in the form of an affidavit of the last witness who heard the two officers in conversation together on the night before their commands separated, and it is conclusive on the point at issue. This evidence is that General Terry returned to General Custer's tent, after giving him the final order, to say to him that on coming up to the Indians he would have to use his own discretion and do what he thought best. This conversation occurred at the mouth of the Rosebud, and the exact words of General Terry, as quoted by the witness, are:

"Custer, I do not know what to say for the last."

Custer replied: "Say what you want to say."

Terry then said: "Use your own judgment, and do what you think best if you strike the trail; and whatever you do, Custer, hold on to your wounded."

This was a most reasonable conversation for the two officers under the circumstances. One had won great distinction as a general in the Civil War; was an able lawyer and department commander, yet entirely without experience in Indian campaigns. The other had won great distinction as one of the most gallant and skillful division commanders of cavalry during the war, commanding one of the most successful divisions of mounted troops; he had years of experience on the plains and in handling troops in that remote country, and he had fought several sharp engagements with hostile Indians.[4]

Dr. Benjamin Andrews uses the same affidavit, via Miles' book, to absolve Custer in his *The United States in Our Own Time*.[5] Brady wrote to Andrews, who replied, giving Miles as his source for the fact of the affidavit, and to Miles, who also replied but did not mention the affidavit specifically. Brady wrote him again and yet again, asking for the name of the affiant. Miles never responded to these later entreaties.

It remained for Colonel William A. Graham, author of *The Story of The Little Big Horn*, to discover the name of the affiant and the circumstances surrounding the swearing of the affidavit, although, as in a great many things he did in his research, Graham went too far and not far enough at the same time, as will become evident.[6]

As Graham says in *The Custer Myth*, he learned the name from E.S. Godfrey, who told Graham that it was Mary Adams, the Custer cook, who had sworn the affidavit, and he further told Graham that Mary Adams had not accompanied the expedition from Fort Lincoln. Graham smelled a rat and began digging for the dirt, first getting a copy of the affidavit from Godfrey, who in turn got it from Mrs. Custer. The affidavit reads as follows:

Territory of Dakota:

County of Burleigh:

Personally came before me Mary Adams, who being first duly sworn, deposes and says: that she resides in the City of Bismarck, D.T., and has resided in said City for three months just past. That she came to Dakota Territory with General George A. Custer in the Spring of 1873. That she was in the employ of General George A. Custer continuously from 1873 up to the time of his death in June 1876. That while in his employ she accompanied him on his military expeditions in the capacity of cook. That she left Fort A. Lincoln in the Spring of 1876 with General Terry's expedition in the employ of the said General Custer, and was present in the said General Custer's tent on the Rosebud River in Montana Territory when General Terry came into said tent, and the said Terry said to General Custer: "Custer, I don't know what to say for the last." Custer replied, "Say whatever you want to say." Terry then said, "Use your own judgment and do what you think best if you strike the trail. And whatever you do, Custer, hold on to your wounded" and further saith not.

    Her

Mary   X   Adams

    mark

Subscribed and sworn to before me this 16th day of January, 1878.

(Notarial Seal)

George P. Flannery, Notary Public, Burleigh Co., D.T.[7]

Now that he had the affidavit and Godfrey's assertion that Mary Adams had not been on the 1876 campaign, Graham set about proving that it was a hoax. He wrote Mr. Flannery, who responded at some length on August 12, 1922, but stated: "I have no recollection about the affidavit referred to by you . . . " and later: "I am sorry I am unable to recall anything in connection with the affidavit. She worked for Mrs. J.W. Raymond for some time after the battle of the Little Big Horn. Mrs. Raymond, I believe, is still living, residing in Pasadena, California."

It is perhaps not so surprising that Flannery could not recall anything about the affidavit, since it had been sworn forty-four years before and he had likely been involved with hundreds, if not thousands of affidavits. But Graham had a lead, so he contacted Mrs. Raymond, who replied to his letter on August 24, 1922. She had no information about the affidavit and only some sketchy information about Mary Adams. She wrote:

> The facts in the case are—that on a visit to Fort Lincoln immediately upon receiving news of the tragedy of the Little Big Horn, I felt that something must be done as soon as possible to get those poor bereaved women to their own people—if they had any. I had been planning to go East soon after, so hastened my going that we might be able to turn over our home to the six widows of the Officers, to use as they would to make ready for the journey.
>
> Mary Adams came with them, and cared for them as long as they remained—afterward keeping house for my husband and a friend until just before I returned to Bismarck—when she left Dakota, as I remember. Since then I have heard nothing.

Mrs. Raymond was in error. Mary Adams did not leave Dakota since she was there in January 1878, when she swore her affidavit. So far, Graham had nothing upon which to close his file, so he pressed onward.

On June 25, 1925, W.A. Falconer had an article published in the *Bismarck Capital* debunking the affidavit and calling it a "frame-up." Falconer claimed that Mary Adams was not with the expedition, and that on June 21 she was at Fort Lincoln so therefore could not have overheard the conversation she attested to hearing. Actually, he does not place her at the post through first-hand knowledge or testimony, but relies on the record of Lieutenant C.L. Gurley of the 6th Infantry, who was one of the officers who broke the news to Mrs. Custer on the morning of July 6, 1876. Falconer quotes Gurley thusly:

> It fell to my lot to accompany Captain McCaskey and Dr. J.V.D. Middleton, our post surgeon, to the quarters of Mrs. Custer. We started on our sad errand a little before seven o'clock on the 6th of July morning. I went to the rear of the Custer house, woke up Maria, Mrs. Custer's housemaid, and requested her to rap on Mrs. Custer's door.

Graham had all he was looking for, even though Falconer's article put Mary Adams at the Fort on July 6, not June 21. Falconer later in the article says: "Mary Adams . . . worked for James W. Raymond for several years . . ." which would have been news to Mrs. Raymond, who said she was there only a short time. Then Falconer ends by declaring that "During the past year I talked with Mr. Flannery who took Mary Adams' oath, and he says that some officer, a friend of Custer, he believed that Captain Carland was the one who drew up the affidavit for Mary Adams to sign. Mr. Flannery is now a resident of St. Paul, Minnesota." And this is the same Flannery who told Graham three years earlier that he couldn't remember anything about the affidavit.

That Falconer had his own axe to grind is found in a comparison of what he says Lieutenant Gurley said and what Gurley actually wrote. This is Gurley's own version, and while the difference is seemingly minor, it is very important. "It fell to my lot to accompany him and Dr. J.V.D. Middleton, our post surgeon, to the quarters of Mrs. Custer, immediately east of those occupied by myself. We started on our sad errand a little before seven o'clock on the sixth. I went to the rear of the Custer house and woke the maid . . . "

Falconer has identified the maid as Mary Adams (actually he said "Maria") while Gurley never named her, and while the language is similar, it is clearly evident that Falconer is not quoting Gurley directly—even though he pretends to do exactly that. But let us suppose that Falconer was right, despite his obviously ulterior motives and that it was Mary Adams. Her presence on July 6 does not negate her presence on the Rosebud on June 21. The question is, or should be, whether there is any positive evidence that she was on the campaign, and the perhaps not-so-startling answer is yes, there most certainly is!

Graham stopped short, because he was happy to deny the validity of the affidavit. He didn't even question Falconer's misquote of Gurley, or Flannery's sudden reversal of memory, or Mrs. Raymond's failure to recall that Mary Adams had worked for the family for several years, not a few weeks. Had he dug further he might have discovered that Mary was mentioned in at least two letters from members of the expedition, both of whom were killed in the fights and neither of whom, quite obviously, had any reason to mention Mary if she hadn't been there.

On June 6, 1876, Captain Tom Custer wrote to his niece, Emma Reed, who was staying at Fort Lincoln, mentioning that he had caught a bunch of sage hens—which he had turned over to Mary, who was going to try to raise them. Then on June 21, 1876—the very day Mary swore she overheard the Terry/Custer conversation that was the subject of her affidavit—Autie Reed, Custer's nephew, wrote to his parents saying that he was in camp at the mouth of the Rosebud; that there was every chance for a success against the Indians, and he mentioned a tame jack rabbit "which Mary thinks all the world of, Mary is staying on the boat."

The validity of the Mary Adams affidavit is not necessary to refute the allegations against Custer of disobedience, so I won't indulge in any attempt to show how Mary could have been on the campaign and not remembered by Godfrey, Varnum or Edgerly. Nor will I try to account for Gurley's statement about the maid (whom he did not name). It seems beyond doubt that she was there and could have heard what she says she heard, but it only shows the lengths to which people like Falconer and Graham would go to "prove" their points.

There is also some question as to whether there might not have been two Adams sisters, one named Mary and the other Maria, and this possibility has been explored at some length by others so the exercise need not be repeated here.[8]

There is one more peripheral matter to look at before we leave the subject of Custer and his "orders," and that is whether or not he had planned all along to do whatever he liked without regard to any instructions. Again, it must be emphasized that this has no bearing on disobedience, because there was none and could not have been any in the circumstances, but it does have a bearing on what kind of man Custer was—and that should be something of extreme interest.

In his rebuttal to the Godfrey *Century Magazine* article and General Fry's added commentary thereto, Colonel Robert P. Hughes, Terry's brother-in-law, who was an aide during the campaign of 1876, advanced the case that Custer had disobeyed his orders and thereby dashed all hopes for Terry's plan to succeed. Aside from his obvious bias, Hughes brought out myriad details of the "plan" and the "intelligence" upon which it had been formulated, because Fry had said that the plan only assumed its importance in Terry's mind after the Custer disaster. Among other things, Hughes reported that Custer had boasted that he would "swing clear" of Terry at the first opportunity. This would illustrate Custer's character, or lack thereof.

Hughes' source for this information was Captain William Ludlow of the Engineers. Custer had reportedly bumped into Ludlow just after leaving Terry's office on the occasion of being reinstated to command of his regiment for the expedition. Hughes also stated that it was Terry who actually composed the letter to President Grant that went out over Custer's signature, after Custer had got down on his knees to beg Terry's intercession. If taken on its face, the report from Ludlow would show Custer to be an ungrateful, disrespectful, scheming and base person.

Hughes also stated that Ludlow had repeated Custer's remarkable comments to Colonel Farquhar, General Ruggles and General Card with a view of having General Terry informed. Hughes does not say why the concerned Captain Ludlow could not have gone straight to Terry on his own rather than waiting until Terry left St. Paul the next day to voice his concerns. In any event, General Ruggles thought he wrote a letter to Terry giving the details. Ludlow had been assigned to the expedition, but had been ordered to Philadelphia and had been replaced by Lieutenant Edward Maguire. Terry supposedly never learned of the matter until his return to St. Paul in September.

That something of the sort happened is beyond doubt. What Custer said to Ludlow and what he meant by it is a horse of another color. Hughes says that Ludlow "was not called upon to remember the exact words which Custer used (until September), and, while these exact words may have faded from his memory, the idea conveyed to him was perfectly clear and was given by him, as above quoted, in a letter to General Terry." So Ludlow, who thought this was so important that he had to have somebody (other than him) get in touch with Terry right away in May, couldn't "remember the exact words" only four months later but he did remember the "idea conveyed to him."

Now, I think it's fair to quibble with all of this as an indictment of Custer, without in any way detracting from the fact that Custer said something to Ludlow. Ludlow supposedly said that Custer said that he would "cut loose from (and make his operations independent of) General Terry during the summer" and that he had "got away with Stanley and would be able to swing clear of Terry."

Even if that is what Custer said, and it may not be, it is not evidence of any ulterior motives. Here was a man who had just been restored to his command and who was obviously just as elated as he had previously been despondent. It would have been perfectly in character for him to have danced Ludlow around in the street and to have said something outrageous. The words themselves convey only what one wants to read into them. In fact Custer not only got his independent command, but he knew all along that he would get it, because that was Terry's plan when the expedition was formed: move into the hostiles' country, fix as much as possible the location of their camp, and then let Custer and the 7th make a big jump at it. Custer knew that; so did Ludlow. All Custer had to do was wait; he did not have to scheme—and he did not.

Terry gave Custer a carte blanche just as he had always planned to do. It was only afterward that Hughes, et al seized upon whatever they could to advance a case against Custer. After all, somebody was going to have to answer for the disaster, and even a chance remark to somebody in the street might be made into some nefarious scheme if used adroitly.

It is just possible that General Ruggles was successful in making Terry aware of what Custer had allegedly said. Perhaps it was only the sort of nasty rumors that jealous men tended to spread about Custer, but certainly there were unkind things being said about Custer and his willingness to serve under Terry that apparently got so much in the open that Custer heard them himself. According to Greene, in his letter to Brady:

> In one of Mrs. Custer's letters to me, narrating what took place during the days of preparation for the General's departure, she wrote: "A day before the expedition started, General Terry was in our house alone with Autie (the General's pet name). A's thoughts were calm, deliberate, and solemn. He had been terribly hurt in Washington. General Terry had applied for him to command the expedition. He was returned to his regiment because General Terry had applied for him. I know that he (Custer) felt tenderly and affectionately toward him. On that day he hunted me out in the house and brought me into the living-room, not telling me why. He shut the door, and very seriously and impressively said: 'General Terry, a man usually means what he says when he brings his wife to listen to his statements. I want to say that reports are circulating that I do not want to go out to the campaign under you. (I supposed that he meant, having been given the command before, he was unwilling to be a subordinate.) But I want you to know that I do want to go and serve under you, not only that I value you as a soldier, but as a friend and a man.' The exact words were the strongest kind of declaration that he wished him to know he wanted to serve under him."

That was Custer all over. And to anyone who knew him—to anyone who can form a reasonable conception of the kind of man he must needs have been to have done for eighteen years what he had done and as he had done it, and won the place and fame he had won—that statement ends all debate. Whatever chagrin, disappointment, or irritation he may have felt before, however unadvisedly the sore-hearted, high-spirited man may have spoken with his lips when all was undetermined and his part and responsibility had not been assigned, this true soldier, knowing the gossip of the camp, conscious possibly it was not wholly without cause, however exaggerated, but facing now his known duty and touched by the confidence of his superior as Custer never failed to be touched, could not part from his commander with a possible shadow resting between them. He knew the speech of men may have carried to Terry's mind the suggestion of a doubt. And yet Terry had trusted him. He could not bear to part without letting General Terry know that he was right to trust him. That statement to Terry was a recognition of whatever folly of words he might before have committed in his grief and anger; it was an open purging of an upright soldier's soul, an act honorably due alike to superior and subordinate; it was, under the circumstances, the instinctive response of a true man to the confidence of one who had committed to him a trust involving the honor and fame of both. Disobedience, whether basely premeditated, or with equal baseness undertaken upon after-deliberation, is inconceivable, unless one imputes to Custer a character void of every soldierly and manly quality.[9]

That Letter of Instruction from Terry to Custer is perhaps the most widely known document connected with the 1876 campaign. Also well documented is the journey of the 7th Cavalry to the Little Horn; but because they kept no written records, unknown at the time was how so many Lakota and Cheyenne people come to be gathered there. That omission can now be rectified.

NOTES

1. *Annual Report of the Secretary of War for 1876*, House Executive Document 1, Second Session, Forty-fourth Congress, Serial volume 1742, p.462.
2. Ibid. The precise language of Terry's order was "He will, however, indicate to you his own views of what your action should be, and he desires that you should conform to them unless you shall see sufficient reason for departing from them."
3. Cyrus Townsend Brady, *Indian Fights and Fighters* (Garden City: Doubleday, 1904).
4. For an analysis of the experience of Custer and the 7th Cavalry with hostile Indians,

see Analysis 4, *Two Controversies: Recruits at the Little Horn and the Indian-Fighting Record of the 7th Cavalry*," particularly the "List of Engagements," as well as [ebook] Appendix 5.5.

5. E. Benjamin Andrews, *The United States in Our Own Time* (New York, 1903).

6. Col. William A. Graham, *The Story of the Little Big Horn* (Harrisburg, 1952).

7. W. A. Graham, *The Custer Myth* (New York: Bonanza Books, 1953), p.280.

8. Shirley A. Leckie, *Elizabeth Bacon Custer And The Making Of A Myth* (Norman: U. of Okla. Press, 1993; Dale T. Schoenberer, *The End of Custer: The Death of an American Legend* (Surrey, B.C.: Hancock House, 1995).

9. Brady, *Indian Fights and Fighters*, p.394, citing the letter to him from Lieutenant Colonel Jacob L. Greene of September 1, 1904. Note that brackets in Mrs. Custer's letter are Greene's.

HOW THE INDIAN BANDS
CAME TOGETHER AT
THE LITTLE HORN

"If you don't find more Indians in that valley than you ever saw together before, you can hang me."—MITCH BOYER, AT THE CROW'S NEST, JUNE 25, 1876

Because of the writings of many past chroniclers of the Custer/Terry campaign—especially Hughes and those other writers who accused Custer of disobedience—it was long thought by most readers that the Indians were definitely known to be located on the Little Horn, at exactly the spot upon which they were encamped. This "fact" accounted for Terry's plan for the destruction of the hostiles and for his instructions to Custer—which, the critics say, if obeyed would have led to a successful conclusion to the campaign. It has already been shown that Terry's instructions were imprecise and non-binding, and that Custer did not disobey any orders. In reality, the location of the hostiles was not known—except in general terms—and it was mere chance that brought them to the Little Horn and kept them on that stream until Custer came upon them.

When attempting to understand the peregrinations of the various Indian bands, it is necessary to keep in mind that there were, in fact, four different "types" of Indians: "agency Indians," who spent virtually all of their time on the reservations, often in close proximity to the agency and who relied upon the agency to fulfill almost all of their needs; "hostiles," who lived free in the unceded territories and who rarely, if ever, visited an agency, except perhaps to trade; "free-roamers," who sometimes visited agencies and might be enrolled at one or more, but who rarely, if ever, resided on one; "agency-roamers," who spent the winters at the agencies, but who spent the summers living the traditional lifestyle, going on buffalo hunts, etc. The nomenclature is arbitrary and informal, just as was the nominal classification of any particular family or band, save the really hardened people who would have nothing at all to do with the whites. Sitting Bull is perhaps the most famous example of the latter, although he was happy enough to trade for necessities, including arms and ammunition.

To understand what combination of circumstances led to Custer finding the Indian village on the Little Horn, I must travel back in time to the winter of 1875–76. The government had ordered all Indians living off their reservations to go to them and register at the appropriate agencies. Few, if any, of the hostiles living in the unceded territories were inclined to obey. The various hostile bands had never had much to do with the agencies and weren't about to start under the duress of the federal ultimatum. At the same time, many of the free-roamers decided to stay out for the winter to see what would transpire—and to support their wilder brethren—and even some agency-roamers went out, or stayed out in the Powder River country. The net effect of all this was that the population scattered throughout the wilds grew considerably, probably by as many as 2,000 people.

When the deadline passed, it became known to the Indians residing on the reservations that the military was preparing to move against their relatives in the Powder River area (the army made no effort to conceal its intentions—quite the contrary), so they sent out couriers with this information. Wooden Leg said that Last Bull, the leading chief of the Fox warrior society, came to his village with the news, which was not readily believed. The Cheyennes thought that they were safe where they were, since they were there legally and had done nothing to warrant punishment by the army. Wooden Leg states that other Cheyennes came, but is not specific as to numbers.

In mid-March, the band to which Wooden Leg's family belonged was camped on the Powder River, forty or fifty miles above the Little Powder. The village consisted of about forty lodges and the leader was Old Bear, one of the old-man chiefs of the Northern Cheyenne. From this camp, Crook's troops were spotted and the village was moved to get away from his column, to just above the confluence of the Powder and Little Powder. This is the village that was attacked in this location by the cavalry under the command of Colonel Joseph J. Reynolds.[1] Note that it was not Crazy Horse's village or Two Moon's band—Two Moon was a minor chief of the Fox society—as popularly supposed and generally reported. This attack, which was pretty much a failure, was the second of the circumstances (the "come in or else" ultimatum being the first) that led to the combination of the bands.

The attack took place on the morning of March 17, and resulted in the almost total destruction of the Cheyenne village and the Indians' property. After getting most of their horses back the same night, the Cheyennes decided to strike out for the village of their friend and ally, Crazy Horse, which was known to be about fifty miles to the north and east. Crazy Horse, although born an Oglala Lakota, had lived many years among the Northern Cheyenne and was almost one of them. This trip took three or four days.

I should say here that every effort has been made to arrive at accurate dates and places and that where possible more than one source has been utilized in order to verify derived information. Still, it is virtually impossible to be 100 percent accurate, since Wooden Leg is the principal primary source for much of the data and he could not be definite in many instances. The "itinerary" is proffered as "best evidence" and I believe that it is nearly exact, as far as it goes.

The Cheyenne were graciously received by the Oglalas, who were happy to help their friends, but less than thrilled by the events which had brought the Cheyenne to them. The Oglala and Cheyenne often visited with each other, so there had been a few Oglala lodges with the Cheyenne at the Battle of Powder River, just as there were a few Cheyenne lodges with the Oglalas in Crazy Horse's village. A council was held and it was decided that the combined bands should go to the Hunkpapa Lakota under Sitting Bull, who were camped to the northeast. This journey occupied another three days, the Hunkpapas being found near present-day Ekalaka, Montana, east of Chalk Butte, about 50 miles east of the Powder. Wooden Leg stated that the Hunkpapas were more numerous than the Oglalas and the Cheyennes together, at this camp. That would put the Hunkpapas at about one hundred lodges, or slightly more.

The area in which the three band circles were located was reasonably conducive to a long stay, so the combined village stayed in the vicinity for more than a week, making only a short move to get away from the refuse. There were a few days of snow.

At about the end of March, Lame Deer and his large band of Mnicoujou Lakota arrived, making four circles. The Mnicoujous ranked third in number, behind the Oglalas but ahead of the Cheyennes, with perhaps fifty lodges. The makeup of the village was now in the order of one hundred lodges of Hunkpapas, sixty of Oglalas, fifty of Mnicoujous and forty of Cheyennes, making a total of about 250. This was a large group, but nothing like what was to come.

Beginning in the first week of April, the Indians began moving north and northwest, trying to put as much distance as possible between themselves and whatever troops might be in the field. Contrary to popular belief, the Indians' military intelligence was not very good and they were not aware of exactly what was going on. As things turned out, the army's own intelligence was neither reliable nor timely, so that military commanders were just as much in the dark as were the Indians. In any event, the moves were neither numerous nor lengthy and the order of march was: first the Cheyennes, who were considered to be actively at war because of the attack upon them; second, the Oglalas, who were the special allies of the Cheyennes and who could be counted upon to fight if it became necessary; next came the Mnicoujous, followed by the Hunkpapas. This order signified a willingness to assist in whatever defensive maneuvering or action might prove necessary, but not necessarily to engage in offensive action. It is doubtful whether the army, however, would have given much thought to the significance of this marching order. As new tribal allies arrived, they took their places behind the Mnicoujous but ahead of the Hunkpapas and this order was maintained as long as the tribal groups remained together.

More Indians were coming in all the time, and while the village was located on Sheep Creek, April 21–23, a band of Blackfeet Lakota joined up, creating a small but separate fifth camp circle. On about April 24, the Indians moved to near the junction of Powder River and Mizpah Creek, where they remained for four or five days. Lame White Man, leading chief of the Elk warrior society of the Cheyenne, arrived here with a substantial following—and Wooden Leg reported that Brules, Santees and Assiniboines were also in this camp. The Santees belonged to the band of Inkpaduta.

The last couple of days of April were occupied by short moves, and on about May 1, the combined village was put up on the Tongue River, very near the mouth of Pumpkin Creek. The village remained in this location for about five days and it was here that Kill Eagle arrived with at least twenty-six lodges of assorted Lakotas, twelve of which were of his own Blackfeet Lakota band.

Kill Eagle had left the Standing Rock Agency in April, as did numerous Indian bands who left the agencies in the spring.

On about May 6, a short move was made up the Tongue so that there would be fresh grass for the ever-increasing pony herd. The size of the combined village was making it difficult to remain long in one place, despite the fact that the hunters were having excellent results in keeping a steady supply of meat and robes for tanning. In this new camp another large contingent of Cheyennes arrived, led by the old chief Dirty Moccasins. Wooden Leg said that there were now about double the number of Cheyenne lodges as had started out, and that all other circles were increased commensurately.

I can now put the Cheyenne count at about 90–100 lodges, with the Oglalas, Sans Arcs and Mnicoujous all in the range of 130–160 and the Hunkpapas at about 250–275. The Brules, Santees and Blackfeet Lakota probably accounted for another seventy-five lodges, while the total of Assiniboines, Yanktonnais and Two Kettles added fifteen to twenty.

The village moved up the Tongue on May 11, and again on the 15th. On May 16, while the Indians were in the latter camp, the smoke of their fires was spotted by Lieutenant Bradley of Gibbon's command, but his Crow scouts cautioned against venturing close enough to try to count the lodges. They said it was a very large village—at least a few hundred lodges, judging by the smoke alone. It was considerably larger than had been expected.

The Indians knew exactly where Gibbon's column was since they had it under almost constant surveillance and a few young men had raided for horses. The chiefs, in council, decided to get as far away from Gibbon as possible and began a series of short moves over to the Rosebud, planning on moving up that stream away from the Yellowstone. They reached the Rosebud on the 19th where they found a huge herd of buffalo waiting for them and moving slowly in the direction they had already planned on going. This was the third circumstance.

A large buffalo hunt was held on the 19th. The date can be fixed from Gibbon's recording that the gunfire could be heard from his camp on the north side of the Yellowstone near the mouth of Little Porcupine Creek. The next couple of days were spent in butchering, scraping, etc., and then the village moved up the Rosebud, in the first of a series of short moves.

After it had moved on about the 25th, Lieutenant Bradley again found the village, this time on the Rosebud, on May 27, about twenty miles above the Yellowstone. Bradley saw not only smoke but also a huge horse herd and some lodges. He suggested that there were 500 lodges, although he had seen only part of the village.

The Indians moved again on May 29 and 30, with more Cheyennes coming in during these moves and the other circles also increasing as the days passed. More Indians were arriving virtually every day, either concentrating from their camps in the wild country or coming out from the agencies. Everyone now knew that this might well be their last summer of freedom, and the overall mood was one of determination to hold on as long as possible and at all costs. The Indians knew almost every move of Gibbon's troops, but they somehow kept missing Bradley. They were not aware of the movements of Terry or Crook, although they knew that other troops would be coming out against them.

June 1 brought the last snow of the year, and a couple of days later the village was moved up the Rosebud to the site where the sun dance was held. This site was on the west side of the Rosebud, between Greenleaf and Lame Deer Creeks, about forty-five miles from the Yellowstone. While at this camp, hunters from the village came across Crook's command, most probably on June 6. Wooden Leg said that it was raining and the 6th was the only rainy day in this camp.

The sun dance itself was held over a couple of days between June 4 and June 7, and it was during this ceremony that Sitting Bull had his famous vision of many soldiers falling into camp. Wooden Leg, who had been one of the hunters who discovered Crook, returned to his camp circle during the next rainy period, which was June 9–11. By the time he got back, the village had moved up the Rosebud to the mouth of Muddy Creek. The returning hunters announced their news and it spread like wildfire throughout the village, the individual band heralds riding about like town criers. Various councils were held and it was decided that scouts would be sent to watch the soldiers, who had been last seen on the upper reaches of the Tongue at Prairie Dog Creek, while the village would head for the Big Horn or Rotten Grass Creek (not to be confused with Greasy Grass—the Little Horn). This decision and change of direction was the fourth circumstance.

The Cheyennes sent out their scouts—Little Hawk, Crooked Nose and a few others—and it is likely that the Lakotas also sent out scouts, although Wooden Leg thought that they depended upon the Cheyennes for the scouting activity. Little Hawk departed from the Muddy Creek site as the villagers were being notified to make ready to move again.

The next campsites were just at the junction of the Rosebud with Davis Creek. The Cheyennes set up their circle on the east side of the Rosebud, across from Davis Creek, while the other Indians erected their lodges in the same order as had been followed all along the "route of march." On the 15th, the combined village moved up Davis Creek toward the divide between it and Ash (Reno) Creek, setting up dry camps just east of the divide. These movements would be strangely echoed by Custer ten days later.

At about the same time that this move was being made, the van of a very large contingent of agency-roamers was reaching the Rosebud about ten miles south of Davis Creek and setting up their own camp circles there. They were, of course, looking to unite with their kinfolk who were known to be somewhere "in the country." It is probable they had also obtained additional information about the movements of the military, and were seeking safety in numbers. The larger group consisted of about 2,500 people, but they had not all reached the Rosebud.

A third group, made up of hostiles and free-roamers, with a few agency-roamers attached, was approaching the divide between the upper Tongue and the headwaters of Lodge Grass Creek from the south and east, having kept a few jumps ahead of Crook's column for the past couple of weeks. Captain Ball was to discover their trail after the Custer disaster while following the trail of the hostiles out of the Little Horn valley. This aggregation numbered almost 2,000, and included some Plains Cree warriors down from Canada to keep a promise made in previous years to help their Lakota friends in time of danger.

On June 16, the camps whose progress I have been tracking moved across the divide and down Ash Creek about 10 miles. Little Hawk returned from his latest scout that same day, reporting that Crook was now approaching the upper Rosebud, evidently intending to march down that stream. He indicated to the council chiefs that Crook would run into the agency-roamers (Crook may have known they were there, as his own Crow scouts had reported a village of 500 lodges about 45 miles from his camp) with his large force and might even be on his way to attack the main gathering. The council deliberated long and hard, and then sent the heralds out to advise the young men to do nothing unless the village was attacked.

This was akin to sending a man to stand in the corner and not think about elephants—it was an order impossible to obey. When night came young warriors began to slip away. Wooden Leg says that they came from every camp circle, but he does not pretend that all the warriors went out, and there is plenty of evidence to suggest that not all of the leading warrior society chiefs went. There was also a contingent of warriors from the agency-roamers' village, but none from the third group, who were still more-or-less invisible to everyone, including their own people.

On the 17th the warriors met Crook in the Battle of the Rosebud, some twenty miles south of Davis Creek, and after their successful fight returned home that evening. The next day, the main village moved overland and also down Ash Creek, to the valley of the Little Horn, setting up shop on the east side of the river very near the mouth of Long Otter Creek, three or four miles south of the mouth of Ash Creek. The village remained in this location for six days and it was here that the other two groups joined, from the east and from the south.

While here, scouts kept a constant watch on Crook and a loose watch on Gibbon. The chiefs knew that Crook had retreated and settled in at Goose Creek, and they apparently did not consider Gibbon much of a threat. They had learned that Custer had taken the field but they didn't know where he was and probably would not have much cared. The now largest congregation of Indians ever in the northwest, fresh from a victory over the hated soldiers, basked in the feeling of its enormous strength, confident that no one dared attack it.

The village had swelled to over 1,700 lodges, and more were arriving every day. Buffalo were plentiful on the bench lands across the river, and the plan was to move up the valley of the Little Horn, but scouts brought word that there were vast herds of antelope west of the Big Horn, so the council decided that the village would move down to the mouth of the Little Horn. Hunters could then go out and obtain the much-desired antelope meat and hides. This was circumstance number five.

On the 24th, the village crossed the Little Horn and moved downstream to the location where Custer found it. There had been no plan to go there, let alone meet there to receive the attack of the soldiers or to set a trap. There is obviously no way that Terry could have known that the village would be there, as the Indians themselves did not decide to go there until June 23. It was chance that took the Indians there and chance that brought the three groups together just when Custer was searching for them and following one of their trails up the Rosebud.

A village of such enormous proportions could never stay together for very long, simply because of the logistical problems involved. There is ample evidence for this statement in the breakup of the gathering after the Custer fight. The Indians were not threatened in any meaningful way by either Terry/Gibbon or Crook, yet still they could not remain as a consolidated body for more than a few days. They split up because they had to, not because they wanted to, and it was Custer's bad luck that he encountered them at the high-water mark of their strength and cohesion. The mere fact that they were forced to separate shows without question just how strong they were. I do not have to indulge in wild speculations to see that strength, and there is certainly nothing in the history of the movements of the various bands that would cause me to shrink from the figures I arrived in this analysis examining the size of the village.

If one wants to indulge in "what-ifs," he can speculate on what might have happened if the army had simply stayed put in their posts and let the Indians stay out in the Powder River country. Maybe most of the Indians would have come in when winter arrived; maybe they would be there yet—hunting buffalo and antelope and nobody the wiser, or poorer, for that matter.

The following is a day-by-day itinerary, with a few gaps, for the main village, showing how it came to be and where it went during the period March 15–June 25, 1876. As mentioned earlier, this information has been derived from many sources, but uses Wooden Leg as a primary source, with other information coming from others where possible.

March 15 & 16	West side of Powder River, about 40–50 miles above Little Powder. Forty lodges under Old Bear.
March 17	Attacked by Reynolds. Village destroyed. Travel northeast toward Crazy Horse.
March 18/19	Travel northeast toward supposed location of Crazy Horse camp.
March 20	Arrive at Crazy Horse camp on creek east of Powder. Oglalas stronger than Cheyennes.
March 21	Hold council, decide to go together to Sitting Bull and his Hunkpapas.
March 22	Preparations made for the journey.
March 23/24	Heading toward Sitting Bull.
March 25	Join Hunkpapas near Ekalaka east of Chalk Butte. Hunkpapas are stronger than Oglalas/Cheyennes.

March 26	Food and clothing distributed and Cheyennes made welcome.
March 27–30	Councils held to decide upon future movements and actions.
March 31	Lame Deer and large band of Mnicoujous arrive.
April 4	Move north to next stream flowing into Powder.
April 9	Move north/northwest.
April 11	Move north.
April 15	Move north.
April 17	Move north. Joined at this camp by a large band of Sans Arcs, about the same size as the Oglalas and Mnicoujous. The village has grown by leaps and bounds and more Indians are arriving daily.
April 21	Move down Sheep Creek. Blackfeet Lakota join at this camp.
April 24	Move to Mizpah Creek/Powder River. Lame White Man arrives with large band of Cheyennes. Santees, Brules and Assiniboines are also in this camp.
April 29	Short move.
April 30	Short move.
May 1	Arrive at Tongue River near Pumpkin Creek. Kill Eagle comes in with at least twenty-six lodges at this camp.
May 6	Short move up the Tongue for new grass. Dirty Moccasins arrives with large band of Cheyennes. All camp circles have grown considerably.
May 11	Move up the Tongue.
May 15	Short move up the Tongue.
May 16	Smoke of this camp seen by Bradley.
May 17	Move northwest.
May 18	Another move northwest.
May 19	Reach the Rosebud, about 8 miles from its mouth.
May 22	Short move up the Rosebud.
May 25	Another short move.
May 27	Part of the camp observed by Bradley.
May 29	Short move. More Cheyennes arrive.
May 30	Another short move up the Rosebud.

June 3	Move to sun dance location.
June 6	Hunters stumble upon Crook's troops.
June 8	Move up Rosebud to Muddy Creek.
June 9	Hunters return with news. Little Hawk and Crooked Nose go out to scout.
June 12	Move up Rosebud to Davis Creek.
June 15	Travel up Davis Creek. Stop short of divide.
June 16	Cross divide and move down Ash Creek. Little Hawk returns from second scout. Many warriors sneak off in night to attack Crook.
June 17	Battle of the Rosebud. Crook pulls back.
June 18	Camps move across country and also via Ash Creek to the Little Horn.
June 20/21	Agency-roamers and free-roamers come in from east and south to this camp. Village almost doubles.
June 24	Move across and down Little Horn to below Ash Creek.
June 25	Custer attacks and is defeated. Reno is besieged.
June 26	Siege continues until the afternoon. In late afternoon, the camps move up the Little Horn valley.

Having examined the population of the camps in the Little Horn valley, it is even more pertinent to look at how many of them represented the fighting force that defeated Custer's vaunted 7th Cavalry.

NOTES

1. Joseph J. Reynolds was a graduate of the West Point Class of 1843 and served as major general commanding a corps during the Civil War. At the Battle of Powder River he commanded a force of 320 soldiers of the 2nd and 3rd U.S. Cavalry, and was subsequently court-martialed for dereliction of duty in connection with the battle, and suspended from rank and pay for one year.

ANALYSIS 3

━━━━━━━━━━━━━━━━━━━━━━━━━

THE NUMBER OF WARRIORS
FACING THE 7TH CAVALRY

" . . . we'll find enough Sioux to keep us fighting two or three days."—BLOODY KNIFE, ON THE ROSEBUD/LITTLE HORN DIVIDE, EARLY MORNING, JUNE 25, 1876

A nother in the seemingly endless questions facing the historian or casual reader is: "How many Indian warriors were there in the fights?" The answer is at once simple and complex. There certainly were enough warriors to defeat the various detachments of the 7th Cavalry in the actual circumstances, and the true number is probably of more value in the field of speculation—"what if Custer hadn't divided his force?"—than in a real understanding of what took place. But it is a matter of some contention, so it behooves me to make an examination of the subject.

In his wonderful book *Centennial Campaign*, John Gray gives a careful and reasoned analysis of this subject, which I would certainly consider required study, but with which I strongly disagree. He concludes that the village numbered only about 1,000 lodges, having a total population of some 7,100, including about 1,800 adult males. He contends that the total fighting force from this village could hardly have exceeded 2,000 and states that this would have been a sufficient number to have inflicted the defeat upon the 7th. With this last statement I would tend to agree, but I cannot do likewise with the remainder.

Before providing my own analysis, I think it wise to quote from what should be reasonably reliable sources, most of whom were actual participants in the fights. Unfortunately, many Indian sources could not be used because they could not express themselves in numbers that are useful—using their own figurative images to convey the fact that there was a vast number, both of lodges and of Indians.

White Man Runs Him, Crow scout, to Colonel Tim McCoy, 1919: "The Indians saw him (Custer) there, and all began running that way. There were thousands of them."

White Man Runs Him again, to General Hugh Scott, 1919: "I would say between 4,000 and 5,000, maybe more. You can ask Curley about that, if you care to do so."

Crazy Horse, Oglala Lakota, in *St. Paul Pioneer Press*, 1877: Quoted as saying that there were 1,800 lodges, 400 wickiups and 7,000 warriors.

Flying By, Mnicoujou Lakota, to Walter Camp, 1910: "Lame Deer had between 600 and 800 tepees. Few Santees there."

Captain F.W. Benteen, in a letter to his wife, July 2, 1876: "There was 5,000 of them—so Genl. Sheridan telegraphs Genl. Terry."

Benteen again, in a letter to his wife, July 4, 1876: "3,000 warriors were there."

Benteen again, in his testimony at the Reno Court of Inquiry: "I thought then there were about twenty-five hundred Indians surrounding us, but I think now that there were eight or nine thousand." Also in the same testimony: "The Indians had picnic parties as large as a regiment standing around in the river bottom, looking on. There was no place to put them. Fully two thousand were around us waiting for a place to shoot from." And also: "Eight or nine hundred Indians was only a small part of what they had." And also: "The village, as I saw it from the high point, I estimated at . . . about eighteen hundred tepees . . . I saw it when it moved away . . . it was . . . about three miles long, and I think a half mile wide, as densely packed as animals could be."

Dr. Charles Eastman, Teton Lakota, in the *Chautauqua* magazine, 1900: ". . . nor were there over 1,000 warriors in the fight . . ."

Major James McLaughlin, Standing Rock Agent, in *My Friend the Indian*, 1910: stated that there were between 2,500 and 3,000 warriors.

Sergeant R. R. Lane, 7th Infantry, in a letter to his brother July 3, 1876: "While the fact is there were over 4,000 of them, as there was a village of 1,300 lodges."

He Dog, Oglala Lakota, to Walter Camp, 1910: "More than 20 lodges (Brules) . . . More Hunkpapas than any other tribe. Minniconjou next. Hunkpapa and Blackfeet together had 600 or 700 lodges. Thirty or forty lodges of Santees . . . (thinks 1,800 lodges in whole village about right)."

Mrs. Spotted Horn Bull, Hunkpapa Lakota, in *St. Paul Pioneer Press*, 1883: quoted as saying that there were 5,000 warriors present.

Lieutenant Charles Varnum, in a letter to his parents, July 4, 1876: "I don't think there is any doubt but that we fought 4,000 of them."

Feather Earring, Mnicoujou Lakota, to General Hugh Scott, 1919: "I know we counted over 5,000, and they were not all there."

Lieutenant Winfield Edgerly, in his Fort Yates statement, 1881: "From what I saw, I think there were as many as 7,000 warriors. I judged from seeing Terry's command—about 500 men—the size of which I knew, ride down where I saw the Indians the day before. Terry's command looked like a handful compared to the Indians."

Edgerly again, in Walter Camp's notes: "Edgerly's estimate of Indians was 4,000 warriors. He based this on number of tepees in village and what he saw when Indians went off on evening of 26th. Says Hare, who had seen large droves of cattle and horses in Texas, remarked there must be more than 20,000 animals in the column."

Tall Bull, Cheyenne, to Walter Camp, 1910: "There were 3,000 population in Cheyenne village."

General A. H. Terry, in his first report June 27, 1876: "Major Reno and Captain Benteen, both of whom are officers of great experience, accustomed to see large masses of mounted men, estimate the number of Indians engaged at not less than twenty-five hundred. Other officers think that the number was greater."

Major M.A. Reno, in a statement in the *New York Herald* August 8, 1876: "The lowest computation puts the Indian strength at about 2,500, and some think there were 5,000 warriors present." Reno again, in a letter in the paper above-noted: ". . . he rode into an ambuscade of at least 2,000 reds." Later, speaking of the fight on the bluffs: " . . .with a force outnumbered ten to one. . ." Reno finally, in his official report, July 5, 1876: While giving an estimate of at least 3,500 warriors, says " . . . the length of the column was fully equal to that of a large division of the cavalry corps of the Army of the Potomac, as I have seen it on the march."

Sergeant Daniel Knipe, in the *Greensboro Daily Record*, 1924: "In that battle there were fully 4,000 Indians besides the squaws, making a total of between 12,000 and 15,000 Indians in all."

Ice Bear, Cheyenne, to Walter Camp, 1910: "Cheyennes had about 3,000 people."

George Herendeen, scout, in the *New York Herald* July 8, 1876: "I think the Indian village must have contained about 6,000 people, fully 3,000 of whom were warriors." Herendeen again, in Walter Camp's notes, 1909: "Thinks there were 1,800 lodges and about 3,500 warriors."

Fred Gerard, interpreter, in *The Arikara Narrative*: "The retreating warriors passed by hundreds close to where we lay hid in the willows . . . "

Gerard again, in Walter Camp's notes, 1909: "He estimated before starting that would find as many as 4,000 warriors and subsequent observations and events have never induced him to lower the estimate."

Wooden Leg, Cheyenne, to Dr. T.B. Marquis: "Almost all of our Northern Cheyenne tribe were with us on the Little Bighorn. Only a few of our forty big chiefs were absent." In a footnote, Marquis states that in 1927, Wooden Leg and some other old men estimated a population of at least 1,600 at the Little Horn. "Three hundred lodges seems to me now as being about the size of our Cheyenne camp. The Blackfeet Sioux [Lakota] had about the same number, or a few less. The Arrows All Gone [Sans Arc] had more. The Minniconjous and Oglalas each had more than the Arrows All Gone. The Hunkpapas had, I believe, twice as many as the Cheyenne." Marquis gives a total village population of about 12,000, based on the estimate of 1,600 for the Cheyennes. Wooden Leg also mentions that a few unmarried young men had "little willow dome and robe shelters." which were generally referred to by whites as wickiups and which are prominently mentioned by several witnesses. Wooden Leg is the only source who gives specific details of the total makeup of the village.

The quoted sources coincidentally are evenly divided between Indians and whites, with all of them, except three, being from actual battle participants—and all being based on information from participants. It is interesting to note that there is a great deal of commonality in the numbers, with the exception of Dr. Eastman's statement that there were fewer than one thousand warriors, although the range is rather wide—2,500 to 9,000. It is also interesting that the Indians tend to have larger estimates than do the whites. What is most striking, however, is the similarity in figures when talking about the number of lodges, as opposed to warriors, present in the great camp. Where the total number of lodges is given, there is a marked tendency to say "1,800," and even where the total population or the number of lodges for a particular circle is estimated, it often is extrapolated to this same total number of lodges.

One need not be a mathematician or statistician to note the common threads of 1,800 lodges total and 3,000–4,000 warriors. There are thirteen estimates of warrior numbers and five estimates of total lodge numbers fitting these parameters. Strangely enough, or perhaps not so strangely, if one takes an average family lodge population of seven persons, which is an accurate round number, the total population for 1,800 lodges becomes 12,600. And using an average of two fighting men per lodge, which is again an accurate figure, leads to a total of 3,600 warriors. Both of these results are well within the range of the estimates shown above and therefore quite reasonable. That does not mean that they are correct, simply that they fit the evidence.

If I try to establish the size of the village by reconstructing the camp circles that were present, I encounter some difficulty right off with the Cheyenne population. Wooden Leg's estimate of 300 lodges does not gibe with his population of 1,600, nor does it correlate with the two other estimates of 3,000 for the Cheyenne population. A count of 300 lodges would translate to about 2,150 people, not 1,600, and 3,000 people would translate to about 420 lodges. So there is no way to reconcile these two statements.

I can, however, work backward from other evidence. Wooden Leg says that the Hunkpapas had twice as many lodges as the Cheyenne. This would give a figure of 600, which is exactly the lower estimate of He Dog, who said that there were 600–700 Hunkpapa and Blackfeet Lakota lodges. Since Wooden Leg didn't include these latter with the Hunkpapa, it is probably safe to allow 600 for the Hunkpapa, and since the Cheyennes were half as many, 300 for them. This will agree with Wooden Leg as to lodges but give slightly more in population, while still being below the numbers given by Ice Bear and Tall Bull.

Flying By states that there were 600–800 Mnicoujou lodges, while He Dog says they were next to the Hunkpapas, who were most numerous. Wooden Leg says the Mnicoujou had more than the Sans Arcs (who had more than the Cheyennes) but fewer than the Hunkpapas, who, at least inferentially, had the most. So I'll make the Mnicoujou count 25 percent fewer than the Hunkpapa, or 450. There is no independent count for the Oglalas, but Wooden Leg states that they had about the same as the Mnicoujou, so let us assign them the same number, 450.

Wooden Leg says that the Blackfeet Lakota had about the same number as the Cheyenne, or a few less, while Flying By included them with the Hunkpapas at 600–700. Since I've given the Hunkpapas 600, I'll give the Blackfeet Lakota the extra 100. That is considerably fewer than per Wooden Leg, but is a safe figure. He Dog gives figures of twenty-plus and thirty to forty for the Brules and the Santees, respectively. It should be safe to use the lower of these estimates.

The Sans Arcs (No Bows, or Arrows All Gone) were, according to Wooden Leg, somewhere between the Cheyennes and the Mnicoujous. If we put them halfway between, we arrive at 375 lodges as their count. There were a few lodges of Yanktons and Yanktonnais, at least one lodge of Southern Cheyennes, and either four or six Arapaho men (who were staying in a Cheyenne lodge); there may have been some Assiniboines. There most certainly were Two Kettles present. I can safely add 20 lodges total to account for these people. So in summary:

Hunkpapas	600
Cheyennes	300
Mnicoujou	450
Oglalas	450
Brule	20
Santees	30
Blackfeet Lakota	100
Sans Arcs	375
Miscellaneous	20

Unfortunately, this represents a total of 2,345 lodges and 16,000–17,000 people, with some 4,700 warriors. This is more than I can manage to fit into the evidence, except perhaps for the number of warriors; in this latter case I can probably allow for a greater than normal ratio of fighting men to lodges because of the circumstances and because of the wickiups that were undeniably present. I could, of course, assume that the evidence is wrong, but it is highly unlikely that an error of the indicated magnitude could have been so consistently made. The interesting thing is that those witnesses who give the numbers for individual camp circles also invariably give a total of 1,800 lodges for the village—when they give any number. So perhaps it would be acting prudently to reduce the total to 1,800 and try to keep the same ratio between the various camp circles, at least as far as the major tribal divisions are concerned. Doing that results in the following lodge figures:

Hunkpapas	440
Cheyennes	220
Mnicoujou	330
Oglalas	330
Brules	20
Santees	30
Blackfeet Lakota	75
Sans Arcs	275
Miscellaneous	20

This gives a total of 1,740 lodges, representing a population of about 12,400 with approximately 3,500 warriors, maybe more if one makes allowances for the higher-than-usual ratio mentioned above. There is now total agreement with virtually all sources as to totals, but not as to specific tribal divisions, though I have maintained the ratio between these. I have also arrived at a Cheyenne population of about 1,600—which fits in very nicely with Wooden Leg/Dr. Marquis, although it is at odds with Ice Bear and Tall Bull.

None of this means that I have discovered the truth, however, only that my conclusion is based upon, and satisfies, the preponderance of evidence. Now I have to see whether I can show what numbers were possible and most probable from sources other than the anecdotal evidence summarized above. Although many researchers might tend to disagree, the only other real sources are the registers and censuses of Indians at the various agencies. Since much has been made of a supposed "vast exodus" from the agencies, a survey of their records should prove to be enlightening.

All sources agree that the number of hostile Lakotas living permanently in the unceded territories in 1875 was approximately 3,000, comprised of several bands of Oglalas and Hunkpapas and a few groups from the other Teton tribal divisions. There were a few hundred Northern Cheyennes, and certainly a few hundred people of other tribal stock. The total of all of these was about 4,000, but they never were to be found camped together in one village, and even the Sioux rarely got together, except perhaps at one of the summer ceremonies at Bear Butte.

It is considerably more difficult to get a handle on the others. There were a lesser number of what I choose to call free-roamers, but a much larger number of agency-roamers, who left the reservations in the late spring each year to hunt buffalo and to renew their lodges and supplies of lodge poles. Although the agency census figures and rolls should give a good idea of at least the total populations, in fact they only confuse the issue. Gray uses these figures to bolster his case for a particular population figure, but does so selectively and, in my opinion, subjectively. He discards as wholly untrustworthy any numbers which do not support his arguments, and finds some way to justify those which do.

Gray says that the Lakota population was virtually static from about 1850 to 1890, and gives a table of selected population estimates and counts to back up this statement and to give a basis for his conclusions. Any numbers which do not fit into his scenario are summarily dismissed. Unfortunately, it is obvious that either the Lakota population was not static or that it was considerably higher than Gray wants to believe—much more in line with the "inflated" counts by agents that he chooses to ignore.

Gray says that the Oglala population was between 2,000 and 3,340 in the years 1850 to 1869, based on estimates from various sources, with an average of 2,558. Then he says that the "reliable" census of 1890 at the Red Cloud Agency showed 4,180 (which is not exactly static). Nearly a century later, the Oglala population in 1975 at Pine Ridge was 11,500, which again is not indicative of a static population—or if the population was indeed static, then it was considerably higher than guessed at in the 1850s and 1860s. The population at Pine Ridge/Spotted Tail was given as 9,610 in January of 1975, and at Red Cloud was either 12,873 or 11,633, depending upon whom you believe. This latter figure included 9,339 Lakotas, 1,202 Northern Cheyennes and 1,092 Arapahoes.

There were 7,400 Brules in 1875 as compared with 5,260 in 1890 and 4,890 Hunkpapas as compared with 1,990. The total Lakota population in 1975 was at least 31,500 for all Teton tribal divisions, as compared with Gray's 19,720 in 1890, and an Indian Department census of 37,391 for the four major agencies taken in January 1875. So it becomes completely confusing to try to make any sense of all of these various numbers. After a while, they just start running into one another and it becomes tempting to grab one or two and take them as gospel.

A military census taken in September 1876 gives a count of 11,660 at the four major Teton agencies, so that whatever one assumes as the 1875 population, there was certainly an exodus from the agencies. It must be remembered also that some families returned to the agencies after the Rosebud fight and that even more went in after the Custer fight. Very few, if any, left the agencies after the Custer fight and before the military census, so it is reasonably safe to suppose that the four-agency population on June 25 was just about 11,000.

If we take a reasonable pre-exodus agency population of 20,000 instead of the 37,000 reported by the agents, we are left with a figure of 9,000 "missing" Lakotas. Obviously, they were not missing but in fact were out in the unceded territory with their "wild" brothers. It can be reasonably assumed that although the vast majority comprised family units, there was a decidedly disproportionate number of young warriors among these Indians. Add to these the 4,000 already in the wilds, the several hundred who did not return to their agencies from their previous year's summer roaming, the Lakotas who left from the other agencies, plus the bulk of the Northern Cheyenne population, and it is obvious that there were, in fact, at least 14,000 Sioux and Cheyenne out in the Powder River country, and probably somewhat more than this.

Not all of them were at the Little Horn. But there is no doubt that the vast majority of them were present, and that there were more warriors *per capita* than there would have been in a normal village or gathering.

The village has invariably been described as being "the largest gathering of Indians in one place at one time" by everyone who saw it—be they Indian or white. The only exception to this statement that I have ever seen was Dr. Charles A. Eastman, who is quoted earlier in this appendix. The gatherings of the Sioux at Bear Butte sometimes brought 10,000 or 12,000 people together. For witnesses to say emphatically that this village was larger is saying all that anyone really needs to know.

Based on the foregoing lodge count, it is not improbable that there were in excess of 12,000 people in the Little Horn village and to put the number of warriors at 3,500 to 4,500. It is not necessary to do this in order to explain the disaster that overtook the 7th Cavalry on June 25–26, and it takes nothing away from the warriors who fought on those two most glorious days in the long history of the Lakotas to establish these numbers as most probable.

In the face of these warrior numbers was the 7th Cavalry—a regiment that was under strength—further weakened by a lack of regular combat experience and the inclusion of a high number of green recruits? Those two questions can be easily resolved by a careful examination of the regimental records.

TWO CONTROVERSIES: RECRUITS AT THE LITTLE HORN AND THE INDIAN-FIGHTING RECORD OF THE 7TH CAVALRY

*"Q. Did you consider those men, in your opinion
as a sergeant, unfit to take into action?
A. Some few I did."*
—Sergeant F. A. Culbertson, A Company:
testimony at the Reno Court of Inquiry

As with most controversial aspects of the Little Horn, I am amazed that these two have not been resolved over the years to the satisfaction of intelligent and reasonable readers and researchers. It would seem a fairly simple task to determine the facts and to let them speak for themselves. Of course, like many other controversies, this one may lie in the eye or mind of the beholder. For example, I might think that a recruit proportion of 15 percent is not very noteworthy and that the number of recruits did not play any part in what happened at the Little Horn, while another might find critical significance in the identical number.

The subject of new recruits and their possible negative contribution to the disaster probably had its genesis at the Reno Court of Inquiry, where Sergeant Culbertson of A Company was allowed to pontificate on the subject in an apparent attempt to remove some of the onus from Major Reno. Culbertson's testimony was not challenged.[1] Benteen noted in his official report that he was reluctant to cross the river because of the high number of recruits in his battalion, and nobody challenged that statement either.[2] Over the years others have attributed varying degrees of responsibility for the disaster to the high number of recruits in the regiment.

A note in Graham's *Story of the Little Big Horn* states: "The proportion of raw recruits in the Seventh Cavalry during the Little Big Horn campaign was very large . . . Generals Edgerly and Godfrey . . . are the authority for the statement that speaking in general terms, the companies contained from thirty to forty percent of recruits without prior service."[3] The note quotes part of Culbertson's testimony (Graham relied very heavily on the Reno Inquiry testimony) and goes on to say that General Godfrey has lately (1925–26) informed the author that K Company took twenty-five recruits at St. Paul, just before the campaign opened. The total strength of the company after leaving the supply camp on the Yellowstone was forty, thus the impression of hordes of recruits is very strongly implanted in the mind of the reader, at least insofar as K Company is concerned.

Thomas B. Marquis puts forth the proposition that Custer's troopers committed mass suicide, and he attributes this action to the "large number of recruits unaccustomed to military discipline and military law."[4] He quotes Graham and Culbertson but also adds his own statistics: "New recruits had been added at Fort Abraham Lincoln during the autumn of 1875. . . . Then, about a month before the start was made, 125 more newly enlisted men arrived to be transformed into instant soldiers. Thus, Custer's Seventh Cavalry . . . consisted at the very least of 30 percent raw soldier material when it set out . . ."

Other writers have tried to correct the record or even gone overboard in the opposite direction. Stewart uses W.J. Ghent as the source for his assertion that only two recruits were in K Company at the Little Horn and that probably none of the other companies had more, but he gives no specifics.[5] Ghent and Stewart were, as will be shown, wrong—there were no recruits in K Company at the Little Horn. John Gray, Joe Sills and Rod MacNeil have explored the subject, but I don't believe that any of these eminent researchers has hit the target.[6]

The subject of the actual Indian record of the regiment is probably not quite so controversial, although some writers have stated that its only action of any consequence was the Battle of the Washita, and have gone on to say that the reputations of both the regiment and its usual field commander were undeserved. There is certainly a smidgeon of truth in there, but it is simplistic to say that the regiment had hardly any experience in Indian fighting and that what it had was too long since to count for much.

Since the experience of the regiment and its members is part and parcel of the recruits' question, it will be addressed first and the findings used to explore the matter of the recruits and their burden upon the regiment.

The 7th Regiment of Cavalry was officially born on July 28, 1866, but none of the companies were actually organized until September 10 at Fort Riley, Kansas. Even then there were few company officers, those that existed being temporarily assigned from the 2nd Cavalry. The 7th's own officers began arriving in October and continued dribbling in until May 1867. Armstrong Custer arrived November 3, 1866 and he was joined by some other officers who were destined to die with him at the Little Horn—Tom Custer, William Cooke, Myles Keogh and others who would fight and survive—Benteen, Moylan and Weir.

The majority of the 7th Cavalry campaigned as part of Hancock's Expedition during the summer of 1867 but there were no engagements with hostiles, except for a few minor run-ins that deserve no inclusion here. There was, however, a sharp fight with a large body of Cheyennes near Fort Wallace, which involved Captain Barnitz and G Company. While elements of the regiment were detailed as guards for the various stage stations across Kansas and into Colorado, many men were exposed to skirmishes with marauding bands, usually small, of Indians intent on making off with livestock, the stage horses being particularly desirable.

The first major fight was the Battle of the Washita on November 27, 1868, where eleven companies of the regiment (L was at Fort Lyon, Colorado) destroyed the village of Black Kettle, a leading Southern Cheyenne chief, and fought an all-day engagement with the occupants of the village and reinforcements from other villages along the river. It is not a part of this review to enter into a debate about the nature of the Indian casualties, or whether Black Kettle was a peace chief, or the Elliott affair—only to note that there was a real fight with real guns and real dead and wounded people—some of whom were 7th Cavalrymen.

The regiment, after recuperating, embarked upon a winter–spring 1869 campaign against the Southern Cheyennes, Kiowas and other nations living or roaming upon the southern plains. This was a long, arduous and successful campaign, but featured little fighting. There was some healthy skirmishing out of Fort Harker in March 1869. The summer saw a couple of company actions; indeed most Indian fights were company or squadron actions. Only rarely was the army able to force a large-scale, set-piece battle upon the Indians.

The 7th was broken up in 1870–71 and was assigned to various duties, mostly reconstruction duty in the South. The regiment was brought back to the plains, this time to Dakota, in 1873. Companies D and I, under the command of Major Reno, were detailed as escort to the Northern Boundary Survey and performed this duty for two years, 1873 and 1874. The remaining ten companies escorted the Northern Pacific Railway survey team (the Stanley Expedition) in 1873, during which there were two sharp engagements with hostile Lakotas on the Yellowstone, very near the battlefield of 1876. Not all of the companies participated in these fights, and I have taken that into consideration in compiling the tables that form part of this analysis.

In 1874 the same ten companies formed the main component of Custer's expedition into the Black Hills. There was no fighting on this summer expedition, which was exploratory in nature. There were a couple of minor actions in 1875.

That is the record. It is not a lengthy one and certainly it would be at least stretching the truth to proclaim that the 7th was the Champion of the Plains. It is true nonetheless that there was much more to the record than the Washita in 1868, and it is equally true that it is an unblemished record, the only failure being the fizzling out of Hancock's campaign without being able to force a fight upon the hostiles. The fact is that not many big Indian fights actually took place in the West—we are dealing with history here, not Hollywood— so that no cavalry regiment really had a great deal of experience (one might argue that the 4th had more experience than the 7th) but the 7th did have experience, some of it relatively recent and had also campaigned in the field extensively.

The matter of recruits is similarly easily dealt with. Although some other writers on the subject have seen fit to divide the recruits into two classes— "raw" and "trained"—I have arbitrarily decided to put them in "1875" and "1876" groups, and have arbitrarily selected September 1, 1875 as the date from which men are classed as recruits. Virtually everything is admittedly arbitrary in classifying these men, and I do not know who received what training, except that they all had their "basic" at St. Louis—but I do know, for the most part, who they were and where they were. I will let the reader make up his own mind as to what effect the recruits had on the outcome of the fights, but will supply as much information as I can to assist in that endeavor.

LIST OF ENGAGEMENTS 1867–75

DATE	PLACE	COMPANIES INVOLVED
June 22, 1867	Near Fort Wallace, Kansas	G and part of I
September 10, 1868	Rule Creek, Colorado	L
September 11–15, 1868	Sand Hills (Cimarron and Canadian Rivers), Kansas	A, B, C, D, E, F, G, I, K
September 17, 1868	Saline River, Kansas	H
October 9 & 10, 1868	Big Bend of the Arkansas River	A, B, C, D, E, F, G, H, I, K, M
October 12, 1868	Big Bend of the Arkansas River	H, K, M
November 3, 1868	Big Coon Creek, Kansas	H
November 27, 1868	Washita River	A, B, C, D, E, F, G, H, I, K, M
January 28, 1869	Solomon River, Kansas	B
March 12–18, 1869	Fort Harker, Kansas	A, B, C, D, E, F, G, H, I, K, H
June 1, 1869	Solomon River, Kansas	H
June 19, 1869	Sheridan, Kansas	H
June 13, 1870	Grinnell Station, Kansas	H
August 4, 1873	Tongue River, Montana	A, B
August 11, 1873	Pease Bottom, Montana	A, B, E, F, G, K, L, H
August 16, 1873	Yellowstone River, Montana	camp attacked
April 22, 1875	Fort Lincoln, Dakota	A, B, E, F, G, L
December 12, 1875	Standing Rock Agency	F, L

It is true that there were large drafts of recruits in late 1875 and early 1876. This was to be expected. The enlistment term of the day was five years and hence one could reasonably expect that about 20 percent of the regiment would be "new enlistments" at any moment in time. Of course, one could also reasonably expect that some of these recruits would actually be re-enlistments, or would have had previous service, or perhaps would have fought in the Civil War. Such was indeed the case.

In compiling the information, lists and tables in this discussion, I have relied on enlistment dates and notations from the official records. This means that the numbers which I provide are in fact "worst-case" figures, since previous enlistments were not always noted, especially if there was a gap in service; some men enlisted under assumed names for various reasons (one of which, strangely enough, was that they had deserted under another name) and foreign or Civil War service was not necessarily referenced.

I have not attempted to determine whether a soldier was actually engaged in an action in which his company took part, except that I have assumed that late 1875 recruits did not take part in the December 1875 action. The number of instances where I give a man credit for experience that he did not in fact have would be compensated for by the number of men with unidentified prior service or military experience. It all evens out, I would think.

The tables which follow indicate, the number of recruits at the Little Horn and the number of experienced soldiers for each company and other component of the regiment. The recruits are separated into 1875 and 1876 groups and the numbers detached are given, while the "experience factor" is categorized as Washita, other Indian fights, other campaigns and Civil War/previous military experience.

It must be noted that men are included in only one category of experience, prioritized in the order given above. Men who had been in service before September 1, 1875 but who did not fall into one of the four categories were not considered as experienced for the purposes of this review, even though they may have been exposed to "military discipline and military law" for more than a year. As a matter of convenience for the reader, I have listed the surnames of those who make up the recruit and experienced categories at the Little Horn in the table at the end of the analysis.

THE RECRUIT FACTOR

Note: The columns represent number of recruits; number having previous enlistments; number having previous military experience; number having fought in the Civil War; number detached prior to the campaign plus number detached at the Powder River Supply Depot.

	1875						1876					
		PREV				AT		PREV				AT
UNIT:	NO	ENL	MIL	CW	DET	LBH	NO	ENL	MIL	CW	DET	LBH
RENO HQ	1	0	0	0	0	1	0	0	0	0	0	0
A CO.	11	1	2	0	0	8	0	0	0	0	0	0
G CO.	3	0	0	0	1	2	17	2	0	0	12	3
M CO.	22	3	2	0	0	17	3	2	1	0	0	0
Totals:	37	4	4	0	1	28	20	4	1	0	12	3
D CO.	14	0	0	0	4	10	1	1	0	0	0	0
H CO.	7	2	1	0	0	4	0	0	0	0	0	0
K CO.	5	0	0	0	5	0	12	6	1	0	5	0
Totals:	26	2	1	0	9	14	13	7	1	0	5	0
PACKS	20	6	0	0	0	14	1	0	0	0	0	1
B CO.	4	3	0	0	0	1	26	2	1	0	17	6
Totals:	24	9	0	0	0	15	27	2	1	0	17	7
CUSTER HQ	3	0	0	0	3	0	3	1	0	0	2	0
C CO.	19	6	0	1	3	9	0	0	0	0	0	0
E CO.	6	3	0	1	1	1	1	1	0	0	0	0
F CO.	11	1	0	1	3	6	4	4	0	0	0	0
I CO.	4	0	0	0	2	2	0	0	0	0	0	0
L CO.	11	2	0	0	1	8	0	0	0	0	0	0
Totals:	54	12	0	3	13	26	8	6	0	0	2	0
REGT	141	27	5	3	23	83	68	19	3	0	36	10

The line "Packs" above refers to the survivors of the Custer companies who were either assigned to the packs or who otherwise wound up with the remnant of the regiment on Reno Hill. With a few exceptions, there is no way of knowing how many of the recruits who were at the Little Horn were assigned to the pack detail. I have assumed that the ratio of recruits to experienced men would have been maintained in such assignments, although the ratio for the five Custer companies was in fact higher, which might seem reasonable in the circumstances. If I had been a first sergeant and had to assign men to the packs, I probably would have leaned toward assigning recruits rather than seasoned veterans, knowing that we were going into a potentially dangerous situation.

The numbers clearly show that the number of recruits at the Little Horn has been consistently overstated. Marquis' 125 recruits assigned about a month before the campaign was in fact sixty-nine—and only eleven of these who were really recruits made it as far as the Little Horn. More than half were deposited at the Powder River Supply Depot, generally because there were not sufficient horses to go around. Even the 1875 recruit number shrinks from a gross number of 140 to a net of eighty-three men who were at the Little Horn.

What does this do to previous portrayals? Obviously it knocks them for a loop. Benteen's excuse for not crossing the river because of the high number of recruits in his battalion proves to be worthless, as the number was only fourteen and not one of these was an 1876 recruit. Culbertson's testimony before the Reno Court of Inquiry is shown to be a fabrication, and the statements of Edgerly and Godfrey turn out to be lapses in memory. Graham's attempt to portray Godfrey's K Company as peopled by a majority of recruits (he gives the impression that twenty-seven of forty-two men were recruits—see above) is shown to be badly misleading, if not an outright fabrication. K Company did not have a single new recruit at the Little Horn—not one.

THE EXPERIENCE FACTOR

Note: Only regular military personnel are included in these tables. Enlisted Indian scouts are not included but it must be pointed out that many of these men had previous enlistments and had fought against the Lakotas. Because of the methodology adopted, there are some men who fall between my definitions of recruit and experienced. These are included in the number present but not in either category under review.

	RECRUITS				EXPERIENCED				
UNIT	PRES	1875	1876	TOTAL	WASH	OTH	CAMP	PREV	TOTAL
RENO									
HQ	5	1	0	1	1	1	1	1	4
A CO.	49	8	0	8	6	31	0	3	40
G CO.	45	2	3	5	9	29	0	1	39
M CO.	56	17	0	17	5	19	9	3	36
Totals:	155	28	3	31	21	80	10	8	119

D CO.	51	10	0	10	10	0	22	1	33
H CO.	46	4	0	4	13	0	23	1	37
K CO.	37	0	0	0	12	21	2	1	36
Totals:	134	14	0	14	35	21	47	3	113
PACKS	72	14	1	15	11	30	15	0	56
B CO.	46	1	6	7	6	29	0	3	38
Totals:	118	15	7	22	17	59	15	3	94
CUSTER HQ	11	0	0	0	5	5	1	0	11
C CO.	38	9	0	9	1	1	23	1	26
E CO.	38	1	0	1	4	28	0	2	34
F CO.	37	6	0	6	6	21	0	2	29
I CO.	36	2	0	2	3	1	28	1	33
L CO.	46	8	0	8	0	33	0	2	35
Totals:	206	26	0	26	19	89	52	8	168
REGT	613	83	10	93	92	249	131	22	494

It can easily be seen that the total number of recruits (ninety-three) is almost matched by the number of men who were at the Washita (ninety-two). More than half the regiment had been in Indian fights, which must come as something of a shock to those readers who have dined only on Graham, Dustin and Brininstool. When other experience is factored in, the regiment is found to be almost exactly 80 percent veterans and only 15 percent recruits. Veterans outnumbered recruits by more than five to one, and remember that the recruits total includes everyone from September 1, 1875 on. In fact, there were only ten recruits of the 1876 variety at the Little Horn, and it is definitely established that at least one of them was with the packs.

The highest percentage of recruits was in the Reno Battalion, but it was still only 20 percent, which is a far cry from the "about half" to which Culbertson testified, or even the 30–40 percent mentioned by Graham. The Reno figures are skewed by those for M Company, which did have 30 percent recruits—the highest of any combat company. The lowest percentage of recruits can be found in Benteen's battalion. This is the same Benteen who reported officially that he did not cross the Little Horn because he knew that the high number of recruits in his command would stand no earthly chance against the veteran Indian warriors he saw over there. Benteen actually had more Washita veterans than any other unit—more than twice as many as his "large element of recruits." While his battalion might not have fared well against those "veteran warriors," it would not have been because of a high number of recruits.

Custer's battalions contained 12 percent recruits and 80 percent veterans, so it cannot be asserted with any basis in fact that the fate of his command was influenced by new men. It would seem safe to draw the same conclusions from the numbers in respect of all of the actions at the Little Horn, and there are good reasons for coming to the same conclusion.

There were very few military movements at the Little Horn which required expert maneuvering on horseback, which is where any deficiencies in training and experience would be bound to show up—as would any lack of experience in the horses (another theory advanced by several writers). Reno made a change in front while moving toward the Indians in the valley and no one has reported that there were any problems in doing so. There were no problems reported with the horses or the horse-holders in the timber. There were no problems reported in the approach to the Little Horn, except a few instances of tired horses; no problems in the advance to Weir Peak and the action there, except Edgerly's difficulty in getting mounted to retreat; no problems with the horses when Godfrey halted and dismounted his company and threw out a skirmish line to check the advance of the Indians during the retreat from Weir Peak, and no problems with his horse-holders taking the horses into the line. Indeed, the only difficulties that we know of for certain are the couple of instances of trooper's horses carrying them into the Indian lines in the valley (and all or most of these men rode back out again) and the testimony of some of Reno's officers that the recruits tended to shoot too high and expend their ammunition too fast. While this most definitely would have helped keep the Indians losses down, it did not account for Reno's defeat in the valley.

The fight on the hilltop did not require that the men do anything more than keep their heads down and keep up a sufficient fire to keep the Indians out of the lines—both of which were done with measures of success. There were no reported instances of insubordination or failure to act when ordered, nor were there any reported flagrant acts of cowardice, although one might make out one or two if one digs deeply enough. But that is just the trouble with the "recruits excuse"—one has to dig too deeply and read too much into nothing to find even the remotest allusion to the supposed cowardice or inexperience of these men causing the great disasters at the Little Horn. If the recruits were cowardly enough to create a panic in the valley, then why were they not cowardly enough to at least stand out on the hilltop? And if they were prone to all of this panic, why is it that four of them (Brant, Callan, Goldin and Thompson) won Medals of Honor for their actions at the Little Horn? Two of these men were 1876 recruits, meaning that two of ten won medals—hardly the performance of men who were thrown into a panic by their first sight of hostile Indians or their first whiff of powder smoke.

As for the Custer battalions, there is nothing here that would make me believe that the performance of recruits therein was anything different from what it was in the other actions. Again, there is absolutely no evidence that any maneuvering done was affected by the performance of rookie men or horses, and while it became fashionable in some circles to describe the action on Custer's Field as a "panic rout" or "regular buffalo hunt," the vast preponderance of physical and anecdotal evidence is to the contrary. There were a few established cases of horses breaking down in the Custer command and I accept these, although it is interesting to note that there were no breakdowns in any of the other units. The truth is that the Custer fight was for the most part a disjointed series of engagements, with little maneuvering and no cause for any panic until, perhaps, the very end—which from all accounts was confused and mixed-up.

Were the 7th Cavalry recruits scared? I would bet they were. I would bet that everyone at the Little Horn was, to one degree or another. Did they shoot high? Quite likely they did—at least some of them and at least for a part of the time. It is easier to shoot up than it is to shoot down. Did they waste ammunition? Probably they did, at first, but there is no credible evidence that a shortage of ammunition affected any of the actions, anywhere, at the Little Horn. Just as there is absolutely no credible evidence that the number of recruits was high or that the recruits who were there influenced the outcomes in any way at all.

This is another example of a "Custer controversy" that has gone on far too long, which should have been cleared up many years ago and which probably could have been—by men of good will and a fair resolve. Unfortunately, until recently, there has been a dearth of these kind of men associated with the history of the fights on the Little Horn and one has only to pore over the testimony from the Reno Court to find the first of the other kind.

THE RECRUITS AND VETERANS AT THE LITTLE HORN

UNIT	CATEGORIES	SOLDIERS
RENO HQ	1875	Abbots
	Washita	Clear
	Fights	Davern
	Campaigns	Hodgson
	Other	Reno
A CO.	1875	Bott, Deal, Gilbert, McClurg, McDonald, Reeves, Seayers, Switzer
	Washita	Moylan, Heyn, Culbertson, Bringes, Armstrong, Siebelder
	Fights	Easley, Hardy, Ailer, Drinan, Durselen, Jonson, Moody, Sullivan, DeRudio, Fehier, McDermott, Dallans, King, Roy, McVeigh, Hamilton, Bancroft, Baumgartner, Blair, Blake, Conner, Foster, Harris, Homsted Johnson, Nugent, Proctor, Rawlins, Stroude, Taylor, Weaver
	Other	Meuring, Cowley, Hook
G CO.	1875	Taylor, Stanley
	1876	Campbell, Dwyer, Goldin
	Washita	Morrison, Botzer, Brown, Northeg, Wells, Grayson, McGonigle, O'Neill, Seafferman
	Fights	Mcintosh, Wallace, Considine, Martin, Cornwall, Graham, Hackett, McDonnell, McEagan, McVay, Moore, Reed, Robb, Rogers, Small, Stevenson, Wallace, Weiss, Hammon, Lattman, Hagemann, Loyd, McCormick, Rapp, Akers, Boyle, Brinkerhof, McGinniss, Petring
	Other	Selby
M CO.	1875	Braun, Cain, Mahoney, Meyer, Morris, Pigford, Rye, Seamans, Senn, Slaper, Smith,

		Sniffin, Stratton, Tanner, Thornberry, Thorpe, Wiedman
	Washita	Ryan, Fisher, Donahoe, Davis, Held
	Fights	French, Carey, McGlone, O'Hara, White, Streing, Weaver, Bates, Golden, Gordon, Kavanaugh, Lorentz, Moore, Neely, Rutten, Severs, Weaver, Williams, Turley
	Campaigns	Scollin, Gallene, Klotzbucher, Meier, Newell, Ryder, Sivertsen, Voigt, Whisten
	Other	Lalor, Summers, Wilber
D CO.	1875	Alberts, Brant, Fox, Harris, Marshall, Meadwell, O'Mann, Randall, Smith, Smith
	Washita	Weir, Martin, Harrison, Bohner, Deetline, Myers, Holden, Kretchmer, Sanders, Wynn
	Campaigns	Edgerly, Russell, Wylie, Chancy, Ascough, Cox, Dann, Dawsey, Fay, Golden, Green, Hall, Hansen, Hardden, Harris, Hayer, Hetler, Horn, Hunt, Hurd, Kavanagh, Keller, Kipp, Manning, McDonnell, Reid, Scott, Stivers, Welch
	Other	Flanagan
H CO.	1875	Channell, Diamond, Nees, O'Ryan
	Washita	Benteen, Gibson, Conneily, Geiger, Maroney, McLaughlin, Glease, Haley, Hughes, Hunt, Kelly, Lawhorn, McDermott
	Campaigns	McCurry, Pahl, Lell, Nealon, Ramell, Volt, Adams, George, Kelly, Black, Cooper, Day, Dewey, Hauck, Jones, McNamara, Meador, Moller, Nicholas, Phillips, Pinkston, Williams, Windolph
	Other	Bishley
K CO.	Washita	Godfrey, Steintker, Burke, Blunt, Burkhardt, Corcoran, Foley, Helmer, Madden, McConnell, Mielke, Murphy
	Fights	Winney, Frederick, Rott, Hose, Penwell,

		Brown, Campbell, Rafter, Boisson, Chesterwood, Coakley, Donahue, Jennys, Raichel, McCue, Robers, Lasley, Siefert, Schwerer, Shauer, Whitlow
	Campaigns	Bresnahan, Gordon
	Other	Schlafer
PACKS.	1875	Brennan, Mahoney, McGuire, Thompson, Watson, Howard, Lyons, Myers, Pickard, Johnson, McShane, Marshall, Moore, Rose
	1876	Chapman
	Washita	Lynch, Sweeney, Hanley, Fitzgerald, Riley, Shields, Kimm, Curtiss, Schleiper, Hunter, Lefler
	Fights	Reese, Finnegan, Mathey, Brommell, Murphy, McKenna, Rooney, Spencer, Miller, Berwald, James, Lang, Liddiard, Clyde, Butler, Walsh, Gregg, Reilley, Shulte, Banks, Brown, Burkman, McHugh, Sullivan, Mullen, Abrams, Logue, Stoffel, Etzler, Bennett
	Campaigns	Ramsey, Fowler, Whitaker, De Lacy, Braun, Cooney, Jones, McNally, Korn, Bennett, Knipe, Farrar, Jordan, Mullin, Nitsche
B CO.	1875	Crowley
	1876	Kelly, Crump, Callan, Criswell, Davenport, McLaughlin
	Washita	Murray, Wetzel, Moore, Crowe, Frank, Ryan
	Fights	McDougall, Criswell, Bailey, Dougherty, Smith, McCabe, Boren, Campbell, Carey, Randall, Pym, Hutchinson, Devoto, Martin, Trumble, Woods, Cunningham, Boam, Shea, Wallace, Carmody, McMasters, Coleman, Dorn, Mask, Spinner, Stout, O'Neill, Sager
	Other	Hill, Barsantee, Thomas

CUSTER	Washita	Custer, Cooke, Voss, McIlhargey, Mitchell
	Fights	Sharrow, Hughes, Vickory, Callahan, Dose
	Campaigns	Lord
C CO.	1875	Kramer, King, Brightsfield, Criddle, Meier, Meyer, Phillips, Shea, Short
	Washita	Custer (T. W.)
	Fights	Finley
	Campaigns	Harrington, Bucknell, Engle, Farrand, Bobo, Howell, Lewis, Hathersall, Finkle, Foley, French, Ryan, Allan, Eisman, Griffin, St. John, Stuart, Rauter, Rix, Russell, Stungerwitz, Van Allen, Wyman
	Other	Warner
E CO.	1875	Farrell
	Washita	Smith, Hohmeyer, Ogden, Smith
	Fights	Mason, Baker, Brogan, James, Brown, Barth, Henderson, Conner, Henderson, Hiley, Rees, Schele, Smith, Torrey, Van Sant, Hagan, Meyer, Knecht, O'Connor, Rood, Stafford, Smith, Stella, Boyle, Davis, Huber, Smallwood, Walker
	Other	Darns, McElroy
F CO.	1875	Brady, Donnelly, Lossee, Monroe, Rudden, Sicfous
	Washita	Yates, Briody, Atchison, Bruce, Klein, Milton
	Fights	Coleman, Nursey, Brandon, Brown, Kenney, Wilkinson, Teeman, Manning, Brown, Burnham, Carney, Cather, Dohman, Hammon, Way, Kelly, Knauth, Lerock, Liemann, Madsen, Omling
	Other	Gardner, Warren
I CO.	1875	Barry, Hetesimer
	Washita	Varden, Kelley, Reed
	Fights	Keogh

	Campaigns	Porter Bustard, Conners, Morris, Staples, Wild, McGucker, Patton, Bailey, Broadhurst, Downing, Driscoll, Gillette, Gross, Holconib, Horn, Lehman, Lehn, Lloyd, Noshang, O'Bryan, Parker, Pitter, Quinn, Rossbury, Troy, Van Bramer, Whaley
	Other	Post
L CO.	1875	Heath, Babcock, Dye, Galvan, Snow, Tarbox, Tweed, Vetter.
	Fights	Calhoun, Burke, Warren, Gilbert, Butler, Cashan, Harrison, Siemon, Adams, Assadily, Seller, Walsh, Cheever, Duggan, Hauggi, Rogers, Scott, O'Connell, Graham, Hamilton, Kavanagh, Lobering, McCarthy, Miller, Harrington, Mahoney, Maxwell, McGue, Reibold, Roberts, Schmidt, Siemonson, Tessier
	Other	Andrews, Crisfield

Whether they were experienced men or newer recruits before the fights on the Little Horn, over 350 officers and men of the 7th Cavalry died there. Who were these casualties and where were they buried?

NOTES

1. [ebook] Appendix 5.17.
2. Captain Frederick W. Benteen: report of July 4, 1876: [ebook] Appendix 4.1.
3. Col. William A. Graham, *The Story of the Little Big Horn* (Harrisburg, 1952), Note 3, p.117.
4. Thomas B. Marquis, *Keep the Last Bullet for Yourself* (Algonac, 1976).
5. Edgar I. Stewart, *Custer's Luck* (Norman: Univ. of Okla. Press, 1955).
6. John S. Gray, *Centennial Campaign* (Fort Collins, 1976); Joe Sills, Jr., "The Recruits Controversy: Another Look," *Greasy Grass*, Vol. 5 (Custer Battlefield Historical & Museum Association, Inc., 1989); MacNeil, Rod, "Custer's Approach to the Little Big Horn River," *More Sidelights of the Sioux Wars* (London: Westerners Publications, 2007).

THE LOCATION OF BODIES
AND THE INITIAL BURIALS OF
THE 7th CAVALRY'S DEAD

"Then beat the drum slowly, play the fife lowly,
Play the dead march as you carry me along,
Take me to the green valley, lay the sod o'er me . . . "
—Streets of Laredo, lyric

The following are excerpts from longer accounts, mostly from participants in the Little Horn fights, pertaining to the initial burials. (Information from these accounts has also been used in the preparation of
Analysis 6.) Only those portions of the accounts dealing with the burials
or locations of the bodies are reproduced and obviously there has been a
great deal of editing involved. I have, however, not edited the excerpts except
as to their pertinence to the subjects at hand—and here we are not so much
concerned with how or why the troops got to where they were, but with
whether or not the locations of the burials coincide with where the bodies
were found.

The condition and mutilation of the bodies are not really peripheral questions, since those are major contributors to determining how much movement, if any, of the bodies was made before and during the initial burials.
Some Indian accounts touching on these subjects are included, but the vast
majority of the Indian reminiscences do not mention much about the location

of the bodies, and deny that any mutilations were done, except, perhaps, by the squaws. Although it was not uncommon for victorious warriors to lariat the bodies of living or dead enemies and drag them about behind their horses as part of a post-battle celebration, not one of the Indian accounts I have seen mentions this having been done. The vast majority of Indian accounts agree on the general location of the troops, i.e. at Calhoun Hill, Keogh Swale, Custer Hill and the slopes leading down from Calhoun and Custer Hills, although there is not always agreement on how the troops got there or in which direction they were moving.

It is interesting to note that there is just as much confusion and contradiction evidenced in these account excerpts as there is in any other area of study of the Little Horn.

Where I have quoted from testimony before the Reno Court of Inquiry, I have omitted the questions and arranged the excerpts in a narrative format. This was done only to simplify reading. Responses have not been otherwise rearranged and are complete, except for edited extraneous material as indicated.

I have not attempted to include every allusion to the condition and location of the bodies since I would only be repeating information contained in the quotes provided. However, nothing of any importance has been omitted. Sources are listed by name.

Adams, Jacob, Private, H Company, packs, 7th Cavalry
Down near the river and before we came to any dead men we found three or four dead horses. Custer lay within a circle of dead horses on a flat place at the end of the ridge. Tom Custer lay back of him and not near the horses. Quite a distance east of Custer (down near Keogh and between Keogh and Custer) the dead bodies lay thick, and among these were identified dead men from all of the five companies. Bodies were mutilated in every conceivable way. One dead body had one leg nicely cut off, as with a sharp knife, at the hip joint . . . some being set up on knees and the hind parts shot full of arrows. . . . Lieut. Gibson and I went to McIntosh's body. The fire had run through the grass and scorched it. Gibson wanted me to get a pack mule and take it up on Reno hill, but I disliked the job and told him I knew of no way to pack it, so he decided to have it buried where it lay, and I buried it there . . . in bottom, Isaiah's body lay not farther from the timber than 40 or 50 yards. Charlie Reynolds's body lay farther from the timber.[1]

Benteen, Frederick W., Captain, H Company, 7th Cavalry
... I did [examine Custer's trail], but I think now I was mistaken. The route I supposed he had gone to that ford was down through a canyon-like ravine or coulee. But I think now that he went around to the right of the second divide and did not go to the ford at all.

On the morning of General Terry's arrival I asked for permission to saddle up my company and go over to the battlefield of General Custer [actually he was ordered to go by Terry, after scoffing at the news that Custer was probably dead with his command, and suggested that he was probably watering his horses in the Big Horn]. I did so and followed down the gorge thinking that was the route taken by General Custer on the 25th of June. Now I am satisfied that was not his route but it was all cut up by horse tracks and pony tracks so that it could not be told from any other trail . . . the nearest body that was found was about six or eight hundred yards from there [Point "B"] . . . there was no line on the battlefield. You can take a handful of corn and scatter it over the floor and make just such lines, there were none [at Calhoun's position where] were the 5 or 6 horses and men I spoke of. Those were his company. I buried that company . . . [bodies were found in a ravine towards the river from Custer's body] probably within 50 to 75 yards [from the river]. If I am not mistaken there were 22. They could not shoot out of the ravine and they certainly did not go into it to shoot out of it. Those men were killed, as I believe, by the Indians with stones and clubs in that ravine, they were unarmed, I think they were wounded men . . . I did not examine them at all. I rode along the ravine and looked down. The bodies had been counted by others. I made no personal examination of them. . . .[2]

Culbertson, Ferdinand A., Sergeant, A Company, 7th Cavalry
... The first body I saw I judge was about 200 yards from there [Point "B"]. The companies were kept together to bury the dead as we came to them and we did but little running around. . . .[3]

DeRudio, Charles C., First Lieutenant, A Company, 7th Cavalry
... They followed the trail of the five companies to the river down Medicine Tail coulee. The whole command of five companies had gone nearly to the river, and two shod horses had gone quite to the river bank and the tracks seemed to indicate that they had shied around quickly in some blue clay as if turned suddenly by their riders. Says Custer's trail was in column of fours

part of the way but in one or two narrow places had changed to column of twos. The first dead man was near Ford B and about 150 yards from river . . . this man was not Sergt. Butler. He was neither stripped nor scalped. . . . On battlefield he counted 214 dead, Bradley counted 214 and Benteen 212. Does not recollect the appearance of dead around Keogh.

Custer lay on top of a conical knoll. Five or six horses lay as if they had been led there and shot down for a barricade, as empty shells lay behind them. These horses were all sorrels from Company C. No one in the group where Custer lay was scalped. DeRudio is positive about this. Riley [Reily] lay near Custer and his body was shot full of arrows. Cooke's sideburn had been scalped from one side of his face and his thighs were cut open in several places.

Does not remember any enlisted men being identified and is not sure about Company E men, but saw a heap of men in a gully and says the dead horses nearest the river were gray ones belonging to Company E. Nowlan found Sturgis' shirt in village and it had a bullet hole . . . Dr. Lord's surgical case was found in village. . . .[4]

Dolan, John, Private, M Company, 7th Cavalry
. . . Private Dolan says he assisted in burying the dead and saw Custer's body. It was stripped, but not mutilated. There were only two shots in him—one in the head and the other in the body.

Tom Custer, his brother, was badly cut up. His heart was cut out and laid beside him. He lay on his back naked. The soldiers lay in companies as if they had fallen by platoons.

. . . There were no arrows in Custer's body. Saw a man named Finley, whose head was crushed in and by whom were lying some twenty of his own cartridge shells.

Charley Reynolds, the guide, fell by the side of his horse, making a breast-work of him. He must have died in a hand-to-hand conflict, for he had a revolver open and empty in his hand.

Isaac, a colored interpreter from Rice, was literally shot to pieces with bullets. He, and many of Co. "M," were horribly mutilated—both their heads and privates being cut off. The stench was awful, and the bodies could not be lifted out of one place and placed in another without falling to pieces. Where Custer made his last stand, there were about 40 men lying around amid their horses just as you might have knocked them down with an axe. The men of companies E and L fell as straight as if they were on a skirmish line.[5]

Edgerly, Winfield S., Second Lieutenant, D Company, 7th Cavalry
. . . Gen'l Custer, Tom Custer and Cook lay at highest point of ridge. Only a few dead on top of ridge . . . but few of the men on the Custer battlefield were scalped . . . Calhoun was not mutilated. Crittenden had numerous arrows sticking in his body . . . Calhoun's men lay in remarkably good line, with the officers in their proper positions for a coolly planned resistance . . . Serg. Bustard found near Keogh. Serg. Varden found near Keogh. I Troop trumpeter also near Keogh . . . one of the shots that went through Comanche struck Keogh's leg, breaking his leg . . . Small stake driven with man's [officer's] name written on it.[6]

. . . All I saw of the trail was on the morning of the 27th when we went to bury the dead. We found the tracks of shod horses on the same side of the river where we were, and on the same side General Custer went down. We formed skirmish lines when we came close to where the battlefield was so as to find all the bodies that might have been killed. We came upon a few bodies about three and a half miles from where we had position on the hill. Each company had orders to bury the dead as they found them and as we came up to the first hill where they were all thick, Major Reno called Captain Moylan to see if he could recognize the bodies there. I went with him and we found Lieutenant Calhoun who was in rear of the first platoon of his company.

About 20 or 30 feet from there was Lieutenant Crittenden lying in the rear of the second platoon, both about 15 or 20 feet in rear of their platoons. I got permission to go ahead and see if I could recognize the bodies of several officers. By that means I left the line and went on till I came to Captain Keogh's company. They were in an irregular line. My impression was that they had formed a line on the left of Lieutenant Calhoun and had fallen back, and some retreated faster than others. Captain Keogh had evidently been wounded as we found that his leg had been broken and the sergeants of his company had got around him and were killed with him. There were no regular lines but still evidence that there had been a line.

After I had recognized Captain Keogh's body I went on towards a high point one or two hundred yards off and came to General Custer's body. About 15 feet from him was his brother's body. A short distance from that was Lieutenant Reily and then Lieutenant Cooke, and there were bodies lying around as far as we could see in every direction in irregular positions. There were a good many soldiers killed round there [Custer] . . . it seemed to be a rallying point for all of them [rather than a company organization]. I think that was where General Custer planted the guidon. It was the last point. It was not as high as some other points around it. It was the highest point in that immediate vicinity; I judge it [the nearest point of fighting to the river] was about half a mile from the ford "B" . . . the nearest one [body] I found was about half a mile from the crossing "B," I think. I am not positive as I did not go over the ground . . . .[7]

Frett, John, civilian packer, 7th Cavalry
. . . Bodies in every stage of decomposition and mutilated in the most shocking manner. . . . Among the bodies whom I recognized . . . was a German named Ackerman, a friend of mine, whose body, by actual count, had seventy-five wounds in it, besides having his limbs all cut off. It was a shocking sight. Lieutenant McIntosh was scalped clear from his forehead to the back of his neck, and he was otherwise horribly mutilated. . . . The body of Bloody Knife . . . was literally hacked to pieces . . . .[8]

Gallene, Jean B. D., Private, M Company, 7th Cavalry
. . . Sergeant Finley, of company C, whose family you are well acquainted with, I have seen, with his head cut off, after having been scalped and also Scollen. . . .[9]

Gerard, Frederic F., interpreter, 7th Cavalry
. . . I accompanied the troops to the Custer battlefield, when the dead were buried. Major Reno instructed me to select some high point and keep a constant lookout for Indians in all directions to avoid any chance of surprise while the men were burying the dead. The men proceeded over the battlefield in formation much like a skirmish line, so as not to overlook any of the scattering dead. As they came to bodies, dirt and sod were thrown over them lightly as they lay. No graves were dug except for the corpse of General Custer.

Identification of the bodies of enlisted men was not attempted, but a good deal of effort was made to find the bodies of all the officers, but there was not entire success in this.

I was present with the group of officers when the bodies of General Custer and Captain Custer were buried. The horror of sight and feeling over the bodies of all these brave men after lying in the hot sun for three days I will not attempt to describe. The eyes of surviving comrades were filled with tears, and throats were choked with grief unspeakable. The stench of dead

men was nauseating. . . . . Custer's body lay on the side of the hill and Tom
Custer on highest point of ridge . . . 20 ft. apart at farthest . . . they had
smashed back of his [Tom's] head in with a stone or hammer and shot an
arrow into top of his skull . . . Genl. Custer was shot through head back of
temples, about halfway between ears and eyes and no powder marks. . . .[10]

Gibbon, John, Colonel, 7th Infantry
. . . After being absent a couple of hours . . . he [Benteen] comes forward, dis-
mounts, and in a low, very quiet voice, tells his story. He had followed Custer's
trail to the scene of the battle [Benteen would afterward claim that he did not
ever see Custer's trail]. . . . As he approached the ground, scattered bodies of
men and horses were found, growing more numerous as he advanced. In the
midst of the field a long backbone ran out obliquely back from the river, rising
very gradually until it terminated in a little knoll which commanded a view
of all the surrounding ground. . . . On each side of this backbone, and sometimes on top of it, dead men and horses were scattered along. These became
more numerous as the terminating knoll was reached; and on the southwestern slope of that lay the brave Custer surrounded by the bodies of several of
his officers and forty or fifty of his men, whilst horses were scattered about
in every direction. All were stripped, and most of the bodies were scalped
and mutilated . . .
    . . . Up to this time [June 29] I had no opportunity to personally visit the
scene of Custer's battle, and . . . I that morning rode up to the spot, and went
over most of the ground.
    . . . As we proceeded up the valley, now an open grassy slope, we sud-
denly came upon a body lying in the grass. It was lying upon its back, and
was in an advanced state of decomposition. It was not stripped, but had evidently been scalped and one ear cut off. The clothing was not that of a soldier,
and, with the idea of identifying the remains, I caused one of the boots to be
cut off, and the stockings and drawers examined for a name, but none could
be found. On looking at the boot, however, a curious construction was observed. The heel of the boot was reinforced by a piece of leather which in
front terminated in two straps, one of which was furnished with a buckle,
evidently for the purpose of tightening the instep of the boot. This led to the
identification of the remains; for, on being carried to camp, the boot was recognized as one belonging to Mr. Kellogg, a newspaper correspondent who
accompanied General Custer's column. Beyond this point, the ground com-

menced to rise more rapidly, and the valley was broken up into several smaller ones, which lead up towards the higher ground beyond. Following up one of these, we reach a rolling but not very broken space, the ground rising higher and higher until it reaches a culminating knoll dominating all the ground in the immediate vicinity [Gibbon is one observer who describes the ground in terms which actually convey a correct impression of what it is like]. This knoll, by common consent now called Custer's hill, is the spot where his body was found, surrounded by those of several of his officers, and some forty or fifty of his men. We can see from where we are numerous bodies of dead horses scattered along its southwestern slope, and as we ride up towards it, we come across another body—lying in a depression just as if killed whilst using his rifle there. We follow the sloping ground, bearing a little to the left or west-ward until we reach the top, and then look around us. On the very top are four or five dead horses, swollen, putrid, and offensive, their stiffened limbs sticking straight out from their bodies. On the slope beyond others are thickly lying in all conceivable positions, and dotted about on the ground in all directions are little mounds of freshly-turned earth, showing where each brave soldier sleeps his last sleep [contrast this with other descriptions of the burials!]. Close under the brow of the knoll several horses are lying nearer together than the rest, and by the side of one of these we are told the body of Custer was found. The top of the knoll is only a few feet higher than the general surface of the long straight ridge, which runs off obliquely towards the river, in the direction of that ford at which it is supposed Custer made the attempt to cross.

Before leaving the prominent point, from which probably Custer surveyed his last battle and took his farewell of earth, let us look around us. There is no point within rifle range which we do not overlook, but the surrounding space, which only a few days ago resounded with the sharp rattle of rifles and the wild yells of the savages, is now silent as the grave and filled with the fetid odor of decaying bodies.

Looking first along the ridge, which, almost level, runs off as straight as an arrow, the eye catches sight on both slopes of dead horses lying here and there, and little mounds showing where the riders fell and are lying. Beyond the end of this, in the direction of the ford, the ground becomes more broken, but still only in gentle slopes, as it descends towards the river. . . . Turning now to the right, and facing the river, the ground is seen to be broken up into rolling hills and valleys, the sides formed of gentle slopes, but now and then, where these valleys approach the river, their bottoms are washed into gulches sometimes ten or fifteen feet deep. One is especially noted, to the right and front [remember that Gibbon is standing on Custer Hill], running in a direction nearly perpendicular to the river, and at the bottom of this one were found some forty or fifty bodies. Arrived at the end of the ridge, the ground opens out, where several other ridges join it, into a kind of level platform. Here evidently a severe struggle took place, for the bodies of men and horses are thickly strewn about. Moving to the far edge of this irregular plateau, the ground is seen to fall away, in a gently sloping valley, towards the ford over which Custer is supposed to have attempted a crossing

The body of our poor guide, Mitch Bouyer, was found lying in the midst of the troopers. . . . The bodies of all the officers but two were found and recognized, and those of all the men, except some twenty or thirty, accounted for. . . By the burial place of each officer was driven the head of a stake, in the top of which a hole was bored, and in this was placed a paper having upon it the name and rank of the officer. . . .[11]

Glease, George W. (real name George W. Glenn),
Private, H Company, 7th Cavalry
. . . In the valley the bodies of McIntosh and Isaiah lay near together. When Benteen took Company H over to Custer ridge on [June] 27, he went up to the ridge via Crazy Horse gully [most think that this was Deep Ravine, but Benteen's comments about Deep Ravine belie that assumption]. The body nearest the river was that of the chief trumpeter, Voss, and near to it was that of Kellogg, the newspaper reporter. Both of these bodies were within a stone's throw of the river. In Crazy Horse gully or washout there were bodies lying thick, and some of the men exclaimed, "Here lies the whole command."

Custer's body lay just below the end of the ridge, and within fifty yards of it lay the body of Tom [Boss] Tweed of Company L, who had once been my "bunky" and whom I recognized. His crotch had been split up with an ax and one of his legs thrown up over his shoulder. He was shot with arrows in both eyes. . . .[12]

Godfrey, Edward S., First Lieutenant, K Company, 7th Cavalry
. . . On Custer battlefield Godfrey buried "Boss" [Boston] Custer, who lay down on side hill some distance below the General . . . Tom Custer lay on his face up on top of the ridge with arrows shot in his back and head and back of

head all smashed in . . . at first thought it was Tom Custer by the shape of his body, and when he was rolled over and stretched out one of his arms they found "T.W.C." tattooed on his arm. Says there were but few bodies between this ridge and the deep ravine . . . .[13]

. . . On the morning of the 28th we left our intrenchments to bury the dead of Custer's command. The morning was bright, and from the high bluffs we had a clear view of Custer's battlefield. We saw a large number of objects that looked like white boulders scattered over the field . . . it was announced that these objects were the dead bodies. Captain Weir exclaimed, "Oh, how white they look!"

. . . one of the nearest to the ford was Sergeant Butler of Tom Custer's troop [Butler was actually first sergeant of L Company]. Sergeant Butler was a soldier of many years' experience and of known courage. The indications were that he had sold his life dearly, for near and under him were found many empty cartridge shells. From knowledge of his personality, and his detached position, I believe he had been selected as courier to communicate with Reno . . .

All the bodies, except a few, were stripped. According to my recollection nearly all were scalped or mutilated, but there was one notable exception, that of General Custer, whose face and expression were natural; he had been shot in the temple and in the left side . . . other bodies were mutilated in a disgusting manner. . . . The ground covered by my company took me two or three hundred yards below the monument. I had just identified and was supervising the burial of Boston Custer [note the location], when Major Reno sent for me to help identify the dead at Custer Hill. When I arrived there General Custer's body had been laid out. He had been shot in the left temple and the left breast. There were no powder marks or signs of mutilation. Mr. F. F. Girard, the interpreter, informed me that he preceded the troops there. He found the naked bodies of two soldiers, one across the other and Custer's naked body in a sitting posture between them and leaning against them, his upper right arm along and on the topmost body, his right forearm and hand supporting his head in an inclining posture like one resting or asleep. . . . When I went to Tom Custer's body it had not been disturbed from its original position. It was lying face downward, all the scalp was removed . . . The skull was smashed in and a number of arrows had been shot into the back of the head and in the body. . . . We rolled the body over . . . in turning the body, one arm which had been shot and broken, remained under the body; this was pulled out and on it we saw "T.W.C." and the goddess of liberty and flag. . . . His belly had been cut open and his entrails protruded. No examination was made to determine if his vitals had been removed.

There were forty-two bodies and thirty-nine dead horses on Custer's Hill. . . . We buried, according to my memoranda, 212 bodies . . . some bodies were moved from where they fell; they were not buried in deep graves or trenches as we did not have the tools necessary to dig them in the hard, dry ground. . . .[14]

. . . I made no examination of the trail. I helped with my company to bury the dead on the 28th. My company was assigned to a certain line of march . . . It was far from [the river], I think, there were one or two companies to my right. I made an examination where the different bodies were. I found a good many cartridge shells . . . I went off from the command to see if there were any evidences of the escape of anybody . . . and was away during the greater part of the time they were carrying on the burials . . . I went down to that ford [Ford "B"] and thought I saw evidences of where shod horses had gone across the ford and I made up my mind at the time that General Custer had attempted to cross there. I saw no evidences of fighting near there. The first body was a long distance off from that, a half or three-quarters of a mile. The bodies that I found where I found the shells were some distance from where General Custer's body was found. I think they had attempted to make a stand there. There were some 15 or 20 bodies buried in one place by my company. All the troops I found there appeared to have made a stand. [They belonged] to different companies, all were not recognizable. They were scattered. I supposed they had been dismounted there and been fighting . . . .[15]

. . . On . . . the highest point . . . the command was dismounted to receive instructions . . . We saw, in bewildered astonishment, what appeared to be white boulders scattered all over the field. "What are they? Are those rocks?" . . . An officer raised his field glasses. In a moment, his arms dropped, limp by his side, and he said, with suppressed feelings: "My God! They are the bodies of the dead!" Colonel Weir, standing by my side, exclaimed with emotion, "Oh, how white they look! How white they look!"[16]

Goldin, Theodore W., Private, G Company, 7th Cavalry
. . . We found the bodies of a number of men and horses of "E" Troop [the white horse]. To all appearances they had angled off across the hillside, finally entering a narrow coulee . . . ending with a high bank in front and on both

sides of them. Here they were . . . shot down, men and horses together. It was impossible to reach them and we shoveled dirt from the overhanging bank to cover them . . . I recall seeing other bodies between the Reynolds marker and the river. These were I believe, as were all who fell near the crossing, buried by the 2nd Cavalry and the 7th Infantry. . . .[17]

. . . the wounds in Custer's body as I saw them June 27 [there was no reason for Goldin to have been on the field on June 27], were made by a gun of smaller caliber than the .45, and we calculated it may have been from a Winchester or Henry. There were no powder marks about the wounds at all. . . .[18]

. . . We turned in at an opening following a well-marked trail of shod horses not very far from the southwest corner of the present fenced enclosure. This brought us to the first group of several soldiers, now marked by headstones, and it was from this point we discovered the faint trail leading along the lower edge of the bluff to the point where we found Smith's troop in what proved to them to be a cul de sac, and men and horses were piled together, and the odor was such that we did not get down to them, but shoveled dirt from the top covering them in one big grave.

From the point where we found the first bodies there was evidence of shod horses in broken order, leading back in the direction where we later found Calhoun's troop. . . .[19]

. . . The bodies were poorly interred . . . we were poorly provided with picks, shovels and axes . . . the ground was so hard it could not be loosened with shovel or spade, and required a pick to make an impression on it . . . the bodies were in such a state of mortification that they could not be handled to move them. I saw instances where men taking hold of an arm often found it to come loose from the body, so all we were able to do was to heap dirt or even sagebrush over the remains and leave them to the mercy of the coyotes, wolves and vultures. I believe that in most cases, at least those that came under my observation, extra efforts were made to inter the bodies of. . . .[20]

. . . "I" Troop lay in a slight depression and looked as though it had been formed in a hollow square with Keogh and one or two others in the center. . . .[21]

. . . When we went over the field on the morning of the 27th before Terry came up, I saw his [Isaiah Dorman's] body together with that of Charley Reynolds, and my recollection is that it lay a bit to the south and east of where Reynolds fell. The body was badly mutilated, scalped but recognizable, as was that of Bloody Knife and Reynolds . . . I was later told by a sergeant of the

Seventh Infantry that Dorman's privates were cut off and stuffed in his mouth [but Goldin apparently did not notice this] . . . .[22]

. . . I have no information as to where he [Benny Hodgson] was finally buried by McDougal but imagine it was, like many of the others, under the picket line where the ground was trampled down by the horses after the shallow graves were filled in . . . .[23]

Hare, Luther Rector, Second Lieutenant, scout detail, 7th Cavalry
. . . On Custer Ridge he saw the dead horses near Custer. The talk at the time was that these had been shot down by the soldiers for barricades but it did not impress him that such was the fact. . . . He buried men near Calhoun . . . Calhoun's and Crittenden's bodies lay near together. An arrow had been shot into Crittenden's eye. Tom Custer was horribly mutilated but his heart was not cut out . . . does not recall any scalped in group with Custer except Cooke, one of whose sideburns had been cut off. Thinks 7th Inf. buried Reno's men in valley. . . .[24]

. . . the first dead man was found about a half mile from the point "B." I saw what was supposed to be General Custer's trail that went down on the left bank. The first evidence of that fight was a dead man of E Company probably about 300 yards from where the final stand was made. There were 28 men of E Company, I assisted in burying the men of E Company and remember more about them. . . . They [the bodies he saw] were mutilated. I don't know that they were changed [in position]. There were evidences on the field of bodies having been dragged off, but I think these were the bodies of dead and wounded Indians . . .[25]

Iron Hawk, Hunkpapa Lakota participant
. . . There are headstones all over there, and the furthest headstone shows where the second man that I killed lies. . . .[26]

Knipe, Daniel, Sergeant, C Company, 7th Cavalry
. . . every man in Custer's command, including Custer, was stripped and . . . many were mutilated with arrows and hatchet blows across forehead, these men being probably not quite dead and killed by squaws in that way. . . . Custer had only one wound and that through chest . . . he had good look at him as he lay with small of his back across another dead soldier and that there was neither wound in his forehead nor burned powder marks on his forehead

or face . . . a dead trooper, with his dead horse, were found on the west side of the Little Big Horn at this point [opposite Medicine Tail ford], or practically in the Indian Camp . . . .[27]

The officers and soldiers seemed to be killed in about the position they were found in the line of march. . . . There was not hardly any horses around where he [Custer] was lying when found. The soldiers lay thick at this point. Custer was lying across two or three soldiers . . . . [he] had no clothing on whatever, nor none of the soldiers. There was nothing left but the foot of a boot, the leg of this being gone, on Custer. There were no mutilated soldiers at this point, except Cooke, who was near Custer, and the mutilation of him was just a long gash on one of his thighs. Custer's wound was in the left breast, near his heart, just one shot. I saw Sergeant Bobo, Finley, Finkle, they were lying along the line of march. . . . Sergeants Finley and Finkle were both mutilated very badly. They showed to be wounded. Their horses were lying near them. Bobo was not mutilated at all. . . .[28]

LeForge, Thomas, interpreter, Gibbon's command
. . . I had been there at times also during the autumn of 1876 . . . Many a grinning skull, ribbed trunk, or detached limb bones I saw on top of the ground or but partly covered up. . . . Even the best of the so-called graves were only a few inches deep.[29]

Logan, William R., Captain, A Company, 7th Infantry
. . . You say that you have been told that the Seventh Infantry buried the dead in a deep coulee on the battlefield, this coulee lying about six or seven hundred yards over the ridge from where the body of the General was found; that your information is that a squadron of men under Sergeant Heaton carried these men's bodies out of the coulee and buried them in the vicinity. Your information on that point is not correct. The bodies were buried where found. The men were killed in bunches, principally each company by itself, and in some cases in company formation, i.e. skirmish formation. We buried the bodies, as I have said, about where they fell. We had no picks and shovels, the graves were dug out with knives and broken plates and other sharp utensils we could obtain. In some cases very little dirt and sage brush were put over the bodies. I was to the battlefield some ten or fifteen days after the burial, and a great many of the bodies had been exposed by the coyotes.[30]

Lynch, Dennis, Private, F Company, packs, 7th Cavalry
. . . saw 7th Inf. men carrying dead men out of deep gully. They had "got 7 men on bank" and he remarked: "There are a whole bunch of them in there yet . . . says these men in gully were carried up and buried on the ridge. Says Serg. Dave Heaton was one of these 7th Inf. men [Heaton was actually a private in K Company, 7th Infantry, and had been placed on special duty with Bradley's mounted detachment] . . . one of men in deep gully was Timothy Donnelly of F Troop . . . identified Briody by sailor's mark on his arm. Vickory and Voss and Donovan lay near Custer. 14 F Troop enlisted men lay around Custer. Saw only one man scalped and looked at a good many. 2nd Cavalry and 7th Inf, and 7th Cavalry all helped to bury. Men with pack train went over with pack mules but did help bury [last two sentences refer to burials in the valley] . . . from vicinity of Calhoun saw 7th Inf. men over at gully and someone said "Let's go over and see what those dough boys are doing." He found them carrying dead bodies up the south side of gully and already had 7 of them laid on the bank . . . .[31]

Martin, John, Orderly Trumpeter, Custer Headquarters, 7th Cavalry
. . . says careful search was made of whole country for dead men down to river—that detachments were sent out and that Serg. Butler was found in this way . . . saw Serg. Butler of L Troop and says his horse was dead with him . . . saw the heap of dead men in deep gully between Custer and the river . . . says on Custer battlefield there were not half as many dead horses as dead men . . . . one of Cooke's sideburns was scalped off, skin and all . . . Keogh had a gold chain and Agnus Dei Catholic emblem on his neck which the Indians had not taken . . . .[32]

Mathey, Edward G., First Lieutenant, pack detail, 7th Cavalry
. . . says that he buried Mark Kellogg's body on June 29. Says it was the last one buried . . . it lay near a ravine and between Custer and the river . . . it had been overlooked or not seen and that he was sent to bury it after all other burying had been done . . . .[33]

McDougall, Thomas M., Captain, B Company, 7th Cavalry
. . . When position was changed on night of June 26 Cos. A. and B went down on bench just above river, B on south side and A on north side of gully run-

ning straight down from H company's line. There Hodgson was buried. Men who recovered Hodgson's body on night of June 26 were Criswell, Private Ryan and Saddler Bailey, all of B Troop. . . . There were few or no dead cavalry horses between top of ridge and deep ravine where Co. E men were found. Says there were only a few bodies between deep gully and where Genl. Custer lay. Is sure there were less than a dozen and might not have been more than ½ dozen . . . he found most of E. Troop in the ravine. Does he mean in the deep gully? Were there as many as 28? Yes. All the bodies in the deep gully were buried in the gully—none was carried out. Hohmeyer was in there and Hughes . . . .[34]

. . . I only went to where I presume the skirmish line was killed. Major Reno then ordered me to take my company and go to the village, and get implements to bury the dead. On returning he ordered me to bury Company E, the one I had formerly commanded for 5 years, and to identify the men as far as possible. I found most of them in a ravine. That [ravine marked "H" on the map] is where most of Company E were found to the best of my recollection, about half were in the ravine and the other half on a line outside . . . all the men were lying on their faces and appeared to have been shot mostly in the sides. I thought they fought the best they could and probably were attacked from both sides. [The skirmish line I spoke of was] about a hundred yards from the ford where I crossed. I think that is the place marked "B" . . . I did not see any bodies but of the one company in the ravine. I did not go over the field at all. . . .[35]

. . . Upon crossing the river I found Keogh's horse in the small bushes, and detailed one of the men to look after him until I reported the same to Reno . . . [who] ordered me to bury Troop "E" which I had commanded so many years. In the ravine I found most of the troop, who had used the upper sides of the ravine for a kind of breastwork, falling to the bottom as they were shot down. In burying the men the stench was so great that the men began to vomit, so we had to pile large chunks of earth upon them, broken off from the sides of the ravine. This was not very far from the village. Only a few men were found upon the ground from the extension of the ravine . . . I knew Sergeant Hohmyer at once; he had one sock left on his foot with his name on it . . . .[36]

Moylan, Myles, Captain, A Company, 7th Cavalry
. . . I did not examine the trail at all. I do not know that I ever saw it until I got to this watering place. It was probably half a mile from there I saw the

first bodies. The evidences of fighting were a great many dead men lying about there. I saw Lieutenant Calhoun's company were killed in regular position of skirmishers. I counted twenty-eight cartridge shells around one man, and between the intervals there were shells scattered. In deploying the men to hunt for the bodies my company was on the left next to the river and there [were] but few evidences of fighting there. But when Lieutenant Calhoun's body was reached, I had permission to go and identify it, as he was a brother-in-law of mine . . . that is the way I happened to see those bodies. After leaving this place, I rode up to this point I think in company with Major Reno. In the ravine marked "H" on the map, we found twenty-odd bodies of E Company. They were undoubtedly fighting and retreating. I could see where they had passed down the edge and attempted to scramble up on the other side, which was almost perpendicular. The marks were plain where they had used their hands to get up but the marks only extended halfway up the bank. That must have been half or three-quarters of a mile [from the river] . . . [It] was not so far, I think [from Custer's body]. There were three officers that I knew that never were found and I think some fifteen or eighteen men. I do not know the exact number. . . . My belief was that those men were buried with the others, but were disfigured to that extent that they could not be identified. There were men I had known ten or twelve years whose bodies could not have been recognized had it not been for certain marks. . . . It was generally understood they [the bodies] were counted . . . I know that there were some men missing that could not be accounted for. I have always been under the impression that the officers were buried with the men. I understood a number of bodies had been found a considerable distance from the field which I think would make up the number . . . .[37]

O'Neill, Thomas F., Private, G Company, 7th Cavalry
. . . helped bury the dead on June 28. He and Hammon personally dug the hole in which Genl. Custer was buried and lay the body in it.

Lieut. Wallace wrote the General's name on a piece of paper, rolled it up and inserted it in an empty cartridge shell and put it by a little stake driven by Custer's head. Before he was covered, Dr. Porter took locks of hair of all the officers . . . says [Custer] was shot clear through head back of both temples and through the chest. Tom Custer was disembowled but breast not cut open. He recognized him by looking at his face . . . .[38]

. . . While O'Neill was digging this trench, Lieut. Wallace came and said:

"O'Neill, I think that will be a good grave to bury Gen. Custer in, and so Custer's body was buried in it . . . .[39]

Petring, Henry, Private, G Company, 7th Cavalry
. . . Henry Dose, trumpeter, orderly for Custer June 25, 1876, was found half way between Custer and Reno with arrows in his back and sides . . . .[40]

Pickard, Edwin F., Private, F Company, pack detail 7th Cavalry
. . . where Custer and five companies fell, the sight was appalling and fearful. Men were slashed, cut and apparently tortured when but slightly wounded, with an ingenuity that left nothing undone that could deface the dead and pain the living, and over all the hot glaring sun poured down on the dead and mutilated bodies. . . .[41]

Red Hawk, Oglala Lakota participant
. . . About a month after the battle some thirty Indians, including Red Hawk, went back to the battlefield and were looking over it. At the mouth of the [unspecified] ravine they found eight (8) dead soldiers lying with their uniforms on and their guns and ammunition and everything by them. Red Hawk said they could not understand how these soldiers were killed down there. They did not, out of respect for their superstition that if they take anything from any person that has been dead a long time that his spirit will haunt them, remove any of the things which belonged to the eight dead soldiers [skeletal remains and old carbines have been found from time to time on the battlefield].[42]

Reno, Marcus A., Major, 7th Cavalry
. . . at 5 a.m. on the 28th, I proceeded with the regiment to the battleground of Custer, and buried 204 bodies, including the following named citizens; Mr. Boston Custer, Mr. Reed . . . and Mr. Kellogg. . . .[43]
. . . our men went to the battleground of that portion that was under General Custer to bury them. Every man with him was killed and stripped. This was the first time I saw them give way. The brave fellows cried like children when they saw the mutilated bodies of their comrades of the day before. . . .[44]
. . . The dead had been mutilated in the most savage way and they lay as they had fallen, scattered in the wildest confusion over the ground, in groups of two or three, or piled in an indiscriminate mass of men and horses. They

had lain thus for nearly three days under the fierce heat of the sun, exposed to swarms of flies and flesh-eating crows . . . Custer lay as if asleep, but all the other men had been most brutally mangled and stripped of their clothing. Many of their skulls had been crushed in, eyes had been torn from their sockets, and hands, feet, arms, legs and noses had been wrenched off. Many had their flesh cut in strips the entire length of their bodies. . . .[45]

Roe, Charles F., Second Lieutenant, F Company, 2nd Cavalry
. . . The 2nd Cav. and 7th Inf. buried McIntosh and some of the soldiers killed with Reno in the bottom . . . Mitch Bouyer's body was found west or northwest [from] where the monument stands on flat ground near the river and the timber line . . . did not see Bouyer's body but at the time believed report about finding it. . . . To settle the report about 20 men getting away from the battlefield and being killed over toward the Rosebud, Roe took a troop of cavalry and deployed them at a suitable interval and marched them all the way to the mountain and found nothing. . . .[46]

Roy, Stanislas, Sergeant, A Company, 7th Cavalry
. . . We then formed skirmish line and buried the dead. On the way over we followed what we supposed was Custer's trail and at one point it led down pretty close to the river.
    The first dead body we came to was that of Corpl. John Foley. I heard several say: "there lies Foley of C Company." I saw him and recognized him easily, as he had bald head and black hair.[47] He was of middle age and I knew him well. Foley was at least three-fourths mile in advance of the first group of dead at C.
    The next body we came to was that of Sergt. Butler, and from him to first group of dead at C the distance was considerable. He lay probably one-half way from Foley to C. There was no dead horse near either Foley or Butler. I helped to bury the bodies on west slope of ridge, and we wound up with E Troop men over near the gully. I then took sick to my stomach from the stench and went to the river to get a drink. . . . When we went to bury the dead . . . we did not follow Dry Creek to the river but cut straight across to the battlefield, going over the little rise between the two coulees. The first body we saw was that of Corpl. Foley of Co. C on this rise, just over toward the coulee running up to the battlefield. Butler lay 200 or 300 yds. beyond and across the ravine. . . .[48]

Runs After the Clouds (Light), Mnicoujou Lakota participant
... Light states that many of the soldiers were killed on the top of the ridge
where the monument stands. Those killed on the side of the ridge were trying
to make their escape ... He also heard that the body of a man wearing a buckskin suit and who resembled Tom Custer [it is not stated how anyone knew
of the resemblance] was first found about a quarter of a mile west of the ridge
marked "C" and who was afterward carried up and placed at "G" [this is eerily
reminiscent of one of the Cheyenne tales, wherein the body of Armstrong
Custer was carried over to Reno field and back again] ... Quite a few men
were killed in gully at "H"—but not as many as at "G,"[49]

Ryan, John M., First Sergeant, M Company, 7th Cavalry
At the top of this bluff we halted, and at foot there was a ford, and this was
where Custer had first encountered the Indians, as we found some of the dead
bodies there two days afterwards ... in burying the dead many of the bodies
were not identified. .... The company commanders went in a body over the
field, to find the bodies of the commissioned officers. The first sergeants of
each troop had orders to advance with their companies over a certain space
of the field, burying what men were found, and keeping an account of the
number and who they were ... we had only a few tools, so we simply dug up
a little earth beside the bodies and threw it over them. In a great many instances their arms and legs protruded. .... Some of the companies ... chopped
down some sage brush and threw it over the bodies. I also saw where 20 or
28 men belonging to Company "E" ... had gotten into a ravine ... got so
steep they could not get out, and we saw the marks where they tried to get
out of there, and where afterwards they were shot by the Indians and fell back
into the ravine.[50]

    ... he sent word to Capt. Custer that if he [Rain-In-The-Face] got the
chance he would kill him and cut out his heart. Sad to relate that from the
appearance of Capt. Custer's remains as I found them, the threat must have
been fulfilled, for on the hillock of death at Little Big Horn, I found his body
frightfully mutilated and this hero would have been buried without identification had I not recognized the initials on his arm that I knew so well ...

    His body laid near his brother Gen. Custer who being considered by the
Indians a brave man was not scalped but his body was pierced in two places
by bullets: one through his skull from ear to ear, the other through his body
from side to side.

We dug a shallow grave about 15 to 18 inches deep at the foot of the hillock. We laid the General in as tenderly as a soldier could with his brother Captain along side of him covering the bodies with pieces of blanket and tents and spreading earth on top. . . . We then took a basket off an Indian "Travois" placing it upside down over the grave and pinning it to the ground with stakes, placing large stones around it to keep the wolves from digging it up, and this . . . was the best of all those heroes . . . and I helped bury 45 enlisted men and commissioned officers of the 5 companies. . . .[51]

Sheridan, Michael V., Captain, L Company, detached, 7th Cavalry
. . . I have a sketch made by Captain Nowlan. It is a rough sketch not made with reference to any scale, and was made for me to exhibit to the Lieutenant General when I came back. It represents the position in which the bodies were found. The first point on the dotted line is where the first body was found back from the ford "B." It is nearly half a mile back. I did not notice any more bodies, or more than one or two, before we came to the crest of the ridge and there we found Lieutenant Calhoun's company, or I was informed they were his company [note that Sheridan was actually the commander of this company, but was on detached duty on his brother's staff]. There I found the men at intervals as though there were a skirmish line or resistance had been made there. There was no other place that showed evidence of resistance having been made. There were other men killed in various positions, and in every direction. Behind the position in which I found Lieutenant Calhoun's body was that of Lieutenant Crittenden who was attached to the regiment at that time. From a quarter to a half mile in rear of that I found Captain Keogh's body. Then they continued in scattered condition to the point of the ridge where we found the remains of 40 or 50 officers and men, among others, those of General Custer, Colonel Custer, Captain Yates, Lieutenant Smith and perhaps one or two others, I don't remember who. . . . It was a rough point or narrow ridge not wide enough to drive a wagon on. It was not a position where successful resistance could be made. Across that ridge were 5 or 6 horses apparently in line, and looked as though they had been killed for the purposes of resistance, but the remains were found in a confused mass. . . .[52]

Slaper, William C., Private, M Company, 7th Cavalry
. . . We were then ordered over to the spot where Custer and his men fell.

Here, with a few spades, we were set to work to bury them. We had but a few implements of any sort. All we could possibly do was to remove a little dirt in a low place, roll in a body and cover it with dirt. Some, I can well remember, were not altogether covered, but the stench was so strong from the disfigured, decaying bodies, which had been exposed to an extremely hot sun for two [three] days, that it was impossible to make as decent a job of interring them as we could otherwise have done. There were also great numbers of dead horses lying about, which added to the horror of the situation.

I did not have time to go over the field and make notes, but from what I did see . . . It struck me that many of them had evidently shot their own horses and used them as breastworks. . . . In one instance we found two men lying between the legs of their dead horses. . . . All the bodies seemed naked . . .

. . . Some of the disfigurations were too horrible to mention. After being scalped, the skulls were crushed in with stone hammers, and the bodies cut and slashed in all fleshy portions. Much of this was doubtless done to wounded men. Many arrows also had been shot into some of the bodies— the eyes, neck, stomach and other members. I observed especially the body of Capt. Tom Custer, which was the worst mutilated of all. Many arrows bristled in it. . . . His body was lying about twenty feet from that of the general, and close beside that of Adjutant Cooke, one side of whose face had been scalped. His body was also badly mutilated.

The body of Gen. Custer had not been touched by the Indians. He had been shot twice . . . Boston Custer was found near the bodies of his brothers. That of Mark Kellogg . . . was close by. These bodies were on the line nearest to the river. . . .

I was working a spade on this end of the line of dead and so had a hand in burying this group. I am sure that we used more earth in covering Custer's body, and made a larger mound for it than for any of the others. . . . The large mound we erected over his body should have been sufficient to identify his burial spot. . . .

After we had buried all the dead on the Custer field, the site of the Reno battle in the river bottom was investigated. The dead were all buried where they fell. All had been horribly butchered. Isaiah Dorman . . . was found with many arrows shot into his body and head, and badly cut and slashed, while unmentionable atrocities had been committed. Corporal Henry Scollen of M Troop was found badly mutilated, with his right leg severed from his body. Jim Turley's body was found with his hunting knife driven to the hilt in one eye. Three others, Gordon, Myers and Summers of M Troop were in an awful state of mutilation. . . .[53]

Thompson, Richard E., Second Lieutenant, K Company, 6th Infantry
. . . Thompson, Capt. Hughes 3rd Inf., Michaelis, Nowlan went all over the battlefield to identify dead on June 27 . . . went with Benteen and Co. H to Custer ridge.

End of ridge was a round hill. . . . It was higher than rest of ridge. Dead horses for a barricade on this hill. Tom Custer lay nearest the peak of round hill . . . lay on his face with head all hacked up with a hatchet in face. The only way he could be identified was by initials tattooed on his arm . . . abdomen had been cut and his bowels had come out. Dr. Lord well identified by . . . Thompson and others. He lay 20 ft. southeast of Custer's body on side hill. Lord had on a blue shirt and lay near Custer. Only about 20 ft. from him. Identified Lord's body for sure. Where each officer buried a piece of tepee pole was driven in ground at his head and the name of officer marked thereon.

Verifies the fact that only 9 or 10 men between gully and Custer. Says many bodies in gully—thinks 34. Says Mark Kellogg lay 3/4 mile from Custer down near river on side hill about 100 yds. from river. Was identified by peculiar shaped boots that he wore.

. . . saw Hodgson's body lying at top of bank of river, perhaps 20 ft. from water . . . .[54]

Turtle Rib, Mnicoujou Lakota participant
. . . He supposed them all killed where they lay. The Indians were so busy caring for their own wounded and going off to fight Reno that they did not stop to scalp or mutilate soldiers. What the squaws did after this he did not know. . . .[55]

Two Eagles, Hunkpapa Lakota participant
. . . There were soldiers killed on the top of the hill at "G" . . . It was the 8 soldiers [markers] west of "C" that came down from "K" [At that time, Two Eagles was on the east side of the ridge at a point between "C" and "D," a little nearer to "D" than halfway between the two points] . . . .[56]

Two Moon, Cheyenne participant
. . . All the soldiers were now killed, and the bodies were stripped. After

that no one could tell which were officers. The bodies were left where they fell. . . .[57]

Varnum, Charles A., Second Lieutenant, scout detail, 7th Cavalry
. . . When dead were buried, Varnum and some scouts were posted on high ground east of Custer battlefield to watch for Indians. This was done by Reno to punish Varnum for adding some additional matter to the notes which Reno had tried to send out of lines on June 26. Varnum was thus not permitted to see any of his friends who had been killed with Custer. Calhoun was identified by filling in his teeth. . . .[58]

. . . We started on the 28th to go down and bury the dead and in going down I was on a trail which I supposed was General Custer's, and when we got to a high hill that had a pile of stones and Indian medicine bags and other things on it, I went there to see what they were and rode off the trail, I suppose, near the point "B" on the map. That point was all cut up by pony tracks and was evidently a watering place. . . . Soon after that I had gone to a ravine and had seen 2 or 3 dead bodies when I received orders from Major Reno to go on some bluffs well out from the river with the Indian scouts as a lookout . . . and I remained there during the burial. I can't give any opinion [as to how far it was from the watering place to the first body]. I just remember seeing one body and someone called out, "Here are some more," . . . It seems to me it must have been 800 or 1,000 yards, that is an approximation on my part entirely. I can't locate it any better by that [distance from the river]. That I don't know [whether the trail led to the river]. I left the trail some distance back and when I came to that watering place I did not come on the trail but over a bluff. The first evidences [of Custer's engagement] were the dead bodies I speak of . . . only the few dead bodies along in those ravines. I judge [the first bodies were] about 2 miles [from Reno's position on the hill]. . . .[59]

Wallace, George D., Second Lieutenant, G Company, 7th Cavalry
. . . [The first dead man was found] back [from Ford B] some two or three hundred yards at the point indicated on the map. [The next was found] after crossing the first ravine as we moved down the river . . . [then] on the ridge, following that dark line on the map to the top of the ridge. There were some few found there until you reached the top of the ridge. . . . The way they were buried was the companies were formed in column-of-fours, and they moved

parallel columns, and each company, as it moved along, would bury the dead it found, and after they had completed this duty the number that each company commander had buried was reported to me and from that the sum total was made up. . . . [Calhoun's company] was found on top of the last ridge, not the one on which General Custer was killed but the one that ran at right angles to it. . . . There was some indication of a skirmish line . . . I afterwards saw in the ravine some men lying in skirmish order but they were at the bottom of a deep ravine and I don't know how it was. [They were] of E Company, Lieutenant Smith. [After leaving Calhoun we found] Captain Keogh's . . . lying halfway down the northern side of the slope. Between Custer and Calhoun, but halfway down the slope, and they appeared to me to have been killed running in file . . . They were killed at intervals, but from their position I don't think they could have been in skirmish line. . . . [Custer] was near that point marked "E" on the map. [The men] were right around. Four or five of them were piled up in a heap beside a horse, and the body of General Custer was lying rather across one of the men. . . . They had apparently tried to lead the horses in a circle on the point of the ridge and killed them there and apparently made an effort for a final stand . . . there were about twenty or thirty [men] but not right around. They were scattered all over the hill, south and east of General Custer . . . .[60]

Windolph, Charles, Private, H Company, 7th Cavalry
. . . From the way the men lay, it was clear that first one troop had been ordered to dismount and fight as a skirmish line. Then a second troop had been posted a little farther on and to the east. Then a third and fourth troop. And finally there on the knob of the hill lay some thirty bodies in a small circle. We knew instinctively that we would find Custer there.

We rode forward at a walk. Most of the troopers had been stripped of clothing and scalped. Some of them had been horribly mutilated.

Custer was lying a trifle to the southeast of the top of the knoll—where the monument is today. I stood six feet away holding Captain Benteen's horse while he identified the General. His body had not been touched, save for a single bullet hole in the left temple near the ear, and a hole in his left breast . . . His brother Tom lay a few feet away. He was horribly mutilated . . .

Captain Benteen found a bit of wood, hollowed out a hole, found an empty shell, wrote Custer's name on a bit of paper and placed it in the shell, and shoved it deep in the hole in the piece of wood. Then he pushed this into the ground at Custer's head. It would make sure that the burial party would identify Custer's body . . .

The following morning we went back to Custer Hill and buried as well as we could, the naked, mutilated bodies of our comrades. It was a gruesome task. . . .[61]

Wylie, George W., Corporal, D Company, 7th Cavalry
. . . On Custer ridge the body of Trumpeter John W. Patton lay across Keogh's breast when first found . . . had opportunity to see only a few bodies around Keogh and was then sent out as vidette to watch for Indians. . . .[62]

NOTES

1. Kenneth Hammer (ed.), *Custer in '76: Walter Camp's Notes on the Custer Fight* (Provo, 1976); various Camp interviews in [ebook] Bibliography, part B.5.
2. Benteen: testimony at the Reno Court of Inquiry; [ebook] Appendix 3.4.
3. Culbertson: testimony at the Reno Court of Inquiry; [ebook] Appendix 3.14.
4. Hammer, *Custer in '76*; various Camp interviews in [ebook] Bibliography, part B.5.
5. *St. Paul Dispatch*, July 19, 1876.
6. Hammer, *Custer in '76*.
7. Winfield Edgerly: testimony at the Reno Court of Inquiry, 1879; [ebook] Appendix 3.21.
8. *St. Paul Dispatch*, July 27, 1876.
9. *St. Paul Pioneer Press*, January 16, 1879.
10. Hammer, *Custer in '76*
11. Colonel John Gibbon, *Gibbon on the Sioux Campaign of 1876* (Bellevue, 1970).
12. Hammer, *Custer in '76*.
13. Ibid.
14. E. S. Godfrey, "Custer's Last Battle," *The Century Magazine* (January 1892), and subsequent revisions and additions thereto.
15. E. S. Godfrey: testimony at the Reno Court of Inquiry, 1879; [ebook] Appendix 3.38.
16. *Billings Record-Herald, Billings,* (June 26, 1916).
17. Goldin: letter to Albert W. Johnson, October 27, 1928.
18. Goldin: letter to Albert W. Johnson, November 6, 1929.
19. Goldin: letter to Albert W. Johnson, January 15, 1930.
20. Goldin: letter to Albert W. Johnson, February 8, 1930.
21. Goldin: letter to Albert W. Johnson, July 27, 1931.
22. Goldin: letter to Albert W. Johnson, January 4, 1933.
23. Goldin: letter to Fred Dustin, June 2, 1934.
24. Hammer, *Custer in '76*.
25. Luther Hare: testimony at the Reno Court of Inquiry; [ebook] Appendix 3.49.

26. J. G. Neihardt, Collection of Personal Papers in Jt Coll., Western History Ms Div., U. of Missouri Library & State Historical Society of Missouri, Columbia.

27. Hammer, *Custer in '76*.

28. Daniel Knipe: from a letter of July 20, 1908 to Walter Camp..

29. Refer to Thomas B. Marquis, *Memoirs of a White Crow Indian* (New York, 1928).

30. William R. Logan: from a letter to Walter Camp May 17, 1909. See also account of Dennis Lynch, below, and comment re: Heaton.

31. Hammer, *Custer in '76*.

32. Ibid.

33. Ibid.

34. Ibid.

35. Captain Thomas McDougall: testimony at the Reno Court of Inquiry, 1879; [ebook] Appendix 3.75.

36. Captain Thomas McDougall: letter to Edward S. Godfrey, May 18, 1909.

37. Captain Myles Moylan: testimony at the Reno Court of Inquiry; [ebook] Appendix 3.81.

38. Hammer, *Custer in '76*.

39. Ibid.

40. Ibid.

41. *Bangor Whig and Courier,* August 16, 1876.

42. Judge Eli S. Ricker, Interview Notes in Nebraska State Historical Society, Lincoln.

43. Marcus A. Reno: report of July 5, 1876; [ebook] Appendix 4.9.

44. *Harrisburg Daily Telegraph,* August 7, 1876.

45. Marcus Reno: unpublished and perhaps unfinished manuscript ostensibly found among his personal effects after his death; statement to the *New York Herald,* August 8, 1876; [ebook] Appendix 3.94, 3.95.

46. Hammer, *Custer in '76*.

47. See commentary in The 7th Regiment of Cavalry, United States Army: Rosters pertaining to regimental assignments, strengths, casualties and battle statistics on the campaign which culminated in the series of actions known as the Battle of the Little Big Horn, June 25 and 26, 1876; [ebook] *Appendix 5.17*.

48. Hammer, *Custer in '76*.

49. Ibid.

50. *The Billings Gazette,* June 25, 1923.

51. From an undated narrative written on the flyleaves of a copy of *Tenting on the Plains,* signed by Ryan.

52. Lieutenant Colonel Michael V. Sheridan: testimony at the Reno Court of Inquiry, 1879; [ebook] *Appendix 5.20*.

53. William C. Slaper, Private, M Company, 7th Cavalry, as told to Earl Brininstool, 1920. Refer to Robert K. Boyd, *Two Indian Battles* (1928).

54. Hammer, *Custer in '76*.

55. Ibid.

56. Ibid.

57. Hamlin Garland, "General Custer's Last Fight as Seen by Two Moon," *McClure's Magazine* (Vol. XI No.5, 1898).

58. Hammer, *Custer in '76.*

59. Charles A. Varnum: testimony at the Reno Court of Inquiry, 1879; [ebook] *Appendix* 3.111.

60. Lt. George D. Wallace: testimony at the Reno Court of Inquiry, 1879; [ebook] *Appendix* 3.113.

61. Frazier Hunt and Robert Hunt, *I Fought with Custer* (Lincoln and London, 1987).

62. Hammer, *Custer in '76.*

BURIALS, MARKERS, AND SURVIVORS

"The evidences of fighting were a great many dead men lying about there."—CAPTAIN M. MOYLAN, A COMPANY: TESTIMONY AT THE RENO COURT OF INQUIRY

T he granite monument that stands atop Custer Hill dominates the whole of the Custer battlefield. A visitor who stands in front of the monument, looks toward the river and then slowly turns to the left to look in the direction of Calhoun Hill, can visualize the fight that took place on this battlefield on June 25, 1876. There is something almost magical about this place. One can smell the rising dust, mixed with the tang of black powder, hear the shouts, wild yells, crash of gunfire and interspersed bugle calls, and see the soldiers and warriors fighting and dying all around. It truly can be a mystical and evocative experience.

One of the factors that contributes to this sensation is, of course, the many portrayals of the battle in books, magazines, films and paintings—so that most of those who come to this field do so with some preconceived notion of what happened and with some sensation already generated within themselves. But perhaps the biggest contributor to their mind-picture is the placement of the many white marble markers which dot the field in lonely isolation or which stand in well-defined groups and which boldly state, upon closer inspection, that a "U.S. Soldier Fell Here" or that a specifically identified person "fell here." There is no other battlefield in the United States which claims to mark the actual locations of where all individual soldiers met their deaths; indeed there is no other that I can name, anywhere on this earth, which does so.

It is these mute markers that say so much and which make it so very easy to picture the struggling troops in our minds' eye. It is these same markers which in recent years have become so important to historians, archaeologists and serious students of the Little Horn fights—for if the markers do what they claim, i.e. mark the spots where soldiers fell, then they also can help us to understand how the soldiers got to where they died. They should therefore help us draw an accurate picture of how the Custer fight progressed and ended. It is only this fight which has been shrouded in mystery and unanswered questions, because the valley and hilltop fights have been well-documented by survivors; and although there have been a few unresolved questions about those fights as well, the focus of historical detectives has always been the Custer fight. So the big question is: do the markers really represent the death scenes of the Custer troopers? To answer this question, I must first explore the history of the placement of the markers.

Senator James Beck of Kentucky had introduced and passed a bill authorizing and funding the placement of formal grave markers. On May 1, 1890, Captain Owen Sweet of the 25th Infantry brought the first markers to the Custer battlefield. He had 249 of them, ostensibly to mark the burial sites of the officers and men of the U.S. Army who fell on that battlefield. In fact, he was about to begin a series of events which would do nothing but confuse matters, but that was not any fault of his. The bureaucrats had done their jobs beforehand, in the way they always seem to. According to the battle statistics, 266 men were killed or died of wounds suffered at the Little Horn. Five of these men died later and were buried elsewhere, leaving 261 interments on the battlefield. However, the monument listed 263 names in total (including James Bennett and Frank Braun who were among the five mentioned previously), so that everything began from a false premise. Somewhere, someone had screwed things up. But why did Sweet have 249 stones, and not 263?

The answer is simple. He was furnished with a sufficient number to mark the known graves of officers and men, not civilians or Indians (although the Indian scouts were enlisted men). In fact, Sweet was given "named" markers for the officers whose burial sites were known. The arithmetic is simple:

Number of names on the monument	263
Less officers listed as missing (Sturgis, Porter, Harrington)	3

Less civilians with Custer (Boston Custer, Reed, Boyer, Kellogg) 4
Less civilians with Reno (DeWolf, Mann, Reynolds, Dorman)   4
Less Indians with Reno (Bloody Knife, Little Brave and
    Bob-tailed Bull)   3
Less grave site already marked (Crittenden)   1
        TOTAL   248

A marker was sent however, for Dr. DeWolf, ostensibly because someone
thought that he was an assistant surgeon (he had flunked the exam), and a
marker was sent with Porter's name on it instead of Benny Hodgson's for some
reason known only to that same (or maybe another) someone. No marker was
sent for John Crittenden, because his grave was already nicely marked by a
stone sent out years earlier by his family. The net effect was that 249 markers
were sent, two of which were to mark bodies that were never there. Sweet,
naturally enough, wound up taking Porter's marker back with him, since he
could not find Porter's grave, and he did not place a marker for Hodgson,
whose grave he did find, because he did not have a marker with Hodgson's
name on it.

Of the 248 markers he left at the Little Horn, Sweet placed only two on
Reno's battlefields—one for Donald McIntosh and the one for Dr. DeWolf.
The rest went to the scene of the Custer fight and were eventually placed
there, all 246 of them. Considering that only 210 men died with the Custer
battalions on June 25, 1876, right off the bat there were thirty-six extra markers on Custer's Field. Actually there were more than that, for it has become
very obvious over the years that at least six or seven men from those battalions
were killed outside the confines of the fenced battlefield. And there would be
more markers to come.

How did Sweet find places for all of those 246 markers? According to his
report and his later correspondence with Walter Camp, Sweet examined every
foot of ground for remains or parts of remains, even going so far as to open
graves to make sure that the marker was placed at the head of the body and
not the foot. This, of course, is utter hogwash, for the battlefield had been
scoured and bones collected so often that there was not a lot left in the way
of complete skeletal remains, save perhaps one or two. There were lots of bits
and pieces in 1890, just as there are today, and since there could not have
been more than 210 actual human grave sites, it is obvious that Sweet did
what any good soldier would do in the circumstances: he marked anything

that remotely resembled a grave. The first 217, he wrote, were fairly easy to place, but he really had to work at finding logical spots for the other twenty-nine, and he spent the better part of twelve days doing it. Wherever there was a stake of wood, he put a marker; wherever there was an indentation that might have been a grave, he put a marker; wherever he found an existing wooden marker with a name on it, he put a marker—until he had used up all 246. There is absolutely no doubt that he marked places where only horse bones had been buried, and there is absolutely no question but that he marked places where nothing at all had been buried.

In 1891, the battlefield and the marker locations were mapped by topographer R.B. Marshall, under the auspices of the U.S. Geological Survey. The enlargement inset of Marshall's map shows 244 markers on Custer's Field, although a legend states that "black dots indicate markers erected where 202 U.S. soldiers fell." Marshall's map has recently been held up to ridicule because it doesn't correlate exactly with the present marker locations, but it is nevertheless of immense value—because it not only shows where the markers were in 1891, but it neatly corroborates the number of men killed with Custer, i.e.:

"markers erected to show where 202 U.S. soldiers fell"	202
missing officers (markers not added until 1910)	3
civilians (Custer, Reed, Kellogg, Boyer)	4
already marked (Crittenden)	1
TOTAL	210

Marshall's map is, in fact, incorrect—but only in a few reasonably minor respects. Much has been made of his count of 244 markers, the statement being repeatedly made that two markers had disappeared in a single year since their placement. However, a comparison of the inset with the surveyed topographical map indicates that the 246 markers were still there and that the inset map is slightly in error, as follows:

- One marker in the Custer Hill group should be removed
- The third marker south of Lord should be deleted
- One marker should be added about 50 yards south of the end of Smith's Command
- One marker should be added in approximately the center of the lower Calhoun Hill

(Finley) grouping
- One marker should be added about 200 feet north of Lord
- One marker should be added just above the "e" in "Lieut."
  J.J. Crittenden
- One marker should be added to the group below the "C"
  in "Command" where it appears beneath "Capt. M.W. Keogh's" .
- One marker should be deleted from the group of four immediately to
  the right of the above group.

This corrects the inset map to the proper total of 246 markers, which is itself considerably in error as compared with the number that should have been there. The truly unfortunate aspect of this is that we do not know with a high degree of certainty which markers in the first placement were spurious. We can only hope that Sweet was conscientious enough to not put markers in frivolous locations merely to get rid of them. The principal indication that he applied himself with a high degree of integrity, in the given circumstances, is the amount of time he devoted to the operation.

In 1896, markers were sent out and put in place for three of the civilians who died with Custer's command: Boston Custer, Autie Reed, and Mark Kellogg. These were placed on and east of Custer Hill, where wooden markers indicated the men had been buried. All of these wooden markers had been present when Sweet placed the original markers, but he did not have any stones for these civilians. None of these new markers went where the men had actually died (Kellogg's is way off), but then the original placements did not have a totally solid foundation in reality either. This brought the total to 249.

In 1910, the mistake made twenty years earlier in respect to Benny Hodgson's marker was finally corrected when a marker was sent out and placed for him on Reno Hill. At the same time, stones were sent for the three missing officers—Sturgis, Harrington and Porter—and these were placed on Custer's Field. Since nobody knew where these three officers had died (their bodies had never been identified), the chances are very good that the markers were not placed accurately. Harrington's marker was placed on Custer Hill, probably because that was where Tom Custer's already had been placed and so was Porter's. There has been speculation that Harrington was killed some distance from the field, being one of the many "he almost got away" riders.

Jack Sturgis' was erected down on the South Skirmish Line, perhaps after consulting Morrow's 1879 photograph. This brought the total number of markers on Custer's Field to 252, which strangely enough is the number that appears on the field today. But between 1910 and today there have been other counts and other maps, so some of them might as well be mentioned.

Walter Camp made a detailed map of Custer's Field, including the marker locations, for his own researches. This map was made sometime between 1905 and 1910 and probably went through several evolutions. Some specific individual burial spots were identified. Camp thought that there were 246 markers. It is rather difficult to count them on his map. Charles Kuhlman, in his *Legend into History*, said that he had counted 246 in 1935 and 1936, but he also said that there were only 202 up until 1896, based on the Marshall inset map mentioned above and that the superintendent of the National Cemetery had requested forty-one additional stones in 1896. Since the first statement is totally incorrect and the latter statement patently false, I see little reason to rely on Kuhlman's count.

The other two great Custer historians, Dustin and Graham, never addressed the question of the markers, although Dustin went to great (but incomplete) lengths discussing the burials and reburials. Dustin visited the field only once; Graham not at all.

Probably the most important and influential mapping and count of the markers was undertaken by an archaeological team in 1984 and 1985. Their count of 252 markers proved to be accurate, but their placement of the markers made a mockery of their criticisms of the 1891 map.[1] Greg Michno presented his own excellent maps, tied to the topography but limited to the South Skirmish Line, in his *The Mystery of E Troop*.[2]

Since there were 252 markers in 1910 and 252 in 1984 and since nobody has admitted to adding or subtracting any in the meantime, one might reasonably assume that Camp and Kuhlman miscounted. Be that as it may, we know how many there are now, we know that they are not all where they should be, and we know that there are many too many.

In terms of positioning, we can draw some valid conclusions as to the relocation of some of the markers. The creation of the parking lot and road led to some disruption in the Keogh and Calhoun areas, with a few markers being moved a bit north or east of where they had originally been placed, plus there are volumes of commentary showing that the Custer Hill group includes many markers that don't belong there and may originally have been elsewhere. Most of these types of discussions are academic anyway, since we already know that all of the marker positions are not and cannot be exact representations of death sites. That they are even close approximations is only possible because of the efforts of the burial parties that were on the field before the markers were placed in 1891.

The first burials following the arrival of General Terry's command occurred on the day of that arrival, June 27, 1876. Those members of the 7th Cavalry who had been killed on the eastern side of the Little Horn under Reno's command were buried. Some—like Hodgson and DeWolf—in individual graves, but most were buried in a mass grave about where Reno's original hospital site had been. The mules and horses were driven over this mass grave site to completely obliterate any traces of it and this proved to be so successful in hiding the spot that it has never been found to this day. It is said that the mass grave held about nineteen bodies. These burials were performed by members of the 7th Cavalry.

The soldiers and civilians killed on the west side of the river, mainly during Reno's retreat, were buried, for the most part, by soldiers from the Terry/Gibbon column, principally the 7th Infantry and by some of the 7th Cavalry survivors. Some bodies were buried where, or very close to where, they had fallen; others were dragged out of the way so as not to impede the setting up of the camp. Most of these burials were rather hasty and unceremonious because, unlike Reno's men killed on the hilltop, the bodies had been savagely mutilated.[3] Even though the soil of the valley floor was more conducive to "proper" interments, there weren't many of these, because the men doing the burying just could not deal with what they had to look at and handle. There is nothing at all mysterious or blameworthy about this; it is one thing to bury a man who has died from a relatively neat gunshot wound to his chest and quite another to deal with a body which has been decapitated, eviscerated and hacked to pieces with an axe. It is hardly surprising that most of the valley burials were seemingly lacking in human compassion. Some, but not all, of the graves were marked.

What happened on Custer's Field was much worse. The men who died there fell on June 25, and their bodies were first discovered on the 27th. It was not until the 28th that burial parties went to the field. The dead on Custer's Field had lain there for three days in a blistering sun. Most of the bodies had been severely mutilated, despite some accounts to the contrary made for public consumption. The burials here were performed by survivors of the 7th Cavalry, men who had just come through two days of intense conflict and who were in no condition to do more than make a perfunctory attempt to hide the grisly remains of what had been living, breathing comrades only a few short days before.

It has been written that the soil of the ridges and ravines above the Little Horn is not of a consistency that would allow for proper interments, and that there were no implements available to allow for digging. Most accounts tell of men scooping up dirt with plates, cups or knives to cover their fallen friends. In fact, there is nothing very much wrong with the soil—there is, after all, a National Cemetery up there so nobody ever had any trouble making proper burials when they really wanted to—and there were sufficient shovels, spades and axes among the joined commands and found in the village. What was in short supply was not good soil and implements, but time—time and human will. These were in short supply only because of an internally generated desire on the parts of almost everyone involved to get the hell away from the disgusting scene on this battlefield and the hostile army which had created it, as quickly as possible. It is not an overstatement to say that there was a great deal of fear pervading that valley, those ridges and those men. And that fear and that sense of urgency are perfectly understandable in the circumstances.

Men tell of the need for speed in order to get the wounded to where they could receive proper medical care, but the wounded didn't go anywhere until the night of the 28th, and not very far then. So there was at least a whole day to bury the 210 bodies on Custer's Field and more than 700 men available to bury them. One need not hold a doctorate in mathematics to be able to figure out that those bodies could have been buried and the graves marked, had there existed the will to do so.

We need not explore at any length the various body counts given by different reporters of the burials. These range from Bradley's initial 196 (he later revised it upward) to Godfrey's 212, and some even much higher (Benteen). Since we know that there were 210 men in Custer's command, we know that Godfrey's count is inaccurate and since several bodies were subsequently discovered unburied (two, including Mark Kellogg, were found the day after the burials by a group accompanying Gibbon to the field), the initial body and burial counts don't mean too much, except to illustrate their inaccuracy.

In any event, the bodies were "buried" in a manner best described as having a bit of dirt or brush thrown over them (or most of them; some were missed). There were a few exceptions, especially Tom and Armstrong Custer, who received more attention, but for the most part the burials were notable only for their haste and imperfection. There is little doubt however, that the vast majority of the bodies were buried where they were found, as the condition of the bodies precluded moving them any distance. The Custers were a notable exception—they were buried together about 20 feet from where they were found. There is also no doubt that the vast majority of the bodies were found where they died. There are no accounts by Indian participants indicating that any bodies were moved, except one which mentions Tom Custer (probably) being carried from Calhoun, or possibly near the river, to Custer Hill, and one which mentions Armstrong Custer's body being carried over to the Reno position and back again.

It is today difficult to believe that Yellowstone had become the United States' first National Park in 1874, two years before the Custer disaster. Even before then, some people traveled to the Yellowstone country just to see the marvels that we have come to accept as commonplace. After the Custer fight, the battlefield became a sort of way stop for some of the travelers to Yellowstone. Not everyone wanted to go there, of course, and there was still some danger attached to travel in that region, despite the presence of thousands of troops. Yet there were visitors to the battlefield as early as a couple of months after the fights, including Tom LeForge, who had been an interpreter with Gibbon's column. Most were horrified by what they found: decaying and half-scavenged horse bodies scattered over Custer's Field, bodies of soldiers left lying to rot in the elements, skulls, bones and decaying flesh everywhere, not a decent grave to be seen anywhere. And hanging like a pall over everything, the sickening stench of decomposition. The scene in August was undoubtedly worse than the scene left on June 28. LeForge, who had not been on the field immediately after the battle because of an injury and who had therefore a high degree of interest in visiting it, described it to Thomas Marquis like this:

> ... I rode over the ground where Custer and his men were buried— or were lying scattered about. I had been there at times also during the autumn of 1876, a few weeks and months after the battle.
>
> Many a grinning skull, ribbed trunk, or detached limb bones I saw on top of the ground or but partly covered up during the year preceding the visit of the reburial squad in early June, 1877. Many times I observed indications of wolves having been at the mutilated human remnants. Some of the bodies had been dismembered and

otherwise hacked and cut up immediately after death. . . . Even the best of the so-called graves were only a few inches deep. . . . A year of rain, sunshine, freezing, thawing, elapsed between the battle and the coming of the second group of their army comrades. All of these conditions combined created a ghastly situation. The mingled odors of decayed horses and humans permeated the air. Furthermore, the foul odors were not all gone for yet another year [1878].

There were, of course, letters of protest and howls of indignation. Two British lords and officers wrote directly to President Grant, asking how any civilized nation could suffer such indignities to the corpses of men who had died defending its colors. Several newspapers took up the cause and the government finally acted, but not until 1877.

The first official expedition to the battlefield was under the command of Lieutenant Colonel Michael V. Sheridan, and its purpose was to recover the bodies of the slain officers and to spruce up the field generally. Sheridan stated that he arrived at the battlefield on the morning of July 2, 1877, and that he left there on July 4, after doing the following:

July 2: "fifty picked men were deployed into a skirmish line, to look up the trenches or graves . . . Whenever the skirmishers came to a grave or trench, the place was marked by a willow stem . . . All the graves of both the men and officers were discovered without difficulty. The remains were found to be scattered over an area of several hundred acres."

July 2: "All that evening . . . the soldiers were converting cedar boughs into stakes . . . three feet long."

July 3: "a fatigue party was ordered out to exhume and re-inter the remains of the soldiers who fell around Custer. There were large and some small trenches. Some contained but few remains. Others contained long rows of separate sets of bones, indicating that as many as a dozen had been buried together . . . In a few hours the thin layer of dirt had been removed from the bones of over two hundred soldiers, and the remains re-interred in the same trenches, but rather more decently than before. Three feet of earth, tastefully heaped and packed . . . was put upon each set of remains, and the head marked by a cedar stake."

July 2, 3, 4: "As some rumors had been circulated last year stating that a party had escaped from the battle-field and been massacred some three or four miles from it, I directed the scouts and Indians to scour the country in a circuit of about ten miles from Custer's hill, with the hope of finding the remains of this party. This search was followed up the next day by a more thorough one, and on the third day by Capt. Nowlan with the greater portion of his company and all the Crow Indians and scouts, and not an indication was met with which would go to show that any portion of the command made its way through the Indians."

July 3 and 4: "The remains of Col. Custer, Capt. Keogh, Capt. Custer, Capt. Yates, Lieut. Cooke, Lt. Smith, Lieut. Calhoun, Lieut. Donald McIntosh, Lieut. Reily, Lieut. Benj. H. Hodgson and Dr. DeWolf, were identified by Capt. Nowlan . . . The remains of each of the above named officers were carefully transferred to pine boxes . . . and taken across the river to my main camp, while those of Lieut. Crittenden were enclosed in a coffin and buried where he fell. In the meantime parties had been sent out in all directions over the field to find and mark the graves of the enlisted men. As soon as these were found, details of burial parties were made [and the work] was carried on until it was concluded on July 4th."

July 4: " After the completion of this work, the command thoroughly searched all the country on the east bank of the river, as far as the cedar bluffs, and extending from Reno's crossing, down the river to within about ten miles of its mouth, for any missing bodies. . . . "

Now if all of this sounds like an awful lot to have been accomplished in approximately two and a half days, it most likely was. While not wishing to brand Mike Sheridan an outright liar, I do believe that he exaggerated his work and results more than somewhat, and there is no question but that he was painting a less-than-accurate picture when he emphasized that everything was done without the slightest difficulty, particularly the identification of the officers' bodies.

Tom LeForge, who had been over the field previously, was with Sheridan's command as a guide/interpreter, and he made the following observation, as recorded by Thomas B. Marquis:

I sat on the ground not more than ten feet distant and watched the soldiers respectfully go through the motions of disinterring and transferring to a box the body of General Custer. On previous visits I had become familiar with the locations of the bodies of the officers, which had been covered up a little more carefully with the sand and sage-brush and whose positions had been specially marked. Hence I knew that at this particular place were the remains indicated as being those of the high officer. But they gathered up nothing substantial except one thigh bone and the skull attached to some part of the skeleton trunk. Besides these, the quantity of cohering and transferable bodily substance was not enough to fill my hat . . . I was right there and looking, and that was all there was. . . .[4]

George Herendeen, who, unlike LeForge, had actually been present at the original burials, told Walter Camp that: "When Custer was buried, there were stakes marked VI and VII for Custer and Tom Custer (the numbers on Nowlan's map are not Roman numerals), and but for me they would have made a mistake and got other remains than Custer's. Already had other remains. I identified Custer's remains . . . "[5] Camp also noted that Herendeen told him, on August 5, 1911, that "out of the grave where Custer was buried not more than a double handful of small bones were picked up."

Sergeant Michael Caddle of I Company had been on detached service at Powder River in June 1876, but he told Joseph Mills Hanson that he was part of the body-recovery detail in 1877. Hanson wrote:

When they came to the body marked Number One on the list and on the stake at its head, and supposed to be that of General Custer, it was placed in the coffin, and then on the ground was found a blouse on which it had been lying. An examination of the blouse revealed . . . it was that of a corporal . . . but the Sergeant goes on to state that later they "found another body and placed it in the coffin. I think we got the right body the second time."[6]

Caddle did not say, however, how they knew that the second "body" was Custer's, or how the stake or corpse was moved in the first place (one or the other had to have been moved).

There were several other statements made to the effect that there was more than a bit of difficulty in identifying Custer's remains, and since he and Tom had reportedly been buried side by side, there is no doubt that this difficulty encompassed Tom's remains as well. The difficulty extended even to the utilization of Nowlan's map, made the previous year. Both Herendeen and Hugh Scott recalled that the stakes bore Roman numerals. Nowlan's map has Arabic figures. To compound the problem, Nowlan's map bears a notation that Custer's grave is number 4 but Caddle says it was number 1, while Herendeen says the two Custer graves were VI and VII. If Armstrong Custer's remains were gathered in July 1877 and now repose at West Point, it is only through good fortune or coincidence. Nowlan's map is incorrect in other respects as well, and there is absolutely no reason to believe that the recovery of any of the other bodies was any more "without any difficulty whatsoever" than that of Armstrong Custer.

In any event, it is obvious that Sheridan's report and statement to the media were both imaginative. His recovery of the bodies was very questionable, as were the re-interments he reported. His command did however mark the obvious grave sites with stakes.[7] All of this is evidenced by subsequent reports from visitors to the battlefield.

Late in the afternoon of the day after Mike Sheridan's party left the battlefield, Philetus W. Norris arrived, accompanied by Sheridan's guide, Jack Baronette. Norris was the newly appointed superintendent of Yellowstone Park and was on his way to take up his duties. He had attempted to catch up with Sheridan's party, but had been unable to overtake it, so he had enlisted Baronette's help when the command returned to Post No. 2. Norris was a long-time friend of Charley Reynolds and was on a mission to recover the latter's body for reburial elsewhere. In this quest he was only partially successful, but he did leave a description of the field which includes the information that "most of the soldiers . . . have stakes driven where they rest." Norris also relates that there was indeed a "sprinkling of earth on each or in groups as they fell last year," and that some bodies were found that had been missed the previous year, although to balance things, some that had been covered in 1876 could not be located in 1877.[8] This latter statement has largely gone unremarked—but it is very interesting.

Consider that the only way one could know that "no trace of some then covered could be found" is if one had some prior knowledge of where those "then covered" were supposed to be. The only 1876 burial spots that were mapped or otherwise specially marked or noted were those of the officers (and those few in the valley mapped for Norris by Fred Gerard). Norris is thus telling us, albeit in a rather circumspect way, that some of the officers' bodies buried in 1876 were not found in 1877, and he undoubtedly got this information or impression from Baronette, who had been on the field with Mike Sheridan. Norris also states that an indescribable odor arose from any place where the ground had been disturbed.

Less than three weeks after Mike Sheridan's detail left the tidied-up battlefield, Mike's older brother, General Philip H. Sheridan, visited the field in company with General George Crook. General Sheridan reported that he found that some graves had been disturbed, he thought by "human coyotes," and his aide, George A. Forsyth, reported that he had a work detail of sixty men spruce up the field, and that "The total skeletons and parts of skeletons reburied were seventeen." Forsyth also stated that "when we returned to camp I do not think there was a human bone unburied on the field."[9]

Others who accompanied that same party were apparently on a different field—at least they saw it differently. Lieutenant John Bourke wrote that he found at least seven skulls lying on the ground, as well as "sticking out from the ground in the ravine . . . the body of a . . . scout" and said that "it was hard to go ten yards in any direction without stepping on portions of the human anatomy and skeletons of horses, singly or mixed together." Private Chris Madsen said that "we found bodies that had been overlooked by the burial party."

There were two points of agreement among these witnesses and others who were there at the same time: the men had been buried where they had fallen, and the graves were marked by stakes. One witness, Lieutenant Homer Wheeler, thought that the graves were marked both at the head and the foot, but the others just said "marked by a cedar stake."[10]

Only a few days later, on July 25, an anonymous correspondent to the New York Sun would write a description of the battlefield that was markedly different from those of Phil Sheridan and Tony Forsyth. He saw the field much as Bourke saw it, and this after the work reportedly done by Forsyth's sixty-man detail. This correspondent wrote that the work had been "so scabbily performed that scarcely a single grave could be found through which the contents did not protrude." He also said that a storm that day had left "not a particle of earth on a single bone of the entire three hundred skeletons," and he ventured a guess that the four companies of Sheridan's escort, who were returning from dropping off the senior officers at Post No. 2 and who were then camped opposite the field, would do nothing to correct the situation. In this observation he was correct. He also reported that the "graves" were "apparently located where the several men fell," and that "teepee poles by the score mark the spots. . ."[11] An identical description appears in a pamphlet by Ami Frank Mulford and appears to have been taken almost directly from the *Sun* article.[12]

In August of the same year, Dr. William Allen led a wagon train through the valley of the Little Horn, and while camped opposite the field paid it a visit. His description indicates that the reburials by Mike Sheridan and Tony Forsyth had been relatively ineffective, but, of more importance to this study, he also reported that he had found "Each soldier lying just where he had fallen, each with a small amount of earth thrown over him, with his head protruding from one end of the grave and his feet from the other."[13]

Other visitors to the field in 1877 and in early 1878 reported much the same thing. While they varied in the level of horror they found, they all agreed that the grave locations were very easy to find and that they were generally marked by wooden stakes.

In August 1878, Captain J.S. Payne of the 5th Cavalry was on the battlefield with the express purpose of making certain measurements in order to clear up the question of how far it was from Custer Hill to Reno Hill, etc. He appeared as a witness at the Reno inquiry, and testified in part as follows:

> Q. What were the evidences also that the place that you measured from was the place where General Custer fell?
>
> A. It was unmistakably the spot where a struggle had taken place. The bones of men and horses were there, and it was the extreme northeast limit of the battlefield.
>
> * * *
>
> Q. Did you see any other evidences of that field of battle at the time that you were there?
>
> A. Nothing except the bones and parts of the bones of men on the Custer battlefield, and one or two pieces of human bones that I found scattered in the grass on the left bank in the bottom.[14]

Payne's testimony clearly indicated that the battlefield gravesites were still readily apparent and that there were still bones strewn about the ridges and hollows. He was part of a larger contingent which included Nelson Miles.

Also accompanying this group was Mamie Sturgis, wife of Colonel Sam Sturgis and mother of the missing Jack Sturgis. Miles, or someone acting under his authority, created a bit of confusion by having a "grave" fabricated for Jack, complete with identifying sign, so as to assuage Mrs. Sturgis' concerns over her missing boy. This wooden marker still existed in 1879 when the next work party came to the battlefield, but it had disappeared by 1890.

The observations and reports of this party, together with the continuing stream of invective from the press led the War Department to issue orders in October 1878 for a cleanup of the field and the erection of a stone cairn housing all exposed remains collected. It was three weeks later and too late in the year to do anything, when the order filtered down to Fort Custer (formerly Post No. 2), but the order was not forgotten, and in April 1879 the assignment was given to Captain George Sanderson of the 11th Infantry.

Sanderson reported that he could not find any rocks within a reasonable distance of the battlefield and so he collected the exposed human and horse bones and interred both, although not together, in and under a pyramidal monument of cordwood.[15] There is a very famous photograph of this monument taken by S.J. Morrow, who accompanied the work party and recorded its work. The photo is misdated 1877. Sanderson reported that:

> Instead of disinterring any remains, I carefully re-mounded all graves that could be found. At each grave a stake was driven, where those that had been previously placed had fallen. Newspaper reports to the effect that the bodies still lay exposed are sensational. From a careful searching of the entire ground, the few remains now buried beneath the mound were all that could be found. I believe the large number of horse bones lying over the field has given rise to some of such statements, and to prevent any such statements being made in the future, I had all the horse bones gathered together and placed in the mound.

Whether or not the field was as neat as Sanderson says he found it, he left the important information that he re-mounded all the sites, made sure that each was marked with a stake, and removed all the horse bones he could find.

In the same year that Sanderson erected the cordwood monument, the granite monument which now dominates Custer Hill was completed and shipped to Fort Custer. The foundation for the monument was poured in the summer of 1880, and the monument was moved to the battlefield early in 1881. In July 1881, Lieutenant Charles F. Roe, who had been a member of Gibbon's command during the 1876 campaign, and who had probably unwittingly been one of the first to see Custer's dead, went to the field to erect the monument and to gather the remains into a mass grave.

Roe spent three weeks at the battlefield and reported that "Ten feet from the foot of the monument, and surrounding it on all four sides, a trench was dug, into which were gathered all the remains of those who fell in that fight, including those who were with Reno, and for this purpose the vicinity was thoroughly scouted, and all were brought together and securely and deeply buried at the foot of the monument." He also stated that he "took great pains in gathering together all the remains from the Custer Battle Field, Reno's Hill and the valley;" that he felt "confident that all the remains are gathered together and placed at base of monument;" and that "Wherever I found the remains of a man, I planted a stake, well in the ground, so that future visitors can see where the men actually fell."[16]

While Roe was not entirely successful in retrieving all of the remains from Custer's Field, he did mark each site from which remains were recovered, and it is obvious from his diligence and his concern for historical rectitude that he would not have had a stake placed where no remains had been found.

Between Roe's work in July 1881 and the tenth-year reunion in June 1886, there was a constant trickle of visitors to the battlefield and cemetery, some of them official parties but most simple tourists and local area workmen. The reports of horrible conditions were no longer widespread and only a few recommendations were made in respect to the gravesites, mainly as to more permanent marking than the wooden stakes. The 1886 reunion attendees left few detailed observations as to the gravesites, but photographs taken at the time clearly show that most of the stakes and other markers had withstood the ravages of time and were still in place.

Captain John French of the 25th Infantry took a work detail to the battlefield in 1889 in order to re-inter bodies removed from the Fort Phil Kearny post cemetery. The fort itself had been razed twenty years earlier as part of the settlement of the Red Cloud War. These remains were buried along and behind Battle Ridge, in three rows running southeast from approximately in the rear of the monument's fenced enclosure. Originally staked, the sites would later be marked by marble stones and still later would be transferred to the cemetery grounds proper. James Campbell came out from Fort Custer as guide to French's command. Campbell had been over the battlefield several times since 1878, and while French took care of the Phil Kearny remains, he led another detail to make sure that the Custer's Field sites were properly marked, reportedly burying the remains of four bodies that had previously been overlooked.[17]

The next mission to the battlefield was Sweet's 1890 placement of the first markers, which has been discussed above. It becomes very clear that between the original shabby burials and the placing of the individual markers there was an almost unbroken chain of events that almost guaranteed that Sweet would find well-marked burial locations. This may seem like a lot of "almosts," but it is as close to a chain of evidence as one can readily find in researching the Little Horn fights. Sweet himself stated that he had no difficulty in finding the first 217 gravesites.

It can be said with a high degree of certainty that the vast majority of the original burial sites were marked by headstones, and that the excess markers in fact mark either nothing or horse bones. While there may be a very few death sites not marked, they could not affect an analysis of movements and positions based in part upon marker sites on the Custer's Field. The body locations that have been noted outside the battlefield boundaries must, of course, be included in any such analysis.[18]

As to the question of survivors of the Custer fight, there is a simple answer: there were none. There were 210 men in the Custer battalions and all of the evidence points to all of them having been killed on Custer's Field on June 25, 1876. Despite the confusion of body count numbers and wild statements by people who should have known better, there were no missing men, only unidentified bodies—and the fact that bodies have been reported found over the years in seemingly out-of-the-way places just reinforces the conclusion that, whatever anyone originally counted, the total would eventually come to 210.

This confusion as to the number of men and the number of bodies led to many tales of survivors and not all of them are obvious wild flights of fancy. But none of them is authentic, either, and the one that perhaps comes as close to being as acceptable as any, that of Frank Finkle,[19] is still too full of holes to really be credible, regardless of Douglas Ellison's and Charles Kuhlman's apparent acceptance of it. Anything may be possible, but if there was a legitimate survivor of the Custer fight, he has never come forward. Then again, perhaps a true survivor never would, and even if there had been a survivor, his existence would do nothing to invalidate the grave marker locations.

The idea that the Custer battalions had fallen in more or less skirmish formations prevailed for years because of the extra markers on the battlefield. To understand just how important it is to eliminate those superfluous markers it is necessary to analyze why and where they came to be placed.

NOTES

1. Douglas D. Scott and Richard A. Fox Jr., *Archaeological Insights into the Custer Battle* (Norman: Univ. of Okla. Press 1987).
2. Gregory Michno, *The Mystery of E Troop* (Missoula: Montana Press, 1994).
3. *See* Analysis 5.
4. Thomas B. Marquis, *Memoirs of a White Crow Indian* (New York: Century Company, 1928), p.284.
5. George Herendeen: account, as given to Walter Camp, 1909; [ebook] Appendix 3.54.
6. Richard G. Hardorff, *The Custer Battle Casualties: Burials, Exhumations, and Reinterments* (El Segundo: Upton & Sons 1990), pp.45–46.
7. Ibid. p.39.
8. Philetus Norris, *New York Herald*, July 15, 1877; reprinted in "Custer's Remains," *Bighorn Yellowstone Journal*, Spring 1992.
9. Richard G. Hardorff, *The Custer Battle Casualties: Burials*, pp.52–53.
10. Ibid., p.54.
11. Ibid., p.58.
12. Ami Frank Mulford, *Fighting Indians in the Seventh U.S. Cavalry* (Corning, 1878); *see also* Hardorff, *The Custer Battle Casualties: Burials*, p.62.
13. Hardorff, *The Custer Battle Casualties: Burials*, p.64.
14. Ronald Nichols (ed.), *Reno's Court of Inquiry* (Custer Battlefield Historical & Museum Association, Inc., 1996), pp.272–3.
15. Capt. C. K. Sanderson, "Report to Post Adjutant Fort Custer April 7, 1879," reprinted in Hardorff, *The Custer Battle Casualties: Burials*, pp.67–68.
16. Charles F. Roe, *Synopsis of his Report of 6 August 1881 as to the placing of the Custer Battle monument* (January 15, 1882).
17. Jerome A. Green, *Stricken Field: The Little Bighorn Since 1876* (Norman: Univ. of Okla. 2008), p.44.
18. The "corrected" marker locations and discussion of the unmarked body locations can be found in Analysis 7.
19. See Douglas W. Ellison, *Sole Survivor: An Examination of the Narrative of Frank Finkle* (Aberdeen, North Plains Press, 1983).

ANALYSIS 7

RECONSTRUCTING THE DEATH SITES ON CUSTER'S FIELD USING MARKER LOCATIONS

"All these months had passed, yet the little band whose brave deeds of heroism will ever remain a matter of history, have not received decent burial."
—AMI F. MULFORD REPORTING ON HIS 1877 VISIT TO THE LITTLE HORN BATTLEFIELD

The burials of the dead and the placement of the markers on Custer's Field have been explored at some length in Analysis 5, wherein it was concluded that the markers undoubtedly give a reasonably accurate representation of the death sites of the Custer battalion's personnel. This analysis will concentrate on an attempt to reconstruct the actual death sites on the field, based upon the placement of the markers, the evidence of eyewitnesses, plus 20th-century skeletal and artifact discoveries. It was also previously shown that there are far too many markers and that the sheer numbers can be extremely misleading.

One might argue that the location of individual bodies is not really necessary to a proper analysis of the Custer fight, but that argument must fail in the light of some very simple questions, such as: What would happen to reconstructions of the action if it could be shown that Custer and the officers who fell with him were not found on Custer Hill, but down by the river, or on Calhoun Hill? What if all of the markers on Custer Hill are spurious? What if thirty markers on the South Skirmish Line actually mark only one or two bodies? What would that do to accounts and analyses of the battle? etc, etc.

Obviously, those are oversimplified and overdramatized questions, but there is enough confusion surrounding the body numbers and locations to require at least an attempt at reconstruction of those, before any credible analysis of the movement of the troops and Indians can be attempted.

The first step is to determine the number of markers that should be on the field. The outside limit is, of course, 210—the total number of men in the Custer command who went beyond Medicine Tail Coulee. Not all of these men however, died within the confines of the fenced area of Custer's Field, and so no markers should appear on that field for them. This is something that few writers on the battle have taken into consideration, although many of these same writers were aware of the "remote" body locations, the most famous of which was that of First Sergeant James Butler of L Company. There has been a great deal of discussion and speculation as to why Butler was where he was when he died, but hardly any mention of the other out-of-place bodies. Even the true location of Butler's original burial is debatable.

The best evidence however, indicates that Butler's body was found on the north side of Deep Coulee and that the remains removed from the south side in 1905 actually were those of Corporal John Foley of C Troop. The Butler marker probably marks neither man's death site.

According to Stanislas Roy:

> The first dead body we came to was that of Corporal John Foley . . . who lay on this rise, just over toward the coulee running up to the battlefield . . . at least three-fourths of a mile in advance of the first group of dead at C [Point C is the rise upon which the Finley group of markers is placed]. The next body we came to was that of Sergeant Butler . . . Butler lay 200 or 300 yards beyond and across a ravine . . . He lay probably half the distance from Foley to point C.[1]

The only coulee that runs up to the battlefield and fits Roy's description is Deep Coulee. On the other hand Edward Godfrey stated that the first body his company came across was that of Butler, while John Martin said only that Butler was found by a party searching "down to the river." Godfrey's find would depend upon the exact route he took to the field, which is not known.

Regardless of who was found where, the evidence is emphatic that both men were found in the area of Deep Coulee and Medicine Tail Coulee, not within the then-fenced area.

At least one body from the Custer battalions was found opposite the Medicine Tail ford on the village side of the river. This body has been identified as Sergeant James Bustard of I Company by Daniel Knipe, and the horse as having been that ridden by Bustard by William Hardy, while both Lieutenant Edgerly and Sergeant James Flanagan identified Bustard with Keogh.[2] On the other hand, James Rooney both wrote and told Camp that the body found on the village side was that of William Brown of F Company. Rooney confused the issue by saying that Brown was found, with his horse, opposite "Crazy Horse Gully," which at least a couple of writers have translated as Deep Ravine (this term gets thrown around rather loosely, sometimes fitting one location, sometimes another).[3] So we have one body, probably Brown's (D Company helped bury Keogh's dead, and both Edgerly and Flanagan belonged to D). They were positive as to Bustard's identification, (while Knipe was rather "iffy"), on the village side of the river, far removed from the markers on Custer's Field.

A human finger bone was found in later years near the mouth of Medicine Tail Coulee, but this is more likely evidence of a careless warrior dropping a trophy than of a casualty.[4] The Cheyennes, after all, were known as "The Cut Finger People," which should be self-explanatory.[5] An almost complete skeleton was, however, discovered in 1928 by Frank Bethune a couple of hundred yards northeast of the 1905 find. These remains would not appear to be connected with either Foley or Butler. A boot found in the same area in 1904 by Joseph Blummer bore the initials "J.D." This must have been a relic of either John Duggan of L Company or John Darris of E, who were the only men with Custer having those initials. There may have been parts of another body discovered at or near this same location, although it appears more probable that there was only one skeleton in total.[6]

There is a preponderance of evidence that Orderly Trumpeter Henry Dose was killed down near the Deep Coulee/Medicine Tail flat, although at least one writer thinks that Dose may account for one of the four skeletons found over the years in three places in the upper area of the Blummer–Nye/ Cartwright–Luce ridges.[7] Henry Petring of G Company told Walter Camp that Dose was found "halfway between Custer and Reno with arrows in his back and sides." James Boyle, also of G, was more specific. He told Camp that

"Dose was found on flat near ford B between two coulees." John Ryan wrote Camp that he understood that the body of one of Custer's trumpeters had been found "where he first attempted to cross the river." This location was verified as the death scene of an unidentified trumpeter by DeRudio, who told the Reno court that he accompanied Benteen to the battlefield on June 27 and that "probably 500 yards from the ford we found a dead body that was the first dead body we found, lying in the bottom of a little coulee. He was so much disfigured that I did not know who he was, only the marks on his pants showed he was a trumpeter." DeRudio also told Walter Camp that "the first dead man was near Ford B and about 150 yards from river. Says this man was not Sergt. Butler."

The balance of DeRudio's description, especially his statements that they went via, "a ford on the north side of the village, on the right bank of the river" and that " . . . there were no signs of the cavalry having forded there at all. We saw tracks of cavalry horses going over the bluff diagonally at that point," caused Camp to decide that Dose had died just south of Deep Ravine and noted to himself that Dose had been slain "at elevation 84," despite all of the positive evidence to the contrary. By no stretch of the imagination can elevation 84 be seen as fitting any of the descriptions given by the enlisted men.

The trumpeter Camp thought was Dose was most probably Henry Voss, the chief trumpeter, whose body was found near the river, but not near Medicine Tail. George Glease and Henry Mechling, both of H Company, went with Benteen on June 27 and each independently told Walter Camp that the body was Voss. Glease said that "the body nearest the river was that of Chief Trumpeter Henry Voss, and near it was that of Mark Kellogg. . . . Both bodies lay within a stone's throw of the river." Mechling agreed, saying that Voss was "nearest the river, about 200 yards from the cut bank, near Crazy Horse Gully." On the other hand, both Tom O'Neill of G Company and Dennis Lynch of F placed Voss near Custer on the hill, which is perhaps where one would expect him to have been.

One might also expect the reporter Mark Kellogg to have been with Custer, but there is absolutely no doubt that Kellogg's body was found near the river, northwest of Deep Ravine, by Colonel Gibbon's party on June 28, having been missed the previous day. E.G. Mathey told Camp that he buried Kellogg on the 29th and that "it lay near a ravine between Custer and the river." Richard Thompson, a lieutenant on Gibbon's staff, told Camp that "Mark Kellogg lay 3/4 mile from Custer, down near the river on a side hill, about 100 yards from the river." Gibbon's description also puts Kellogg near the river.[8] All of "100 yards from the river," "200 yards from the cut bank" and "a stone's throw from the river" lie outside the old boundary fence. There are no markers near the river. Kellogg's marker is east of the monument. It may very well be that Voss and Kellogg are still buried where they were originally found.

The evidence is convincing that Voss, Kellogg and Dose were found outside the old battlefield fence. This brings the total number of men killed "outside" to seven: the three named plus Butler, Foley, Brown or Bustard, and unidentified (Darris or Duggan). There are however, more to come.

It was mentioned previously that it was speculated that Dose was among the four skeletons found near the Blummer and Luce ridges.[9] The basis for this speculation is Dose's status as an orderly—it being natural for him to have been sent, perhaps with an escort, as a messenger to Benteen or Reno or the pack train. As has been established, Dose could not have been found in this area, unless one would care to claim that Custer tried to first ford the river at Luce Ridge. The fact remains that four human skeletons and three horse skeletons were found in this area. It cannot be established whether these men were the first casualties of the Custer fight or were killed later in the conflict, only that they were found here and that their markers should not be within the fenced perimeter. Now there are eleven.

About 1,000 yards north of this area, just across a wash separating Blummer Ridge from the next divide, a fragment of a human phalanx was found, indicating a probable death site, perhaps that of one of the ubiquitous "last dash" attempted escapees. It is unlikely that a body was dragged to this out-of-the-way spot. Also just outside the northwest battlefield fence line, about 650 yards from the northwest corner, a human leg bone was found. This would not appear to be battlefield detritus, but the remains of yet another dead trooper, the location militating against a dragging scenario.

So now the grand total is thirteen, or at least thirteen. The Oglala Red Hawk told Nicholas Ruleau that "about a month after the battle some thirty Indians, including himself, went back to the battlefield and were looking over it. At the mouth of the ravine [once again an imprecise location that might have been just about anywhere] they found eight dead soldiers lying with their uniforms on and their guns and ammunition and everything by them."[10]

It is now possible to state with absolute certainty that there should not be more than 197 markers on Custer's Field, so instead of having to consider—as most do who are even aware of the discrepancies—forty or forty-two spurious grave markers, fifty-five must be found and removed—and as nearly as possible, they must be the right fifty-five.

This effort can be helped enormously by the record made by the team of archaeologists who worked Custer's Field in 1984 and 1985.[11] While I do not agree with all of their conclusions as to how the battle was fought, and find some errors in their mapping of the markers, there can be no doubt as to what they discovered when they excavated individual and paired marker locations.

The archaeologists excavated at thirty-seven marker locations, including eleven sets of pairs. Their most important finding, in terms of this particular study, was that all of the paired markers they excavated indicated that only one body had been buried there, except for one—and it contained absolutely nothing. Four of the fifteen single digs turned up empty, while the other eleven contained some small remnant of a human body. The vast majority, eighteen of twenty-one of the excavations which contained human remains, also contained other relics of the fight, such as bullets, cartridge cases, buttons, etc., indicating that they were indeed death/burial sites.

While a direct extrapolation from these findings might be adventurous and slightly presumptuous—the sample is not large—it at least has a solid basis. Coupled with anecdotal evidence from the men who performed the burials and reburials, or who visited the field out of respect or curiosity, it should be possible to begin a valid reconstruction of the original death sites. The 1891 Marshall plotting will be used for this purpose where the plotting of the 1984/1985 team is in error, although there must always be reference to the latter for utilization of marker numbers (see also Analysis 6). There is not, however, any direct correlation between the 1891 and 1984/1985 plottings, although they are in broad general agreement as to the groupings of the markers—that is, they each show areas of concentration at Custer Hill, Calhoun Hill, Keogh Swale and the South Skirmish Line, as well as a string of isolated markers between Calhoun Hill and the South Skirmish Line.

One must have a starting point, and Custer Hill itself will serve as well as any. The 1984/85 mapping shows fifty markers within the fenced grouping and four situated outside it to the northwest. The referenced marker numbers are 59–110, except 92 and 93, within the fence and 92, 93, 57 and 58 outside. The 1891 mapping shows fifty-three markers in total, the corrected number (see Analysis 6) being fifty-two. The difference in markers can be partially explained by those for Harrington, Reed and Boston Custer, which were definitely added after 1890, but the most important consideration is that the 1891 map had too many markers to begin with.

Edward S. Godfrey was very specific as to the number of bodies found on Custer Hill. He wrote that there were "forty-two bodies and thirty-nine dead horses" there on June 28.[12] John Ryan, First Sergeant of H Company, stated that he was part of the burial party on the 28th and that he "helped to bury 45 of Custer's men," including Custer, Cooke, Tom Custer and two other officers.[13] Ryan was obviously speaking of the bodies on Custer Hill. Colonel John Gibbon thought that there were "40 or 50" bodies on the hill.[14]

Attempting to identify all of the specific individuals found on Custer Hill is an impossible task, as the burial locations of the enlisted men were not, for the most part, identified—although most of the men probably were—and there is considerable disagreement as to the whereabouts of some people, such as Henry Voss and Robert Hughes. The number of bodies is, however, of paramount importance and it would seem to make sense to use Godfrey's figure of forty-two, which is not only precise but which fits in neatly with the other estimates found in the literature.

Some of these forty-two bodies were found on top of the then-existing knob or "conical knoll"[15] where the monument now stands, the remainder occupying the ground now enclosed below the monument on the side of the ridge. Edgerly told Camp that there were only a few dead on top of the ridge, including Tom and Armstrong Custer and Cooke. Hare told him that he saw dead horses up there, as well as Cooke. Godfrey said that Tom Custer was there; DeRudio saw Armstrong Custer, Reily and five or six horses, "all sorrels from Company C." On the other hand, Knipe wrote Camp that "there was not hardly any horses around" where Custer was lying when he was first found, and that Custer was lying across "two or three soldiers." Custer was on the very peak of the hill, Knipe said. Fred Gerard told Camp that Tom and Armstrong lay within 20 feet of each other, Tom on the very top of the hill and Armstrong on the side.

Richard Thompson agreed that Tom was "nearest the peak of round hill." He also told Camp that he and others identified Dr. Lord's body about "twenty ft. southeast of Custer's body on side hill." George Wallace told the Reno court that there was a pile of four or five men beside a horse and that Armstrong Custer lay across one of them. Charles F. Roe is positive that there were ten men on top of the little knob, "Custer, nine men and officers were found lying behind their horses on the top of the ridge;" and he stated that there were twenty-five men on the western slope of the hill, "Just west on the slope, in a very small space, we found twenty-five men and numerous horses."[16] Edward McClernand gave the number as thirty or forty.[17]

Trumpeter William Hardy of A Company told Walter Camp that privates John Parker and Edward Driscoll, both of I Company, were found lying together "on riverside of hogback, on ground a little higher up than Adjutant Cooke," which may indicate that they were on the little knoll, although the "higher up" may actually be a reference to a river relationship, which would put them over toward the Keogh position, where one might expect to have found them.[18]

Several other enlisted men have been identified as having fallen "near Custer," but the descriptions as to location are too vague to pinpoint them. They undoubtedly were among the bodies strewn over the slope.

About 200 yards to the northwest of the monument, two markers were placed in 1890. Charles Woodruff told Camp that one of the "two men farthest north" was William Sharrow, sergeant major of the regiment. These two locations are therefore most likely genuine and it is unlikely that Godfrey included them in his count of forty-two on the hill, since they were so far away. Indeed, Godfrey may have been totally unaware of their presence, since he had been called upon to identify Tom Custer, not to make a survey for bodies. There are no markers there today, but the 1984/85 survey did disclose wooden stake fragments in that area.

So utilizing the information from all of these reports, it is possible to assume, with a high degree of certainty, that there were two bodies remote to the northwest of Custer Hill, eight or ten bodies on the knob, and thirty-two to thirty-four bodies on the slope, together with numerous dead horses, perhaps three dozen or so. Since the knob is now leveled and occupied by the monument, and since the bodies on the hillside were within a small space, moving ten markers to the knob[19] and reducing the number on the hill to thirty-two (Godfrey's forty-two minus ten) and putting two to the northwest (as per the 1891 map and Woodruff) will give an accurate picture of what was reality in 1876.

The removal or otherwise of specific markers is made easier by the 1984/85 survey results and by using the "small space" description to pare away some of the edges. The first step is to recreate the small knoll where the monument is and to put some bodies on top of it. It has been shown that this number is approximately ten, so take ten markers from the group and put them on top of the knoll. It makes sense to take markers 70, 109, 102 and 110 (Tom and Armstrong Custer, Cooke, and Reily) along with five from the fringes, say 59, 77, 81, 84 and 85. The reason for selecting only five is that room must be left for Dr. George Lord, as will be discussed below.

This leaves forty-three markers on the hillside and two to the northwest. Numbers 63 and 67 were excavated by the archaeological team and no remains were found in either. These may be deleted. The team also excavated at a pair of markers, 86 and 87, and found human remains in only one excavation unit, the remains being consistent with one body. Delete number 86. There are, to my way of looking at things, five other pairs of markers on the hill proper: 79/80, 73/74, 94/95, 65/66, and 101/102. Number 102 (Cooke) has already been placed on top of the hill, so 101 can be considered spurious, as can one of each of the other pairs. Delete 101, 79, 73, 94 and 65.

The pair of markers, 57/58, which are shown on the 1984/85 plotting some 60 meters outside the fenced area on the hill have no specific counterpart on the 1890 map and can be considered spurious for that reason, also because they fall within the "pairs theory." They may be deleted. It is well known that Lieutenant Harrington's body was never identified, and yet marker number 93 purports to indicate his resting place. This marker also has no equivalent on the 1890 map. Markers 82 and 83 bear the names of Autie Reed and Boston Custer, but the evidence from both Edgerly and Godfrey is that these two were found some distance down the slope, about 100 yards from the other Custers.[20] That would put them well outside the fenced area and between the Custer Hill group and the South Skirmish Line. Delete 82, 83 and 93.

Before leaving Custer Hill, one addition must be made and that is in respect to the marker for Dr. George Lord. This marker is currently located on the South Skirmish Line, although Marshall originally had it about 200 yards northeast of its present location. In fact, it should be on Custer Hill, at least according to Richard E. Thompson, who told Walter Camp that he had positively identified Lord.[21] Add number 17 about "20 feet southeast of Custer's body on side hill."

This process, which has not been totally arbitrary, has resulted in exactly the situation that Godfrey described: 42 bodies on Custer Hill, the only difference being that the new mapping places 10 of these on top of the hill and 32 on the side slope. It is important to note that it is the evidence which has led to the result and not the other way around. Forty-four of the Custer dead have now been accounted for—the forty-two on the hill, and the two to the northwest.

The next large grouping of markers to be considered is that now known as the South Skirmish Line. This area has been a bone of contention ever since the South Skirmish Line theory was first advanced by Charles Kuhlman in 1951. Traditional histories of Custer's disaster mention a large number of bodies of E Company men found in "a deep ravine" or "deep gully." The generally accepted number is twenty-eight, although higher and lower numbers have been mentioned. This would have been only ten men short of the entire combat strength of E Company[22] and no-one has yet satisfactorily explained what almost an entire company was doing in a very unlikely combat position, which was good for neither offense nor defense.

If the traditional histories are correct, then, the argument goes, at least twenty-eight of the markers on the South Skirmish Line are spurious and should be in Deep Ravine, but that would not leave sufficient markers to indicate that any meaningful action took place on the South Skirmish Line, or that indeed such a line ever existed. Even Kuhlman argued that markers should be in Deep Ravine, despite the fact that his argument fought against his own South Skirmish Line theory. And a member of the 1984/85 archaeological team, Richard Fox, stated that:

> Revealed through archaeology, the historical evidence reduces the much celebrated South Skirmish Line to nothing more than a minor killing field. Clearly, there are no archaeological data to support a tactical battle line in this sector. Historical accounts when properly interpreted, find consonance with archaeological reality. Quite clearly also, the thin "line" of bodies stretching to Deep Ravine can be attributed to men fleeing from the Custer Hill sector. Thus, some 28 marble markers on the upper segment of the South Skirmish Line sector are spuriously located; they belong in the ravine.[23]

The archaeological digs of 1984/85 were, however, unable to find any evidence whatsoever of bodies in Deep Ravine, despite repeated and specific attempts by the team to do just that. So the team's boast that "we know with almost 100 percent certainty where the twenty-eight missing men who supposedly were buried in Deep Ravine will be found" came to nothing. Indeed, only two or three artifacts of any kind can even remotely be associated with

Deep Ravine. Dr. Fox knew that nothing had been found, since he was a prominent member of the team, and yet he repeated the traditional story as though it had been proven by the digs.

The 1984/85 archaeological team mapped fifty-eight markers below (i.e. toward the river) the Custer Hill group, including those on the South Skirmish Line proper, some stragglers between that line and Custer, and some beyond the line, and a few "inside" and "outside" the line. These markers are numbers 1 to 56 inclusive, plus numbers 233 and 255 on the "inside" of the line toward Deep Ravine. This mapping is incorrect in several respects. Markers 40 and 41 are not isolated "outside" the line, but are on the line itself. The same can be said of number 28, substituting "inside" for "outside." Marker 2 is actually about 160 yards north of its mapped location, while 20 and 21 are about 75 yards north. Number 233, which is shown "inside" the line, is really part of the large concentrations in Keogh Swale, a mere hop, skip and jump to the northeast, provided one has legs a hundred yards long.

As to the "evidence" of burials along this line, one need refer only to *Archaeological Perspectives*, which Fox co-authored and wherein it is shown that only two of the eight markers or pairs excavated came up empty of human remains and those two were numbers 5 and 6 on the far side of Deep Ravine at the extreme end of the "stragglers." All of those on the line proper disclosed evidence of burials: one was even positively identified as that of Mitch Boyer. The establishment of this position as fact and the identification of Boyer were perhaps the most exciting and startling results of the work done in 1984–5, along with the failure to find anything in Deep Ravine, yet Fox apparently forgot both. The evidence shows that there were men killed in that sector, and whether or not one chooses to call it the South Skirmish Line or simply the Southwest Position, one certainly cannot argue that it did not exist or that twenty-eight of the markers belong in Deep Ravine, based on that same evidence and more particularly if one participated in the gathering of that evidence.

The actual findings of the digs were as follows: at paired markers 52/53 the remains of one person were found; at number 42 the bones of one hand were found; at 33/34 the remains of Mitch Boyer were found and identified; at 9/10 the almost complete skeleton of one person was found; number 7 yielded the sparse remains of another individual; the same result was obtained from the unit at number 2; units at markers 5 and 6 yielded nothing. Delete markers 52, 33, 9 and 233.

The absence of evidence at markers 5 and 6 should allow both of them to be deleted also, but there is an unusual circumstance here. These markers were erected in an area where there is a mere two inches of dirt covering bedrock. It seems unlikely that bodies would have been buried there and dead certain that no stakes could have been driven there, which leaves one to ponder what it was that caused Sweet to erect a marker in this area (he erected only one). The authors of *Archaeological Perspectives* suggested that perhaps the stones were meant to mark burials which had occurred in Deep Ravine, but it would not have been an onerous task to place the markers in the ravine—and nothing has ever been found in the ravine. It would appear that there was another and very good reason for the placement, and it might be argued that, because of the soil conditions, a complete recovery of remains which had been covered by sagebrush was made in 1877 or 1879. The archaeological evidence is that nothing was found there, but it is obvious that the marker placement by Sweet was done after some lengthy reasoning exercise, and although that process is unknown, it must be credited and number 6 retained. Delete number 5.

Marker number 17—that for Dr. George E. Lord—has been moved to Custer Hill as part of this exercise, so it must be deleted as well. The death site of Lieutenant James G. Sturgis is ostensibly marked by number 48, but it has been established that the original marker for Sturgis was erected in 1878 as part of a conspiracy to soothe his mother's concerns. Sweet then placed a marble marker where the original had stood. Nobody knows where Sturgis' body was buried. That spot may very well be marked by one of the other stones along the line, but it is not number 48, which should be deleted.

There are, in my eyes, six pairs of markers that were not excavated in 1984/85. These are 55/56, 38/39, 30/31, 29/32, 18/19 and 12/13. Applying the "pairs theory" to these would result in the deletion of one marker from five of these pairs and the total elimination of the other. This becomes a rather arbitrary exercise at this point, since there is no criterion for selecting the pair to be eliminated, but it probably makes most sense to take it from the most populous area. Eliminate markers 38, 39, 29, 30, 18 and 12. Markers 55 and 56 were not paired when originally erected, so they will stay, moved slightly apart. These latter markers are in the area described as containing the bodies of Boston Custer and Autie Reed.

A comparison of the 1984/85 and 1891 mappings is instructive as to other deletions and additions, always bearing in mind that both maps are in error as to the number of markers that should be on the field.

In addition to what has already been noted, one marker should be added—where the wooden stake (artifact 1635) is shown on the 1984/85 map. Markers 28, 40 and 41 should be moved onto the line proper. Markers 1 and 43 should be deleted. It might be assumed that two or three other markers down this line are spurious, but none can be deleted without being entirely arbitrary in both the number and the specifics.

The maps resulting from this process of reasoning now indicate 44 markers stringing down from below the Custer Hill grouping, including one marker which has been added, and not including fifteen which have been deleted. Not counting the "stragglers," there are two distinct groupings, which for the sake of simplicity I have named "Upper South Skirmish Line" and "Lower South Skirmish Line," these designations referencing the relative position on the "line," with "Upper" being nearest the Custer Hill group.

These maps do not agree with the popularly held belief of "bodies in Deep Ravine," because the preponderance of the evidence from accounts, which is nicely presented and summarized by Gregory Michno in *The Mystery of E Troop*, together with the absolute logic of events, indicates that the historical references to bodies in a ravine or gully cannot and therefore do not pertain to Deep Ravine. Of course, one might select only those accounts which tend to support one's own arguments or theories, but there is no getting away from the logic forced by the nature of the ground itself.

Deep Ravine holds no attraction militarily except as a covered approach to or from the river. Anyone in the ravine is completely at the mercy of anyone outside it, unless otherwise protected by forces also outside it. Custer might have used the ravine to move toward the river, or to withdraw from it, but he would have had to post strong forces outside to protect against attack while in the ravine. No one in his right mind would choose Deep Ravine as either a defensive or offensive position to be held for any length of time, because of the absolute vulnerability of the force within it.

The Indians, from all accounts, did utilize this approach to the battlefield. They were able to do so because the soldiers were being kept busy by warriors in other positions. Toward the end of the fight, this approach was literally crammed with warriors and onlookers trying to get to the scene of the fighting. It would have been the last choice of anyone trying to escape the carnage of Custer Hill and the slope leading down from it. The ridge, or slope, which separates Deep Ravine and Cemetery Ravine, is the natural route for flight, and the last few straggling markers in this area are consistent with the accounts of a few men trying to run away at the last, or the last of the men moving up toward the high ground.

Greg Michno argues that the bodies that were not in Deep Ravine were actually in Cemetery Ravine, although there was no meaningful number of markers put there either. It is conceivable that some markers in that area were moved to the slope in order to make room for the Fort Phil Kearny dead that were relocated to Battle Ridge (the subject of marker movement was not always well documented in cemetery or battlefield records). It is not necessary, however, to put them in another ravine. The descriptions and accounts are so hazy and contradictory that a reference to a ravine, no matter how "deep," might have been meant to apply to the slope of the ravine, not the bottom of it. It might also well be, although no one would want to admit it, that the whole story of the deep ravine that made it impossible to go down and bury the bodies was a handy fabrication to cover the fact that everybody had just got so sick of the stench of mortification and the sight of savaged corpses that they could not deal with another one.

One of the best witnesses for the presence of bodies on the South Skirmish Line slope is Colonel John Gibbon, who visited the field on June 29, 1876, and approached by a small valley to the north of Deep Ravine. Gibbon did not see any signs of either bodies or burials in any ravine except one, which he noted ran "nearly perpendicular to the river" and was "to the right and front" as he looked toward the river from Custer Hill. There he saw "some forty or fifty bodies," obviously referring to gravesites. If these had been in the bottom of any deep ravine or gulch, Gibbon could not have seen them, especially considering that the burial sites were hardly distinguishable from the surrounding terrain, the burials, such as they were, having been made two days previously. Gibbon also wrote that the "body of our poor guide, Mitch Bouyer, was found lying in the midst of the troopers," and some of Boyer's remains were found by the 1984/85 archaeological team at Marker 34 on the South Skirmish Line.[24] Lieutenant John G. Bourke saw much the same thing a year later,[25] including the body of a scout among thirty or forty bodies of men he thought had been fleeing toward the river.

While it is impossible to be absolutely certain as to the exact number of men who were killed in this area, there is no question but that it was between thirty and fifty, probably between forty and fifty. The number arrived at through the process outlined above is forty-four, not at all inconsistent with the numbers given by the witnesses.

The next area for consideration is that comparatively vast space between the "bottom" of the South Skirmish Line and the "bottom" of Calhoun ridge (the "Finley group"). It may be overstating the case to say that these two lines are "connected," as there is only a very loose string of markers between them. This string gives the impression of men killed while going from one point to the other, although it is generally thought that the troopers probably were fugitives running for their lives. Since none of these men were identified in accounts of the burials, it is impossible to make any statements relative to them that have a solid basis in historical evidence.

What can be stated is that the 1984/85 survey indicated that there were ten markers comprising this loose string, one of which, number 252, showed no evidence of a burial, Marshall's 1891 mapping shows only eight markers in the string, with only a slight, but very important, variation in marker positions from the 1984/85 survey. In the absence of any evidence to the contrary, the 1891 locations will be used in this reconstruction, and number 257, which has no equivalent on the 1891 map but which did give up evidence of being a burial site, will be added. One other location, at Marker 128, was excavated by the archaeologists. An almost-complete skeleton was recovered there, along with several battle-related artifacts.

The important difference in locations mentioned above involves three markers (125, 126, and 127), which the 1984/85 survey shows on a line between numbers 124 and 128. Indeed, the 1984/85 survey gives a very strong impression of a line of markers, with only number 121 located off the line. The 1891 mapping, however, clearly indicates that the three markers mentioned were not on any line and were, in fact, near the top of Greasy Grass Ridge, on the side away from the river. The positioning of these three markers tends to indicate men in a static defensive position rather than fleeing or moving from one point to another. Men fleeing battle do not run uphill into an enemy position in order to escape. The 1984/85 positioning puts these markers in Calhoun Coulee, which is the more natural route for men seeking safety from Calhoun Ridge or Battle Ridge. The inferences drawn from the combination of body locations and historical evidence are discussed elsewhere.

Following this "string" of markers leads to the bottom of Calhoun Ridge, so named because virtually all accounts indicate that Calhoun's L Company was positioned in this area and perished here, and on Calhoun Hill which is the high point of the ridge. The lower rise is often called simply "Finley," after Walter Camp's familiar usage, or "the Finley group," as this is where the body of Sergeant Jeremiah Finley of C Company was ostensibly found and identified on June 27. Camp also marked this Finley position as C on his battlefield map.

There is a confusion of numbers at Finley. The enlarged Marshall shows sixteen at Finley, while the 1984/85 survey portrays fourteen markers, numbers 129 through 142. Both of these figures are too high.

The archaeologists excavated two units at Finley, number 131 and the pair at 134/135. Nothing was recovered from 131; remains consistent with one person were found at 134/135. Delete 131 and 134. There is one other pair in this area, 138/139. In keeping with the "pairs theory" 138 can be deleted. This reduces the number of markers to eleven, based upon evidence or the lack thereof. The positioning of the markers is, however, another story.

There is no doubt but that the construction of the battlefield road, while making it easier to traverse the field and perhaps enhancing the views, caused some serious relocation of markers in the Calhoun Ridge area. This is evidenced by a superimposition of the roadway on the 1891 mapping, as well as a comparison of the 1984/85 with the 1891. The 1891 will therefore be used for locating the body sites. It is also possible that the relocation mentioned may have destroyed actual burial locations and that there should be more than eleven markers here. It is conceivable that the roadwork moved bone fragments and other relics from one spot to another, further confusing the issue. But some number must be selected, and the eleven chosen can at least be rationalized.

Anecdotal evidence is entirely lacking as to the number of bodies found in this area, and only Sergeant Jeremiah Finley of C Company was identified for posterity. Both Daniel Knipe and John Creighton identified Finley as being where marked on Camp's map.[26] Knipe said that Finley had been "mutilated very badly" and had "twelve arrows through him." Knipe speculated that Finley had been wounded when found by the squaws and young Indian boys, hence the mutilation. On the other hand, virtually everybody on the field had suffered more or less mutilation. Knipe reported that Finley's horse (Carlo) was dead with him. The mutilation was confirmed by Jean De Gallene in a July 5, 1876 letter to Father Genin.[27]

There is some evidence, in the form of notes by Walter Camp from a statement by the Mnicoujou Flying By,[28] that someone in the Finley group may have been the last man killed. According to Flying By, the last man killed "rode a horse" and "fell over near where Sergeant Finley was found later."

Between the Finley group and the group of markers on Calhoun Hill are seven markers in three sets of two and one single. None of these was excavated, but the pairs theory can be applied to the two pairs, resulting in the deletion of markers 145 and 122 and the reduction of the number to five. Marshall's 1891 map agrees with the 1984/85 in numbers but there is a slight variance in locations. The 1891 map will be used for placement; but it must be noted that neither the number nor the positioning of the markers indicates any valid military disposition, certainly not a skirmish line. These markers covered a distance of about 220 yards, indicating that the men were probably killed while moving and not while holding a position that was destroyed or overrun. Daniel Knipe told Walter Camp[29] that Sergeant August Finckle of C Company was among the men "on the way between Finley and Calhoun."

Arriving at the Calhoun Hill area groupings, yet another variation between 1891 and 1984/85 is found. Marshall indicates sixteen markers as opposed to the twelve shown by the 1984/85 survey. The caveat about movement of markers and relics on account of road construction must be repeated in respect to this area, so the 1891 mapping will be utilized for positioning.

The archaeological survey was very helpful in determining the correct number of markers. Excavations at Marker 148 and paired 152/155 disclosed the presence of human remains, with artifacts showing up at 152/155. The remains at 152/155 were consistent with one person and were found in the Marker 152 unit. Delete 155. Marker 150 is a pair with 148 (where some bone fragments were found) and can also be deleted. A unit was excavated at Marker 153 and nothing was found there. Delete 153. The number of markers has now been reduced to nine and it is quite obvious that they do not represent any "stand" of L Company, despite often dramatic accounts to the contrary. Even the addition of the four markers "missing" from 1891 to 1984/85, or the more audacious acceptance of the 1891 mapping as gospel would not alter that statement. Even sixteen bodies would not represent the wreckage of an L Company stand.

Indeed, the only L Company bodies positively identified in this whole area were those of Lieutenants Calhoun and Crittenden. That is only two out of twenty-five. There were five enlisted men from L identified on the field and elsewhere (Butler, Graham, Harrington, Tweed and Hughes). Not one of them was on what has commonly been accepted as the L Company line; Graham's being the closest, having been identified halfway between Keogh and Calhoun.[30]

Between Calhoun Hill and the main Keogh Swale positions is a string of thirteen markers, numbers 160 through 171 plus 174, which latter is actually almost 200 yards northeast of the line, near the boundary fence. The line itself starts some 200 yards from the center of the Calhoun Hill group of markers, and lies along a gentle drainage from Calhoun Hill and the slope from Battle Ridge toward the large swale or "ravine" between Battle Ridge and the higher ridge to the east. It is not on Battle Ridge proper and never was. There were no excavations at any of these markers and there is only one pair, 169/170, so only 169 may be deleted under the pairs theory.

There is absolutely no doubt that bodies were found along this line, and the number, twelve, agrees exactly with the corrected 1891 map, although again there is some difference in actual locations. The 1891 map has been used to ascertain the body sites, and the number will be used as well, although the same anonymous correspondent quoted below as to Keogh counted ten bodies on the line in regular order, and then "several scattered graves" before reaching Crittenden's cross. Had he seen the isolated body, he would have counted eleven graves.

It was noted above that Charles Graham of L Company was identified on this line. John Creighton told Walter Camp that he "lay between Lieutenant Calhoun and Captain Keogh." Creighton also told Camp that Sergeant John Vickory lay "in the ravine between Lieutenant Calhoun and Captain Keogh," although other testimony places this body elsewhere. Daniel Knipe said that Sergeant Bobo's horse was on this line, two thirds of the way to Keogh, but that Bobo himself was found near Keogh. Other witnesses, including later visitors to the field, got the impression that the whole command lay beyond Calhoun Hill, which is very nearly the truth. Certainly to anyone standing on Calhoun Hill and looking toward Custer Hill, the trail of carnage would give that impression. Even the stark white markers convey something of that nature today. The twelve bodies, including the remote one, are located on the map as they probably were found on June 27, 1876.

The markers in Keogh Swale proper represent a greater challenge to reconstruction of actual locations. There are twenty-seven markers in the main Keogh group, i.e. in reasonably close proximity to Keogh's own marker. These are numbered 172 through 199, less 174, 182 and 196, with the addition of 188B and 230A. Marker 174 has already been plotted. 182 and 196 do not exist.

There is no doubt that a great many bodies were found in this area. Obviously Captain Keogh was found here, and several witnesses say that he was surrounded by the sergeants of his company. Edgerly told Camp that Sergeant Bustard and First Sergeant Varden were found near Keogh, as was an I Company trumpeter. George Wylie said that this trumpeter was John Patton and that he actually lay across Keogh's body when found. Daniel Knipe reported that "when I came to the pile of men lying around Keogh I recognized [First] Sergeant [Edwin] Bobo [of C]." John Wild also was found near Keogh, as evidenced by photographs showing a headboard bearing his name near Keogh's elaborate original headboard.

Perhaps the most helpful evidence is the account of an unnamed visitor to the field in 1877, shortly after Michael Sheridan's trip to remove the officers' bodies: "Passing down to and up the canyon, we met first the carcass of a horse, then several heaps of bones close together, and in the center thereof a rough unplaned pine cross, upon which is inscribed: 'COL. KEOGH and 18 SOLDIERS of Co. I, 7th Cavalry, killed here June 25th, 1876.' Upon a more unpretentious tablet are inscribed the words: 'WILD I Co. 7th.' "[31]

This is the only account that is specific as to numbers of graves in particular locations, although the reporter does not give numbers for all areas and it is often difficult to know just where he is talking about. It is not however, a stretch to assume that the signboard he saw was correct as to the number of bodies with Keogh, and therefore nineteen will be used to create the map of this group. It should be mentioned that there are two identical photographs of two officers viewing this scene in 1877. One caption states that Keogh and thirty-eight men died there, the other states that the number around Keogh was twenty-eight. In confirmation of the anonymous account quoted above is a photograph taken after the erection of the markers, which clearly shows Keogh's cross with eighteen markers surrounding it. This latter photograph appears in *Contributions to the Historical Society of Montana* (Vol. IV, 1903).

The 1984/85 archaeological survey excavated at two pairs of markers, 194/195 and 183/199 plus one single in this group, the single, number 178, being the supposed death site of Myles Keogh himself. Some bone fragments were discovered at Marker 178 (not sufficient to establish any connection to Keogh) as well as at the two other excavation units. Both of the latter were consistent with the remains of only one individual. Delete numbers 183 and 194. There is one other pair, 176/177, in this group. Delete 176. This brings the number down to twenty-four, which happens to be the number of markers on the 1891 mapping after adjustments.

Paring the group by another five is somewhat problematical and arbitrary, but there are some indications as to which other markers are more probably spurious. The anonymous reporter quoted above noted eighteen bodies in six distinct piles. This observation may or may not have been his first glimpse of the Keogh group—from a close reading of his account, it would seem that it could refer to the space between Custer Hill and the Keogh group, which latter does not readily break down into "six piles"—and the wooden marker definitely says eighteen men plus Keogh. The 1891 map shows a rather compact grouping here, while the markers today are more widely scattered. Accounts of survivors and later visitors confirm the more compact grouping. Deleting markers 172, 173, 175 and 184 restores the compactness of the historical grouping and reduces the number to twenty. It also restores the distance between the Keogh group and the end of the "string" leading from Calhoun Hill, so this step is not wholly arbitrary. Determining the final marker to be removed is, however, strictly guesswork; but since the positions will be changed to conform more nearly to 1891 and to the photograph of the markers, the marker number is not particularly important. Delete 230A, which appears to have been a late addition to the group.

To the northwest, i.e. toward Custer Hill, a more scattered bunch of markers lies in almost a double line, separated from the Keogh group by only a short, but obvious, space. There are thirty-five markers in this loose grouping, numbers 200 to 234, less 210 plus 211B. The 1984/85 team excavated units at 200 and 201/202, finding remains consistent with the remains of one individual. Delete 200 and 202. There are also four other pairs of markers in this grouping: 222/223, 233/234, 217/218 and 227/228. Delete 222, 233, 217 and 227. This reduces the number of markers to twenty-nine.

The corrected 1891 mapping shows thirty-two markers in this same area but in different positions from the 1984/85 mapping. Since the archaeological excavations mentioned above found bone fragments and larger bones between markers, it is obvious that there has been some dislocation of the markers over the years, as well as the addition of three markers for unknown reasons. There is no doubt that bodies lay thick in this area, but there is no direct identification of any of them in post-battle accounts. As noted above, the anonymous reporter of 1877 may have been referencing this area when he spoke of bodies in six distinct piles, but he noted only eighteen bodies, which is far fewer than the number of markers arrived at through the process of deduction. The 1891 mapping will be used for locating the twenty-nine burial sites determined to be in this area. Some of these markers were much closer to the top of Battle Ridge than they are now, having been moved to facilitate the road construction.

The next group of markers to be considered is the "North Keogh Swale" bunch, which includes the spurious Mark Kellogg marker, number 247. There are thirteen markers in this area, compared to twelve on the Marshall map. Aside from the Kellogg marker, which should be deleted, there are four paired markers, which results in the deletion of numbers 235, 237, 241 and 243. This reduces the number of markers to eight, and these will be plotted in accordance with the 1891 mapping, which indicates that one group of these markers was originally on the ridgeline. There were no excavations in this area by the 1984/85 team, nor was there any identification of individuals in accounts of the burials.

Finally, the string of markers that now lies on the river side of the ridge, paralleling the Keogh Swale, must be considered. In 1891 there were ten markers here, the same number as currently, 111 through 120. The 1984/85 team excavated at the pair of markers 112/113, uncovering both bones and artifacts. The bones were found between the markers and were consistent with the remains of one person. Delete 112. This leaves nine markers to plot according to the 1891 map, which shows them generally closer to the ridgeline. There is no doubt that a couple of these were displaced by the road construction. There were no identifications of bodies in this area.

The reconstruction of death sites has now been completed and the corrected locations mapped as follows:

2	Northwest of Custer Hill
10	Top of Custer Hill
32	Slope of Custer Hill
44	South Skirmish Line and stragglers
9	String between South Skirmish Line and Finley group
11	Finley group
5	String between Finley group and Calhoun Hill
9	Calhoun Hill
12	String between Calhoun Hill and Keogh group
19	Keogh group
29	Mid Keogh Swale group
8	North Keogh Swale

9   River side of Battle Ridge

199   TOTAL CORRECTED NUMBER OF MARKERS

This corrected total is much more in line with what should be recalled as the maximum number, 197 and the positioning of the markers can now be used for a meaningful examination of the action on June 25, 1876. It would be a simple matter to remove two more markers and so reach 197, but there would be absolutely no basis upon which to rest the selection of those two, and 197 is not an absolutely reliable figure, only a maximum limiting quantity. It is, however, astonishing, what a difference this new plotting lends to the interpretation of existing evidence and to a recreation of the battle based upon that evidence.

The maps indicating the probable positions of the bodies on June 25, 1876 have been largely based upon the positioning shown on the Marshall 1891 mapping. Marker numbers used have been taken from the 1984/85 survey and are used on the maps only to correlate with the reasoning exercises undertaken in the text and to simplify matters for the reader. The markers that appear without numbers are additional markers mentioned in the text. It is not intended that the number shown on a marker indicate anything more than the correlation mentioned; indeed, the numbers might just as easily have been left off.

The scale of the maps is approximate and the orientation of the bodies is based upon Marshall, which probably means nothing much. There is no way to tell, except in some very few specific cases, which way a body was facing or pointing when found. The scale of the markers themselves is not meant to be exact. It is a mistake to read too much significance into the locations and especially the orientation, of the individual markers—it is the number of markers and the general layout of the same that are important to historians and researchers today.

NOTES

1. Richard G. Hardorff, *The Custer Battle Casualties: Burials, Exhumations and Reinterments* (El Segundo: Upton & Sons 1990), pp.113–4. I have edited the statement as to form only.
2. Ibid., p.109.
3. Ibid., p.108.

4. Jerome A. Greene, *Evidence and the Custer Enigma: A Reconstruction of Indian-Military History* (Kansas City Posse of the Westerners, 1973), p.18.
5. [ebook] Bibliography, *Sec. B 4.*
6. R. G. Cartwright, Research Notes; J. J. Boesl: letter to W. M. Camp, September 4, 1911.
7. Jerome A. Greene, *Evidence and the Custer Enigma*... (Olympic Valley, 1978); Jerome A. Greene, *Evidence and the Custer Enigma*...(Golden, 1986); and R. Dutch Hardorff, *Markers, Artefacts and Indian Testimony* (Short Hills, 1985).
8. Colonel John Gibbon: excerpts from his narrative of 1877; [ebook] *Appendix 3.34.*
9. [ebook] Bibliography, *Sec. B 4.*
10. Oglala: Stories from the Hostiles; [ebook] *Appendix 3.83.*
11. Douglas D. Scott and Richard A. Fox Jr. *Archaeological Insights*... *Custer Battle* (Norman: U. of Okla., 1987); Douglas D. Scott, Richard A. Fox Jr., Melissa A. Connor, & Dick Harmon, *Archaeological Perspectives on the Battle of the Little Big Horn* (Norman: U. of Okla., 1989).
12. Anonymous, "Handwritten statement as to the dead and wounded," *Montana Historical Society Contributions* (Vol. IV, 1903).
13. 1st Sgt. John M. Ryan, "Narrative of the Custer Fight," *Hardin, Montana Tribune,* June 22, 1923.
14. Col. Jn. Gibbon, "Last Summer's Expedition against the Sioux & Its Great Catastrophe," *American Catholic Quarterly Review* (April 1877); Colonel John Gibbon, *Gibbon on the Sioux Campaign of 1876* (Bellevue, 1970).
15. Kenneth Hammer (ed.), *Custer in '76: Walter Camp's Notes on the Custer Fight,* (Provo, Utah: Brigham Young University Press, 1976).
16. Charles F. Roe, *Custer's Last Battle* (New York, 1927).
17. Ibid.
18. Luther R. Hare, Re: Little Horn, Camp Field Notes, folder 16 B.Y.U.
19. *See* Roe's figures in Charles F. Roe, *Custer's Last Battle* (New York, 1927).
20. Refer to [ebook], Appendices 5.1–5.20.
21. David Humphreys, Miller, *Custer's Fall: The Indian Side of the Story* (New York, 1972).
22. The 7th Regiment of Cavalry, United States Army: Rosters pertaining to regimental assignments, strengths, casualties and battle statistics on the campaign which culminated in the series of actions known as the Battle of the Little Big Horn, June 25 and 26, 1876; [ebook] *Appendix 5.17.*
23. Richard Fox, *Archaeology, History, and Custer's Last Battle* (Norman, 1993).
24. Colonel John Gibbon: excerpts from his narrative of 1877; [ebook] *Appendix 3.34.*
25. See Forsyth in General Sheridan and Major George A. Forsyth: reports of April 8, 1878, relative to a visit to the Custer Battlefield, July 1877, and some commentary from other members of the same group; [ebook] *Appendix 5.18.*
26. Kenneth Hammer, *The Glory March* (Monroe, 1980); John C. Creighton, *Re: Little Horn.*
27. Jean B. D. Gallene: letter to Father Genin, July 5, 1876, giving abstract of his journal re: fights, *Saint Paul Pioneer Press,* January 16, 1879.
28. Mnicoujou Flying By Lakota: interview with Walter Camp July 27, 1912, at Standing Rock Agency; [ebook] *Appendix 3.23.*
29. Hammer, *Custer in '76.*

30. John C. Creighton: interview with Walter Camp, undated; [ebook] *Appendix 3.12.*
31. Ami Frank Mulford, an excerpt from his *Fighting Indians in the Seventh U.S. Cavalry,* plus the report of an unidentified visit to Custer's Field in July 1877 and a description by Dr. William A. Allen; [ebook] *Appendix 5.12.*

THE ENLISTED MEN'S PETITION

A week after the "rescue" of the shattered remnants of the 7th Cavalry by the Montana column under Gibbon and Terry, the surviving enlisted men of the 7th made up a petition requesting that the vacancies resulting from the deaths of their officers be filled by "Officers of the Regiment only." This petition, popularly known as "The Enlisted Men's Petition," has been used by some writers to advance the causes of Marcus Reno and Frederick Benteen and has been sloughed off as meaningless by other historians, because nothing came of it. It has also been used by Custer advocates as a vehicle of exoneration.

The petition and General Sherman's response to it were, however, exhibits 10 and 11 at the Reno Court of Inquiry and cannot be so easily dismissed, since the court must have considered them to one extent or another in arriving at its conclusions. The petition was drawn up and signed between June 28 and July 4. It reads as follows:

> Camp near Big Horn on Yellowstone River, July 4th 1876.
> To His Excellency the President and the
> Honorable Representatives of the United States.
> Gentlemen,
> We the enlisted men the survivors of the battle on the Heights of Little Horn River, on the 25th and 26th of June 1876, of the 7th Regiment of Cavalry who subscribe our names to this petition, most earnestly solicit the President and Representatives of our Country,

that the vacancies among the Commissioned Officers of our Regiment, made by the slaughter of our brave, heroic, now lamented Lieutenant Colonel George A. Custer, and the other noble dead Commissioned Officers of our Regiment who fell close by him on the bloody field, daring the savage demons to the last, be filled by the Officers of the Regiment only. That Major M.A. Reno, be our Lieutenant Colonel vice Custer, killed: Captain F.W. Benteen our Major vice Reno, promoted. The other vacancies to be filled by officers of the Regiment by seniority. Your petitioners know this to be contrary to the established rule of promotion, but prayerfully solicit a deviation from the usual rule in this case, as it will be conferring a bravely fought for and a justly merited promotion to officers who by their bravery, coolness and decision on the 25th and 26th of June 1876, saved the lives of every man now living of the 7th Cavalry who participated in the battle, one of the most bloody on record and one that would have ended with the loss of every officer and enlisted man on the field only for the position taken by Major Reno, which we held with bitter tenacity against fearful odds to the last.

To support this assertion—had our position been taken 100 yards back from the brink of the heights overlooking the river we would have been entirely cut off from water; and from behind those heights the Indian demons would have swarmed in hundreds picking off our men by detail, and before midday June 26th not an officer or enlisted man of our Regiment would have been left to tell of our dreadful fate as we then would have been completely surrounded.

With prayerful hope that our petitions be granted, we have the honor to forward it through our Commanding Officer.

Very Respectfully,

[There followed 237 signatures, ostensibly representing enlisted men who had survived the fights on the Little Horn].

As noted in the closing, the petition was forwarded through the commanding officer, Major Reno, and it went through official channels as far the desk of General Sherman, the Commanding General of the Army, where it apparently stopped, never making it to the President. Sherman's reply was returned through the same channels:

Headquarters of the Army, Adjutant
General's Office, Washington, August 10, 1876
Major M.A. Reno, 7th Cavalry
(Thro' Headquarters Military Division of the Missouri)

Sir:

Referring to the petition of the enlisted men of the 7th Cavalry (forwarded by you the 15th ultimo) for the promotion of yourself and other officers of the regiment who participated in the engagement of June 25, 1876, I have the honor to enclose herewith, for the information of the officers and enlisted men concerned, a copy of the remarks of the General of the Army with reference to the request contained in the petition.

Very respectfully

Your obedient servant

E.D. Townsend, Adjutant General

Headquarters Army of the United States,
Washington, D.C., Aug. 5, 1876

The judicious and skillful conduct of Major Reno and Captain Benteen is appreciated, but the promotions caused by General Custer's death have been made by the President and confirmed by the Senate; therefore this petition cannot be granted. When the Sioux campaign is over I shall be happy to recognize the valuable services of both officers and men by granting favors or recommending actual promotion.

Promotion on the field of battle was Napoleon's favorite method of stimulating his officers and soldiers to deeds of heroism, but it is impossible in our service because commissions can only be granted by the President on the advice and consent of the Senate, and except in original vacancies, promotion in a regiment is generally if not always made on the rule of seniority.

W.T. Sherman, General.

Official: E.D. Townsend,

Adjutant General

There is no question but that Sherman's reply was exactly that which had been anticipated by both Reno and whoever dreamed up the petition in the first place. The wonder is that Reno and Benteen, both of whom knew very well how the army worked, allowed the document to be forwarded at all. Since it appeared to be at once self-serving and doomed to failure, it could not reasonably be expected to impress the chain of command in a positive manner. It did, however, accomplish the feat of putting a positive spin on the conduct of Reno and Benteen for future readers of the petition, and it became a piece of the official record which could be summoned up when needed. Even Sherman's opening line, which reads like a standard psychological preparation for the let-down which follows, can be taken out of context and used as a commendation from the highest army authority.

These papers—the petition and the reply—were as a matter of course reproduced in the *Army and Navy Journal,* and Reno saw to it that they appeared in the newspapers of the day; and so they properly should have, for they were indeed part of the historical record.

The principal contemporary use of the petition and reply were as exhibits at the Reno inquiry, as mentioned previously, but they saw harder duty in the first half of this century when writers hostile to Custer and friendly to Reno, especially, and also to Benteen used them to buttress their arguments.

William A. Graham reproduced the petition and the reply in his *The Story of The Little Big Horn,* using the mere existence of the petition to exculpate both Reno and Benteen from any and all accusations. "It is highly significant," Graham wrote. "Had there existed in fact any such condition as the imputations against Reno and Benteen infer [that they abandoned Custer to his fate] it is beyond belief that such a request would have been almost unanimously made by the surviving enlisted men."

Graham's analysis of the battle and his research were accepted almost without question for a half century. His conclusions seemed reasonable; but they proved to be based, purposely or not, on faulty data.

Graham accepted the petition without reservation simply because it had been introduced as evidence at Reno's inquiry hearings—and Graham was a member of the Judge Advocate General's service, a lawyer at heart and in fact. Apparently he felt that anything admitted as evidence in the hearing must be taken as gospel and he did just that, using the transcript copy that he had made as his primary source for his book. One would have expected, perhaps, a more jaundiced view from an experienced lawyer—it is hardly surprising to find fraudulent, deceitful or prejudiced testimony in trial situations. Many other writers have followed the lead of Colonel Graham, most notably Fred Dustin and Earl Brininstool, who uncritically accepted the testimony given at the inquiry, or even more uncritically, Graham's version of it.

Graham went to great lengths to defend the petition's veracity and authenticity, since so much of his reasoning and conclusions rested upon it. In his correspondence with Captain Robert G. Carter, as reproduced in *The Custer Myth*, Graham explains away a statement by General Godfrey relative to several old veterans denying that they had signed the petition, by saying that they said they did not remember signing it, which is admittedly a different thing entirely.

The fact of the matter is that the petition is authentic—at least from the standpoint that it was drawn up and submitted exactly as reproduced above and received the response also reproduced. As to its veracity—well, that is another question entirely.

Graham wrote that it would be "beyond belief that such a request would have been made almost unanimously" had Reno and Benteen been culpable in any real sense. Graham's problem in this instance, as it was in several others, is that he rarely approached evidence with any measure of disbelief if it fit neatly into his personal view of things. Had he bothered to check the petition closely after Godfrey's statement, he might have found some interesting anomalies, but it did not occur to him that maybe these old veterans were correct in stating that they did not sign the petition.

The petition was not "almost unanimously" signed by the surviving enlisted men. There were 624 enlisted men who marched to the Little Horn. 243 of these men were killed in action or died of wounds, seventy others were missing, wounded and on the *Far West*, or not invited to sign (scouts). This left 311 "we the enlisted men the survivors" to sign, and there are 237 signatures. Graham wrote that about 80 percent had signed, which is accurate, assuming that the signatures are all genuine. They are not.

In 1954, the Federal Bureau of Investigation was asked by Major Edward S. Luce to analyze the document and the signatures. The FBI did so and responded that in their opinion seventy-nine of the signatures were in all probability forgeries, although they could not offer an opinion as to the identity of the forger. In fact there were many more errors and inconsistencies in the signatures, and I have drawn up a table, by company, based upon my own researches and conclusions, to help illustrate these problems.

Signatures on the Enlisted Men's Petition

CO.	ELIGIBLE	SIGNED	XED OUT	FORGED	ILLIT	INCONSIST	GOOD SIGN
A	32	27	0	13	0	1	13
B	42	38	0	7	2	0	29
C	12	8	0	1	1	1	5
D	45	41	0	2	3	1	35
E	12	5	0	1	1	0	3
F	18	8	0	1	0	1	6
G	28	3	0	0	0	0	3
H	33	31	0	14	4	2	11
I	10	3	0	0	0	1	2
K	33	33	1	25	0	0	7
L	12	5	0	1	2	0	2
M	34	35	1	12	5	5	12
TOTALS	311	237	2	77	18	12	128

Legend

FORGED: indicates an almost-certainly forged signature.
ILLIT: denotes that a man who could not write supposedly signed his name.
INCONSIST: includes signatures of men who did not exist in regimental records, who were on detached service at the time, who horribly misspelled their names, or who signed twice.

As can be readily seen, the number of actual signers ("good sign") shrinks considerably under the harsh light of close scrutiny—by almost half—and instead of Graham's 80 percent, there is now a signing rate of a little more than 40 percent. While this still might be viewed as an endorsement of Reno and Benteen, it certainly cannot be seen as a ringing endorsement, and one is left to wonder why the forgeries and subterfuge were thought necessary by whoever dreamed up and circulated the petition. The obvious answer is that it was felt, or realised, that a majority of the men would not sign. It is hardly a wonder that several veterans would tell Godfrey forty years later that they did not sign the document.

Surprisingly, not many of the men who belonged to Reno's battalion put their names to the petition. Just twenty-eight of ninety-four eligible men from companies A, G and M signed. Indeed, only eleven men from Benteen's own company really signed, although the number of forgeries made it seem as if more had done so. Had it not been for the high percentage of signatures from companies B and D and the spurious signatures, it is highly unlikely that the petition would ever have seen the light of day—which it could not have stood had anyone harbored even a modicum of suspicion. Can anyone really imagine the petition going to the President with only 128 signatures? In any event it now stands totally repudiated as a vehicle for boosting Reno and Benteen.

It has been suggested that the inspiration for the petition was Benteen and not the more obvious Reno, and that First Sergeant Joseph McCurry of H Company is the most logical "suspect" for the petition itself and for its attendant forgeries. While it would most definitely be in keeping with what is known of Benteen's character and of his marked propensity for working deviously through others to accomplish his purposes, I can find no hard evidence linking him or McCurry to the petition. Indeed, had McCurry drafted and circulated the petition, he most likely would have started with his own company, and would in all likelihood have been put off by the lack of response from his comrades. I cannot see him continuing when he would have had to start off by forging so many names.

Reno too must stand blameless in the matter, as there is nothing to show that he was in any way involved in the preparation or circulation of the petition. Somebody did do it, however, and really botched the job, although nobody bothered to find this out for seventy or eighty years. Who stood to gain?

Reno and Benteen did stand to gain from the petition, but only in the sense that it cast their conduct in a favorable light at the time and that it established a record for future reference. They both could guess that the requests would not be granted, and indeed neither of them received any promotions or special favors from Sherman after the campaign. Reno, of course, was kicked out of the army within five years, and Benteen finally received a brevet for the Little Horn (and Canyon Creek) in 1894, almost twenty years later, when he was already on the retired list.

Custer's reputation also stood to gain, but only in a roundabout way. Had it been shown at the time that the document was so largely a fraud, Reno and Benteen would look considerably less heroic. It must be remarked that the truth about the petition is in no way a defense of Armstrong Custer. Even if it could be shown that Reno and Benteen cooked up the whole thing and signed all the signatures themselves (which they did not), that would reflect only upon them. It would not affect what Custer did or did not do, or what responsibility he must bear for his own actions.

As a matter of interest, I have shown how the officer vacancies were in fact filled.

	OFFICERS KILLED	REPLACEMENTS
Lieutenant Colonel	George A. Custer	Elmer S. Otis
Captains	Myles W. Keogh	Henry J. Nowlan
	George W. Yates	James M. Bell
	Thomas W. Custer	Henry Jackson
First Lieutenants	William W. Cooke	George D. Wallace
	Algernon E. Smith	Andrew H. Nave
	James E. Porter	Luther R. Hare
	Donald McIntosh	Ernest A. Garlington
	James Calhoun	Charles A. Varnum
		Winfield S. Edgerly
		Charles Braden
		Edwin P. Eckerson
		William W. Robinson
		John W. Wilkinson
Second Lieutenants	Benjamin Hodgson	William J. Nicholson
	Henry M. Harrington	Horatio G. Sickel Jr.
	William Van W. Reily	Hugh L. Scott
	James G. Sturgis	John C. Gresham
		Loyd S. McCormick
		Albert J. Russell
		J. Williams Biddle
		Herbert J. Slocum
		Ezra B. Fuller
		Edwin P. Brewer

Note that Lieutenants Lord and Crittenden, who were also killed, were not officers of the regiment.

EPILOGUE

BY GORDON RICHARD

"The making of a book, like the making of a clock, is a craft;
it takes more than wit to be an author."—JEAN DE LA
BRUYERE, *Les caracteres ou les mouers de ce siècle* (1688)

I n this book we have been privileged to share Gordon Harper's insights
on the Fights on the Little Horn, developed over the lifetime he spent
looking into every aspect of what happened on June 25–28, 1876 at the
place the Lakota called the Greasy Grass.

Although he left behind a vast body of written and computer records,
his untimely death deprived all of us with an abiding interest in "Custer's Last
Stand" of a unique depth of knowledge in the subject. This book represents
but a relatively small part of the immense amount of research he did and the
work he created. The constraints of modern publishing budgets, especially
where specialist matters are concerned, mean that the bulk of the reference
work he compiled presently remains unpublished.

The end result of Gordon Harper's diligence and dedication deserves
to be made available to an audience fascinated by every little nuance of this
world-renowned historical event, and that audience would be entranced by
the special overview of the author, who brings a singular understanding to
the interpretation of the many documents he uncovered. These include rare
correspondence written almost immediately after the Fights, such as the letters of July 4, 1876 from Lieutenants W.S. Edgerly and F.M. Gibson to their

wives, and from Lieutenant C.A. Varnum to his parents. Then there are the Gall Narratives, Fred Gerard's interview of January 31, 1879 with the *St. Paul Pioneer Press* and information concerning the affidavit purportedly given by Captain Thomas B. Weir. All these are enhanced by Gordon Harper's comments, and finally, there is a reference section that would become a 21st-century "Custer Myth."

What else that extraordinary man would have furnished to us if he had lived longer we will never know. The knowledge he gained from his close friendship with the Northern Cheyenne tribe perhaps, or analyses of the Reno Scout, the march of the Montana column to the Little Horn and General Terry's plan. Those possibilities are now lost to us, but it is to be hoped that what is not lost to us will eventually appear in print for the benefit of us all.

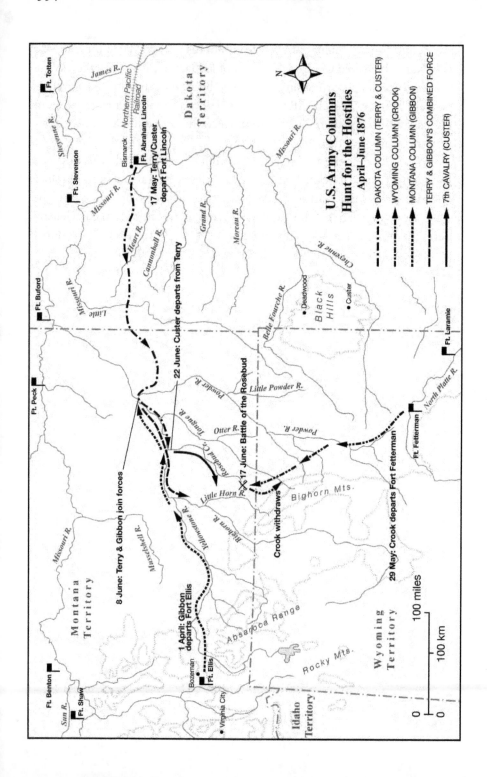

U.S. Army Columns
Hunt for the Hostiles
April–June 1876

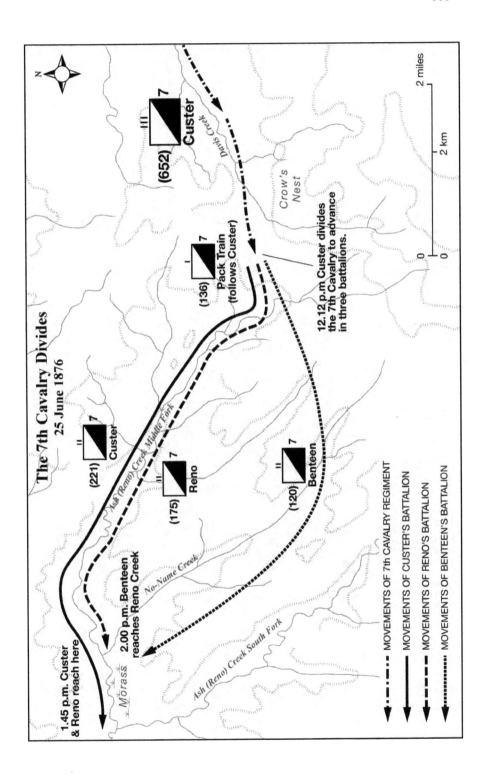

The 7th Cavalry Divides
25 June 1876

N

(652) 7 III
Custer

(136) 7 I
Pack Train
(follows Custer)

(221) 7 II
Custer

(175) 7 II
Reno

(120) 7 II
Benteen

Davis Creek

Crow's Nest

Ash (Reno) Creek Middle Fork

No-Name Creek

Ash (Reno) Creek South Fork

Morass

12.12 p.m. Custer divides
the 7th Cavalry to advance
in three battalions.

2.00 p.m. Benteen
reaches Reno Creek

1.45 p.m. Custer
& Reno reach here

0   2 km

0   2 miles

MOVEMENTS OF 7th CAVALRY REGIMENT

MOVEMENTS OF CUSTER'S BATTALION

MOVEMENTS OF RENO'S BATTALION

MOVEMENTS OF BENTEEN'S BATTALION

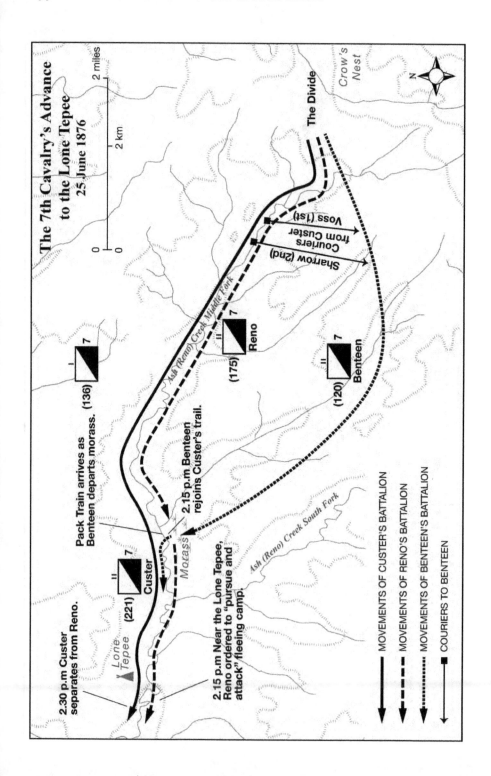

The 7th Cavalry's Advance to the Lone Tepee
25 June 1876

2 miles
2 km
0
0

N

Crow's Nest

The Divide

Voss (1st)
Couriers from Custer
Sharrow (2nd)

Ash (Reno) Creek Middle Fork

7 Reno
II
(175)

7 Benteen
II
(120)

7
I
(136)

Pack Train arrives as Benteen departs morass. (136)

2.15 p.m Benteen rejoins Custer's trail.

Morass

Ash (Reno) Creek South Fork

7 Custer
II
(221)

Lone Tepee

2.30 p.m Custer separates from Reno.

2.15 p.m Near the Lone Tepee, Reno ordered to "pursue and attack" fleeing camp.

MOVEMENTS OF CUSTER'S BATTALION
MOVEMENTS OF RENO'S BATTALION
MOVEMENTS OF BENTEEN'S BATTALION
COURIERS TO BENTEEN

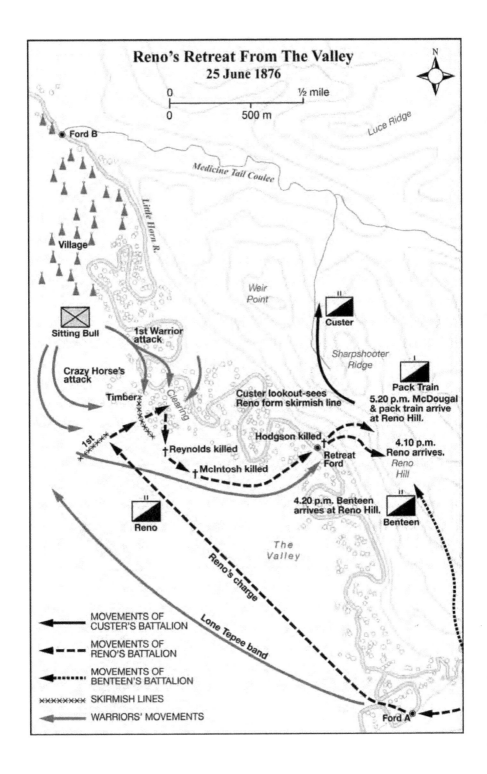

Reno's Retreat From The Valley
25 June 1876

Ford B

Luce Ridge

Medicine Tail Coulee

Little Horn R.

Village

Weir Point

Sitting Bull

Custer

1st Warrior attack

Sharpshooter Ridge

Crazy Horse's attack

Pack Train
5.20 p.m. McDougal & pack train arrive at Reno Hill.

Timber

Clearing

Custer lookout–sees Reno form skirmish line

1st

Reynolds killed

Hodgson killed

4.10 p.m. Reno arrives.

Retreat Ford

Reno Hill

McIntosh killed

4.20 p.m. Benteen arrives at Reno Hill.

Reno

Benteen

The Valley

Reno's charge

Lone Tepee band

MOVEMENTS OF CUSTER'S BATTALION

MOVEMENTS OF RENO'S BATTALION

MOVEMENTS OF BENTEEN'S BATTALION

×××××××× SKIRMISH LINES

WARRIORS' MOVEMENTS

Ford A

0 ½ mile
0 500 m

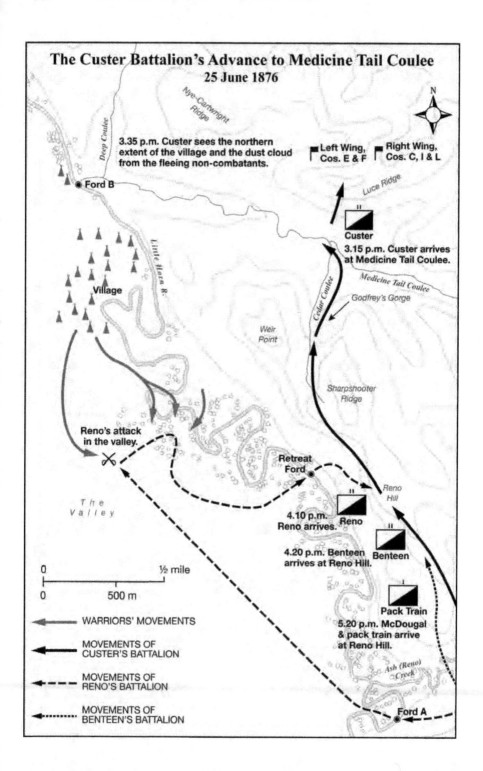

The Custer Battalion's Advance to Medicine Tail Coulee
25 June 1876

3.35 p.m. Custer sees the northern extent of the village and the dust cloud from the fleeing non-combatants.

Nye-Cartwright Ridge

Deep Coulee

Ford B

Little Horn R.

Village

Left Wing, Cos. E & F

Right Wing, Cos. C, I & L

Luce Ridge

N

Custer

3.15 p.m. Custer arrives at Medicine Tail Coulee.

Medicine Tail Coulee

Godfrey's Gorge

Cedar Coulee

Weir Point

Sharpshooter Ridge

Reno's attack in the valley.

Retreat Ford

Reno Hill

4.10 p.m. Reno arrives.

Reno

The Valley

4.20 p.m. Benteen arrives at Reno Hill.

Benteen

0   ½ mile

0   500 m

Pack Train

5.20 p.m. McDougal & pack train arrive at Reno Hill.

WARRIORS' MOVEMENTS

MOVEMENTS OF CUSTER'S BATTALION

MOVEMENTS OF RENO'S BATTALION

MOVEMENTS OF BENTEEN'S BATTALION

Ash (Reno) Creek

Ford A

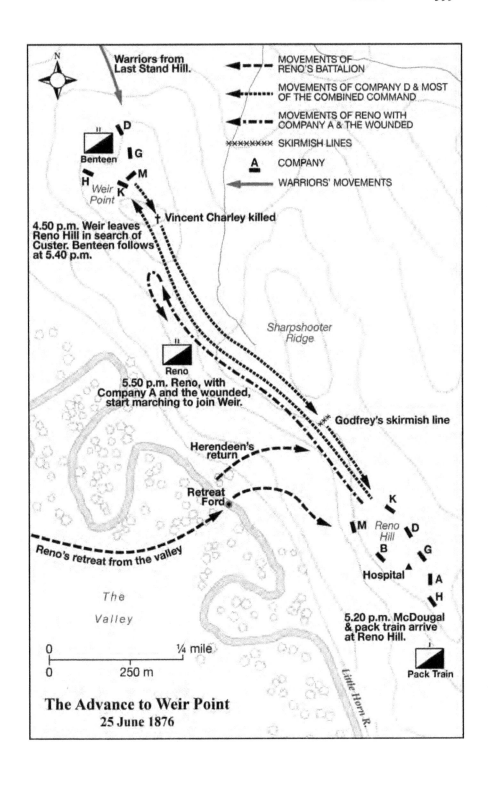

Warriors from Last Stand Hill.

MOVEMENTS OF RENO'S BATTALION

MOVEMENTS OF COMPANY D & MOST OF THE COMBINED COMMAND

MOVEMENTS OF RENO WITH COMPANY A & THE WOUNDED

×××××××× SKIRMISH LINES

A COMPANY

WARRIORS' MOVEMENTS

D

Benteen G

H Weir K M
Point

4.50 p.m. Weir leaves Reno Hill in search of Custer. Benteen follows at **5.40 p.m.**

† Vincent Charley killed

Sharpshooter Ridge

Reno

5.50 p.m. Reno, with Company A and the wounded, start marching to join Weir.

Godfrey's skirmish line

Herendeen's return

Retreat Ford

K

Reno's retreat from the valley

M Reno D
Hill

B G

Hospital A

H

The Valley

0 ¼ mile

0 250 m

5.20 p.m. McDougal & pack train arrive at Reno Hill.

Little Horn R.

Pack Train

The Advance to Weir Point
25 June 1876

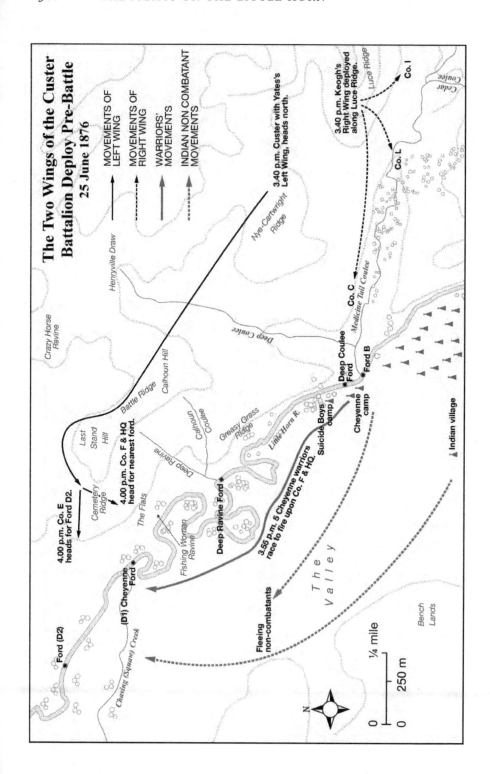

The Two Wings of the Custer Battalion Deploy Pre-Battle
25 June 1876

MOVEMENTS OF LEFT WING

MOVEMENTS OF RIGHT WING

WARRIORS' MOVEMENTS

INDIAN NON COMBATANT MOVEMENTS

3.40 p.m. Custer with Yates's Left Wing, heads north.

3.40 p.m. Keogh's Right Wing deployed along Luce Ridge.

Luce Ridge

Co. I

Cedar Coulee

Co. L

Co. C

Nye-Cartwright Ridge

Medicine Tail Coulee

Deep Coulee

Hentyville Draw

Crazy Horse Ravine

Battle Ridge

Calhoun Hill

Last Stand Hill

Cemetery Ridge

The Flats

Deep Ravine

Calhoun Coulee

Greasy Grass Ridge

Little Horn R.

Ford B

Deep Coulee Ford

Cheyenne camp

Suicide Boys camp

3.55 p.m. 5 Cheyenne warriors race to fire upon Co. F & HQ.

Indian village

4.00 p.m. Co. E heads for Ford D2.

4.00 p.m. Co. F & HQ. head for nearest ford.

Deep Ravine Ford

Fishing Woman Ravine

(D1) Cheyenne Ford

Ford (D2)

Chasing (Squaw) Creek

Fleeing non-combatants

The Valley

Bench Lands

N

¼ mile

250 m

0

0

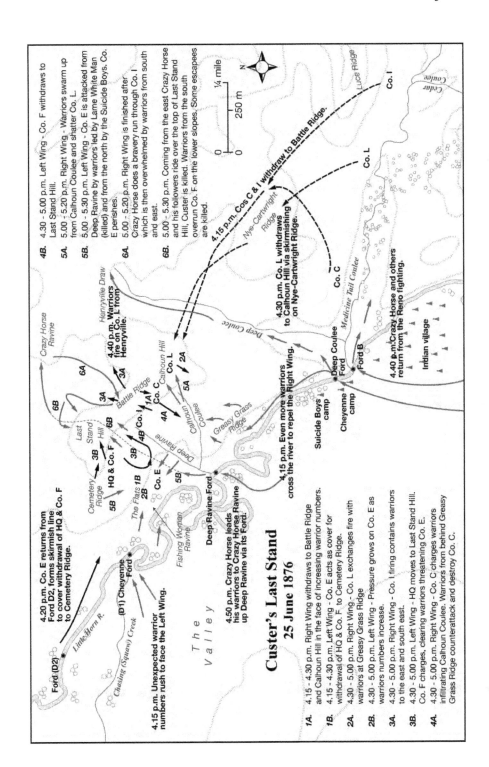

Custer's Last Stand
25 June 1876

1A. 4.15 - 4.30 p.m. Right Wing withdraws to Battle Ridge and Calhoun Hill in the face of increasing warrior numbers.

1B. 4.15 - 4.30 p.m. Left Wing - Co. E acts as cover for withdrawal of HQ & Co. F. to Cemetery Ridge.

2A. 4.30 - 5.00 p.m. Right Wing - Co. L exchanges fire with warriors at Greasy Grass Ridge

2B. 4.30 - 5.00 p.m. Left Wing - Pressure grows on Co. E as warriors numbers increase.

3A. 4.30 - 5.00 p.m. Right Wing - Co. I firing contains warriors to the east and south east.

3B. 4.30 - 5.00 p.m. Left Wing - HQ moves to Last Stand Hill. Co. F charges, clearing warriors threatening Co. E.

4A. 4.30 - 5.00 p.m. Right Wing - Co. C charges warriors infiltrating Calhoun Coulee. Warriors from behind Greasy Grass Ridge counterattack and destroy Co. C.

4B. 4.30 - 5.00 p.m. Left Wing - Co. F withdraws to Last Stand Hill.

5A. 5.00 - 5.20 p.m. Right Wing - Warriors swarm up from Calhoun Coulee and shatter Co. L.

5B. 5.00 - 5.30 p.m. Left Wing - Co. E is attacked from Deep Ravine by warriors led by Lame White Man (killed) and from the north by the Suicide Boys. Co. E perishes.

6A. 5.00 - 5.20 p.m. Right Wing is finished after Crazy Horse does a bravery run through Co. I which is then overwhelmed by warriors from south and east.

6B. 5.00 - 5.30 p.m. Coming from the east Crazy Horse and his followers ride over the top of Last Stand Hill. Custer is killed. Warriors from the south overrun Co. F on the lower slopes. Some escapees are killed.

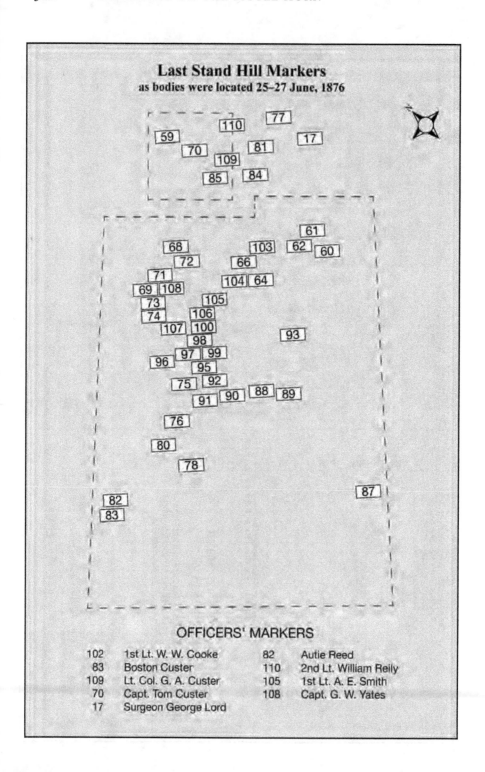

Last Stand Hill Markers
as bodies were located 25–27 June, 1876

OFFICERS' MARKERS

102	1st Lt. W. W. Cooke		82	Autie Reed
83	Boston Custer		110	2nd Lt. William Reily
109	Lt. Col. G. A. Custer		105	1st Lt. A. E. Smith
70	Capt. Tom Custer		108	Capt. G. W. Yates
17	Surgeon George Lord			

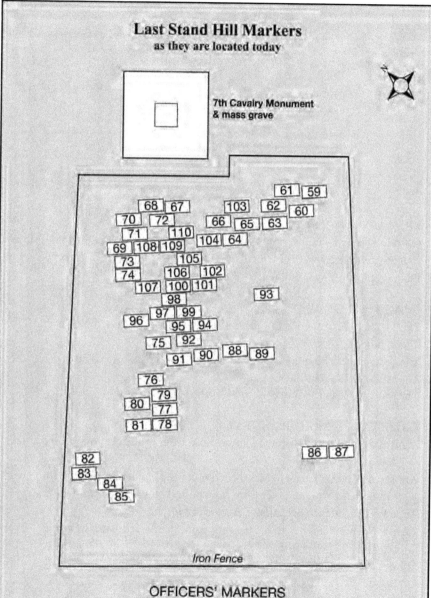

Last Stand Hill Markers
as they are located today

7th Cavalry Monument
& mass grave

Iron Fence

OFFICERS' MARKERS

102	1st Lt. W. W. Cooke	82	Autie Reed
83	Boston Custer	110	2nd Lt. William Reily
109	Lt. Col. G. A. Custer	105	1st Lt. A. E. Smith
70	Capt. Tom Custer	108	Capt. G. W. Yates
93	Lt. Henry Harrington		

BIBLIOGRAPHY

PRIMARY SOURCES
Gordon Harper's manuscript is based almost entirely on the following primary sources, complete copies of which are available in the e-book of Appendices and Bibliography for *Fights on the Little Horn*

CAMPAIGN ORDERS
The Letter of Instructions to Lieutenant Colonel Custer issued by General Terry on June 22, 1876
The order establishing the command structure of the Dakota column
The order for the Reno scout
The order to Custer to move the 7th Cavalry to the Rosebud

CAMPAIGN CORRESPONDENCE
Armstrong Custer: an attributed anonymous letter to the *New York Herald*, dated June 22, 1876
Armstrong Custer: letters to his wife from the 1876 Yellowstone Expedition, with additional correspondence from his wife and other members of his family
Autie Reed: a letter to his parents, June 21, 1876
Charles Varnum: a letter to his parents, from the *Lowell Weekly Journal*, August 1876
Charles Varnum: two letters to A. W. Johnson
Dr. Holmes O. Paulding: excerpts from his correspondence of 1876
Dr. James DeWolf: a letter to his wife, June 21, 1876
Edward Godfrey: a letter commenting upon some actions of Luther Hare at the Little Horn
First Lieutenant John Carland, 6th Infantry: a letter to Elizabeth Custer, December 4, 1877

Francis M. Gibson: a letter to his wife, July 4, 1876

Fred Gerard: a letter to his daughters, July 5, 1876

Frederick Benteen: a letter to his wife, written in dated installments, commencing July 2, 1876

Frederick Whittaker: a letter to the *New York Sun*, February 1879, published February 26, 1879

Frederick William Benteen: a letter to his wife, July 4, 1876

General Alfred H. Terry: a letter to General Sherman regarding his Dispatch from the Little Horn Battlefield, December 9, 1876

General Alfred H. Terry: the letter to General Crook July 9, 1876, notifying Crook of Terry's campaign progress and of Custer's disaster on the Little Horn

James H. Bradley: a letter to *The Helena Herald*, published July 25, 1876

Jesse M. Lee: a letter to Elizabeth Custer, June 27, 1897

John Gibbon: letter to Captain D. W. Benham, June 28, 1876; and from Benham to Division Headquarters in Chicago, July 5, 1876

Luther Hare: a letter to an unidentified correspondent, June 11, 1929

Marcus Reno: a letter to T. L. Rosser, July 30, 1876

Mark Kellogg: letters of June 21, 1876

Robert Newton Price: a letter to the *Philadelphia Times*, March 1879, published March 13, 1879

Sergeant Riley Lane, 7th Infantry: a letter to his brother, July 3, 1876

Thomas French: a letter to the mother of William W. Cooke, June 16, 1880

Thomas L. Rosser: a letter to Marcus Reno, August 16, 1876

Thomas L. Rosser: a letter to the *St. Paul Pioneer Press* and *Minneapolis Tribune*, July 8, 1876

Walter Camp and the Kanipe letters

Walter Camp: a letter to Charles A. Woodruff, February 28, 1910

Winfield Scott Edgerly: a letter to his wife, July 4, 1876

CAMPAIGN AND BATTLE ACCOUNTS

Alfred H. Terry: excerpts from his field diary of 1876

Billy Jackson: account from *the L.A. Times*, January 17, 1914

Captain E. G. Mathey: testimony at the Reno Court of Inquiry, 1879

Captain F. W. Benteen: statement to the *New York Herald*, August 8, 1876

Captain Myles Moylan: testimony at the Reno Court of Inquiry, 1879

Captain Thomas B. Weir: alleged statement concerning the Little Horn fights and Reno's conduct therein, from the files of the *Saint Paul Pioneer Press* and the *New York Herald*

Captain Thomas M. McDougall: testimony at the Reno Court of Inquiry, 1879

Charles A. Varnum: undated statement found in the papers of Charles Francis Bates

Charles A. Varnum: testimony at the Reno Court of Inquiry, 1879

Charles Windolph: story as given to John P. Everitt and published in the *Sunshine* magazine, September 1930

Cheyenne participants: stories from the Hostiles

Colonel John Gibbon: excerpts from his narrative of 1877

Colonel John Gibbon: testimony at the Reno Court of Inquiry, 1879

Crazy Horse, Oglala: attributed narrative as published in the *Saint Paul Pioneer Press*, May 28, 1877

Crow King, Hunkpapa Lakota: story given at Fort Yates, Dakota, July 30, 1881

Curley, Crow scout: several and varied narratives of 1876 et sub.

Curley: 1881 narrative as told to Charles Francis Roe, from *The Army and Navy Journal*, March 25, 1882

Daniel A. Knipe: narrative from *the Greensboro Daily Record*, April 27, 1924

Daniel Knipe: account, 1903, from *Montana Historical Society Contributions*, Volume 4, 1903

Daniel Newell: account as given to John P. Everitt and published in the *Sunshine* magazine, September 1930

Doctor H. R. Porter: testimony at the Reno Court of Inquiry, 1879

Dr. Henry Porter: account from the *St. Paul Pioneer Press*, May 3, 1878

Edward G. Mathey: interview with Walter Camp, January 19, 1910

Edward S. Godfrey: excerpts from his field diary, June 1876

Edward S. Godfrey: narratives of 1892 and 1908

Edward S. Godfrey: testimony at the Reno Court of Inquiry, 1879

Edwin Pickard: account of 1923

F. I. Geist: interview with Walter Camp, undated

Feather Earring, Mnicoujou Lakota: account as given to Hugh L. Scott, September 1919

First Lieutenant George D. Wallace: testimony at the Reno Court of Inquiry, 1879

Flying By, Mnicoujou Lakota: interview with Walter Camp July 27, 1912, at Standing Rock Agency

Foolish Elk, Oglala Lakota: narrative as given to Walter Mason Camp, September 22, 1908

Francis Johnson Kennedy: account, circa 1899

Francis M. Gibson: account, undated, from a manuscript in the collections of the North Dakota Historical Society

Fred Gerard: another account in response to DeRudio's testimony at the Reno court, taken from the *St. Paul Pioneer Press*, January 31, 1879

Fred Gerard: testimony at the Reno Court of Inquiry, 1879

Frederic F. Gerard: account from *the Arikara Narrative*

Frederic F. Gerard: narrative of 1909

Frederick Whittaker: anonymous narratives from his life of General Custer, 1876

Frederick William Benteen: lengthier narratives and his testimony at the Reno Court of Inquiry

Gall, Hunkpapa Lakota: two narratives from the Tenth Anniversary Reunion of the fights on the Little Horn, June 25 and July 14, 1886

Gen. Edward J. McClernand: interview with Walter Camp, undated

George Herendeen: account, as given to Walter Camp, 1909

George Herendeen: letter to *the New York Herald*, January 4, 1878

George Herendeen: statement of July 7, 1876, as published in *the New York Herald*, July 8, 1876

George Herendeen: testimony at the Reno Court of Inquiry, 1879

Goes Ahead, the Crow scout: narratives from the *Arikara Narrative* and as given to Walter Camp, August 5, 1909

Good Voiced Elk, Hunkpapa: interview with Walter Camp, May 21, 1909, at Standing Rock Agency

Hairy Moccasin, Crow scout: interview with Walter Camp July 17, 1910, at Crow Agency

Hairy Moccasin, Crow scout: narratives from the *Tepee Book* 1916, and as related to Walter M. Camp February 23, 1911

Harvey A. Fox and John A. Bailey: interview with Walter Camp, undated

He Dog, Oglala Lakota: narrative from an interview with Walter Mason Camp, July 13, 1910

Henry W. B. Mechling: letter to James Braddock, July 16, 1921

Henry W. B. Mechling: Walter Camp interview, undated

Hump, Mnicoujou Lakota: narrative given at Fort Yates, Dakota, July 30, 1881

Hunkpapa and Brule participants: stories from the Hostiles

Iron Thunder: account given at Fort Yates, July 30, 1881

James M. Rooney: interview with Walter Camp

James R. Boyle: interview with Walter Camp, February 5, 1913

John Burkman: interview with Walter Camp, undated

John C. Creighton: interview with Walter Camp, undated

John E. Hammon: interview with Walter Camp, undated

John Frett: accounts as given to and published in the *Saint Paul Dispatch* and the *Chicago Tribune*, July 27 & 28, 1876

John Frett: testimony at the Reno Court of Inquiry, 1879

John Hammon: account dated February 28, 1898

John M. Ryan: narrative published in *The Hardin Tribune*, June 22, 1923

John Stands In Timber: account from *American Heritage*, Volume XVIII, No. 3, 1966

John Stands In Timber: interview conducted by Don Rickey, August 18, 1956

Kate Bighead, Southern Cheyenne: her narrative as interpreted by Dr. Thomas B. Marquis, 1927

Kill Eagle, Blackfoot Lakota: narrative of September 1876

Left Hand and Waterman, Arapahoes: narratives of 1920

Lieutenant Alfred B. Johnson: account from July 1876

Lieutenant Charles C. DeRudio: stories from various sources, 1876 and subsequent and testimony at the Reno Court of Inquiry, 1879

Lieutenant Edward J. McClernand: narrative

Lieutenant James H. Bradley, Gibbon's Chief of Scouts 1876/1877: excerpts from his journal

Little Sioux, Arikara scout: narratives from the *Arikara Narrative* and from a Walter Camp interview, circa 1912

Low Dog, Oglala Lakota: narrative given at Fort Yates, Dakota, July 30, 1881

Luther Rector Hare: testimony at the Reno Court of Inquiry, 1879

Major Marcus A. Reno: testimony at Reno Court of Inquiry, 1879

Marcus A. Reno: an unpublished and perhaps unfinished manuscript ostensibly found among his personal effects after his death

Marcus A. Reno: statement to the *New York Herald*, August 8, 187

Mnicoujou and Two Kettles: stories from the Hostiles

Oglala: stories from the Hostiles

One Bull and White Bull: to Walter Camp, 1912, Standing Rock Indian Reservation

One Man: interview with Camp, 1912, Standing Rock Indian Reservation

Orderly-trumpeter John Martin: account as contained in *the Cavalry Journal*, July 1923

Patrick Corcoran: interview with Walter Camp, undated

Private Edward Davern of F Company, Reno's orderly: testimony at the Reno Court of Inquiry, 1879

Rain-In-The-Face, Hunkpapa: personal story as told to W. Kent Thomas, August 12, 1894, appearing in *Outdoor Life*, March 1903

Red Bear, Arikara scout: narratives of from the *Arikara Narrative* and from an interview with Walter Mason Camp, July 22, 1912

Red Horse, Mnicoujou Lakota: narratives of 1877 and 1881

Red Star, Arikara scout: account taken from the *Arikara narrative*

Ring Cloud, Blackfoot Lakota: interview with Walter Camp

Sergeant Ferdinand A. Culbertson: testimony at the Reno Court of Inquiry.

Sitting Bull: story of the fights on the Little Horn, given at Fort Walsh, Northwest

Territories, Canada, October 17, 1877 and published in the *New York Herald*, November 16, 1877

Soldier, Arikara scout: from the *Arikara narrative* and from an interview with Walter Mason Camp, C. July 1912

Spotted Horn bull (Mrs.), Hunkpapa: as published in the *Saint Paul Pioneer Press* May 19, 1883 and as given by Major J. S. McLaughlin in his *My Friend the Indian*, 1910

Strikes Two and Young Hawk: interviews with Walter Camp

Strikes Two, Arikara scout: narratives as given to Walter Camp, July 23, 1912 and from the *Arikara Narrative*

Strikes Two: another interview with Walter Camp\

The Arikara scouts with Custer on the Little Horn Campaign: accounts from *the Arikara Narrative*

The Mnicoujou people: their involvement in the fights on the Little Horn, as transcribed from their oral history by their historians on the Cheyenne River Reservation and reproduced with their permission

Theodore W. Goldin: *Army Magazine* article and a letter to Frederick Benteen

Theodore W. Goldin: stories as reflected in his correspondence from 1904 to 1934

Thomas F. O'Neill: interview with Walter Camp

Thomas W. Harrison: interview with Walter Camp, undated

Two Moon, Northern Cheyenne: account from "Custer's Last Fight as seen by Two Moon" as told to Hamlin Garland and published in *McClure's Magazine*, September 1898

White Bull, Mnicoujou Lakota: narratives as given to Walter S. Campbell [Stanley Vestal], 1930 and 1932

White Man Runs Him, Crow scout: narratives

William E. Morris: excerpts from his accounts from correspondence and as published in an unidentified newspaper, in the period 1894–1923

William G. Hardy: interview with Walter Camp, undated

William Heyn: interview with Walter Camp, undated

William J. Bailey: interview with Walter Camp, October 8, 1910

Winfield Edgerly: testimony at the Reno Court of Inquiry, 1879

Winfield S. Edgerly: account given at Fort Yates, Dakota, July 30, 1881, as published in the *Leavenworth Weekly times*, August 18, 1881

Winfield S. Edgerly: later narrative, date unknown but definitely after 1909

Wooden Leg, Northern Cheyenne warrior: from conversations over several years with Doctor Thomas B. Marquis

Young Hawk, Arikara scout: accounts from the *Arikara Narrative* and from interviews with Walter Mason Camp, circa 1912

CAMPAIGN AND BATTLE REPORTS

Brigadier General Alfred H. Terry: reports on the dead and wounded

Brigadier General Alfred H. Terry: two reports (including "The Confidential")

Brigadier General George Crook: his reports relative to the "Battle of the Rosebud," dated June 19 & 20, 1876

Brigadier General Terry: third "Report," sent to his headquarters in Saint Paul

Captain Frederick W. Benteen: report of July 4, 1876

Colonel John Gibbon: Report of the 1876 Campaign: October 17, 1876

First Lieutenant George Daniel Wallace: report and the question of rapid and excessive marches, worn-out horses and exhausted men

J. S. Poland: two reports relative to the treatment of the Indians at Standing Rock Agency and to the fights on the Little Horn, July 14 & 24, 1876

Johnathan D. Miles, agent: report of August 4, 1876

Lieutenant Edward J. McClernand: report as found in the annual report of the Chief of Engineers for the

Lieutenant William Philo Clark: report of September 14, 1877

Major Marcus A. Reno: message to Terry June 27, 1876

Major Marcus A. Reno: report of July 11, 1876, to the Chief of Ordnance regarding the functioning of the cavalry carbines at the fights on the Little Horn and the question of carbine extractor failure

Major Marcus A. Reno: report of the fights on the Little Horn, July 5, 1876

Sergeant James E. Wilson: report of January 3, 1877

MISCELLANEOUS

A. F. Mulford's 1877 visit to the Little Horn

Ami Frank Mulford, an excerpt from his *Fighting Indians in the Seventh U.S. Cavalry*, plus the report of an unidentified visitor to Custer's field in July 1877 and a description by Dr. William A. Allen

Brigadier General Godfrey letter

Brigadier General Godfrey: a letter to E. S. Paxson

Captain Frederick Benteen concerning the battle of the Washita

Captain George K. Sanderson: report of April 7, 1879, relative to reburials on Custer's field

Captain J. S. Payne, 5th Cavalry: excerpts from his testimony before the Reno Court of Inquiry, January 27, 1879

Edward S. Luce: some letters and a statement from the superintendent of Custer battlefield 1941–56, as to some interesting discoveries on the field

First Lieutenant Edward Maguire, engineer corps: testimony at the Reno Court of Inquiry

George Armstrong Custer: the findings, sentence and remission of sentence, relative to the Court Martial of 1867 and 1868

George Armstrong Custer's military record

Lieutenant Colonel Michael V. Sheridan: official report of July 20, 1877 and his account given to the *Chicago Times* July 25, 1877

Lieutenant Colonel Michael V. Sheridan: testimony at the Reno Court of Inquiry, 1879

Major General Sheridan and Major George A. Forsyth: reports of April 8, 1878, relative to a visit to the Custer battlefield July 1877 and some commentary from other members of the same group

Organization chart of a Cavalry Regiment, indicating the authorized strength of the headquarters and combat companies as at June 25, 1876

Philetus W. Norris, Superintendent of Yellowstone park: a July 1877 counterpoint to Michael Sheridan's report

Reno Court of Inquiry: the Summations and Findings of the Reno court, January and February 1879

Walter Mason Camp: a letter to Edward S. Godfrey, November 6 1920, regarding the markers on the Custer battlefield

SECONDARY SOURCES

Gordon Harper's complete bibliography, available in the e-book of Appendices and Bibliography of *Fights on the Little Horn,* while not presented as an exhaustive list of every publication related to Custer and the Little Bighorn, nevertheless comprises approximately 2500 secondary sources and may be considered a complete reading list of significant secondary works published between 1876 and 2013. The publications are grouped as follows:

Maps, published and other
Books: Biographical and Autobiographical
Books: History and Sociology
Books: The Fights on the Little Horn
Newspapers and Periodicals
Technical Studies
Collections, Manuscripts and Interviews
Official Reports and Records

The following secondary sources, some of which contain primary sources, are cited in the text:

Benjamin, Andrews E. *The United States in Our Own Time* (New York, 1903)

Bradley, James H., *The March of the Montana Column* (Norman: University of Oklahoma Press, 1961)

Brady, Cyrus Townsend, *Indian Fights and Fighters* (Garden City: Doubleday, 1904)

Carroll, J.M., *General Custer and the Battle of the Little Big Horn: The Federal View* (New Brunswick, New Jersey: The Garry Owen Press, 1976)

Carroll, John M. Ed., *A Seventh Cavalry Scrapbook #11* (Bryan, Tx, 1978)

Clark, George M., *Scalp Dance: The Edgerly Papers on the Battle of the Little Big Horn* (Oswego, New York: Heritage Press, 1985)

Coffeen, Herbert A., *The Custer Battle Book* (New York: Carlton Press, 1964)

Coffeen, Herbert A. *The Tepee Book*, Volume II, No.VI, June 1916 (Sheridan, Wyoming: Coffeen, 1916)

Dixon, Joseph K., *The Vanishing Race: The Last Great Indian Council* (Amsterdam, The Netherlands: Fredonia Books, 2004)

Donahue, Michael N., *Drawing Battle Lines; The Map Testimony of Custer's Last Fight* (El Segundo, California: Upton and Sons, Publishers, 2008)

Douglas W. Ellison, *Sole Survivor: An Examination of the Narrative of Frank Finkle* (Aberdeen: North Plains Press: 1983)

Dustin, Fred, *The Custer Tragedy* (El Segundo, California: Upton & Sons Publishers, 1987)

Eastman, Dr. Charles, *The Story of the Little Big Horn: Chautauquan Magazine*, Volume XXXI, No.4, 1900

Fox, Jr., Richard Allan, *Archaeology, History, and Custer's Last Battle* (Norman & London: University of Oklahoma Press, 1993)

Gibbon, Col. John "Last Summer's Expedition against the Sioux & Its Great Catastrophe," *American Catholic Quarterly Review*, April 1877

Gibbon, Col. John, *Gibbon on the Sioux Campaign of 1876 :Hunting Sitting Bull* (Bellevue, Nebraska: The Old Army Press, 1970, Reprinted from The American Catholic Quarterly Review, October 1877)

Godfrey, E.S. *Custer's Last Battle 1876* (Olympic Valley, California: Outbooks, 1976)

Godfrey, E.S., *The Field Diary* (Portland, Oregon: The Champoeg Press, 1957)

Graham, Col. William A., *The Story of the Little Big Horn* (Harrisburg, 1952)

Graham, W.A., *The Custer Myth: A Source Book of Custeriana* (Harrisburg, Pennsylvania: The Stackpole Company, 1953)

Gray, John S., *Centennial Campaign* (Fort Collins, 1976)

Green, Jerome A., *Stricken Field: The Little Bighorn Since 1876* (Norman: Univ. of Okla. 2008)

Greene, Jerome A. *Evidence and the Custer Enigma*, Olympic Valley, 1978

Greene, Jerome A. *Evidence and the Custer Enigma*, Golden, 1986

Greene, Jerome A., *Evidence and the Custer Enigma: A Reconstruction of Indian-*

Military History (Kansas City Posse of the Westerners, 1973)

Grinnell, George Bird, *The Fighting Cheyennes* (Norman: University of Oklahoma Press, 1983)

Hammer, Kenneth, Ed., *Custer in 76: Walter Camp's Notes on the Custer Fight,* (Provo, Utah: Brigham Young University Press, 1976)

Hammer, Kenneth, *Men With Custer* (Hardin: Custer Battlefield Historical & Museum Association, 1885)

Hammer, Kenneth, *The Glory March* (Monroe, 1980)

Hammer, Kenneth, Ed., *Custer in 76: Walter Camp's Notes on the Custer Fight,* (Provo, Utah: Brigham Young University Press, 1976)

Hardorff, Richard G., *Markers, Artifacts and Indian Testimony* (Short Hills, 1985)

Hardorff, Richard G. *On the Little Bighorn with Walter Camp: A Collection of W.M. Camp's Letters, Notes and Opinions on Custer's Last Fight* (El Segundo, California, Upton & Sons, Publishers, 2002

Hardorff, Richard G., *Cheyenne Memories of the Custer Fight* (Spokane, Washington: The Arthur H. Clark Company, 1995)

Hardorff, Richard G., *Lakota Recollections of the Custer Fight* (Spokane, Washington: The Arthur H. Clark Company, 1991)

Hardorff, Richard G., *The Custer Battle Casualties: Burials, Exhumations and Reinterments* Vol. 1 (El Segundo: Upton & Sons 1989)

Hardorff, Richard G., *The Custer Battle Casualties: Burials, Exhumations and Reinterments,* Vol 2 (El Segundo, California: Upton and Sons, Publishers, 1991)

Hardorff, Richard G., *Walter M. Camp's Little Bighorn Rosters* (Spokane, Washington: The Arthur H. Clark Company, 2002)

Hart, John P., *Custer and His Times Book Four: The Fight in Fishing Woman Ravine,* by Bruce A. Trinque, (Dexter, Michigan: Thomson-Shore, Inc., Little Big Horn Associates, Inc., 2002)

Historical Society of Montana, *Montana Historical Society Contributions, Volume 4, 1903* (Helena, Montana: Rocky Mountain Publishing Company, 1903)

Hunt, Frazier and Hunt, Robert, *I Fought with Custer* (Lincoln and London, 1987)

John B. Hart, *Custer and His Times: Book Four: Bigelow Neal and Dr. Porter,* by Ralph Heinz (Dexter, Michigan: Thomson-Shore, Inc., Little Big Horn Associates, Inc., 2002)

Johnson, Barry C., *George Herendeen: The Life of a Montana Scout in 'More Sidelights of the Sioux Wars'* (London: Westerners Publications Limited, 2004)

Leckie, Shirley A. *Elizabeth Bacon Custer And The Making Of A Myth* (Norman: U. of Okla. Press, 1993)

Schoenberer, Dale T., *The End of Custer: The Death of an American Legend* (Surrey, B.C.: Hancock House, 1995)

Leslie Tillett, *Wind On The Buffalo Grass: The Indians' Own Account of the Battle at the Little Big Horn River, & the Death of their life on the Plains* (New York: Thomas Y. Crowell Company, 1976)

Libby, O. G., *The Arikara Narrative of the Campaign Against the Hostile Dakotas June, 1876* (New York: Sol Lewis, 1973)

Liddic, Bruce R. and Harbaugh, Paul, Eds., *Camp On Custer: Transcribing the Custer Myth* (Spokane: The Arthur Clark Co., 1995)

Mackintosh, John D., *Custer's Southern Officer: Captain George D. Wallace 7th U.S. Cavalry* (Lexington, South Carolina: Cloud Creek Press, 2002)

MacNeil, Rod, "Custer's Approach to the Little Big Horn River," *More Sidelights of the Sioux Wars* (London: Westerners Publications 2007)

Marquis, Thomas B. *Memoirs of a White Crow Indian* (New York: Century Company, 1928)

Marquis, Thomas B., *Keep the Last Bullet for Yourself* (Algonac, 1976)

Marquis, Thomas B., *Rain-in-the-Face/Curly, The Crow* (Scottsdale, Arizona: Cactus Pony, 1934)

Marquis, Thomas B., *Wooden Leg: A Warrior who Fought Custer* (Lincoln and London: University of Nebraska Press, 1971)

McCreight, M. I., *Firewater and Forked Tongues: A Sioux Chief Interprets U.S. History* (Pasadena, California: Trails End Publishing, 1947)

McLaughlin, James, *My Friend The Indian* (Boston & New York: Houghton Mifflin Company, 1910)

Merington, Marguerite *The Custer Story: The Life and Intimate Letters of General George A. Custer and His Wife Elizabeth* (Lincoln & London: University of Nebraska Press, 1987)

Michno, Gregory, *the Mystery of E Troop* (Missoula: Montana Press 1994)

Miller, D.H., *Echoes of the Little Bighorn* (American Heritage 22 (4), 1971)

Miller, David Humphreys, *Custer's Fall: The Indian Side of the Story* (Lincoln & London: University of Nebraska Press, 1985)

Miller, David Humphreys, *Custer's Fall: The Indian Side of the Story* (New York, 1972)

Neihardt, J.G., Coll. of Personal Papers in Jt Coll., Western History Ms Div., U. of Missouri Library & State Historical Society of Missouri, Columbia

Nichols, Ronald H. *Reno Court of Inquiry Proceedings of a Court of Inquiry in the case of Major Marcus A. Reno,* (Hardin, Montana: Custer Battlefield Historical & Museum Association, Inc., 1996)

Philetus Norris, *New York Herald,* July 15, 1877; reprinted in "Custer's Remains," *Bighorn Yellowstone Journal,* Spring 1992

Raymond J. DeMallie, *The Sixth Grandfather: Black Elk's Teachings Given to John G. Neihardt,* (Lincoln & London: University of Nebraska Press, 1984)

Richard G. Hardorff, *The Custer Battle Casualties,* Vol. 1 (El Segundo: Upton & Sons 1989)

Ricker, Judge Eli S., Interview Notes in Nebraska State Historical Society, Lincoln

Roe, Charles F. *Synopsis of his Report of 6 August 1881 as to the placing of the Custer Battle Monument,* January 15, 1882

Roe, Charles F., *Custer's Last Battle,* (New York, 1927)

Ryan, 1st. Sgt. John M. "Narrative of the Custer Fight," *Hardin, Montana Tribune,* June 22, 1923

Scott, Douglas D. and Fox, Richard A. Jr. *Archaeological Insights into the Custer Battle* (Norman: Univ. of Okla. Press 1987)

Scott, Douglas D., Fox, Jr., Richard A., Fox, Connorm Melissa A., and Harmon, Dick, *Archaeological Perspectives on the Battle of the Little Bighorn* (Norman and London: University of Oklahoma Press, 1989)

Sills, Joe Jr., "The Recruits Controversy: Another Look," *Greasy Grass,* Vol. 5 (Custer Battlefield Historical & Museum Association, Inc., 1989)

Smith, Jay, Little Big Horn Associates, *Research Review, Vol. 3, No.1, June 1989: The Indian Fighting Army* (Dexter, MI: Thomson-Shore, Inc. 1989)

Smith, Jay, Little Big Horn Associates, *Research Review, Vol. 6, No.2, June 1992: What Did Not Happen at The Battle of the Little Big Horn* (Saline, MI: McNaughton & Gunn, Inc., 1992)

Stands In Timber, John & Liberty, Margot, *Cheyenne Memories* (Lincoln & London: University of Nebraska Press, 1972)

Stewart, Edgar I., *Custer's Luck* (Norman: Univ. of Okla. Press, 1955)

Thomas B. Marquis, *Custer On The Little Bighorn: She Watched Custer's Last Battle* (Lodi, California: End-Kian Publishing Company, 1967)

Thompson, Peter, *Thompson's Narrative of the Little Bighorn Campaign 1876* (Glendale, Calif.: The Arthur H. Clark Co. 1974)

Usher L. Burdick, *David F. Barry's Indian Notes on "The Custer Battle,"* (Baltimore: Wirth Brothers, 1949)

Vestal, Stanley, *Interview with White Bull (Mnicoujou) in 1932,* in the personal papers of Walter Stanley Campbell at The University of Oklahoma Libraries

Vestal, Stanley, *Warpath: The True Story of the Fighting Sioux: Told in a Biography of Chief White Bull* (Lincoln & London: University of Nebraska Press, 1984)

Yellow Nose, "Yellow Nose Tells of Custer's Last Stand" *Bighorn Yellowstone Journal* (Howell: Powder River Press, Vol.1. No.3, Summer 1992)

INDEX